VISUAL QUICKPRO GUIDE

FLASH 5
ADVANCED

FOR WINDOWS AND MACINTOSH

Russell Chun

 Peachpit Press

Visual QuickPro Guide
Flash 5 Advanced for Windows and Macintosh
Russell Chun

Peachpit Press

1249 Eighth Street
Berkeley, CA 94710
510/524-2178
800/283-9444
510/524-2221 (fax)

Find us on the World Wide Web at: http://www.peachpit.com
Published by Peachpit Press, a division of Addison Wesley Longman,
in association with Macromedia Press.
Copyright © 2001 by Russell Chun

Editor: Rebecca Gulick
Production Coordinator: Lisa Brazieal
Copyeditor: Elissa Rabellino
Compositor: Melanie Haage
Cover design: The Visual Group
Indexer: Karin Arrigoni

Notice of rights

Notice of liability

Trademarks

ISBN 0-201-72624-6

9 8 7 6 5 4 3 2 1

Printed and bound in the United States of America

Thank you

Many thanks to everyone at Peachpit Press, especially my dedicated editor, Rebecca Gulick, who jumped into this project head first, giving me the support throughout the process and the polish to my words. Your late nights and weekends at the office have not gone unnoticed. Thanks also to the tremendous help from Elissa Rabellino, Marjorie Baer, Lisa Brazieal, Melanie Haage, Victor Gavenda, Kristine Kurovsky, and Nancy Ruenzel.

Special thanks to Steve Vargas, my fellow Flash instructor, for cheerfully writing the sections on XML, Generator, and the CGI GET and POST methods and making sense out of these complex topics.

Thanks to Eric Stickney for providing many of the great illustrations; Derek Jimenez, the skateboarder, and Ross "Hogg" Viator, the DJ, for lending their talents to video; SadSadFun (A. Gass, B. Chulada, F. Parsa, and M. Chulada) for their music; and Bryan Chun for photos of my nephew and niece, David and Alexandra Chun. Additional images and sound provided courtesy of Addison Wesley Longman, Corel Photo, Damnhot.com, Gary Fisher bikes, Greenjem.com, Music4Flash.com, and Vecta3D.

CONTENTS AT A GLANCE

TABLE OF CONTENTS

INTRODUCTION

Macromedia Flash is one of the hottest technologies on the Web today. Leading corporate Web sites use its streamlined graphics to communicate their brands, major motion picture studios promote theatrical releases with Flash animations, and online gaming and educational sites provide rich user experiences with Flash interactivity. As a vector-based animation and authoring application, Flash is ideal for creating high-impact, low-bandwidth Web sites incorporating animation, interactivity, and sound. In fact, this tool is becoming the standard for delivering dynamic content across various browsers and platforms.

As the popularity of Flash increases, so does the demand for animators and developers who know how to tap its power. This book is designed to help you meet that challenge. Learn how to build complex animations; integrate sophisticated interfaces and navigation schemes; and dynamically control graphics, sound, and text. Experiment with the techniques discussed in this book to create the compelling media that Flash makes possible. It's not an exaggeration to say that Flash is revolutionizing the Web. This book will help you be a part of that revolution. So boot up your computer and get started.

Who Should Use This Book

This book is for the designer, animator, and developer who want to take their Flash skills to the next level. You've mastered the basics of tweening and are ready to move on to more complex tasks involving video, masking, dynamic sound control, or movie-clip collision detection. You may not be a hard-core programmer, but you're ready to learn how ActionScript can control graphics, sounds, and text. You're ready to combine buttons and movie clips to create complex pull-down menus, to integrate interactivity with your animations to create arcade-style games, and to learn how Flash communicates with outside applications such as Web browsers and Macromedia Generator. If this description fits you, then this book is right for you.

This book explores the advanced features of Flash 5, so you should already be comfortable with the basic tools and commands for creating simple Flash movies. You should know how to create and modify shapes and text with the drawing tools, and be able to create graphic and button symbols. You should also know how to apply motion and shape tweens, and how to work with frame-by-frame animation. You should know your way around the Flash interface—moving from the Stage to symbol-editing mode to the Timeline, to manipulate layers and frames. You should also be familiar with importing and using bitmaps and sounds and assigning basic actions to frames and buttons for navigation. Review the tutorials that come with the software or pick up a copy of *Macromedia Flash 5: Visual QuickStart Guide,* by Katherine Ulrich.

Goals of This Book

Many books present material in one of two ways: Either they list every command one-by-one and explain its function in an ency-clopedic fashion, or they provide specific case studies for you to look at and copy. This book does neither. Its aim is to demonstrate the advanced features of Flash 5 in a logical approach emphasizing how techniques are applied. You will learn how techniques build on each other, and how groups of techniques can be combined to solve a particular prob-lem. Each example you work through puts another skill under your belt, so by the end of this book you'll be able to create sophisti-cated interactive Flash projects.

For example, creating a pull-down menu illustrates how simple elements—invisible buttons, mouse events, button-tracking options, and movie clips—come together to make more complex behaviors. Examples illustrate the practical application of tech-niques, and additional tips explain how to apply these techniques in other contexts.

How to Use This Book

The concepts in this book build on each other, so the material at the end is more complex than that at the beginning. If you're familiar with some of the material, you can skip around to the subjects that interest you, but you'll find it more useful to learn the techniques in the order in which they appear.

As with other books in the Visual QuickPro Guide series, tasks are presented for you to do as you read about them so that you can see how a technique is applied. Follow the step-by-step instructions, look at the figures, and try them on your computer. You'll learn more by doing and by taking an active role in experimenting with these exercises.

Tips follow the specific tasks to give you hints on how to use a shortcut, warnings on common mistakes, and suggestions on how the technique can be extended.

Occasionally, you'll see sidebars in gray boxes. Sidebars discuss related matters that are not directly task-oriented. You'll find interesting and useful concepts that can help you understand how Flash works.

What's in This Book

This book is organized into five parts:

♦ Part I: Approaching Advanced Animation

This part covers advanced techniques for graphics and animation, including strategies for motion tweening, shape tweening, masking, and using QuickTime video and 3D graphics.

♦ Part II: Understanding ActionScript

This part introduces ActionScript, the scripting language Flash uses to add interactivity to a movie. You'll learn the basic components of the language and how to use the Actions panel to construct meaningful code.

♦ Part III: Navigating Timelines and Communicating

This part teaches you the ways in which Flash accepts input from the viewer and how complex navigation schemes can be created with multiple Timelines. You'll also see how Flash communicates with external files and applications such as Web browsers.

♦ Part IV: Transforming Graphics and Sound

This part demonstrates how to dynamically control the basic elements of any Flash movie—its graphics and sound—through ActionScript.

♦ Part V: Working with Information

The last part focuses on how to retrieve, store, modify, and test information to create complex Flash environments that can respond to interactions with the viewer.

♦ Appendixes

Three appendixes give you quick access to the essential ActionScript objects, actions, and key code values.

What's on the CD

Accompanying this book is a CD-ROM that contains nearly all the Flash source files for the tasks. You can see how each task was created, study the ActionScripts, or use the ActionScripts to do further experimentation. You'll also find a demo copy of Flash 5 as well as a list of Web links to sites devoted to Flash, showcasing the latest Flash examples, with tutorials, articles, and advice.

Additional Resources

Use the Web to your advantage. There is a thriving, international community of Flash developers; within it you can share your frustrations, seek help, and show off your latest Flash masterpiece. There are bulletin boards and mailing lists for all levels of Flash users that are free to everyone. Begin your search for Flash resources with the list of Web sites on the accompanying CD and with the Macromedia Dashboard, a panel within the Flash application that provides links to the Flash developer community on the Web.

GOALS OF THIS BOOK

What's New in Flash 5

A number of new features in Flash 5 will appeal to both beginners and advanced users. The following are just a few that make Flash 5 even more powerful, flexible, and easy to use.

Improved Interface

Many of the tools and commands are now accessible through panels—small windows that you can rearrange to suit your work environment. The Movie Explorer, a new panel, displays a hierarchical overview of your movie, letting you search for and modify particular elements. Flash 5 also provides customizable keyboard shortcuts and a new look to the Timeline, which makes it easier to see and edit frames and keyframes.

New Drawing Aids

New tools that help you draw include a Bézier pen tool to define more accurate curves, draggable guides, enhanced color controls, and new selection highlights that make it easier to identify fill colors.

Shared Libraries and SmartClips

New features such as shared Libraries and SmartClips make it easier to work on large projects. Shared Libraries allow multiple movies to share common assets, while SmartClips give you a way to make templates for specialized movie clips.

Increased Integration

Flash 5 recognizes more file formats such as MP3 sound files, and can import FreeHand and Fireworks PNG files directly into Flash while preserving layers, text, and other elements. Flash also supports basic HTML text formatting and XML objects.

Expanded Interactivity

The expansion of ActionScript adds objects, methods, and properties, as well as new actions and functions such as printing and collision detection. A new ActionScript panel makes scripting easy, and a Debugger panel helps you troubleshoot your movie by letting you watch and modify variables and properties during playback.

Part I: Approaching Advanced Animation

BUILDING COMPLEXITY

The key to creating complex animations in Flash is to build them from simpler parts. Just as the movement of a runner is essentially a collection of rotating limbs, you should think of your Flash project as a collection of simpler motions. Isolating individual components of a much larger, complicated motion allows you to treat each component with the most appropriate technique, simplifies the tweening, and gives you better control with more refined results.

For example, to animate a head that's quickly turning to face the camera, you would first consider how to simplify the animation into separate motions. Animating the entire sequence at once would be difficult, if not impossible, because the many elements making up the head change in different ways as they move. The outline of the head could be a frame-by-frame animation to show the transformation from a profile to a frontal pose. Some of the features of the face could be symbol instances that you squash and stretch in a motion tween to match the turn of the head. And the hair could be a shape tween that lets you show its flow, swing, and slight bounce-back effect when the head stops.

Learning to combine different techniques and break down animation into simpler parts like this not only solves difficult animation problems, but forces you to use multiple layers and establish symbols of the component parts. By doing so, you set it up so the animation is easy to manage now and revise later.

This chapter describes approaches to building complex animations through the layering, combining, and extending of basic Flash capabilities.

Motion Tweening Strategies

Motion tweening lets you interpolate any of the instance properties of a symbol, such as its location, size, rotation, color, or transparency. Because of its versatility, motion tweening can be applied to a variety of animation problems, making it the foundation of most Flash projects. Since motion tweening deals with instance properties, it's a good idea to think of the technique in terms of instance tweening. Whether or not actual motion across the Stage is involved, changing instances between keyframes requires motion tweening. Thinking of it as instance tweening will help you distinguish when and where to use motion tweening as opposed to shape tweening or frame-by-frame animation.

Creating Seamless Animated Loops

Animated loops are important because they provide a way to continue motion by defining only a few keyframes. You see animated loops in interface elements such as rotating buttons and scrolling menus as well as cyclical motions like a person walking, a butterfly's wings flapping, or a planet revolving. The important point in making seamless loops is to make sure the last and first keyframes are identical or nearly identical so that the motion is continuous.

Here we consider ways of doing two of the most common types of animated loops, scrolling graphics and graphics on closed motion paths.

Scrolling graphics are familiar effects in interface elements such as menu options that cycle. You can also use this technique to create background animations that loop endlessly in a scene that waits for user interaction.

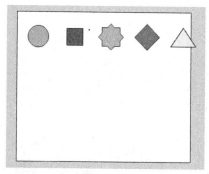

Figure 1.1 Five objects placed across the Stage as they would appear when they begin scrolling across from right to left. The objects could be buttons or simple graphics.

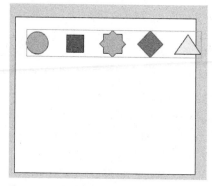

Figure 1.2 Group the objects together by choosing Modify > Group.

First group   *Second group*

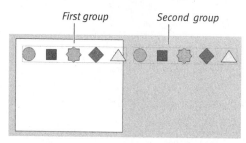

Figure 1.3 Create a pattern by copying and pasting the group.

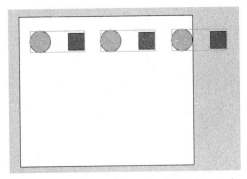

Figure 1.4 This group only has two objects. Repeat the groups to extend well past the Stage.

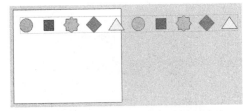

Figure 1.5 Create a single group of the entire pattern.

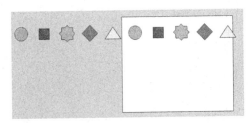

Figure 1.6 The second repeated group is moved to where the first group was originally.

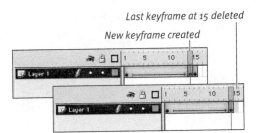

Figure 1.7 Create a new keyframe (top) and delete the last keyframe (bottom).

To create a continuous scrolling graphic:

1. Create the necessary elements that will scroll across the Stage, and place them as they would appear at any given moment (**Figure 1.1**).

2. Select all the elements, and choose Modify > Group (**Figure 1.2**).

3. Copy the group and paste the copy next to the original group to create a long band of repeating elements. For example, if your elements scroll from right to left, place the second group to the right of the first group (**Figure 1.3**).

   Your scrolling elements will usually be larger than the Stage size, but if your first group is smaller, you'll need to duplicate it more than once to create a repeating pattern that extends beyond the Stage (**Figure 1.4**).

4. Select all your groups and group them into one single group (**Figure 1.5**). Having a single group allows you to motion tween it across the Stage.

5. Create a keyframe at a later point in the Timeline.

6. Select the group in the last keyframe, and move it so that the second repeated group of elements aligns with the first. When you move your group, use its outlines to match its previous position (**Figure 1.6**).

7. Apply a motion tween between the keyframes.

8. Insert a new keyframe just before the last keyframe, and delete the last frame altogether (**Figure 1.7**).

   This makes the animation not have to play two identical frames and creates a smooth loop.

MOTION TWEENING STRATEGIES

A motion path in a guide layer provides a way to create smooth movement along a path from the beginning point to the end point. If you make the end point of the path match the beginning point, you can create a seamless loop and effectively close the motion path.

To make a closed motion path:

1. Create a graphic symbol, and place an instance of it on the Stage (**Figure 1.8**).

2. Create a guide layer by clicking the Add Guide Layer icon under your layers.

   A new guide layer appears, and your first layer becomes a guided layer (**Figure 1.9**).

3. Draw an empty ellipse in the guide layer.

4. With the Snap modifier for the arrow tool turned on, place the registration point of your instance on the path of the ellipse (**Figure 1.10**).

5. Add frames to both layers, and create a new keyframe in the last frame of the guided layer.

   The first and last keyframes remain the same in order to create the animated loop (**Figure 1.11**).

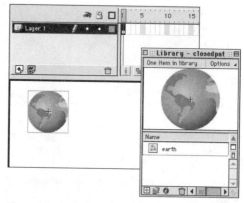

Figure 1.8 An instance of a graphic symbol is placed on the Stage for motion tweening along a path.

Figure 1.9 The guide layer above Layer 1 will contain the motion path.

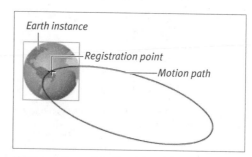

Figure 1.10 The registration point of the earth instance snaps to the motion path.

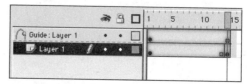

Figure 1.11 The position of the earth at keyframe 1 and at keyframe 14 in Layer 1 are the same.

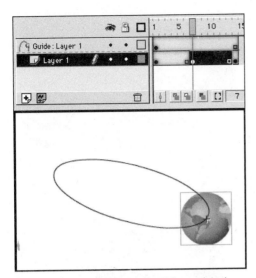

Figure 1.12 The registration point of the earth in the middle keyframe is positioned at the far side of the ellipse.

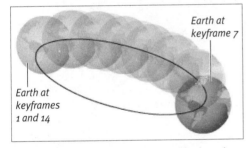

Figure 1.13 The earth bounces back and forth on the same segment of the ellipse.

Earth at keyframe 7

Earth at keyframes 1 and 14

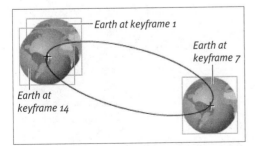

Earth at keyframe 1

Earth at keyframe 7

Earth at keyframe 14

Figure 1.14 The three keyframes of the earth. The first instance is closer to the middle instance on the top path of the ellipse, while the last instance is closer to the middle instance on the bottom path of the ellipse.

6. Select the middle frame of the guided layer, and insert a new keyframe. Move your instance in this intermediate keyframe to the opposite side of the ellipse (**Figure 1.12**).

7. Select all the frames between the three keyframes, and from the Frame panel choose Motion Tweening.

   Your instance now travels along the path of the ellipse. However, it returns on the same segment of the ellipse rather than making a complete circuit (**Figure 1.13**).

8. Grab the instance in the last keyframe of the guided layer and move it slightly closer to the instance in the middle keyframe while maintaining its registration point on the path (**Figure 1.14**).

(continued on next page)

Flash tweens two instances by taking the most direct path, so by shortening the distance between the last two keyframes on the bottom segment of the ellipse, you force Flash to use that segment of the ellipse.

Your instance now travels along both sides of the ellipse (**Figure 1.15**).

✔ Tip

■ You can also accomplish the same kind of looping effect by deleting a small segment of your path. When you create a gap, you essentially make an open path with beginning and end points for your instance to follow (**Figure 1.16**).

Using Multiple Guided Layers

A single guide layer can affect more than one guided layer, letting multiple motion tweens follow the same path. This is a good approach for creating complex animations that require many objects traveling in the same direction, such as marching soldiers, blood cells coursing through an artery, rapid gunfire, or a stampeding herd of cattle. While the individual instances may vary slightly, you maintain control over their general direction with the guide layer.

For example, several leaves blowing across the Stage could be animated to follow one guide layer. The guide layer establishes the wind's general direction, while the leaves could still have slight individual variations by being offset in separate guided layers. Just by your changing the path in the guide layer, all the leaves change accordingly. Using a single path to guide multiple layers this way is an example of how you build complex animations—in this case, swirling leaves—from very simple parts—one guide layer and one leaf symbol.

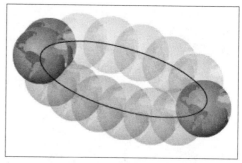

Figure 1.15 The earth moves around the closed path.

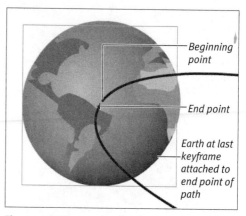

Figure 1.16 A tiny gap provides beginning and end points for your motion path.

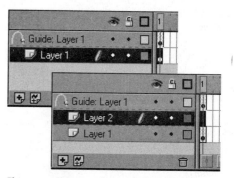

Figure 1.17 Selecting the guided layer (top) and inserting a new layer automatically modifies the new layer as a guided layer.

MOTION TWEENING STRATEGIES

Drag Layer 2 under the guide layer

Figure 1.18 A normal layer (Layer 2) can be dragged under the guide layer to become a guided layer.

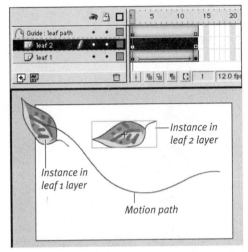

Figure 1.19 An instance on the Stage in the leaf 2 Layer.

Instance in leaf 2 layer

Instance in leaf 1 layer

Motion path

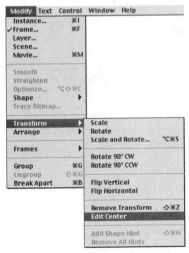

Figure 1.20 Select the instance in the second guided layer, and choose Modify > Transform > Edit Center.

To assign a second guided layer to a guide layer:

◆ Select the first guided layer, and click the Insert Layer icon.

A second guided layer appears above the first (**Figure 1.17**).

◆ Alternatively, click and drag an existing normal layer under the guided layer.

The normal layer becomes a guide layer (**Figure 1.18**).

To offset a second guided layer:

1. Create the second guided layer, and drag in an instance that you want to tween (**Figure 1.19**).

2. Select the instance in the second guided layer. Choose Modify > Transform > Edit Center (**Figure 1.20**).

A white cross appears on your instance, marking the current registration point (**Figure 1.21**).

3. Drag the registration point cross to a new position.

4. Deselect the instance by clicking in the Stage.

5. Select the instance again.

The new registration point will appear where you just placed it (**Figure 1.22**).

(continued on next page)

Registration point

Figure 1.21 The editable registration point of the leaf.

New registration point

Figure 1.22 The new registration point of the leaf.

MOTION TWEENING STRATEGIES

6. With the Snap modifier for the arrow tool on, grab the instance by the registration point and attach it to the beginning of the guide layer path (**Figure 1.23**).

7. Insert a new keyframe in the last frame.

The newly created instance in the last keyframe will have the same registration point as the edited instance.

8. Now attach the instance in the last keyframe to the end of the guide layer path.

The motion tween in the second guided layer follows the same path as the first guided layer. The new registration point of the instance in the second guided layer, however, offsets the motion (**Figure 1.24**).

To vary the timing of a second guided layer:

1. Drag the first keyframe of the second guided layer to a later point in time.

The motion tween for that guided layer will begin after the first one starts, but both of the animations will end at the same time (**Figure 1.25**).

2. Drag the last keyframe of the first guided layer to an earlier point in time.

The keyframe will move, but a new keyframe appears just after it with a broken motion tween.

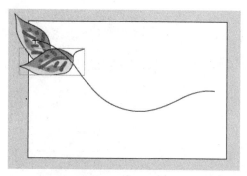

Figure 1.23 The registration point of the leaf, shown selected here, is attached to the path.

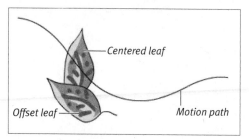

Figure 1.24 The two tweens follow the same motion path. The second leaf is offset because of its moved registration point.

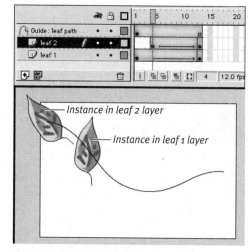

Figure 1.25 The leaf in the leaf 2 layer follows the motion path only after the one in the leaf 1 layer has already started.

MOTION TWEENING STRATEGIES

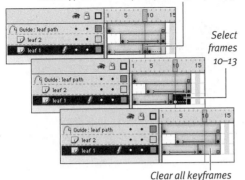

Last keyframe moved from frame 13 to frame 9

Select frames 10–13

Clear all keyframes

Figure 1.26 Move the last keyframe in the leaf 1 layer closer to the first keyframe (top). Select the broken tween and empty keyframe (middle), then clear all keyframes (bottom).

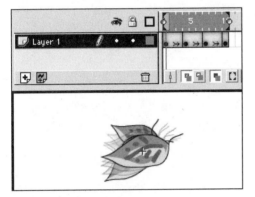

Figure 1.27 An animated graphic symbol of a leaf moving up and down.

Figure 1.28 Play the movie to see how the leaves follow the motion path while going through their own animation.

3. Clear all the frames of keyframes by selecting them and choosing Insert > Clear keyframe (**Figure 1.26**).

   The motion tweens following the path in the guide layer are staggered relative to each other.

4. Refine the timing of the motion tweens by moving the first and last keyframes in both guided layers.

✔ Tips

- Create variations in the second guided layer by placing the instances on any point along the path in the guide layer. They do not have to lie at the very beginning or end of the path in order for the motion tween to work.

- You can increase complexity by using animated graphic symbol instances along the guide layer's motion path. Animated loops within graphic symbols provide localized motion that still follows the guide layer on the main Timeline.

To add local variations to multiple guided layers:

1. Enter symbol-editing mode for the graphic symbol you use on the motion path.

2. Select the contents of this symbol, and convert it to a graphic symbol.

   You create a graphic symbol within another graphic symbol. This allows you to create a motion tween within your first graphic symbol.

3. Create a looping motion tween (**Figure 1.27**).

4. Exit symbol-editing mode and play the movie to see how the motion tween of the graphic symbol gets incorporated with the motion tween on the main Stage (**Figure 1.28**).

MOTION TWEENING STRATEGIES

✔ Tips

- In the Instance panel, under the Behavior options, adjust the play mode parameter and First parameter to vary how the animated graphic instances play (**Figure 1.29**). By having your loops begin with different frames, you avoid having them all synchronized with each other (**Figure 1.30**).

- Rotating your instances at this point can produce even more complex, interesting, and seemingly random movements. Experiment with rotating your instances as they travel along the motion path.

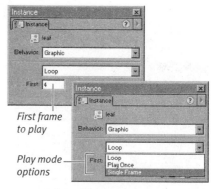

First frame to play

Play mode options

Figure 1.29 The First parameter is set to 4 (top) so that the leaf graphic will loop beginning with frame 4. The other play mode options in the pull-down menu include Play Once and Single Frame.

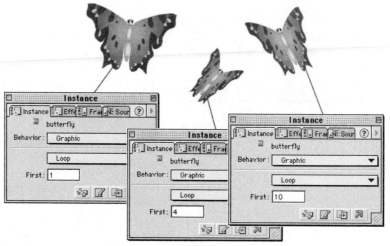

Figure 1.30 Three instances of the same graphic symbol with different First frame play options. The left butterfly loops beginning with frame 1. Its wings will start to close. The middle butterfly loops beginning with frame 4. Its wings are already closed and will start to open. The right butterfly loops beginning with frame 10. Its wings are opening up.

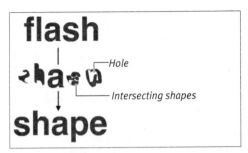

Figure 1.31 An attempt to shape tween "flash" to "shape." Notice the breakups between the "s" and the "p," and the hole that appears between the "h" and the "e."

Figure 1.32 Select the first keyframe of the shape tween, and choose Modify > Transform > Add Shape Hint.

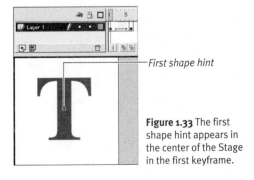

Figure 1.33 The first shape hint appears in the center of the Stage in the first keyframe.

Shape Tweening Strategies

Shape tweening is a technique for interpolating amorphous changes that can't be accomplished using instance transformations such as rotation, scale, or skew. Fill, outline, gradient, and alpha are all shape attributes that can be shape tweened.

Flash applies a shape tween using what it considers the most efficient, direct route. This method sometimes has unpredictable results, creating overlapping shapes or seemingly random holes that appear and merge (**Figure 1.31**). These undesirable effects are usually the result of keyframes containing shapes that are too complex to tween all at once. As with motion tweening, simplifying a complicated shape tween into more basic component parts and separating those parts in layers will result in a more successful interpolation. Shape hints give you a way to tell Flash what point on the first shape corresponds to what point on the second shape. Sometimes, adding intermediate keyframes will help a complicated tween by providing a transition state and making the tween go through many but more manageable stages.

Using Shape Hints

Shape hints force Flash to map particular points on the first shape to corresponding points on the second shape. By placing multiple shape hints, you can more precisely control the way your shapes will tween.

To add a shape hint:

1. Select the first keyframe of the shape tween. Choose Modify > Transform > Add Shape Hint (**Figure 1.32**).

   A red-circled letter appears in the middle of your shape (**Figure 1.33**).

   (continued on next page)

2. Move the first shape hint to a point on your shape.

Make sure the Snap modifier for the arrow is turned on to snap your selections to vertices and edges.

3. Select the last keyframe of the shape tween and move the matching circled letter to a corresponding point on the end shape.

This shape hint turns green and the first shape hint turns yellow, signifying that both have been moved into place correctly (**Figure 1.34**).

4. Continue adding shape hints, up to a maximum of 26, to refine the shape tween (**Figure 1.35**).

✔ Tips

■ Place shape hints in order either clockwise or counterclockwise. Flash will more easily understand a sequential placement than one that jumps around.

■ Shape hints need to be placed on an edge or a corner of the shape. If you place a shape hint in the fill or outside the shape, the shape hints will remain red and be ignored.

■ To view your animation without the shape hints, choose View > Show Shape Hints. Flash unchecks the Show Shape Hints option, and the shape hints are hidden.

■ If you move your entire shape tween using Edit Multiple Frames, you will have to reposition all your shape hints. Unfortunately, there is no way to move all the shape hints at once.

Figure 1.34 The corresponding shape hint in the last keyframe.

The cross of the T absorbs into the I

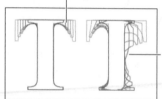

This T goes through some unnecessary changes to get to the I

Figure 1.35 Changing from a "T" to an "I" with shape hints (left) and without shape hints (right).

First keyframe   *Second keyframe*

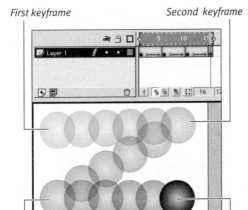

Third keyframe   *Final keyframe*

Figure 1.36 A complicated motion tween requires several intermediate keyframes.

Intersecting shapes

Figure 1.37 Changing a "Z" to an "S" all at once causes the shape to flip and cross over itself.

Figure 1.38 An intermediate shape.

Figure 1.39 The "Z" makes an easy transition to the intermediate shape (middle), from which the "S" can tween smoothly.

To delete a shape hint:

◆ Drag the shape hint off the Stage entirely. The matching shape hint in the other keyframe will be deleted automatically.

To remove all shape hints:

◆ Choose Modify > Transform > Remove All Hints.

Using Intermediate Keyframes

Adding intermediate keyframes can help a complicated tween by providing a transition state that creates smaller and more manageable changes. Think about it in terms of motion tweening: Imagine you want to create the motion of a ball starting from the top left of the Stage, moving to the top right, then to the bottom left, and finally to the bottom right (**Figure 1.36**). You wouldn't just create two keyframes, one with the ball at the top left and one with the ball on the bottom right, and expect Flash to tween the zigzag motion. You would need to establish the intermediate keyframes so that Flash could create the motion in stages. It's the same with shape tweening. You can better handle a dramatic change between two shapes by using intermediate keyframes.

To create an intermediate keyframe:

1. Study how an existing shape tween fails to produce satisfactory results when tweening the letter "Z" to the letter "S" (**Figure 1.37**).

2. Insert a keyframe at an intermediate point within the tween.

3. In the newly created keyframe, edit the shape that provides a kind of stepping stone to the final shape (**Figure 1.38**). The shape tween has smaller changes to go through, with smoother results (**Figure 1.39**).

Sometimes providing an intermediate keyframe isn't enough, and you need shape hints to refine the tween even more. Here are three ways you can add shape hints to a shape tween that uses an intermediate keyframe.

To use shape hints across multiple keyframes:

◆ Select the intermediate keyframe, and add shape hints as if it were the first keyframe.

Keep track of which shape hint belongs to which tween by their respective colors. Yellow is the shape hint for the beginning keyframe, and green is the shape hint for the end keyframe (**Figure 1.40**).

◆ Insert a new keyframe adjacent to the second keyframe, and begin adding shape hints.

A new keyframe allows you to add shape hints without the confusion that overlapping shape hints from the previous tween may cause (**Figure 1.41**).

◆ Create a new layer that duplicates the intermediate and last keyframes of the shape tween, and begin adding shape tweens on this new layer.

By duplicating the intermediate keyframe, you keep shape hints on separate layers, which also avoids overlapping the shape hints (**Figure 1.42**).

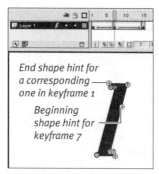

End shape hint for a corresponding one in keyframe 1

Beginning shape hint for keyframe 7

Figure 1.40 This intermediate keyframe contains two sets of shape hints. Some are the ending shape hints for the first tween, and others are the beginning shape hints for the second tween.

Figure 1.41 A shape hint on a new keyframe.

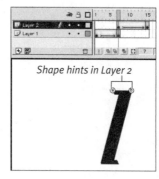

Shape hints in Layer 2

Figure 1.42 Layer 2 keeps the beginning shape hints for the tween from frames 7 to 15 separate from the end shape hints for the tween from frames 1 to 7.

SHAPE TWEENING STRATEGIES

Figure 1.43 A hole appears at the outline of the first shape when a shape tween is applied to change an "F" to a "D."

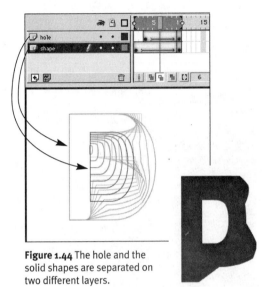

Figure 1.44 The hole and the solid shapes are separated on two different layers.

Using Layers to Simplify Shape Changes

Shape tweening lets you create very complex shape tweens on a single layer, but doing so can produce unpredictable results. Use layers to separate complex shapes and create multiple but simpler shape tweens.

For example, when a shape tween is applied to change the letter "F" to the letter "D," the hole in the last shape appears at the edges of the first shape (**Figure 1.43**). Separating the hole in the "D" and treating it as a white shape allows you to control when and how it will appear. Insert a new layer and create a second tween for the hole. The compound tween gives you better, more refined results (**Figure 1.44**).

SHAPE TWEENING STRATEGIES

Animating Your Masks

Masking is a simple way to selectively reveal portions of the layer or layers below it. This requires making one layer a mask layer and the layers below the masked layers.

By adding tweening to either or both the mask layer and the masked layers, you can go beyond simple, static peepholes and create dynamic masks that move, change shape, and reveal moving images. Use animated masks to achieve such complex effects as moving spotlights, magnifying lenses that enlarge underlying pictures, or "x-ray" types of interactions that show more detail within the mask area. Animated masks are also useful for creating cinematic transitions such as wipes, in which the first scene is covered up as a second scene is revealed; and iris effects, where the first scene collapses in a shrinking circle, leaving a second scene on the screen.

Inserting layers above and below masks can add even more complexity to animated masks. For example, a shape filled with an alpha gradient can make the hard edges of a mask slowly fade out for a subtle spotlight.

To tween the mask layer:

1. In Layer 1, create a background image or import a bitmap.

2. Insert a new layer above the first layer.

3. Select the top layer, and choose Modify > Layer. Select Mask Type. Select the bottom layer, and choose Modify > Layer. Select Masked Type.

   The top layer becomes the mask layer, and the bottom layer becomes the masked layer (**Figure 1.45**).

4. Create a shape tween or a motion tween in the mask layer (**Figure 1.46**).

5. Insert sufficient frames in your masked layer to match the number of frames in the tween in your mask layer.

Mask layer — Masked layer

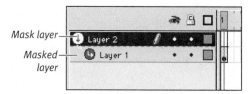

Figure 1.45 Layer 2 is the mask layer, and Layer 1 is the masked layer.

Shape tween in Layer 2   Diver in Layer 1

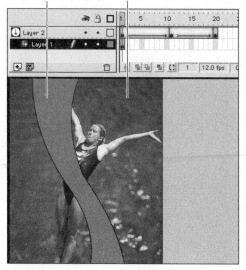

Figure 1.46 A shape tween of a moving vertical swirl is on the mask layer. The diver image is on the masked layer.

Figure 1.47 The shape tween uncovers the image of the diver.

ANIMATING YOUR MASKS

Figure 1.48 The moving spotlight in the mask layer (spotlight) uncovers the stained-glass image in the masked layer (bitmap). A duplicate darker image resides in the bottom, normal layer (dark bitmap).

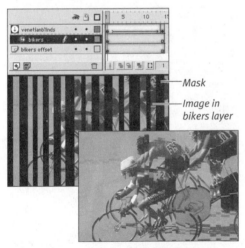

Mask

Image in bikers layer

Figure 1.49 The moving vertical shapes in the mask layer (top) uncover the image of bicyclists in the masked layer. A duplicate image in the bottom normal layer is shifted slightly to create the rippling effect (bottom).

6. Lock both layers to see the effects of your animated mask on the image in the masked layer (**Figure 1.47**).

✔ Tips

- Place duplicate images that vary slightly in a normal layer under both the mask and masked layers. This makes the animated mask act as a kind of filter that exposes the underlying image. For example, add a bright image in the masked layer and a dark version of the same image in a normal layer under the masked layer. The mask becomes a spotlight on the image (**Figure 1.48**). Explore other duplicate-image combinations, such as a sharp and a blurry image, a grayscale and a color image, or an offset image (**Figure 1.49**).

- Place a tween of an expanding box in the mask layer that covers the Stage to simulate cinematic wipes between images (**Figure 1.50**).

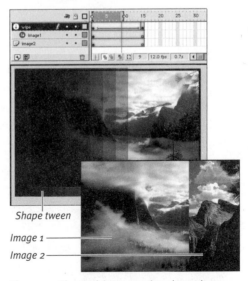

Shape tween

Image 1

Image 2

Figure 1.50 The mask layer contains a large shape tween that covers the entire Stage (top). This creates a cinematic wipe between an image in the masked layer and an image in the bottom, normal layer.

To tween the masked layer:

1. Beginning with two layers, modify the top to be the mask layer and the bottom to be the masked layer.

2. Draw a filled shape or shapes in the mask layer (**Figure 1.51**).

   This becomes the area through which you see your animation on the masked layer.

3. Create a shape tween or a motion tween in the masked layer that passes under the shape in the mask layer (**Figure 1.52**).

4. Lock both layers to see the effects of your animated masked layer as it shows up from behind your mask layer (**Figure 1.53**).

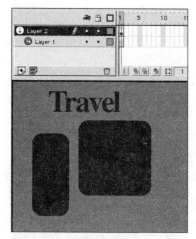

Figure 1.51 Shapes in the mask layer.

Image of castle moving under mask

Figure 1.52 The motion tween in the masked layer (Layer 1) moves under the shapes in the mask layer.

Figure 1.53 The image of the castle moves under the masks. The background color is the color of the Stage.

✔ Tip

■ This approach is a useful alternative to using shape tweens to animate borders or similar types of objects that grow, shrink, or fill in. For example, imagine animating a fuse that shortens to reach a bomb (**Figure 1.54**). Create a mask of the fuse, and animate the masked layer to slowly become smaller, making it look like just the fuse is shortening (**Figure 1.55**).

Figure 1.54 The fuse of a bomb shortens.

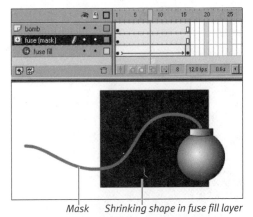

Mask   Shrinking shape in fuse fill layer

Figure 1.55 The bomb's fuse is a thin shape in the mask layer. The rectangular tween in the masked layer shrinks, making it appear as though the fuse is shortening.

ANIMATING YOUR MASKS

In the mask layer, Flash sees all fills as opaque shapes, even if you use a transparent solid or gradient. As a result, all masks have hard edges. To create a softer edge, place a gradient with a transparent center either under or over the mask to hide the edges.

To create a soft-edged mask:

1. Create a mask layer and a masked layer.

2. Place or draw a background image in the masked layer.

3. Draw an ellipse in the mask layer.

4. Copy the ellipse.

5. Insert a new layer between the mask layer and the masked layer.

   Your new layer will become a masked layer.

6. Choose Edit > Paste in Place. A new ellipse appears in the new masked layer, right under the ellipse in the top mask layer (**Figure 1.56**).

7. Fill the pasted ellipse with a radial gradient defined with a transparent center to an opaque perimeter in the same color as the Stage (**Figure 1.57**).

8. Lock all three layers to see the effects of the mask (**Figure 1.58**).

   The mask layer lets you see through an elliptical area. The top masked layer hides the edges of the ellipse by creating a gradual fade toward the center. The bottom masked layer holds the contents of your background image (**Figure 1.59**).

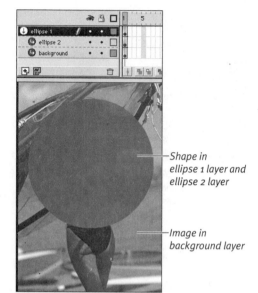

Shape in ellipse 1 layer and ellipse 2 layer

Image in background layer

Figure 1.56 The same ellipse appears in both the mask layer (ellipse 1) and the top masked layer (ellipse 2). The image of the windsurfer is in the bottom masked layer (background).

100% Alpha

0% Alpha

Figure 1.57 A radial gradient with a transparent center in the top masked layer.

Figure 1.58 The resulting soft-edged mask.

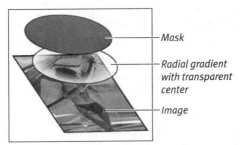

— Mask

— Radial gradient with transparent center

— Image

Figure 1.59 The soft-edged mask is the combination of the mask in the top layer (mask layer), a radial gradient in the middle layer (top masked layer), and the background image in the bottom layer (bottom masked layer).

Creating soft edges with radial transparent gradients works well with circular masks, but if the shapes of your masks are more complicated, you'll need to resort to customizing the fades of your edges.

To create a soft-edged mask with a complex shape:

1. Create a mask layer and a masked layer.

2. Place or draw an image in the masked layer.

3. Draw a complex shape in the mask layer.

4. Copy the shape.

5. Insert a new masked layer between the mask layer and the first masked layer.

6. Choose Edit > Paste in Place.

   Your complex shape appears in the new masked layer right under the original shape in the top mask layer (**Figure 1.60**).

(continued on next page)

Figure 1.60 A complex shape in the top masked layer above an image in the bottom masked layer.

ANIMATING YOUR MASKS

7. Draw an outline with the oval or rectangle tool around your shape (**Figure 1.61**).

8. Fill the area between your shape and the outline with the background color, and delete the fill in the original shape.

Your complex shape is now the "hole" of a larger shape (**Figure 1.62**).

9. Select the entire shape and choose Modify > Shape > Soften Fill Edges (**Figure 1.63**).

The Soften Edges dialog box appears (**Figure 1.64**). The Distance determines the thickness of the soft edge. The Number of steps determines how gradual the transition will be from opaque to transparent. The Direction determines which way the edge softening will take place.

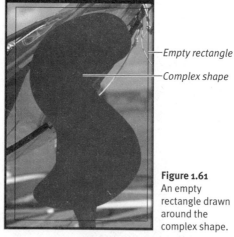

Figure 1.61 An empty rectangle drawn around the complex shape.

Figure 1.62 By filling the area between the shape and the rectangle and deleting the shape, you create a hole.

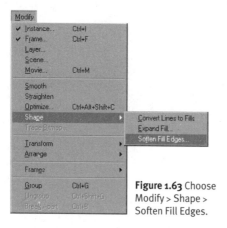

Figure 1.63 Choose Modify > Shape > Soften Fill Edges.

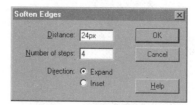

Figure 1.64 The Soften Edges dialog box.

Figure 1.65 The softened edges expand into the "hole" where it is visible through the mask in the top mask layer.

Figure 1.66 The soft edges of a non-circular mask created with Modify > Shape > Soften Fill Edges.

10. Enter the Distance in pixels and the Number of steps, and select Expand for the Direction.

    All the edges around your shape soften. Since the entire shape expands, the actual hole shrinks (**Figure 1.65**).

11. Lock all three layers to see the effects of the mask (**Figure 1.66**).

Although Flash allows multiple masked layers under a single mask layer, you cannot have more than one mask layer affecting any number of masked layers (**Figure 1.67**). To create multiple mask layers, you must also duplicate the masked layers (**Figure 1.68**). Why would you need to have multiple mask layers? Imagine creating an animation that has two spotlights moving independently on top of an image (**Figure 1.69**). The two moving spotlights have to be on separate layers to be tweened, so you need two mask layers.

To create multiple mask layers:

1. Place your image on a masked layer.

2. Create the first mask in the mask layer above your image (**Figure 1.70**).

3. Duplicate your image in a separate masked layer above the first mask.

4. Create the second mask in another masked layer above the duplicate image (**Figure 1.71**).

   Each of the identical images is affected by one of the mask layers, so, in essence, your image is affected by both masks. Increase the number of mask layers by duplicating the image on new masked layers.

This layer will not work as a mask layer

Figure 1.67 Layer 3 and Layer 2 are both defined as mask layers, but only Layer 2 affects Layer 1, the masked layer.

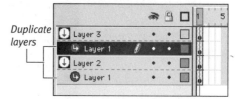

Duplicate layers

Figure 1.68 Layer 2 and Layer 3 can both affect Layer 1 only by duplicating Layer 1.

First mask

Second mask

Figure 1.69 Two independent spotlights over an image, each on separate mask layers.

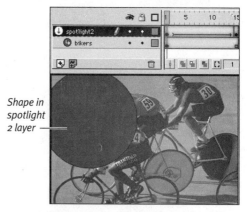

Shape in spotlight 2 layer

Figure 1.70 The first moving spotlight is a motion tween in the mask layer.

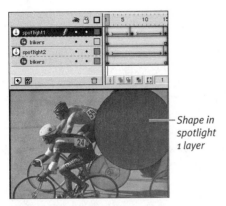

Shape in spotlight 1 layer

Figure 1.71 The second moving spotlight is a motion tween in a second mask layer over a duplicate masked layer.

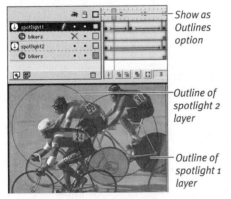

Show as Outlines option

Outline of spotlight 2 layer

Outline of spotlight 1 layer

Figure 1.72 Viewing your masks as outlines lets you see the image underneath; choose the Outlines option in the Layers Properties dialog box, or click on the Show as Outlines icon in your layer.

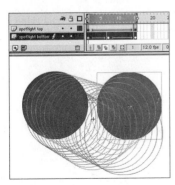

Figure 1.73 Two moving spotlights created within a graphic symbol.

✔ Tips

- To see what your masks are uncovering, use either a transparent fill or choose the Outlines option in your Layers Properties (**Figure 1.72**).

- Flash doesn't allow more than one mask layer to affect a masked layer on the same Timeline, so you need to duplicate the masked layers as outlined in the last task. If you try to get around this problem by creating a graphic symbol with several layers (**Figure 1.73**) and then placing an instance of that symbol in the mask layer (**Figure 1.74**), Flash will only use the bottom layer as the mask (**Figure 1.75**). You won't fare much better using a movie-clip instance in your mask layer. Mask layers with a movie-clip instance show only the first frame of the bottom layer as the mask.

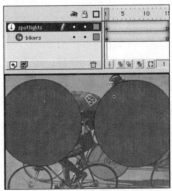

Figure 1.74 The instance of the animated graphic symbol is in the mask layer.

Figure 1.75 Flash only uses the bottom layer of the animated graphic symbol as a mask.

Nesting Masked Layers

Creating multiple masks lets you have each mask layer affect an image or animation equally. In the previous task, each spotlight affected the image independently from the other. If, instead, you want one mask to affect another mask so your masks are cumulative rather than independent, you need to nest the first mask inside a masked layer. Build your first mask and masked layers in a graphic symbol (**Figure 1.76**). Placing an instance of this symbol into a masked layer of the main Timeline will let you build a second mask to affect the instance (**Figure 1.77**). By nesting graphic symbol instances in the masked layer, you can create cumulative masking effects.

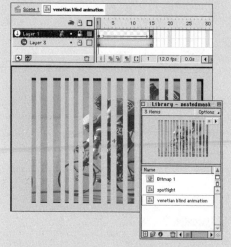

Figure 1.76 The moving vertical stripes mask the bicyclists' image. This moving mask is within a graphic symbol (venetian blind animation).

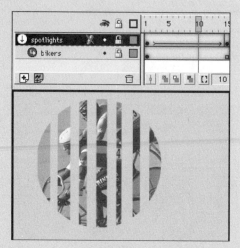

Figure 1.77 The moving spotlight masks the instance of the venetian blind animation. The result is two moving masks, but the venetian blinds are applied first, and then the spotlight is applied.

WORKING WITH VIDEO AND 3D

This chapter explores the exciting possibilities of using media created outside of Flash in your Flash project. Combining digital video or 3D graphics with Flash lets you develop imagery with all the interactivity of Flash ActionScript but without the limitations of the Flash drawing tools. For example, you can create truly interactive movies by importing your videos into Flash, adding buttons, sounds, and graphics, and then exporting the integrated file as a QuickTime movie. Another way is to use an imported video to serve as a guide for your Flash animation, or transform the video completely by applying Flash's editing tools that turn your video into vector drawings. This kind of effect is used often on Flash Web sites promoting theatrical releases or music videos. Short video clips of band members are imported into Flash as a series of bitmap images, simplified into vectors, and sprinkled throughout other graphics and animation to play along with a soundtrack.

Similarly, working with 3D graphics literally adds another dimension to your Flash projects. Although Flash can't actually import and display 3D models, third-party applications let you use models in true 3D space, play with lighting, set camera angles, and export a Flash-compatible vector image. Use 3D objects and animations in Flash as interface elements, buttons, or even feature characters.

Integrating Flash and QuickTime

While several popular formats for digital video exist, QuickTime, MPEG, and AVI formats among them, Flash supports only Apple's QuickTime format. You can import QuickTime movies into Flash; add Flash graphics, animation, and interactivity; and then save the integrated file as a QuickTime movie for playback with the QuickTime Player.

There are several ways to acquire digital video. You can shoot your own footage using a digital video camera, or you can shoot with an analog video camera and convert the video using a digitizing board that you install in your computer. Alternatively, you can use copyright-free video clips that have already been digitized and are available on CD-ROM from commercial image stock houses.

Figure 2.1 Importing a QuickTime movie puts a reference to the source movie in the Library and an instance of the movie on the Stage in Layer 1.

To import a QuickTime movie into Flash:

1. From the File menu, choose Import. The Import dialog box appears.

2. Select the QuickTime file you wish to import, and click Import (Mac) or Open (Windows).

   Flash imports the QuickTime file into your document and places an instance on the Stage in the active layer (**Figure 2.1**). Flash puts a reference to the source movie in the Library. Note that only the first frame of the QuickTime movie is displayed. To play the entire QuickTime movie, the Flash Timeline needs enough frames to accommodate the length of the movie; when you import it, you only see the portion on the Timeline where you have enough frames.

Figure 2.2 This QuickTime movie is 18.4 seconds long. The Flash frame rate is 12.0 frames per second. That means you need 221 frames (18.4 seconds x 12.0 frames per second) to see the whole movie. At frame 221 we see the last frame of the QuickTime movie.

Figure 2.3 The placeholder on the Stage means you're past the end of the QuickTime movie and there are no more frames available to display.

3. Insert enough frames in your Timeline to accommodate your QuickTime movie. To calculate how many frames you will need, multiply the length of your QuickTime movie (in seconds) with the frame rate of your Flash document (the default setting is 12 frames per second). The result is the number of frames needed in the Flash Timeline for the QuickTime movie (**Figure 2.2**).

4. If you add more frames than are needed, Flash will display a placeholder on the Stage when the playhead goes past the end of the QuickTime movie. (**Figure 2.3**). Select the excess frames, and choose Insert > Remove Frames.

✔ Tips

■ For Macintosh users, to quickly import a file, simply drag and drop your QuickTime file from the desktop on the Stage.

■ Flash can only display the video track of an imported QuickTime file, not the sound track, so if your original QuickTime file has sound, you won't be able to hear it within Flash. When you publish your Flash movie as a QuickTime file, the sound will be audible once again.

INTEGRATING FLASH AND QUICKTIME

Keeping track of QuickTime files

Flash maintains a link, or path, to your source QuickTime file instead of embedding it in your document as it does with bitmaps and sounds. This keeps your Flash document small. However, it's important that you preserve the same name and location of your source QuickTime file. If you move or rename your original QuickTime file, new (and existing, if you use Windows) instances of the video, you will get an empty placeholder because Flash can't locate it (**Figure 2.4**).

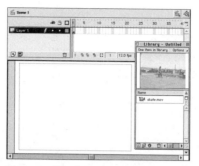

Figure 2.4 The empty placeholder on the Stage means that Flash can't find the original QuickTime movie you've imported, so you'll need to reset the movie's path.

To set a new path for your imported QuickTime movie:

1. Double-click the video icon or the preview window in your Library.

   or

   Select the video symbol in the Library, then from the Library Options menu, choose Properties (**Figure 2.5**).

   The Video Properties dialog box appears, showing the symbol name and the original QuickTime file's location (**Figure 2.6**).

2. Click the Set Path button.

3. Navigate to the new location or renamed QuickTime file, select it, and click Open.

   The new path and filename appear in the Video Properties dialog box next to Path.

4. Click OK.

   Flash will now be able to locate the QuickTime movie, and the empty selection box will be filled with your chosen video.

Figure 2.5 Choose Options > Properties from the Library to get information about the selected symbol.

✔ Tip

- The Name field in the Video Properties dialog box is not the name of your original QuickTime file, but rather the name of your symbol in the Library. These two names can be different as long as the path to the QuickTime file is correct.

Figure 2.6 The Video Properties dialog box shows the name of the symbol and the location of the original QuickTime file.

Figure 2.7 Choose Options > Edit with from the Library to use another application to make changes to your QuickTime file.

Titles and border added on top of QuickTime movie

Smoke added on top of QuickTime movie

Imported QuickTime movie in the bottom layer

Figure 2.8 Add Flash graphics and animation over your imported QuickTime movie. This example shows two animated titles, a mask that uncovers a border, and the special effect of the shape-tweened smoke behind the skateboarder's foot.

Flash allows you to edit your original QuickTime video with either the QuickTime Player or another external digital video editor. Note that if you use the QuickTime Player, you will need QuickTime Pro, the upgrade you buy from Apple, to do any copying, pasting, or resaving of files.

To edit the original QuickTime video:

1. In the Library, select the video symbol you wish to edit.

2. From the Library Options menu, choose Edit with QuickTime Player or Edit with (**Figure 2.7**).

   The external application will launch and open your QuickTime file.

3. Edit the QuickTime file and save it.

4. Return to Flash, delete the current instance of the QuickTime movie on the Stage, and drag a new instance from the Library in order to see the changes to your video.

   Flash will use the new QuickTime file that you just edited and saved.

Once you have imported your QuickTime file, you can add animated Flash elements over the movie, such as titles or special effects.

To overlay Flash animation on the QuickTime movie:

1. For this example, set the Stage size to the same size as the imported QuickTime file (320 by 240 pixels), and position the movie to cover the Stage exactly.

2. Add layers to create animated titles, graphics, or special effects. **Figure 2.8** shows a few animated elements super-imposed on the imported QuickTime file. Check out the Flash and QuickTime files provided on the CD.

(continued on next page)

INTEGRATING FLASH AND QUICKTIME

3. Once you publish your Flash movie as a QuickTime file (covered in this section), both your Flash graphics and the QuickTime movie will play together.

By adding buttons with simple navigation actions, you can create a Flash interface that controls QuickTime content.

To create interactive controls:

1. Create four buttons: a play button, a pause button, a skip to end button, and a skip to beginning button.

2. Place your four button instances in a new layer above the layer containing the imported QuickTime file (**Figure 2.9**).

4. Assign actions to all four button instances by selecting them and opening the Actions panel (**Figure 2.10**).

- ◆ Give the play button the action
  play();

- ◆ Give the pause button the action
  stop();

- ◆ Give the Skip to end button the Action
  gotoAndStop(221);

- ◆ Give the Skip to Beginning button the action gotoAndStop(1);

For more information on the Actions panel, see Chapter 3.

5. Once your Flash movie is published as a QuickTime file (see the next section), your custom Flash buttons will let you navigate to different spots on the Timeline without relying on the standard QuickTime controller (**Figure 2.11**).

Four button instances placed on a layer above the QuickTime movie

Figure 2.9 Add button instances to let your users navigate within the QuickTime movie. These buttons are placed on a separate layer.

Click and hold to select any Action

Action scripts appear in this window

Single-click to expand and choose from a list of Basic Actions

Figure 2.10 Assign basic actions to the on (release) statement using the Object Actions panel. Choose these basic actions from the plus icon or the Basic Actions expandable menu.

INTEGRATING FLASH AND QUICKTIME

Figure 2.11 The exported QuickTime file has the option of leaving out the standard playback controls, letting you use the buttons and actions you've customized.

Export QuickTime

Dimensions:	Width	Height	
	320	X 240	⊠ Match Movie

Alpha: Auto

Layer: Auto

Streaming Sound: ☐ Use QuickTime Compression

[Settings...]

Controller: None

Playback: ☐ Loop
☐ Paused At Start
☐ Play every frame

File: ⊠ Flatten (Make self-contained)

OK   Cancel   Help

Figure 2.12 The Export QuickTime dialog box.

To integrate Flash and QuickTime, you need to publish or export your movie as a QuickTime movie. Although you can display QuickTime movies within the Flash authoring environment, the Flash Player doesn't support QuickTime playback. If you test a Flash movie that contains an imported QuickTime file by choosing Control > Test Movie, you can see all your Flash graphics but no QuickTime movie.

To publish your Flash movie as a QuickTime movie:

1. From the File menu, choose Export Movie. The Export Movie dialog box appears.

2. Name the destination file, and choose QuickTime from the pull-down menu. The Export QuickTime dialog box appears (**Figure 2.12**).

    or

    As an alternative to steps 1 and 2, choose File > Publish Settings. From the Formats tab, check the box next to QuickTime and deselect the others. Select the QuickTime tab.

3. Select the following parameters for QuickTime:

    ◆ **Dimensions:** Allows you to set alternate height and width sizes in pixels.

    ◆ **Alpha:** Controls how the Flash elements are displayed with the QuickTime movie. Choose Copy to make the Flash Stage opaque. Choose Alpha-transparent to make the Flash Stage transparent. Choose Auto to make the Flash Stage transparent or opaque depending on the stacking order of Flash graphics and the QuickTime file.

    ◆ **Layer:** Controls where you want the Flash track to lie in the exported QuickTime file. Choose Auto for the layering to follow your Flash layers.

(continued on next page)

INTEGRATING FLASH AND QUICKTIME

◆ **Streaming Sound:** Lets any sounds in Flash be converted to a QuickTime sound track using QuickTime compression settings.

◆ **Controller:** By choosing None, you can create a QuickTime file that doesn't contain the standard QuickTime playback controls. Use this option if you've created custom navigation buttons with Flash (**Figure 2.13**).

◆ **Playback:** Check these options to control how the movie will play. Avoid using the "Play every frame" option because it will disable any audio in the QuickTime sound track.

◆ **File:** The Flatten option creates a single file incorporating all externally referenced media. This eliminates the need to keep the original imported QuickTime file together with the final exported QuickTime file. The Flatten option also makes the file compatible on both Mac OS and Windows.

4. Click OK or Publish.

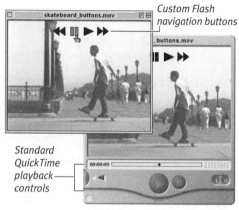

Custom Flash navigation buttons

Standard QuickTime playback controls

Figure 2.13 Two QuickTime movies, with (bottom) and without (top) the standard playback controls.

Not All Flash Features Work in QuickTime Movies

It's very important to understand that only Flash 3 features are currently supported by QuickTime 4. This means that many of the more complicated interactive functions in Flash 5 movies won't work properly or at all when exported as a QuickTime file.

Moreover, some Flash features, even if they are in version 3 or earlier, will not work predictably when played within the QuickTime Player. Here are some of the known problems:

◆ getURL actions assigned to keyframes have no effect.

◆ loadMovieNum actions do not work.

◆ The cursor may not always appear as a hand when passing over the hit state of a button.

◆ Masking a QuickTime movie doesn't work.

You should design your Flash files with these limitations in mind if your intended destination is the QuickTime Player.

QuickTime, QuickTime Video, and AVI

The Export Movie option (File > Export Movie) gives you the choice of QuickTime, and either QuickTime Video or AVI, depending on whether you're using a Mac or a Windows computer. These produce very different formats even though they are all "movie" files.

The QuickTime option allows you to integrate your Flash content into a separate track of the QuickTime file. The Flash content maintains its functionality and its vector information, so the Flash graphics are still resolution-independent.

On the Mac, the QuickTime Video option rasterizes your Flash content and puts it on the video track along with the imported QuickTime movie. All interactivity is lost, and buttons become simple graphics that are locked in at a set resolution (**Figure 2.14**). Choose this option if you wish to create simple, linear movie files from Flash that don't require the latest version of the QuickTime player.

On a Windows computer, you have the option of exporting a movie to AVI format. This also rasterizes Flash content into a linear movie and disables all interactivity (**Figure 2.14**).

QuickTime

QuickTime Video or AVI

Figure 2.14 QuickTime (top) separates Flash content on a different track, maintaining Flash's vector information. QuickTime Video and AVI (bottom) combine Flash graphics with the video so that vector information is lost. Recompression of the original imported QuickTime file also results in degraded picture quality.

Rotoscoping

Rotoscoping is a traditional animator's technique that involves tracing live-motion film to create animation. This process is named after an actual machine, the Roto-scope, which projected live-action film onto an animation board. There, an animator could easily trace the outline of an actor, frame by frame, in order to get a natural motion that would be too difficult to animate by hand.

You can use Flash to import and display QuickTime movies, and do the rotoscoping yourself.

To copy the motion of a QuickTime movie:

1. Import a QuickTime file, and extend the Timeline to accommodate the entire movie (**Figure 2.15**).

2. Add a new layer.

3. Begin tracing the actors or the action in the new layer in keyframe 1 with any of the drawing tools (**Figure 2.16**).

4. Add a blank keyframe by choosing Insert > Blank Keyframe.

    An empty keyframe appears in frame 2.

5. Trace the actors or action in the empty keyframe you just created.

Figure 2.15 A QuickTime movie that is good for rotoscoping contains dramatic action with a clear distinction between background and foreground.

Lock the layer containing the QuickTime movie to prevent you from accidentally moving it

A loose tracing of this trapeze performer was made with the pencil tool set on the Smooth Modifier

Figure 2.16 Zoom in to the area you wish to trace, and use the imported QuickTime file as your guide.

ROTOSCOPING

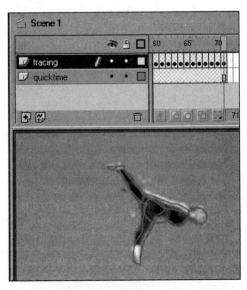

Figure 2.17 Rotoscoping this trapeze artist results in a layer of keyframes with drawings that follow her motion.

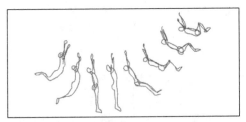

Figure 2.18 When you play the finished rotoscoped animation, watch how natural the animation appears even if the tracings are very loose.

6. Continue the process of adding blank keyframes and tracing until your sequence is complete (**Figure 2.17**).

7. Delete the layer that contains the QuickTime movie to see the final rotoscoped animation (**Figure 2.18**).

   In this example, rotoscoping produces a very loose tracing of the action, but you can trace any level of detail depending on the desired effect.

✔ Tip

■ To make it easier to see the QuickTime movie under your tracings, you can use the Show Layers as Outlines option in your active layer, or you can use a semi-transparent color temporarily until you finish the entire sequence.

ROTOSCOPING

Sometimes the QuickTime movie you are trying to rotoscope has too many frames, making the motion unnecessarily smooth and the tracing too tedious. You can reduce the number of frames that the QuickTime movie occupies in the Flash Timeline by changing the frame rate.

To reduce the number of available frames:

1. Choose Modify > Movie.

   or

1. Double-click the Frame Rate display under the Timeline (**Figure 2.19**).

2. In the Movie Properties dialog box that appears, enter 6 in the Frame Rate field, and click OK (**Figure 2.20**).

3. The QuickTime movie now occupies only half of the previous frames (**Figure 2.21**). Because you're squeezing the same amount of action into fewer frames, the motion will be choppier, but there will be fewer tracings to do.

Frame Rate display

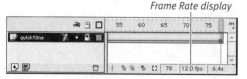

Figure 2.19 The Frame Rate display shows 12.0 fps (frames per second). Double-clicking the display brings up Movie Properties.

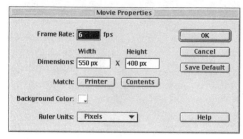

Figure 2.20 The Movie Properties dialog box with the frame rate lowered.

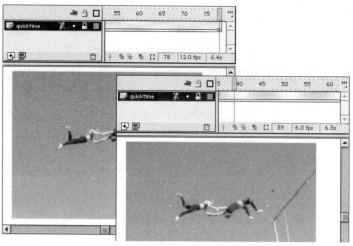

Figure 2.21 At 12.0 fps (left), the trapeze movie ends at Frame 78. Cutting the frame rate in half to 6.0 fps (right) puts the same point in the trapeze movie at Frame 39.

Figure 2.22 Setting the frame rate to 8.0 fps and only allocating 14 frames limits the number of exported bitmaps.

Simulating Video

Because Flash cannot display QuickTime movies in the Flash Player, you have to use a sequence of bitmap images, each in its own keyframe, to simulate video. Essentially, you must create a frame-by-frame animation with bitmaps. Although this process can be laborious and relatively low-tech, the rewards are enormous. When you work with bitmap sequences entirely within Flash, you are no longer restricted by the functionality limitations that the QuickTime Player imposes. You have full access to Flash ActionScripting. You can also tap into Flash's animation and drawing tools, which you can use to trace the bitmaps to vector shapes. This reduces file size and allows for resolution-independent scaling.

To create sequential bitmaps from a QuickTime movie:

1. Import a QuickTime file.

2. You will be importing the same number of images as you have frames, so you have to take care not to create too big a series. Change the frame rate so that the total number of frames occupied by your imported QuickTime movie equates to a manageable number of individual images (**Figure 2.22**).

3. Change the dimensions of the Stage to fit the dimensions of your imported QuickTime movie.

4. Choose File > Export Movie.
   The Export Movie dialog box appears which lets you choose a file format and destination folder.

(continued on next page)

5. Click New folder to create a new destination folder. Enter a name for your exported image files and from the pull-down menu, choose PICT sequence (Mac) or Bitmap sequence (Windows) (**Figure 2.23**). Click Save.

The Export PICT dialog box appears (Mac only). Click the "Match Screen" button to make sure the Width, Height, and Resolution numbers match your Stage size at screen resolution. From the Color Depth pull-down menu, choose the appropriate bitmap level. Check the "Smooth bitmap" option (**Figure 2.24**). Click OK.

Flash will export a series of bitmap images and append a numerical suffix to the filename to keep them in series.

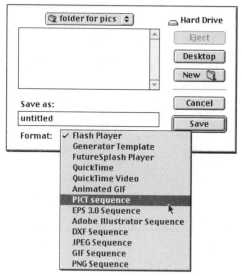

Figure 2.23 The Export Movie dialog box. The Format pulldown menu gives you the choice of export file types.

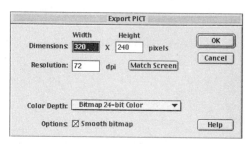

Figure 2.24 The Export PICT dialog box.

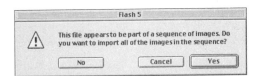

Figure 2.25 The warning dialog box. Click Yes to import the entire sequence.

Each keyframe contains one bitmap   *Fourteen individual bitmaps are saved in the Library*

Figure 2.26 After you import a bitmap series, each image is placed in a separate keyframe and also automatically saved in the Library.

6. Open a new Flash file, and import the first of the images you just created. Flash recognizes that this first image is part of a sequence (**Figure 2.25**), and asks you if you want to import the entire sequence. Click Yes.

Flash places each bitmap in a new keyframe and aligns them all with each other in the active layer (**Figure 2.26**).

✔ Tips

- For Mac users, be sure to bump up your memory partition for the Flash application if you plan to import a large PICT sequence. Working with bitmaps can take up a large amount of memory, and imports will often fail because of insufficient memory.

- If you have movie files in other formats (AVI or MPEG), you have to use another application to generate a sequence of bitmaps, or use an application that converts those files to QuickTime files.

Your file size increases significantly when you use sequential bitmaps to simulate video, to the extent that it can be prohibitive. One way to reduce the file size is to convert all the bitmaps into vectors using Trace Bitmap. This technique for reducing file size can produce cool effects as a bonus. For example, you can achieve interesting poster-ized effects by limiting the number of colors, or create dramatic silhouettes by deleting background elements after the conversion.

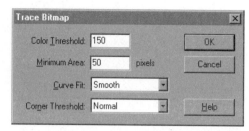

Figure 2.27 The Trace Bitmap dialog box.

To convert the bitmaps into simplified vectors:

1. Select the first keyframe or bitmap on the Stage.

2. Choose Modify > Trace Bitmap.

   The Trace Bitmap dialog box appears (**Figure 2.27**). The parameters in the dialog box determine how accurate the tracing will be to the bitmapped image.

   ◆ **Color Threshold** (a number between 1 and 200): Controls the tolerance level when Flash is deciding whether neighbor-ing pixels should be considered one color or two colors. Flash compares RGB values of two neighboring regions, and if their difference is less than the Color Threshold, then the color is considered to be the same. This means the lower the Color Threshold, the more colors Flash will see and reproduce.

   ◆ **Minimum Area** (a number between 1 and 1000): Controls how large an area Flash will consider when making the color calculations.

   ◆ **Curve Fit:** Controls the smoothness of the contours around shapes.

   ◆ **Corner Threshold:** Determines whether Flash will create sharp or smooth corners.

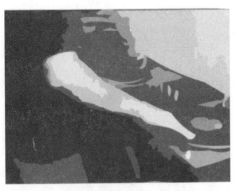

Figure 2.28 This image is the result of a color threshold of 150 and a minimum area of 50.

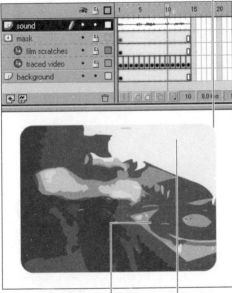

A rectangle with rounded corners masks the traced bitmaps

Animated random lines are added to give the effect of film scratches

The background in the traced bitmaps is deleted

Figure 2.29 Deleting the background in every traced bitmap of the sequence lets you experiment with a more dynamic, animated backdrop. This example masks the traced series, and adds sound and other animated elements.

3. After making the first tracing, select the bitmap in the next keyframe and apply Trace Bitmap. Continue this process until all the bitmaps in the sequence have been traced (**Figure 2.28**).

4. Add, delete, or change shapes and colors as needed in each keyframe by using the drawing and selection tools in the Toolbar (**Figure 2.29**).

Look at the finished Flash file on the CD that accompanies this book to see how this short traced video has been modified.

✔ Tips

■ The Trace Bitmap menu command doesn't have a default keyboard shortcut, but you can create one yourself by choosing Edit > Keyboard Shortcuts. With keyboard shortcuts for Trace Bitmap and Step Forward (>), the process of converting a long sequence of bitmaps becomes much easier.

■ You should be careful not to select too low a Color Threshold value. A traced bitmap that has too many shapes will be a huge drain on performance and will often make the Flash file size larger than if you used the bitmap itself.

SIMULATING VIDEO

Although they are vector shapes, sequences of traced bitmaps still can take up a fair amount of space, so it's important to consider ways to maximize their use and get the most bang for your buck.

Copy your keyframes containing the traced animation and paste them into a graphic symbol or a movie-clip symbol. This allows you to treat them as a single instance, which makes them easier to manipulate.

Here are a few simple strategies you can use to make your one traced animation symbol seem like many different clips (**Figure 2.30**).

To use the traced animation:

◆ Try to keep your simulated video sequences short and small. Most times you only need a few frames (fewer than ten) to suggest a particular motion if you focus on the most dramatic action of a central character.

◆ Modify the instances by changing the brightness, tint, or alpha effect. Repetition of graphics with color variations can create Warhol-inspired designs and maintain really small Flash file sizes.

◆ Transform the instances by flipping them horizontally or vertically, or changing rotation or scale. An enlarged mirror-image animation can provide a dramatically different backdrop.

◆ Apply motion tweens to the instances. Create more variety by moving something that's already moving. For example, tweening instances of an Olympic diver sequence can result in many dive varieties.

First instance of a traced videoclip symbol   *Second instance of the same symbol, flipped, enlarged, and set to begin playing at a different frame*

Figure 2.30 A single traced video clip of a DJ spinning some records gets reproduced twice on the Stage. The background instance has been flipped horizontally, enlarged, and made transparent. The foreground instance moves across the Stage and begins looping at a different frame. The circles are extra animated elements.

◆ Keep some of the instances static in different frames while looping others with different starting frames. In the Instance Panel, choose among three options (Loop, Play Once, and Single Frame) and designate the First frame to play. Setting these play-mode options will prevent multiple instances on the Stage from being synchronized with each other.

Figure 2.31 A series of vector images that have been imported into Flash. A 3D model rendered as a vector image in Swift 3D (left) and an animation rendered as a series of vector images in Vecta3D (right).

Simulating 3D

Like video playback in the Flash Player, true 3D must be faked because Flash has no native support for handling 3D models. But with help from other applications, a little patience, and some ingenuity, you can create vector versions of 3D models and give the illusion of 3D motion.

Third-party applications

There are two basic kinds of applications that can create 3D images for Flash. The first kind are programs like David Gould's Illustrate! and IdeaWorks3D Ltd.'s Vecta3D, which are plug-ins for 3D Studio Max, a traditional 3D program for 3D modeling, rendering, and animation. Illustrate! and Vecta3D output 3D models and animations created in 3D Studio Max as vector images compatible with Flash. They are sometimes called cel shaders because they render the final images to look like cartoons that were drawn on traditional sheets of acetate, or cels. The second kind of program, such as Electric Rain Inc.'s Swift 3D or Adobe Systems Inc.'s Dimensions, are standalone tools that can generate 3D models and animations on their own. Swift 3D will import 3D models and let you build models with primitive objects and extruded text. Adobe Dimensions doesn't support importing 3D models, but has tools for extruding text, revolving objects, and mapping artwork around objects. Vecta3D is also available as a standalone tool, with functions for both importing 3D models and extruding text.

Both kinds of applications output single vector images or vector image series that can be easily brought into Flash in individual keyframes (**Figure 2.31**). In this respect, the process is no different than importing sequential bitmaps to simulate video, except that the conversion to vectors has already been done.

SIMULATING 3D

To animate a 3D title using Flash and a third-party 3D tool

1. Create extruded text in a third-party 3D tool and export it as a Flash-compatible vector file (**Figure 2.32**).

2. Convert each of the letters into graphic symbols, and apply a motion tween to each instance to finish the 3D animation.

When you don't require a complex 3D model and only need a simple object that appears to be moving in 3D space, you can use Flash's existing animation tools (Frame by Frame, motion tween, or shape tween) to create the effect. The result is a much smaller file size and quicker download time.

By simplifying an object's motion, you can break down its three-dimensionality into flat, individual surfaces and tween those shapes. For example, a simple rotating cube consists of rectangles that change shape in a cyclical fashion. The challenge becomes one of defining the keyframes.

To create a 3D rotation:

1. Create the cube in Keyframe 10 as two adjacent, filled rectangles with the seam in the center (**Figure 2.33**).

   To keep the perspective correct, it helps if you use a 3D program to create the initial cube and import it into Flash.

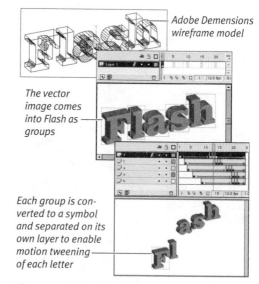

Adobe Demensions wireframe model

The vector image comes into Flash as groups

Each group is converted to a symbol and separated on its own layer to enable motion tweening of each letter

Figure 2.32 Adobe Dimensions creates extruded text (top). Flash imports the shaded image as groups (middle) that can be animated within the Flash environment (bottom).

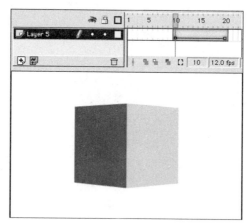

Figure 2.33 A cube is shown as two rectangular shapes.

This cube will rotate from right to left, so this surface will start big (Keyframe 1) and end as a small sliver (Keyframe 20)

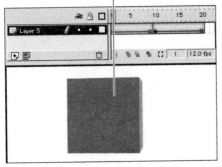

Figure 2.34 Establish one extreme of the cube's rotation in Keyframe 1.

This surface of the cube began in Keyframe 1 as a small sliver

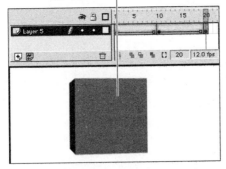

Figure 2.35 Establish the other extreme of the cube's rotation at Keyframe 20.

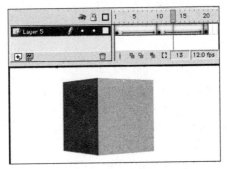

Figure 2.36 Shape tweening provides a smooth transition between the rectangular shapes.

2. Create a keyframe at Frame 1 of the rectangles with more of the left side showing (**Figure 2.34**).

3. Create a keyframe at Frame 20 of the rectangles with more of the right side showing (**Figure 2.35**).

4. Apply a shape tween between all three keyframes (**Figure 2.36**).

The filled rectangles change shape, giving the illusion that a cube is rotating in space.

You can use this same approach with even more complicated rotations, as long as you consider how each surface is moving and changing shape. For a cube that's tilted so that three surfaces are visible instead of two, you need to separate the three surfaces on different layers and apply three shape tweens (**Figure 2.37**).

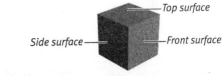

Top surface
Side surface
Front surface

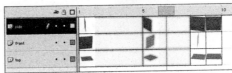

Figure 2.37 The side, front, and top shapes of the cube are separated into three layers for more effective shape tweening. The keyframe at the end lets the shape in the "front" layer disappear.

SIMULATING 3D

Part II: Understanding ActionScript

GETTING A
HANDLE ON
ACTIONSCRIPT

ActionScript is Flash's scripting language for adding interactivity to your graphics and movies. You can use ActionScript to create complex navigation within your Flash movie, Web graphics that react to the location of the viewer's pointer, arcade-style games, and even full-blown e-commerce sites with dynamically updating data. In this chapter you'll learn how to construct ActionScripts to create effective Flash interaction. Think of it as learning the grammar of a foreign language: First you must learn how to put nouns and verbs together, and integrate adjectives and prepositions; then you can expand your communication skills and have meaningful conversations by building your vocabulary. This chapter will teach you the basics of ActionScripting and the skills to increase your vocabulary of Flash actions.

If you are familiar with JavaScript, you'll notice some similarities between it and ActionScript. In fact, ActionScript is based on JavaScript, which is a popular object-oriented programming language for adding interactivity to a Web page. While JavaScript is intended to control the Web browser, ActionScript controls the interactivity within Flash content, so there are slight differences between the two scripting languages. However, the basic syntax of scripts and the handling of objects—reusable pieces of code—remain the same.

Even if you've never used JavaScript, you'll see in this chapter that Flash makes basic scripting easy. You'll learn about the logic of objects and how the Actions panel can automate much of the scripting process while giving you the flexibility to build more sophisticated interaction as your skills improve.

About Objects and Classes

At the heart of ActionScript are objects and classes. Objects are data types, such as sound, graphics, text, or numeric values, that you create in Flash and use to control the movie. For example, a date object is used to retrieve information about the time and the date. And an array object is used to manipulate data stored in a particular order. All of the objects you create belong to a larger collective group known as a class. Flash provides certain classes for you to use in your movie. These predefined classes are also referred to as objects, but they are named and capitalized. For example, the Color object is a class from which different color objects are created. Learning to code in ActionScript centers on understanding the capabilities of these objects and their classes, and using them to interact with each other and with the viewer.

In the real world, we are familiar with objects like a cow, a tree, or a person (**Figure 3.1**). Flash objects range from visible things, such as a spinning ball, to more abstract concepts, such as the date, pieces of data, or the detection of keyboard inputs. Whether concrete or abstract, however, Flash objects are versatile because once you create them, you can reuse them in different contexts. Before you can use objects, you need to be able to identify them, and you do so by name just as we do in the real world. Say you have three people in front of you, Adam, Betty, and Zeke. All three are objects that can be distinguished by name. All three belong to the collective group known as humans. You could also say that Adam, Betty, and Zeke are all *instances* of the human class (**Figure 3.2**). In ActionScript, instances and objects are synonymous, and the terms are used interchangeably in this book.

Figure 3.1 Objects in the real world include things like a cow, a tree, and a person.

Human class

Adam   Betty   Zeke

Figure 3.2 Adam, Betty, and Zeke are three objects of the human class. Flash doesn't have such a class, but this analogy is useful for understanding objects.

Figure 3.3 Adam, Betty, and Zeke are human objects with different properties. Properties differentiate objects of the same class.

About Methods and Properties

Each object of a class (for example, Zeke of the humans) is different from the others in its class by more than just its name. Each person differs because of several characteristics that define the individual such as height, weight, sex, and hair color. In object-oriented scripting, we say that objects and classes have *properties*. Height, weight, sex, and hair color are all properties of the human class (**Figure 3.3**). In Flash, each class has a predefined set of properties that let you establish the uniqueness of the object. The String class has just one property called length, which is a measure of how many characters there are in the object. The MovieClip class, on the other hand, has many properties, such as _height, _width, and _rotation, which are measures of the dimensions and orientation of a particular movie-clip object. By defining and changing the properties of objects, you control what each object is like and how each object differs from the others.

Objects also do things. Zeke can run, sleep, or talk. The things that objects can do are known as *methods*. Each class has its own set of methods. For example, a Sound class has a setVolume method that will play its sound louder or softer, and a Date class has a getDay method that retrieves the day of the week. When an object does something using a method, we say the method is *called,* or that the object *calls* the method.

It's important that you understand the relationships between objects, classes, properties, and methods. Putting objects together so that the methods and properties of one influence the methods and properties of another is what drives Flash interactivity. The key to building your ActionScript vocabulary is learning the properties and methods of different classes.

✔ Tip

■ It helps to think of objects as nouns, properties as adjectives, and methods as verbs. Properties describe their objects, while methods are the actions they perform.

Writing with Dot Syntax

As with other foreign languages, you must learn the rules of grammar in order to put words together. Dot syntax is the convention that ActionScript uses to put objects, properties, and methods together into *statements*. You connect objects, properties, and methods with dots (periods) to describe a particular object or process. For example,

```
Zeke.weight = 188
```

```
Betty.weight = 135
```

The first statement assigns the value 188 to the weight of Zeke. The second statement assigns the value 135 to the weight of Betty. The dot separates the object name from the property (weight) (**Figure 3.4**).

```
Betty.shirt.color = gray
```

This statement describes the object Betty that is linked to the object shirt. The object shirt, in turn, has the property color, which is assigned the value gray. Notice that with dot syntax you use multiple dots to maintain object hierarchy. When you have multiple objects linked in this fashion, it's often easier to read the statement backward. So you could read it as, "Gray is the color of the shirt of Betty."

```
Zeke.run ()
```

This statement causes the object Zeke to call the method run. The parentheses after run signify that run is a method and not a property. You can think of this construction as noun-dot-verb (**Figure 3.5**). Methods will often have *parameters,* or *arguments,* within the parentheses. These affect how the method is executed. For example,

```
Zeke.run (fast)
```

```
Adam.run (slow)
```

Betty.weight = 135   Zeke.weight = 188

Figure 3.4 The hypothetical weight property describes Betty and Zeke. In Flash, the properties of objects can be evaluated and modified with ActionScript.

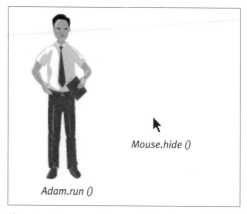

Mouse.hide ()

Adam.run ()

Figure 3.5 Dot syntax lets you make objects call methods. Just as the hypothetical method run() could make the Adam object begin to jog, the real Flash method hide(), when applied to the Mouse object, makes the pointer disappear.

Both of these statements will make the Zeke and Adam objects call the run method, but because each method contains a different argument, the way the run is performed is different: Zeke runs fast, while Adam runs slowly.

Each method will have its own set of arguments. For example, consider the basic Flash action `gotoAndPlay("Scene 1",20)`. `gotoAndPlay` is a method of the MovieClip class. The parenthetical arguments, ("Scene1", 20), refer to the scene and the frame number, so the playhead of the object will jump to Scene 1, Frame 20, and begin playing.

✔ Tip

■ The dot syntax replaces the slash syntax used in previous versions of Flash. Although you can still use the slash syntax, it's recommended that you use the dot syntax because it's more compatible with all the new actions.

More on Punctuation

The dot syntax allows you to construct meaningful processes and assignments with objects, properties, and methods. Additional punctuation symbols let you do more with these single statements.

The Semicolon

In order to terminate individual ActionScript statements and start new ones, you use the semicolon. It functions as a period does in a sentence: It concludes one idea and lets another one begin. For example,

```
stopAllSounds ();
```

```
play ();
```

The semicolons separate the statements, so that first all the sounds stop, then the movie begins to play. Each statement is executed in order from the top down, like a set of instructions or a cookbook recipe.

✔ Tip

■ Flash will still understand ActionScript statements even if you don't have the semicolons to terminate each one. It is good practice, however, to include them in your scripts.

Curly Braces

Curly braces are another kind of punctuation that ActionScript uses frequently. Curly braces group together related blocks of ActionScript statements. For instance, when you assign actions to a button, those actions appear within curly braces of the on (release) statement.

```
on (release) {
    stopAllSounds ();
    play ();
}
```

In this case, both the stopAllSounds action and the play action are executed when the mouse button is released. Notice how the curly braces are separated on different lines to make it easier to read the related ActionScript statements.

The Actions Panel

The Actions panel is the Flash dialog box that lets you access predefined ActionScripts and build custom scripts. You can create, delete, and edit actions in two modes, Normal and Expert, depending on your level of expertise. The Actions panel can automate some of the scripting process; for example, it generates punctuation, such as semicolons and curly braces, automatically.

In Flash, the name of the Actions panel appears as both Object Actions and Frame Actions, depending on which element you currently have selected. In either case, the contents of the panel remain the same, so this book always refers to it as the Actions panel.

To open the Actions panel:

◆ From the Windows menu, choose Actions.

or

◆ From the Launcher bar at the bottom-right corner of the Stage, click the Show Actions button (**Figure 3.6**).

Depending on what is currently selected, either the Frame Actions or the Object Actions panel appears.

or

◆ Double-click a keyframe or Alt-Double-click (Win) or Option-Double-click (Mac) an instance on Stage.

The Frame Actions or Object Actions panel appears so that you can attach actions to either the keyframe or the instance, respectively (**Figure 3.7**).

Show Actions button

Figure 3.6 The Launcher bar at the lower-right corner of your Flash file gives you access to the Show Actions button.

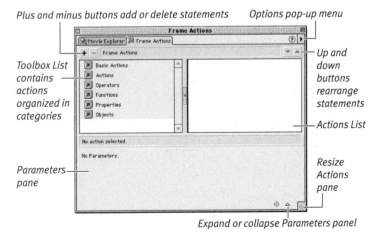

Figure 3.7 The Actions panel in Normal mode.

Normal Mode

The Normal mode of the Actions panel features three different sections and multiple ways to enter ActionScript statements.

Expert Mode

The Expert mode of the Actions panel is for experienced ActionScript developers who don't need the structured scripting help provided in Normal mode. The Expert mode allows you to enter scripts in the Actions List freely as if you were typing in a text-editing application (**Figure 3.8**).

Figure 3.8 The Actions panel in Expert mode.

✔ Tips

- ■ Each script maintains its own mode, so if you create actions in one keyframe in Normal mode and in another keyframe in Expert mode, your Actions panel will switch modes depending on which keyframe is selected.

- ■ Be careful of switching modes while writing one group of ActionScripts. Switching from Expert to Normal will reformat your statements, stripping them of extra white space and indentations. Flash won't allow you to switch from Expert to Normal unless your script is free of errors.

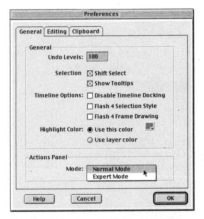

Figure 3.9 The options menu in the Actions panel gives you the choice of Normal or Expert mode.

Figure 3.10 Choose the General tab in the Preferences dialog box to change the default mode for the Actions panel.

To choose Normal or Expert mode:

1. With the Actions panel open, click the right triangular button at the upper right-hand corner.

   The options pop-up menu appears (**Figure 3.9**).

2. Select Normal (Command-N for Mac, Ctrl-N for Windows) or Expert (Command-E for Mac, Ctrl-E for Windows) mode from the menu.

✔ Tip

■ You can set the Actions panel to automatically open to either Normal or Expert mode. From the Edit menu, choose Preferences. Under the General tab of the Preferences dialog box, select either Normal or Expert Mode from the pull-down menu (**Figure 3.10**).

THE ACTIONS PANEL

Table 3.1

Differences Between Expert Mode and Normal Mode		
FEATURE	NORMAL MODE	EXPERT MODE
Direct text entry of ActionScript	No	Yes
Parameters pane	Yes	No
Basic Actions category in Toolbox List	Yes	No
Minus button	Yes	No, select statement and press Delete key
Up and down buttons	Yes	No, use Copy, Cut, and Paste to rearrange statements

To add an action in Normal mode:

1. Select the instance or frame where you want to assign an action. In the Toolbox List, expand an action category by clicking on it.

2. Double-click the desired action.

   The action appears in the Actions List (**Figure 3.11**).

or

1. Select the instance or frame where you want to assign an action. In the Toolbox List, expand an action category by clicking it.

2. Select the action, and drag it into the Actions List or into one of the empty fields in the Parameters pane (**Figure 3.12**).

   The action appears in the Actions List or the Parameters pane.

or

1. Select the instance or frame where you want to assign an action. Click the plus button above the Toolbox List, and select the action from the pull-down menus (**Figure 3.13**).

   The action appears in the Actions List.

or

1. Select the instance or frame where you want to assign an action. Using the shortcut key commands that are listed under the plus-button menu, first press the Escape key.

2. Type in the two-letter code corresponding to the action you want.

   The action appears in the Actions List. For a full list of shortcut key commands for actions, see Appendix C.

Figure 3.11 Add an action by choosing a statement from the Toolbox List.

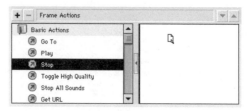

Figure 3.12 Add an action by dragging the statement to the Actions List on the right. The pointer changes temporarily to show you where you can drop the action.

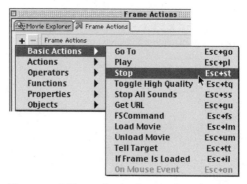

Figure 3.13 Add an action by choosing from the plus-button pull-down menus.

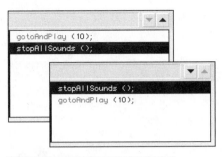

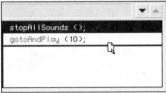

Figure 3.14 Move the stopAllSounds () statement by using the arrow buttons (top) or by dragging it to a new location (bottom). The bold horizontal line shows you where it will be once you release it.

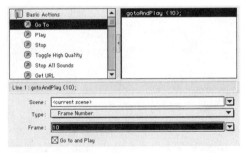

Figure 3.15 The Parameters pane lets you change the parameters of a selected action. The Go To action has two parameter fields, a pull-down menu, and a check box that affect the way it will work. Entering 10 in the Frame field and checking the Go to and Play button change the statement in the Actions List and make the playhead go to Frame 10 and begin playing.

To edit actions in Normal mode:

◆ Select the action and use the up and down arrow buttons to rearrange it in the Actions List, or select the action and drag it to its new location (**Figure 3.14**).

◆ Select the action and use the minus button to delete it from the Actions List, or press the Delete key.

◆ Enter values in the empty fields, check boxes, and pull-down menus of the Parameters pane to change the arguments for a selected action. The Actions List shows the action with the parameters in place (**Figure 3.15**).

✔ Tips

■ You can drag actions directly into Parameter fields or the Actions List.

■ You can still use familiar editing commands such as Copy, Cut, and Paste to create and rearrange ActionScripts. However, when you paste a copied script, the new script appears after the selection rather than replacing it as it would in a text-editing application.

■ Use the Shift key to select multiple selections to Copy or Cut.

THE ACTIONS PANEL

63

To modify the Actions panel display:

◆ Drag or double-click the vertical splitter bar, or click the arrow button that divides the Toolbox and Actions windows, to collapse or expand them (**Figure 3.16**).

◆ Click the triangle at the bottom-right corner of the Actions panel to collapse or expand the Parameters pane (**Figure 3.17**).

Vertical splitter bar being dragged

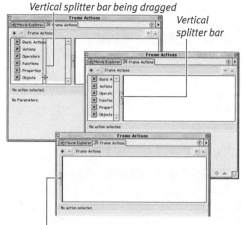

Vertical splitter bar

Vertical splitter bar on a completely expanded Actions List

Figure 3.16 Resizing the Actions panel windows by dragging (top) or clicking the vertical splitter bar. The Actions List window can be resized (middle) or completely expanded (bottom).

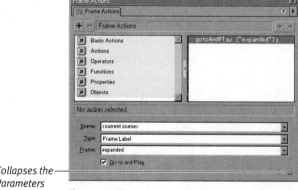

Collapses the Parameters pane

Figure 3.17 The Actions panel with the Parameters pane.

THE ACTIONS PANEL

ActionScript Categories

You've seen how objects, methods, and properties are essential components of ActionScript, but how do they relate to the categories of actions in the Toolbox List in the Actions panel? And what are the other categories of actions? In Normal mode, Flash organizes all actions hierarchically into six categories: Basic Actions, Actions, Operators, Functions, Properties, and Objects. Some contain subcategories of actions. The following is a brief description of the categories.

◆ Basic Actions contain simple actions that mostly deal with navigation, such as play(). The category includes actions to play different frames of your movie, load external movies or Web sites, and assign mouse responses.

◆ Actions contain the Basic Actions plus more complex actions to control the movie. This category includes actions that manipulate variables (placeholders), expressions (formulas that combine variables), and conditional statements. This category also includes actions that work with movie clips, such as startDrag(mySpaceship). In general,

you will be accessing many of the actions in this category to set up your objects and to modify, compare, or call their properties and methods.

◆ Operators contain the symbols and statements that actually transform variables and expressions or test one value against another. They include the common mathematical symbols such as addition and subtraction as well as symbols to modify text elements.

◆ Functions contain actions such as hitTest(bullseye) that retrieve specific pieces of information based on data that you supply. You can think of functions as an input-output machine that returns useful information for you to use.

◆ Properties contain the properties of objects that you can modify or evaluate, such as _rotation. Most of them are properties of movie clips only, and some are properties that affect the entire Flash movie.

◆ Objects contain all the objects, and their unique methods and properties, for example, Selection.getFocus().

Using Objects

Now that you know what objects are and how to operate the Actions panel, you can begin to script with objects and call their methods, or evaluate and assign new properties.

Flash provides preexisting classes that it calls "objects." There are really two definitions of objects here. The Array object, the Boolean object, the Color object, and all the other objects that Flash provides in the Objects category of the Toolbox List are referred to as objects because they are predefined classes. Objects in the general sense still refer to single instances of a class. So the Array object should really be called the Array class, and will still have an object created from itself. In this book, we refer to the Flash predefined classes as objects with capitalized names since that's the way they are categorized in the Actions panel Toolbox List. These Flash classes have methods and properties that control different elements of your Flash movie, such as graphics, sound, data, time, or mathematical calculations. You can also build your own classes from scratch by combining some of the preexisting classes and actions with functions (see Chapter 11, Manipulating Information).

Predefined Classes

Flash's predefined classes reside in the Objects category in the Actions panel (**Figure 3.18**). To use these classes, first you must create an instance of the class by giving it a name. The process is similar to creating an instance of, or instantiating, a symbol; you need to create an instance of the class in order to use it in ActionScript, and you do so by naming it. Use the action set variable to assign a unique name to a new instance of the class.

```
Adam = new Human ();
```

```
myColor = new Color ();
```

Figure 3.18 Flash's predefined objects control different kinds of information.

These two statements create new objects that you can now use and manipulate. The statement that contains the new operator in front of the class, as shown in the examples above is called a *constructor function*. Constructor functions are specialized functions that create new instances from classes.

The next step involves calling an object's methods, or evaluating and assigning new properties. You can call a method by simply choosing the evaluate action and entering an expression using dot syntax:

```
myColor.setRGB(0x00CC33)
```

This statement calls the method setRGB to change the color associated with the myColor object.

✔ Tip

■ Some of the Flash objects, such as the Key object, the Math object, and the Mouse object, do not need a constructor function to instantiate an object. You can use their methods and properties immediately without having a named object. You can tell which of the Flash objects don't require a constructor function by looking in the Objects category in the Toolbox List. Those that don't require a constructor function won't list it among their methods and properties.

USING OBJECTS

First you'll see how to use the actions `set variable`, `new`, and `evaluate` to construct and use new objects. Later chapters introduce you to specific objects, properties, and methods and show you how to use them to control your Flash movie.

The following tasks demonstrate instantiating the Date object and setting a variable to retrieve the current date.

To create an object:

1. Open the Actions panel in Normal mode.

2. From the Toolbox List or the plus button, choose Actions > set variable.

   A new statement appears in the Actions List with empty fields in the Parameters pane (**Figure 3.19**).

3. In the Variable field, enter the name you wish to call your object (**Figure 3.20**).

4. Place your pointer in the Value field. Choose Objects > Date > new Date, or drag new Date into the Value field.

   The constructor function `new Date` appears in the Value field (**Figure 3.21**).

5. Delete the highlighted arguments within the parentheses of the `new Date` constructor function. Check the Expression box next to the Value field (**Figure 3.22**).

   The quotation marks around the `new Date` constructor function in the Actions List disappear. This makes sure that Flash recognizes that the name of your instance evaluates a new Date object and is not assigned to the actual characters contained in the Value field.

   The Actions List shows the full statement, which assigns the variable name to the object. Your Date object is instantiated and ready to use (**Figure 3.23**).

Figure 3.19 The set `variable` action requires a variable and a value.

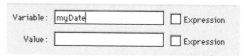

Figure 3.20 Enter `myDate` as the name of the Date object.

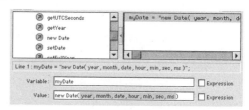

Figure 3.21 The constructor function `new Date` has the optional arguments year, month, date, hour, min, sec, and ms.

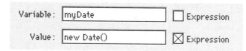

Figure 3.22 The `new Date` constructor function, without any arguments, doesn't assign specific properties to the myDate object.

Figure 3.23 The finished statement creates the object called myDate from the Date object.

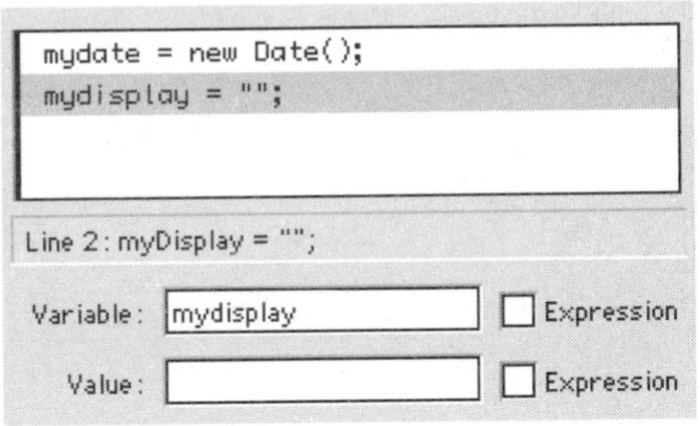

```
mydate = new Date();
mydisplay = "";
```
Line 2: myDisplay = "";

Variable: mydisplay   ☐ Expression

Value: _____   ☐ Expression

Figure 3.24 Enter mydisplay for the Variable name, and leave the Expression box unchecked.

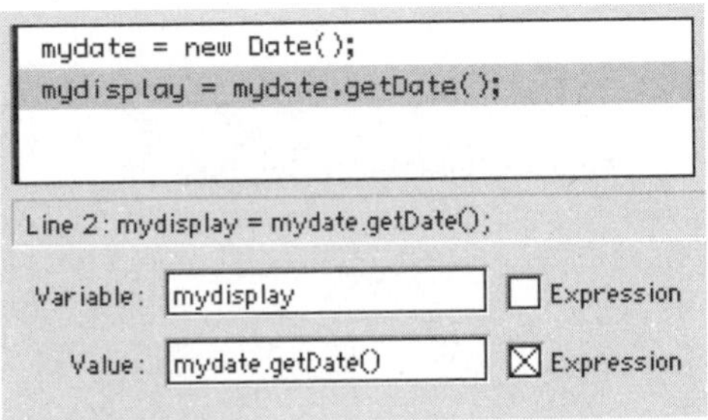

```
mydate = new Date();
mydisplay = mydate.getDate();
```
Line 2: mydisplay = mydate.getDate();

Variable: mydisplay   ☐ Expression

Value: mydate.getDate()   ☒ Expression

Figure 3.25 The variable mydisplay will hold the information that the getDate method retrieves from the mydate object.

To call a method of an object:

1. Continue with the previous task. In the Actions panel, choose Actions > set variable.

   A new statement appears below the first.

2. In the Variable field, enter the name of a variable (**Figure 3.24**).

3. In the Value field, enter the name of the Date object you created in the last task (myDate, in this example).

4. With your pointer still in the Value field, choose Objects > Date > getDate. Check the Expression box (**Figure 3.25**).

   The getDate method appears in the Value field after the object called myDate. The completed statement gets the current date and puts that information into the variable called mydisplay. The information that this method gets is called the *returned value*.

About the Expression Box

Checking the Expression box takes off the quotation marks in the Value field, changing what is known as a *string literal* to an *expression*. A string literal is always contained within quotation marks and represents the actual collection of characters—numbers, letters, or symbols. An expression, on the other hand, is a formula that may contain variables, or placeholders, that Flash needs to evaluate before knowing what the entire expression represents. For example, the string literal of "3+2" is just the three characters, 3+2. The expression of 3+2, however, is 5. We'll work more with expressions and variables in Part V: Working with Information.

USING OBJECTS

5. Select your text tool, and drag out an empty selection on the Stage. Under the Text Options panel, choose Dynamic Text from the pull-down menu, and in the Variable field enter the name of the variable that holds the current date (**Figure 3.26**).

The dynamic text box on the Stage displays the value of its variable during playback of the movie. You will learn more about dynamic text in Chapter 10.

6. Test your movie by choosing Control > Test movie.

Flash instantiates a Date object, and then makes the object call the `getDate` method. The returned value (the date) is put into the variable called mydisplay. You see the value of this variable in the text field on the Stage.

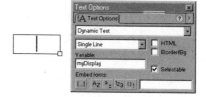

Figure 3.26 The text field at the left is set to Dynamic Text with the variable mydisplay.

✔ Tip

- In this task, you used the action `set variable` to assign a variable to the returned value of a method. This was necessary so that you could see the results of the method. Other methods may not need to have a variable assigned to them. For example, the method for the Sound object `start()` simply begins to play a sound file. In this case, you can use the action `evaluate` to call the method.

Symbols and Classes

Symbols are *not* classes. Symbols are not even objects. It's true that a movie clip is both a symbol and an object, but this is the one exception, and perhaps the source of some confusion. Graphics, buttons, sounds, bitmaps, and QuickTime video clips are all symbols that appear in the Library, but they are not objects or classes because they do not have methods and properties that you can control with ActionScript. Buttons do things not because they have methods but because you assign actions to their instances.

There are some parallels between classes and symbols. Symbols are reusable assets created in or imported to the Library. With these symbols you create instances, or copies of the symbols, to use in your movie. Classes, as you have seen, also have instances made from them to be used in your movie.

```
// instantiate the mydate object
mydate = new Date();
// retrieve the date and put it
// in the variable called mydisplay
mydisplay = mydate.getDate();
```

Figure 3.27 Comments interspersed with ActionScript statements help make sense of the code.

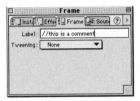

Figure 3.28 Double slashes indicate a comment in a Frame label.

Using Comments

Once you have built a strong vocabulary of Flash actions and are constructing complex statements in the Actions panel, you should include remarks in your scripts to remind yourself and your collaborators of the goals of the ActionScript. Comments help you keep things straight as you develop intricate interactivity and relationships among objects (**Figure 3.27**).

To create a comment:

◆ In the Actions panel, select Actions > comment. In the Comment field in the Parameters pane, enter your comments.

◆ In Expert mode only, type two slashes (//) in the Actions List. Enter your comments after the two slashes.

Comments appear in a different color than the rest of the script, making them easy to locate.

✔ Tips

■ If you have a long comment, break it up with multiple comment statements. That way, you'll have separate lines and you won't have to scroll the Actions List to see the end of a long remark.

■ Don't worry about creating too many comments. They are not compiled with the rest of the script, so they won't bog down performance. Also, because they aren't included in the exported SWF file, they don't increase file size.

■ The slash convention for creating comments in ActionScripts is the same for creating them in the Frame panel. When you modify a frame, begin with two slashes (//) to indicate a comment rather than a label (**Figure 3.28**).

Part III: Navigating Timelines and Communicating

ADVANCED BUTTONS AND USER INPUT

4

Creating graphics and animation in Flash is only half the story. You can then incorporate interactivity via buttons and ActionScript to give the viewer control over those graphics and animations. Interactivity is essential for site navigation and e-commerce interfaces on the Web, as well as for game development, online tutorials, or anything that requires that the viewer make choices.

What makes a movie interactive? Interactivity is the back-and-forth communication between the user and the movie. In a Flash movie, the user might react to something that's going on by moving the pointer, clicking the mouse button, or pressing a particular key on the keyboard. That action may trigger a response from the Flash movie, which in turn prompts the user to do something else. It's the user's reactions to things that happen, or what Flash calls *events,* that make up interactivity. Flash uses a combination of ActionScript assigned to frames, button instances, and objects to handle these events in statements conveniently known as *event handlers.*

This chapter first explores button symbols and more advanced applications of buttons. You'll learn how to extend their functionality by creating invisible buttons, tweening button instances, and creating fully animated buttons. You'll tackle the issues involved in creating a more complex button, such as pull-down menu, which includes different mouse events, tracking options, and movie clips. Finally, you'll see how to control user input via the keyboard using key events with button instances and the Key object. In addition to the mouse event and the key event, a third kind of event, the clip event, is important for controlling user interaction. Since clip events are associated with movie clips, they will be discussed in Chapter 5, which focuses on the movie clip and the control of Timelines.

Invisible Buttons

Flash lets you define four special keyframes of a button symbol that describe how the button looks and responds to the mouse, the Up, Over, Down, and Hit states. The Up state shows what the button looks like when the pointer is *not* over the button. Over shows what the button looks like when the pointer is over the button. Down shows what the button looks like when the pointer is over the button with the mouse button depressed. And Hit defines the actual active, or "hot," area of the button (**Figure 4.1**).

You can exploit the flexibility of Flash buttons by defining only particular states. If you leave empty keyframes in all states except for the Hit state, you create an invisible button. An invisible button contains only a Hit state, which defines the area that responds to the pointer (**Figure 4.2**). Invisible buttons are extremely useful for creating multiple, generic hot spots to which you can assign actions. By placing invisible button instances on top of graphics, you essentially have the power to make anything on the Stage a button. For example, if you have several blocks of text you want the user to read in succession, you can set it up to have the user click on each paragraph to advance to the next one. Instead of creating separate buttons out of each text block, make just one invisible button, and stretch instances to fit each one. Assign actions to each invisible button instance that covers the paragraphs (**Figure 4.3**).

When you drag an instance of an invisible button onto the Stage, you actually see the Hit area as a transparent blue shape, allowing you to place it precisely. When you choose Control > Enable Simple Buttons, the button disappears.

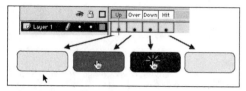

Figure 4.1 The four keyframes of a button symbol.

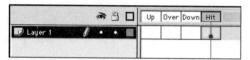

Figure 4.2 An invisible button only has the Hit keyframe defined.

Two instances of the same invisible button symbol

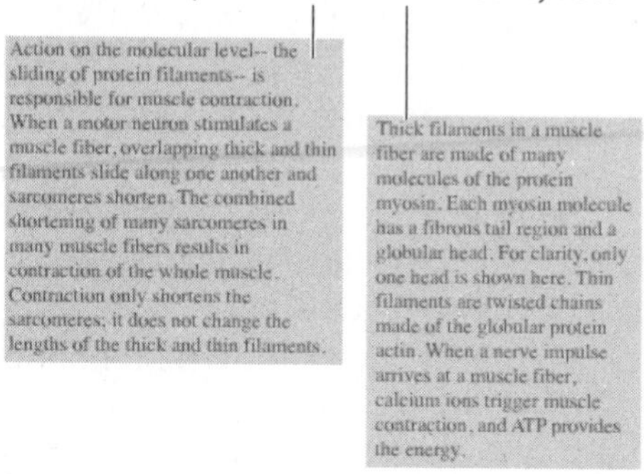

Action on the molecular level-- the sliding of protein filaments-- is responsible for muscle contraction. When a motor neuron stimulates a muscle fiber, overlapping thick and thin filaments slide along one another and sarcomeres shorten. The combined shortening of many sarcomeres in many muscle fibers results in contraction of the whole muscle. Contraction only shortens the sarcomeres; it does not change the lengths of the thick and thin filaments.

Thick filaments in a muscle fiber are made of many molecules of the protein myosin. Each myosin molecule has a fibrous tail region and a globular head. For clarity, only one head is shown here. Thin filaments are twisted chains made of the globular protein actin. When a nerve impulse arrives at a muscle fiber, calcium ions trigger muscle contraction, and ATP provides the energy.

Figure 4.3 Invisible button instances over text blocks.

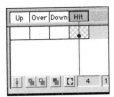

Figure 4.4 An invisible button symbol. The rectangular shape in the Hit keyframe defines the active area of the button.

To create an invisible button:

1. From the Insert menu, choose New Symbol.

   The Symbol Properties dialog box appears.

2. Type in the name of your button, and choose Button as the Behavior. Click OK.

   A new button symbol is created in the Library, and you enter symbol-editing mode.

3. Select the Hit keyframe.

4. From the Insert menu, choose Keyframe.

   A new keyframe is created in the Hit state.

5. With the Hit keyframe selected, draw a generic shape that serves as the hot spot for your invisible button (**Figure 4.4**).

6. Return to the main Timeline.

7. As with any button symbol, drag an instance of the symbol from the Library onto the Stage.

   A transparent blue shape appears on the Stage indicating the Hit state of your invisible button.

8. Move, scale, and rotate the invisible button instance to cover any graphic.

9. From the Actions panel, assign an action to the button instance.

   When you enable simple buttons, the transparent blue area disappears, but your pointer changes to a hand to indicate the presence of a button.

INVISIBLE BUTTONS

Tool tips or helpful pop-up reminders can also be created using invisible buttons. Create a short message in the Over state of an invisible button, and position these instances wherever the little messages apply (**Figure 4.5**).

To create pop-up tool tips with invisible buttons:

1. Create an invisible button as illustrated in the previous task.

2. Select the Over state and insert a new keyframe.

3. In the Over state, create a graphic that guides users about a particular feature that may be scattered through your Stage or movie (**Figure 4.6**).

4. Return to the main movie Timeline and place instances of your invisible button over all the appropriate spots.

✔ Tips

■ Be careful about rotating and scaling your instance because it will also affect the button's Over state (**Figure 4.7**).

■ Be conscious of the stacking order of invisible buttons and how they are placed in your layers. The topmost button will take precedence over any button underneath it, effectively disabling its action.

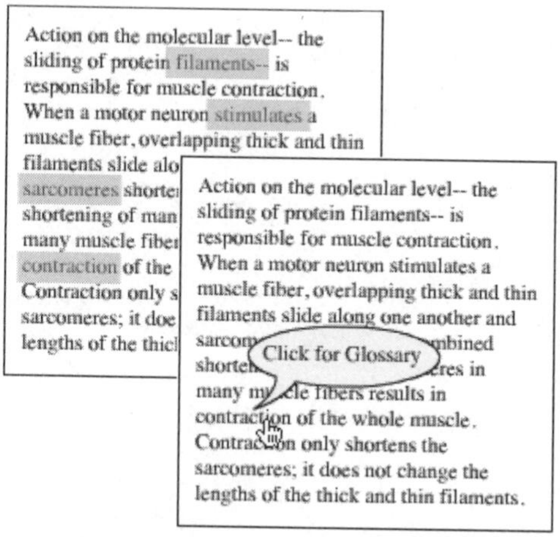

Figure 4.5 The Over state of this invisible button has a balloon with directions to go to the Glossary. Multiple instances can be used to cover different words.

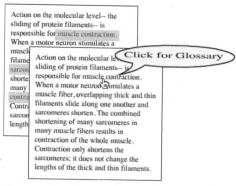

Figure 4.6 When only the Over state is defined in an invisible button, it will appear to pop up when the mouse rolls over the active area.

Figure 4.7 The instance over "muscle contraction" is stretched, making the Over state of the button stretched as much.

```
on (release) {
    gotoAndPlay ("happy birthday");
}
```

Figure 4.8 The action attached to this balloon button instance makes you go to the label *happy birthday* and begin playing.

Motion tweens of the button instance — gotoAndPlay (1) action

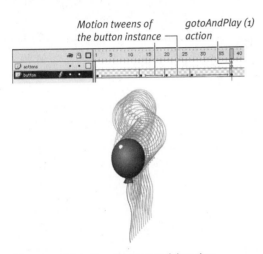

Figure 4.9 This balloon floats up and down in a constant loop.

Actions assigned to the Button Instance in this Keyframe will hold true until the next Keyframe

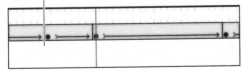

Figure 4.10 Actions assigned to tweened instances. The actions assigned to the first instance of any tween are the ones that are followed.

Tweening Buttons

Since buttons in Flash are a type of symbol, you can tween them just like any other kind of symbol instance. By giving motion to your buttons, you can create moving menus and interfaces that still respond to the pointer and carry out actions assigned to them.

To apply a motion tween to a button:

1. From the Insert menu, choose New Symbol and create a button symbol.

2. Return to the main movie Timeline, and drag an instance of it onto the Stage.

3. Select the instance and open the Actions panel in Normal mode. Add an action to your button instance (**Figure 4.8**).

4. Create a motion tween as you would normally for a graphic instance. Insert new keyframes, move or transform each instance, then choose Motion Tween in the Frames panel.

5. At the end of your motion tween add the action gotoAndPlay(1).

   Flash creates an endless loop for your motion-tweened button (**Figure 4.9**).

5. Create a spot on the Timeline where the action assigned to the button Instance takes the user.

6. Test your movie. Throughout its tween, the button instance is active and responds to your pointer.

✔ Tip

- Tweened button instances use the actions that are assigned to the first keyframe of the motion tween (**Figure 4.10**). It's a good idea to assign an action to the button instance first, and then create your motion tween. That way, all subsequent inserted keyframes will contain the same instance with the same actions.

Animated Buttons and the Movie Clip Symbol

Animated buttons display an animation in any of the first three keyframes (Up, Over, and Down) of the button symbol. For example, a button can spin when the pointer rolls over it because there's an animation of the spinning button in the Over state. How do you fit an animation in only one keyframe of the button symbol? The answer is to use a movie clip.

Movie clips are a special kind of symbol that allow you to have animations that run regardless of where they are or how many actual frames the instance occupies. This is possible because a movie clip's Timeline runs independently of any other Timeline, including other movie-clip Timelines and the main movie Timeline in which it may reside. This independence means that as long as you establish an instance on the Stage, a movie-clip animation will play all of its frames regardless of where it is. Placing a movie-clip instance in a keyframe of a button symbol makes the movie clip play whenever that particular keyframe is displayed. That is the basis of an animated button.

For example, an animation of a butterfly flapping its wings may take ten frames in a movie-clip symbol. Placing an instance of that movie clip on the Stage in a movie that has only one frame will still allow you to see the butterfly flapping its wings (**Figure 4.11**). This functionality is useful for cyclical animations that play no matter what else may be going on in the current Timeline. Blinking eyes, for instance, can be a movie clip placed on a character's face. No matter what the character does—whether moving or static in the current Timeline—the eyes will blink continuously.

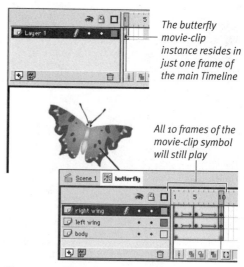

The butterfly movie-clip instance resides in just one frame of the main Timeline

All 10 frames of the movie-clip symbol will still play

Figure 4.11 Movie clips have independent Timelines.

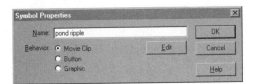

Figure 4.12 Create a new movie-clip symbol by naming it and selecting the behavior.

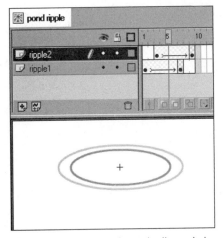

Figure 4.13 The pond ripple movie clip symbol contains two tweens of an oval getting bigger and gradually fading.

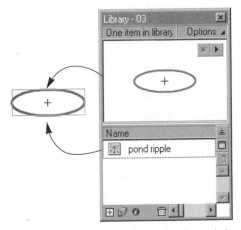

Figure 4.14 Bring an instance of a movie-clip symbol onto the Stage by dragging it from the Library.

The movie clip is unique in that it is also a Flash object. This means that along with its independent Timeline, the movie clip has methods and properties you can control with an action script. You'll learn how to control a movie clip's Timeline as well as its methods and properties in the upcoming chapters. For now, we'll look at how to use a movie clip in the context of buttons.

To create a movie clip:

1. From the Insert menu, choose New Symbol.

   The Symbol Properties dialog box appears.

2. Type in a descriptive name for your movie-clip symbol, choose Movie Clip as the Behavior, and click OK (**Figure 4.12**). You will enter symbol-editing mode.

3. Create the graphics and animation on the movie-clip Timeline (**Figure 4.13**).

4. Return to the main Stage.

   Your movie clip is stored in the Library as a symbol, available for you to bring onto the Stage as an instance (**Figure 4.14**).

✔ Tip

■ New instances of movie clips will automatically begin playing from the first frame. This also applies to instances in different scenes. For example, imagine that you build a movie-clip animation of a clock whose hand makes a full rotation starting at 12 o'clock. If you place an instance in Scene 1 and continue your movie in Scene 2, Flash will consider the instance in Scene 2 as new, and will reset the movie clip animation and begin playing the clock animation at 12 o'clock.

To create an animated button:

1. Create a movie-clip symbol that contains an animation as described in the previous task.

2. Create a button symbol and define the four keyframes for the Up, Over, Down, and Hit states (**Figure 4.15**).

3. Select either the Up, Over, or Down state in the Symbol-Editing mode of your button, depending on when you would like to see the animation.

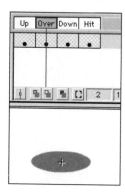

Figure 4.15 A simple button symbol with ovals in all four keyframes.

Comparing a Movie-Clip Instance with a Graphic Instance

How does a movie clip instance differ from a graphic instance? If you create the same animation in both a movie clip symbol and a graphic symbol, and then place both instances on the Stage, the differences become clear. The graphic instance shows its animation in the authoring environment, displaying however many frames are available in the main Timeline. For example, if the graphic symbol contains an animation lasting ten frames and the instance occupies four frames of the main Timeline, then you will see only four frames of the animation. Movie clips, on the other hand, do not work in the Flash authoring environment. You need to export the movie as a SWF to see any movie clip animation or functionality. When you do export the movie, Flash plays the movie-clip instance continuously, regardless of the number of frames the instance occupies, and even when the movie itself has stopped.

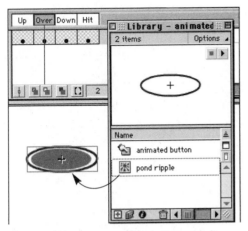

Figure 4.16 The Over state of the button symbol. Place an instance of the pond ripple movie clip in this keyframe to play the pond ripple animation whenever the pointer moves over the button.

Figure 4.17 The completed animated button. When the pointer passes over the button, the pond ripple movie clip plays.

4. Place an instance of your movie-clip symbol on the Stage (**Figure 4.16**).

5. Return to the main movie Timeline, and drag an instance of your button on the Stage.

6. From the Control menu, select Test Movie.

Your button instance plays the movie-clip animation continuously as your pointer interacts with the button (**Figure 4.17**).

✔ Tip

■ Stop the continuous cycling of your movie clip by placing a stop action in the last keyframe of your movie-clip symbol. Because movie clips have independent Timelines, they will respond to frame actions. Graphic symbols do not respond to frame actions.

Complex Buttons

You can use a combination of invisible buttons, tweening buttons, animated buttons, and movie clips to create complex buttons such as pull-down menus. The pull-down (or popup) menu is a kind of button, common in computer systems and Web interfaces, that is useful for presenting several choices under a single heading. The functionality consists of a single button that expands to show more buttons, then collapses once a selection has been made (**Figure 4.18**).

To build your own pull-down menu, the basic strategy is to place buttons inside a movie clip. The buttons control which frames within the movie-clip Timeline to play. Whether the menu is expanded or collapsed is all determined within the movie clip. Placing an instance of this movie clip on the Stage allows you to access either the expanded or collapsed state independently of what's happening in your main movie.

To create a simple pull-down menu:

1. Create a button symbol that will be used for the top menu button as well as the choices in the expanded list. Fill the Up, Over, Down, and Hit keyframes with a filled rectangle (**Figure 4.19**).

2. Create a new movie-clip symbol. Enter symbol-editing mode for the movie clip.

3. Insert a new keyframe at a later point in the movie-clip Timeline.
   You now have two keyframes. The first one will contain the collapsed state of your menu, and the second one will contain its expanded state (**Figure 4.20**).

4. Drag one instance of your button symbol into the first keyframe. Add text over the instance to describe the button.
   This is the collapsed state of your menu.

Figure 4.18 Typical pull-down menus: the Mac OS file menu (left) and a Web menu from Netscape Navigator (right).

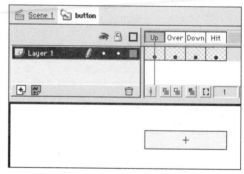

Figure 4.19 A generic button with the four keyframes defined.

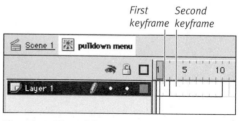

Figure 4.20 The pulldown menu movie-clip Timeline contains two keyframes, one at frame one, and another at frame three.

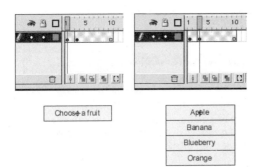

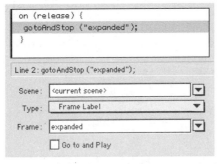

Figure 4.21 The two states of your pull-down menu. The collapsed state is in the first keyframe (left); the expanded state is in the second keyframe (right). The expanded state contains four button instances which represent the choices for the menu.

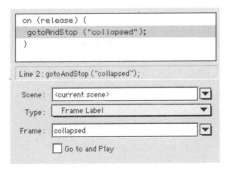

```
on (release) {
  gotoAndStop ("expanded");
}
```

Line 2: gotoAndStop ("expanded");

Scene:	<current scene>	▼
Type:	Frame Label	▼
Frame:	expanded	▼
	☐ Go to and Play	

Figure 4.22 This button sends the Flash playhead to the frame labeled expanded and stops there.

```
on (release) {
  gotoAndStop ("collapsed");
}
```

Line 2: gotoAndStop ("collapsed");

Scene:	<current scene>	▼
Type:	Frame Label	▼
Frame:	collapsed	▼
	☐ Go to and Play	

Figure 4.23 This button sends the Flash playhead to the frame labeled collapsed and stops there.

5. Drag several instances of your button symbol into the second keyframe and align them with each other. Add text over these instances to describe the buttons.

   This is the expanded state of your menu (**Figure 4.21**).

6. Add a new layer and place labels to mark the collapsed and expanded keyframes. In the Frame panel in the Label field, enter collapsed for the first keyframe and expanded for the second keyframe.

   The labels let you to see clearly the collapsed and expanded states of your movie clip and let you use the gotoAndStop action with frame labels instead of frame numbers.

7. Select the instance in the first keyframe. In the Actions panel, choose Basic Actions > Go To.

8. In the Type pull-down menu, choose Frame Label. In the Frame field, enter expanded. Uncheck the Go to and Play box (**Figure 4.22**).

9. Select each of the instances in the last keyframe. In the Actions panel, choose Basic Actions > Go To.

10. In the Type pull-down menu, choose Frame Label. In the Frame field, enter collapsed. Uncheck the Go to and Play box (**Figure 4.23**).

(continued on next page)

COMPLEX BUTTONS

11. Add a third layer, and in the first keyframe assign the action `stop`.

Without this `stop` in the first frame of your movie clip, you would see the menu repeatedly opening and closing because of the automatic cycling of movie clips. The `stop` action ensures that the movie clip stays on frame 1 until you click the menu button (**Figure 4.24**).

12. Return to the main movie Timeline and place an instance of your movie clip on the Stage.

13. From the Control menu, select Test Movie to see how your pull-down menu works.

When you click and release the first button, the buttons for your choices appear because you direct the playhead to go to the expanded keyframe on the movie-clip Timeline. When you click and release one of the buttons in the expanded state, the buttons disappear, returning you to the collapsed keyframe of the movie-clip Timeline. All this happens independently of the main movie Timeline, where the movie-clip instance resides (**Figure 4.25**).

At this point, you have created a complex button that behaves like a pull-down menu, but still does not actually do anything (except modify itself). In Chapter 5 you'll learn how to have Timelines communicate, which enables you to create complex navigation systems.

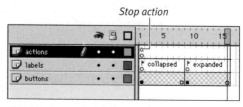

Stop action

Figure 4.24 The completed movie-clip Timeline for the pull-down menu. A `stop` action is assigned to the first frame in the top layer.

Movie clip in collapsed Keyframe

Movie clip in expanded keyframe

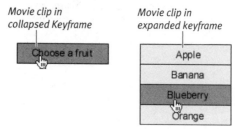

Figure 4.25 The two states of the pull-down menu work independently of the main Timeline.

COMPLEX BUTTONS

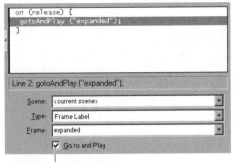

check this box to toggle from
gotoAndStop *to* gotoAndPlay

Figure 4.26 Actions assigned to the first button in the *collapsed* keyframe of the pull-down menu.

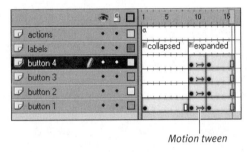

Motion tween

Figure 4.27 The pull-down menu movie clip. The expanded-menu buttons are separated on different layers in order to motion-tween them.

Once you understand the concept behind the simple pull-down menu, you can create more elaborate ones by adding animation to the transition between the collapsed state and the expanded state. For instance, instead of having the expanded state suddenly pop up, create a tween that makes the buttons scroll down gently.

To create an animated pull-down menu:

1. Create a simple pull-down menu as described in the last task.

2. Enter symbol-editing mode for your movie clip.

3. Instead of a gotoAndStop action on the button instance in the first keyframe, assign the actions
   gotoAndPlay ("expanded");
   This makes the playhead go to the label expanded and begin playing (**Figure 4.26**).

4. Create motion tweens for your button instances in the last keyframe (**Figure 4.27**).

5. In the last frame of the movie clip, insert a keyframe and assign the frame action stop.

6. Return to the main movie Timeline and place an instance of your movie clip on the Stage.

7. From the Control menu, select Test Movie to see how your pull-down menu works.

   When you click and release the first button, the playhead jumps to the label expanded in the movie clip and begins playing, showing the motion tweening of your button choices.

Event Handlers

Event handlers are actions that control the response to certain things, called *events,* that the viewer does in a Flash movie. Pressing and releasing the mouse button and pressing a key on the keyboard are all examples of events. Event handlers detect these events and perform certain actions as a response. For example, in the previous tasks, you assigned actions to buttons that detect the mouse release event. In response, you had Flash go to either the expanded keyframe or the collapsed keyframe.

Mouse events are all the events associated with the movements and button clicks of the viewer's mouse. When you assign an action to a button instance, Flash automatically brackets that action with the default mouse event Release:

```
on (release) {

}
```

The Release mouse event is the typical trigger for mouse interactivity. When the mouse button is released inside the Hit state of a button symbol, any action within the curly braces is performed. This allows viewers to change their mind and release the mouse button over a safe spot outside the Hit area even after they've already clicked a button. Other types of mouse events make possible a range of mouse interactions. All the mouse events are listed in **Table 4.1.**

To select a mouse event:

1. In the Actions panel in Normal mode, select Actions > on. In the Parameters pane, the different kinds of events appear with checkboxes (**Figure 4.28**).

2. Check the event you want, based on the interaction you require.

3. Choose an action as a response to the selected event.

Table 4.1

Mouse Event Descriptions	
MOUSE EVENT	**TRIGGERED WHEN**
on (press)	When the pointer is over the Hit area and the mouse button is depressed.
on (release)	When the pointer is over the Hit area and the mouse button is depressed and released.
on (releaseOutside)	When the pointer is over the Hit area, then the mouse button is depressed, then released outside of the Hit area.
on (rollOver)	When the pointer moves over the Hit area.
on (rollOut)	When the pointer moves from the Hit area off the Hit area.
on (dragOver)	When the pointer is over the Hit area, and the mouse button is depressed, then the pointer is moved off the Hit area and back over the Hit area while the button remains depressed.
on (dragOut)	When the pointer is over the Hit area, and the mouse button is depressed, then the pointer is moved off the Hit area while the button remains depressed.

Figure 4.28 The Parameters area of the on action contains a checkbox list of the various events.

Figure 4.29 The pull-down menu with the Roll Over event. When the mouse simply moves over the top button, the menu immediately expands.

```
on (press, release) {
    play ();
}
```

Line 1 : on (press, release) {

Event: ☒ Press   ☐ Roll Over
       ☒ Release   ☐ Roll Out
       ☐ Release Outside ☐ Drag Over
       ☐ Key Press: [   ] ☐ Drag Out

Figure 4.30 If the Press event or the Release event is detected, this script will carry out the action play.

This keyframe should only contain graphics or movie clips.

🖱 **button symbol**

🐾 🔒 ☐ | Up | **Over** | Down | Hit |

Object Actions

t Actions

```
on (rollOver) {
    play ();
}
```

Figure 4.31 The Over state of the button symbol (top) defines how the button looks when the pointer is over the Hit state. A Roll Over event handler assigned to the instance (bottom) defines what the button does when the pointer is over the Hit state.

4. From the Control menu, choose Test Movie to see the behavior of different mouse events (**Figure 4.29**).

✔ Tips

■ All the mouse events except Release require that you use Control > Test Movie in order to see the behavior of the button instance. These mouse events don't work in the editing environment when you choose Control > Enable Simple Buttons.

■ It's possible to assign more than one selection of mouse events within one on action. For example, the action on (press, release) will detect when the mouse is depressed as well as when the mouse is released, and will execute any action within its curly braces if either of those two mouse events occurs (**Figure 4.30**).

■ Within one button instance, if you want one event to have a different consequence from another event, you must create separate on action statements. For example, to have the Roll Over event make your movie play and the Roll Out event make your movie stop, your actions would look like this:

```
on (rollOver) {
    play ();
}
on (rollOut) {
    stop ();
}
```

■ Don't confuse the Roll Over mouse event with the Over keyframe of your button symbol. Both involve detecting when the pointer is over the Hit area, but the Over state describes how your Button looks when the mouse is over the Hit area while the Roll Over mouse event assigns an action when that event actually occurs. So the keyframes of a button symbol define how it looks, and the mouse-event action defines what it does (**Figure 4.31**).

Button Tracking Options

A button instance can be defined in one of two ways in the Instance panel: Track as Button or Track as Menu Item (**Figure 4.32**). These two tracking options determine whether button instances can receive a mouse event even after the event has started on a different button instance. The Track as Menu Item option allows this to happen, while the Track as Button does not. The default option, Track as Button, is the more typical behavior for buttons and causes one mouse event to affect one button instance. More complex cases, such as pull-down menus, require multiple button instances working together. For example, imagine that you press and hold down the menu button to see the pop-up choices, then drag your mouse to your selection and then release the mouse button. You need Flash to recognize the Release event in the expanded menu, even though the Press event occurred in the collapsed menu on a different button instance (in fact, on a different frame altogether). Choosing Track as Menu Item allows these events to be accepted and gives you more flexibility to work with a combination of mouse events.

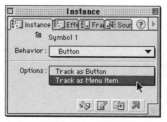

Figure 4.32
The Instance panel button tracking options.

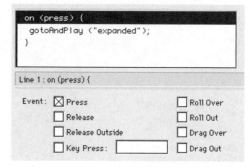

Figure 4.33 The collapsed menu button is assigned the Press event.

To set Track as Menu Item with the Press event:

1. Create a pull-down menu as shown in the previous task, and go to symbol-editing mode for the movie clip.

2. Select the button instance in the first keyframe, and change the mouse event to Press (**Figure 4.33**).

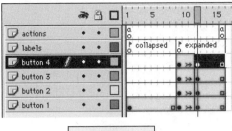

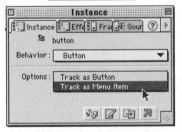

Figure 4.34 Each button instance in the expanded section of the Timeline needs to change to Track as Menu Item. This includes buttons 1 through 4 in keyframes 9 and 12.

3. Select each button instance in the expanded keyframe, and in the Options area of the Instance panel choose Track as Menu Item (**Figure 4.34**).

   The button instances in the expanded menu will now accept a Release event after the Press event occurs on a different instance.

4. Return to the main Timeline and test your movie.

   You now must click and hold down the mouse button in order to keep the menu open.

✔ Tip

■ When you set Track as Menu Item for this pull-down menu, the expanded button instances display their Down state as you move your pointer over them. This is because your mouse button is, in fact, depressed, but that event occurred earlier on a different instance.

BUTTON TRACKING OPTIONS

Refine the pull-down menu with a Drag Over mouse event so that the menu collapses even if no selection is made. This is important to keep pull-down menus expanded only when your viewer is making a choice from the menu.

To set Track as Menu Item with the Drag Over event:

1. Continuing with the pull-down menu constructed in the previous tasks, go to symbol-editing mode for the movie clip.

2. Add a new layer under the existing layers.

3. In the new layer, create an invisible button, and place an instance in a new keyframe corresponding to the expanded keyframe. Your invisible button instance should be slightly larger than the expanded menu (**Figure 4.35**).

4. Select the invisible button instance, and in the Instance panel choose the Track as Menu Item option.

5. In the Actions panel, assign the Actions:

```
on (dragOver) {
    gotoAndStop ("collapsed");
}
```

6. Return to the main Timeline and test your movie.

   The invisible button instance under the expanded menu detects whether the pointer leaves any of the other button instances. If it does, it sends the movie clip back to Frame 1 and collapses the menu.

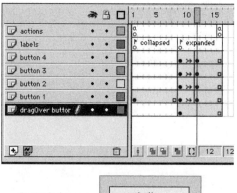

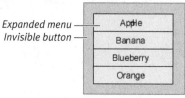

Expanded menu —
Invisible button —

Figure 4.35 When the pointer leaves one of the buttons in the expanded state of the menu, it is dragged over the invisible button that sits in the bottom Layer. The Drag Over mouse event is detected in that button, signaling the playhead to jump to the keyframe labeled collapsed.

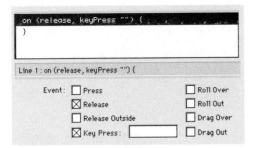

Figure 4.36 The Parameters area of the on action contains the Key Press event.

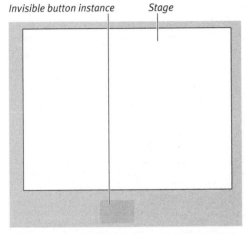

Invisible button instance   *Stage*

Figure 4.37 Placement of the button instance for a Key Press event, just off the Stage.

Keyboard Input

The keyboard is just as important an interface device as the mouse, and Flash lets you detect events occurring from single key presses. This opens up the possibility of having navigation based on the keyboard (using the arrow keys or the number keys, for example), or having keyboard shortcuts that duplicate mouse-based navigation schemes. Flash even lets you control live text that's entered by the viewer into empty fields in a movie; however, these text fields are not usually associated with events and merit a separate discussion in Chapter 10. Here we will focus on single keystrokes that trigger things to happen using the Key Press event and the Key object.

Key Events

The Key Press event is an option in the Parameters area of the on action (**Figure 4.36**). To use the Key Press event, you need to create a button symbol and place an instance of that button in the Timeline. The button instance acts just as a container for the event and associated actions, so you should either make the button invisible or place the instance just off the Stage so you can't see it in the final exported SWF.

To create a Key Press event:

1. Create an invisible button symbol as demonstrated earlier in this Chapter.

2. Place an instance of the button on the Stage or just off the Stage in the first keyframe (**Figure 4.37**).

3. Select the instance, and open the Actions panel.

4. Choose Actions > on.

   The on (release) event handler appears in the Script window.

(continued on next page)

5. In the Parameters area, deselect Release and select Key Press.

6. Choose a specific keyboard character or symbol by simply typing it into the empty field next to the Key Press checkbox (**Figure 4.38**).

7. Select an action that will be executed upon detection of the key press (**Figure 4.39**).

8. From the Control menu, choose Test Movie to see how the Key Press event responds (**Figure 4.40**).

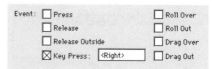

Figure 4.38 The Key Press field lets you enter a single character—in this case, the right arrow.

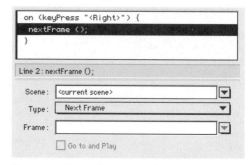

Figure 4.39 The Go To action is selected with the Type set to Next Frame.

Stop *action*   *Images on Stage in separate keyframes*

Invisible button instance with key event

Figure 4.40 This movie has four successive images on the Stage. The on (keyPress "<right>") event with the response set to nextFrame allows you to advance to the next image by simply pressing the right arrow key.

Figure 4.41 A new on action is added after the end curly brace of the first on action.

Figure 4.42 Another Key Press event requires two separate on action statements.

Button instance

Figure 4.43 The right arrow button is assigned two events, an on (release) and an on (keyPress "<right>") event. Either event will advance the movie to the next frame.

✔ Tips

- When your Flash movie plays inside a browser, you must first click on the movie before any Key Press events can be detected. This is an issue of window "focus."

- The Escape key and function keys are not valid keystrokes.

- The Key Press event does not recognize combination keystrokes. However, Flash does distinguish between upper- and lowercase letters.

To create multiple Key Press events:

1. Select the button instance that contains the first Key Press event.

2. Open the Actions panel.

3. Add a separate on action (**Figure 4.41**).

4. In the Parameters area of the second on action, change the event to Key Press and select another key.

5. Add a different action to be executed upon detection of the second key press (**Figure 4.42**).

   Although multiple keystrokes can be handled with one button instance, each one of them requires a separate on statement.

To combine a Key Press event and a Mouse event:

1. Create a button symbol that has its Up, Over, Down, and Hit states defined.

2. Place an instance of the button on the Stage.

3. Select the instance and open the Actions panel.

4. Choose Actions > on.

5. In the Parameters area of the on action, keep the Release checkbox selected and also select the Key Press checkbox.

6. Select an action for the event handler, and test your movie (**Figure 4.43**).

   Either clicking the button on the Stage or pressing the key on the keyboard will make your movie perform the action you selected.

The Key Object

The Key object is an ActionScript class that handles the detection of keystrokes on the keyboard (**Figure 4.44**). In Chapter 3, you learned that you must instantiate a class before you can use it. However, the Key object is one of a few top-level objects that don't require a constructor function to create an instance before you can use it.

The Key object has methods that allow you to retrieve the exact key that was last pressed or to test whether a certain key was pressed. The most common method is isDown, whose argument is a specific key on the keyboard. This method checks if that key has been pressed, and if it has, returns a value of true.

All keys in Flash have a specific number associated with them, known as their key code value (Appendix B). You use these codes in conjunction with the isDown method to construct a conditional statement that creates the keyboard interaction. For example, Key.isDown(32) returns a true or a false depending on whether the spacebar (whose key code value is 32) is pressed.

Figure 4.44 The Toolkit window in the Actions panel contains the methods and properties of the Key object.

The Key Object vs the Key Press Event

Why would you use the Key object and its methods and properties instead of a button with a Key Press event? It's really a matter of sophistication versus ease of use and simplicity. The Key object is much more powerful than a Key event assigned to a button instance because you can construct more complex ActionScript code around the Key object. For example, you can test for key combinations by requiring two isDown methods to be true before performing certain actions as a response. Using key code values also opens up virtually the entire keyboard. The function keys and the Escape key have key code values, so they are available to the Key object.

However, Key Press events are much easier to use. If your Flash movie doesn't require much in terms of keyboard interaction, or if you simply want to have a keyboard shortcut accompany a Mouse event, then use the on (keyPress) action.

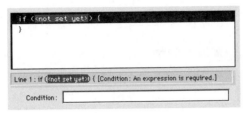

Figure 4.45 The if statement has a condition that it tests. If that condition is true, then the actions within the curly braces will be carried out.

Figure 4.46 The Condition field in the Parameters area of the if statement. The method isDown expects a key code value.

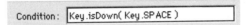

Figure 4.47 The property key.SPACE is in place as the key Code for the method isDown.

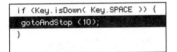

Figure 4.48 The Script window shows the response if the spacebar is pressed.

Fortunately, you don't have to use clumsy key codes all the time. The most common keys are conveniently assigned as properties of the Key object. These properties are constants that can be used in place of the key codes. For example, the statement Key.isDown(32) is the same as Key.isDown(Key.SPACE).

For the full list of Key object methods and properties, refer to Appendix A.

To use the Key object isDown method:

1. Select the first keyframe on the Timeline, and open up the Actions panel in Normal mode.

2. Choose Actions > if.

   The incomplete if statement appears in the Actions List, with an empty Condition field in the Parameters pane (**Figure 4.45**).

3. Select the empty Condition field in the Parameters area.

4. Choose Objects > Key > isDown, or drag the isDown method into the Condition field.

   The isDown method appears in the Condition field. The argument keyCode is required for this method (**Figure 4.46**).

5. Choose Objects > Key > SPACE, or drag the SPACE property into the Condition field.

   The property Key.SPACE appears as the argument for the isDown method (**Figure 4.47**).

6. Choose a basic action as the response for this conditional statement (**Figure 4.48**).

(continued on next page)

KEYBOARD INPUT

7. Insert a new keyframe after the first one, and assign the frame action `gotoAndPlay(1)`.

This second keyframe loops back to the first so that the conditional statement is continuously checked. This is the simplest way to have the `if` statement tested (**Figure 4.49**). We'll explore more refined ways of dealing with conditionals and Action loops later. For now, you are able to test the `isDown` method and different Key object properties using this basic loop.

To create key combinations with the Key object isDown method:

1. Select the first keyframe of the previous task, and open the Actions panel in Normal mode.

2. Select the `if` statement.

The Parameters area shows the Condition with the Key object method and property.

3. In the Parameters area, click the Condition field and type in a space, then choose Actions > Operators > &&. Type in another space (**Figure 4.50**).

4. In the Condition field after the && operator, choose Objects > Key > isDown.

The `isDown` method appears in the Condition field after the && operator. Another argument is required for this method (**Figure 4.51**).

5. Choose Objects > Key > CONTROL, or drag CONTROL into the Condition field (**Figure 4.52**).

The property `key.CONTROL` appears as the argument for the second `isDown` method. The conditional will only perform the action within the curly braces if both the spacebar and the Control key are pressed.

The Key method called and tested — gotoAndPlay(1) action creates loop

Hi-jumper image in frame 10

Press the Spacebar to continue

Figure 4.49 This movie loops between frames 1 and 2 until the spacebar is pressed.

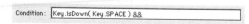

Figure 4.50 Add the operator && from the Toolkit window or simply enter it into the Condition field after the first Key method.

Figure 4.51 The second `isDown` method follows the first, connected with the && operator.

Figure 4.52 Both the spacebar and the Control key have to be pressed before this condition can be met.

KEYBOARD INPUT

MANAGING FLASH COMMUNICATION

To create interactivity and direct your users to see, hear, and do exactly what you want them to, you have to know how to control the Flash playhead on different Timelines. The playhead displays what is on the Stage at any time, plays back any sound, and triggers any actions attached to the Timeline. Jumping from frame to frame on the main movie Timeline is simple enough, using basic actions you're familiar with, such as Go To, Play, and Stop. But when you bring movie clips into your movie, you introduce other Timelines that can be individually controlled. Your main Timeline can control a movie clip's Timeline; a movie clip's Timeline can, in turn, control the main Timeline; and the Timeline of one movie clip can even control the Timeline of another. Handling this complex interaction and navigation between Timelines is the subject of this chapter.

Navigating Timelines with Movie Clips

The independent Timelines of movie-clip symbols make complicated navigation schemes possible (**Figure 5.1**). While the main Timeline is playing, other Timelines of movie clips can be playing as well, interacting with each other and telling what frames to play or when to stop. It's quite common, in fact, to have enough movie clips on the Stage all talking to each other that the main movie Timeline need only be a single frame for the entire movie to work. Driving all this navigation between Timelines is, of course, ActionScript. The basic actions used to navigate within the main Timeline (Go To, Stop, and Play) can also be used to navigate the Timeline of any movie clip. This is possible because movie clips are part of a Flash-defined movie-clip class, allowing you to work with movie clips as objects.

The fact that the movie clip is both a symbol and an object makes it unique in its function and in its creation. As a symbol instance, a movie clip can be used for animation loops and in animated buttons. When it is an object, you call its methods to guide the playhead or evaluate properties to transform the way it appears. You create movie clips and store them in the Library as you would other symbols. Using them as objects, however, requires that you instantiate them. Once instantiated, movie-clip objects become available to all the methods and properties of the movie-clip class.

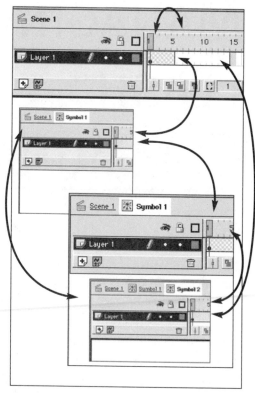

Figure 5.1 A movie can contain many Timelines that interact with each other. This example shows Scene 1 as the main Timeline. It contains two movie clips. One of the movie clips contains another movie clip. The arrows show just a few of the possible lines of communication.

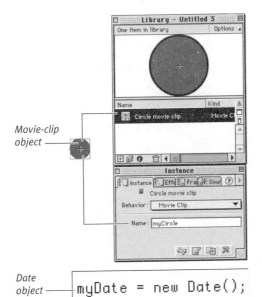

Movie-clip object

Date object —— `myDate = new Date();`

Figure 5.2 Instantiation of a movie-clip symbol versus instantiation of a Date object.

Figure 5.3 The Instance panel for a movie clip. The name of this movie clip object is myCircle.

Naming Instances

Instantiation of your movie-clip symbol involves two steps: placing an instance on the Stage and naming that instance. These two steps accomplish the same task as the constructor function does for other Flash objects (**Figure 5.2**). The result is the same—a named object or instance is created from a class that you can then use by calling its methods or evaluating its properties.

To name a movie-clip instance:

1. Create a movie-clip symbol.

2. Drag an instance of the movie clip from the Library onto the Stage.

3. Select the instance.

4. In the Instance panel in the Name field, type in a unique name for your movie-clip instance (**Figure 5.3**).

   Your movie-clip instance can now be identified with ActionScipt, using this name.

✔ Tip

- The name of your movie-clip symbol (the one that appears in the Library) and the name you give it in the Instance panel are two different identifiers (**Figure 5.4**). The name that appears in the Library is a symbol property and is basically just an organizational reminder. The name in the Instance panel is more important because it is the actual name of the object and will be used in targeting paths. Although the two names can be the same, try to give your symbol a generic name and the instance a more specific name to distinguish them.

Movie-clip symbol name

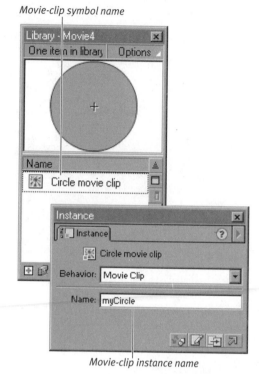

Movie-clip instance name

Figure 5.4 The name of the movie-clip symbol appears in the Library, while the name of the movie-clip instance appears in the Instance panel.

NAMING INSTANCES

Target Paths

A target path is essentially an object name, or a series of object names separated by dots, that tells Flash where to find a particular object. To control movie clip timelines, you specify both the target path for a particular movie clip and a basic action. The target path tells Flash which movie-clip instance to look at, and the action tells Flash what to do with that movie-clip instance. The basic actions that control the playhead are Go To, Play, and Stop. For example, if you name a movie-clip instance bigClock, you can write the ActionScript statement

bigClock.gotoAndStop(37), and the playhead within the movie-clip instance called bigClock will move to frame 37 and stop there. bigClock is the target path, and gotoAndStop is the action.

In the Parameters pane of the Actions panel, the Insert Target Path button opens the Insert Target Path dialog box which provides a visual way to insert a target path (**Figure 5.5**). All named movie-clip instances are shown in a hierarchical fashion in the display window. You can select individual movie clips, and the correct target paths appear.

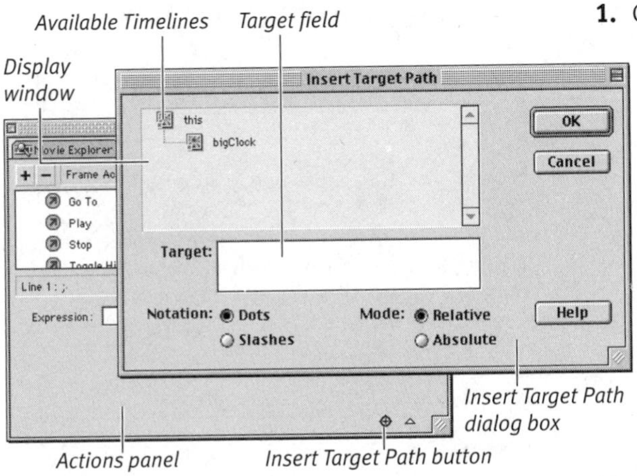

To target a movie-clip instance from the main Timeline:

1. Create a movie-clip symbol and place an instance of it on the Stage. In the Instance panel, give the instance a name.

2. Create a button symbol and place an instance of it on the Stage along with the named movie-clip instance (**Figure 5.6**).

   The button on the main Timeline will control the movie-clip Timeline.

   (continued on next page)

Available Timelines Target field
Display window
Insert Target Path dialog box
Actions panel Insert Target Path button

Figure 5.5 The Insert Target Path dialog box allows you to choose a target path by clicking a movie clip within the hierarchy.

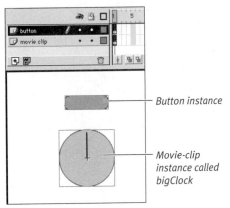

Button instance

Movie-clip instance called bigClock

Figure 5.6 Button and movie-clip instances on the main Timeline.

3. Select the button instance and open the Actions panel.

4. Choose Actions > evaluate.

   A new ActionScript line appears under the on (release) event handler (**Figure 5.7**).

5. In the Parameters area, click the Insert Target Path button.

   The Insert Target Path dialog box appears.

6. Select Relative mode, and choose the movie-clip instance from the display list.

   The target path appears in the Target field (**Figure 5.8**).

7. Click OK.

   The target path appears in the Expression field (**Figure 5.9**).

8. In the Expression field after the Target Path, enter a dot, then the desired method with any applicable arguments (**Figure 5.10**).

9. Test your movie.

   Your button instance controls the Timeline of the targeted movie clip.

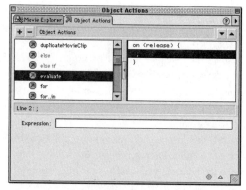

Figure 5.7 Use the evaluate statement to specify a target and an action for that target.

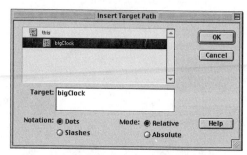

Figure 5.8 The Insert Target Path dialog box. Selecting the movie clip from the display window enters the target path in the Target field.

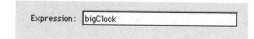

Figure 5.9 The Expression field of the Actions panel.

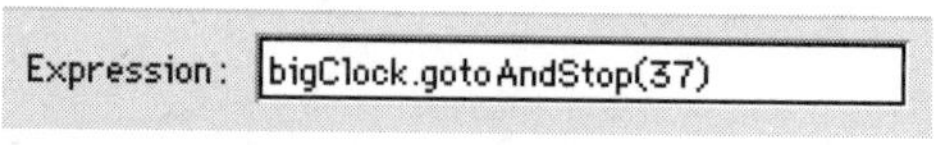

Expression : | bigClock.gotoAndStop(37) |

Figure 5.10 The action gotoAndStop(37) is the method of the movie-clip object called bigClock. This statement moves the playhead in the bigClock Timeline to Frame 37 and stops.

TARGET PATHS

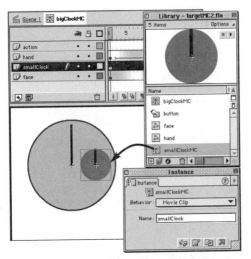

Figure 5.11 Place an instance of the smallClock movie clip inside the bigClockMC movie clip. Name the embedded movie clip instance smallClock and the movie clip instance that's on the stage bigClock. The parent is bigClock and the child is smallClock.

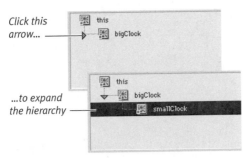

Click this arrow... ... *to expand the hierarchy*

Figure 5.12 The display window of the Insert Target Path dialog box. The hierarchy shows parent-child relationships.

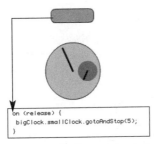

```
on (release) {
  bigClock.smallClock.gotoAndStop(5);
}
```

Figure 5.13 The button (top) moves the playhead of the child movie clip smallClock to Frame 5 and stops while the parent movie clip bigClock keeps going.

You can have a movie clip within another movie clip. The first is the *parent*. The second is the *child*. Any transformation you do to the parent will also affect the child. To control the Timeline of a child movie clip from the main Timeline, use both the parent and the child name in the target path.

To target a child of a movie-clip instance from the main Timeline:

1. Create a movie-clip symbol, place an instance on the Stage, and name it.

2. Create another movie-clip symbol, and place an instance inside the first movie-clip symbol. In the Instance panel, give the embedded instance a name (**Figure 5.11**).

3. Create a button symbol, and place an instance on the Stage in the main Timeline. You will use this button to control the Timeline of the movie-clip child.

4. Select the button instance, and open the Actions panel. Select Actions > evaluate.

5. In the Parameters area, click the Insert Target Path button, and in the Insert Target Path dialog box choose Relative mode.

6. From the display window, click the triangle in front of the parent movie clip. The hierarchy expands, showing the child movie clip within the parent (**Figure 5.12**).

7. Select the child movie clip as the target path. Click OK. The target path in the form of `Parent.Child` appears in the Expression field of the Actions panel.

8. In the Expression field, enter a dot, then an action for the targeted object.

9. Test your movie. When you click and release the button, the action affects the child but not the parent movie clip (**Figure 5.13**). Despite the parent-child relationship, their Timelines remain independent.

Absolute and Relative Paths

Flash gives you two mode options in the Insert Target Path dialog box: relative and absolute. In the last example, the method `bigClock.smallClock.gotoAndStop(5)` originated from a button residing on the main Timeline. When Flash executes that action, it looks within that Timeline for the object called bigClock that contains another object called smallClock. This is an example of a path that uses the relative mode. Everything is relative to where the action statement resides—in this case, the main Timeline. An alternative way of inserting a target path is to use absolute mode, which has no particular frame of reference. You can think of relative target paths as directions given from your present location, as in "go two blocks straight, then turn left." Absolute target paths, on the other hand, are directions that work no matter where you are, as in "go to 555 University Avenue."

Why would you use one mode over the other? If you need to target a Timeline that sits at a higher level than the current Timeline you're working in, you need to use absolute mode. For example, imagine that you want to have a movie clip control the main Timeline in which it resides. With relative mode, you only see the Timelines that are inside the current one. With absolute mode, you see all the Timelines no matter where you are. In absolute mode, it's as if you have a bird's-eye view of all the movie clips on the Stage at once.

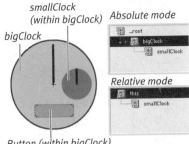

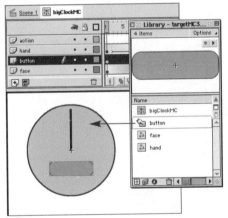

Figure 5.14 Absolute mode versus relative mode of target paths. This example shows both a button and the smallClock movie clip within the bigClock movie clip. When assigning a target path to the button, this in relative mode refers to bigClock in absolute mode.

Figure 5.15 Place a button instance inside the bigClockMC movie clip. An instance of the movie clip (called bigClock) sits on the Stage.

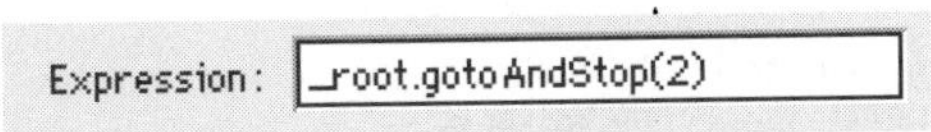

Expression : _root.goto AndStop(2)

Figure 5.16 The Expression field of the Actions panel.

Using This and _root

With relative mode, the current Timeline is called this. All other Timelines are relative to the this Timeline. With absolute mode, the main movie Timeline is called _root. All other Timelines are organized relative to the _root timeline (**Figure 5.14**).

To target the main Timeline from a movie-clip instance:

1. Create a movie-clip symbol, and place an instance of it on the Stage. In the Instance panel, give the instance a name.

2. Create a button symbol, and place an instance of it inside the movie-clip symbol. You will use this button to control the main Timeline (**Figure 5.15**).

3. Select the button instance, and open the Actions panel. Select Actions > evaluate.

4. In the Parameters area, click the Insert Target Path button.

5. In the Insert Target Path dialog box choose Absolute mode.

   All the movie clips and the main Timeline of the movie appear, not just those inside the current movie-clip Timeline.

6. Select the main Timeline as the target path. Click OK.

   The target path _root appears in the Expression field.

7. In the Expression field, enter a dot, then an action for the targeted object (**Figure 5.16**).

(continued on next page)

ABSOLUTE AND RELATIVE PATHS

8. Test your movie.

When you click and release the button, Flash will jump outside the current Timeline and look for the _root Timeline to perform the action there (**Figure 5.17**).

To target a movie-clip instance from another movie-clip instance:

1. Create a movie-clip symbol, and place an instance of it on the Stage. In the Instance panel, give the instance a name.

2. Create another movie-clip symbol, and place an instance of it on the Stage. In the Instance panel, give the instance a name.

3. Create a button symbol, and place an instance of it inside the first movie-clip symbol.

You will use this button to control the second movie clip (**Figure 5.18**).

4. Select the button instance, and open the Actions panel. Select Actions > evaluate.

5. In the Parameters area, click the Insert Target Path button. In the Insert Target Path dialog box choose Absolute mode.

6. Select the second movie-clip instance. Click OK.

The target path _root.secondClock appears in the Expression field of the Actions panel.

7. In the Expression field after the target path, enter a dot, then an action for the targeted object.

8. Test your movie.

When you click and release the button, Flash will start looking from the _root Timeline, drill down to the object called secondClock, and perform the action on that object (**Figure 5.19**).

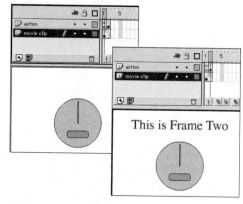

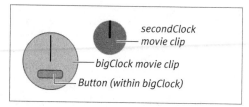

Figure 5.17 The button inside the big clock movie clip moves the playhead in the root or main Timeline to Frame 2.

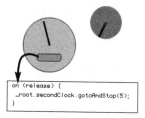

Figure 5.18 Two movie clips on Stage, with a button inside one of them.

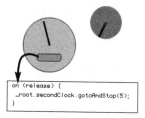

```
on (release) {
    _root.secondClock.gotoAndStop(5);
}
```

Figure 5.19 This button action targets the secondClock movie clip sitting on the root Timeline.

ABSOLUTE AND RELATIVE PATHS

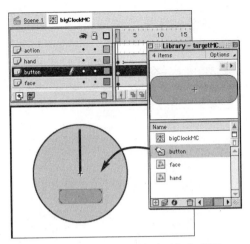

Figure 5.20 Place a button inside the bigclockMC movie clip. An instance of the movie clip (called bigClock) sits on the Stage.

```
on (release) {
    this.gotoAndStop(37);
}
```

```
on (release) {
    _root.bigClock.gotoAndStop(37);
}
```

```
on (release) {
    gotoAndStop (37);
}
```

Figure 5.21 Three equivalent actions to target the bigClock Timeline from within bigClock itself.

To target a movie clip's own Timeline:

1. Create a movie-clip symbol, and place an instance of it on the Stage. In the Instance panel, give the instance a name.

2. Create a button symbol, and place an instance of it inside the movie-clip symbol.

    You will use this button to control the movie clip's own Timeline (**Figure 5.20**).

3. Select the button instance, and open the Actions panel. Select Actions > evaluate.

4. Click the Insert Target Path button to open the Insert Target Path dialog box. Choose Relative mode and select this.

    or

    Click the Insert Target Path button to open the Insert Target Path dialog box. Choose Absolute mode and select the absolute target path.

    or

    Don't use the evaluate action in Step 3. Instead, simply use any of the basic actions—Go To, Stop, or Play (**Figure 5.21**).

✔ Tip

■ Using this or an absolute path to target a movie clip's own Timeline is unnecessary, just as it is unnecessary to use this or _root when navigating within the main Timeline. It's understood that actions residing in one movie clip pertain, or are scoped, to that particular movie clip.

ABSOLUTE AND RELATIVE PATHS

Using _parent in Target Paths

Although it does not appear in the Insert Target Path dialog box, you can also use the relative term _parent. Use _parent to target the movie clip at the next-higher level from the current Timeline.

To target the parent of a movie clip:

1. Create a movie-clip symbol, and place an instance of it on the Stage. In the Instance panel, give the instance a name.

2. Create another movie-clip symbol, and place an instance of it inside the first movie-clip symbol. In the Instance panel, give the child instance a name.

3. Create a button symbol, and place an instance within the child movie clip (**Figure 5.22**).

4. Select the button instance, and open the Actions panel. Select Actions > evaluate.

5. In the Expression field, enter _parent, then a dot, then an action.

6. Test your movie.

   When you click and release the button, Flash will look at the Timeline that holds the current object (the parent) and perform the action there (**Figure 5.23**).

   Table 5.1 and **Figure 5.24** summarize the ways you can use absolute and relative paths to target different movie clips.

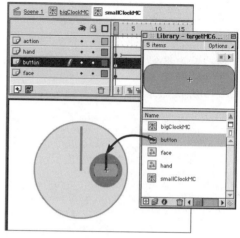

Figure 5.22 Place a button inside the "small clock" movie clip. An instance of the smallClockMC (called smallClock) is inside the bigClockMC movie clip. An instance of the bigClockMC (called bigClock) sits on the Stage.

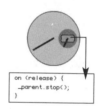

Figure 5.23 The button within the "small clock" movie clip targets the "big clock" movie clip with the relative statement _parent.

```
on (release) {
    _parent.stop();
}
```

ABSOLUTE AND RELATIVE PATHS

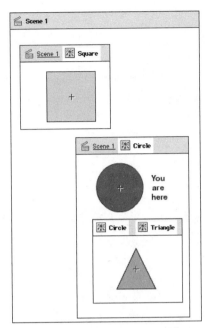

Figure 5.24 A representation of a movie with multiple movie clips. The main Timeline (Scene 1) contains the Square movie clip and the Circle movie clip. The Circle movie clip contains the Triangle movie clip. These names represent instances. **Table 5.1** summarizes the absolute and relative target paths for calls made within the Circle movie clip (you are here).

Why Relative Paths?

Why use relative paths at all? Absolute paths seem to be a safer construction because they explicitly identify an object no matter where you are.

There are at least two places where relative paths are useful:

If you create a movie clip with actions that affect other movie clips relative to itself, you can move the entire ensemble and still have the target paths work using relative terms. This makes it easier to work with complex navigation schemes because you can copy and paste and move the pieces without having to rewrite the target paths. A direct parallel is in Website management and maintaining Web links. If you were to create absolute paths to links to your résumé and then move your home page to a different server, you'd have to rewrite your links. The more practical method would be to establish relative links within your home page.

The other place is in situations where you dynamically create movie clips. You will learn how to create movie-clip objects from existing movie clips and name them on the fly with ActionScript. In these cases, movie clips are not static, and relative target paths are required to follow them around.

Table 5.1

Absolute versus Relative Target Paths

TO TARGET... (FROM CIRCLE)	ABSOLUTE PATH	RELATIVE PATH
Scene 1	_root	_parent
Square	_root.Square	_parent.Square
Circle	_root.Circle	this
Triangle	_root.Circle.Triangle	Triangle

Using the With Action to Target Movie Clips

An alternative way to target movie clips is to use the action with. Instead of calling a single action for an object with the evaluate action, the with action allows multiple actions to be performed for an object. The with action statement is written like this:

```
with (bigClock) {

    gotoAndStop (5)

}
```

This with action temporarily sets the target path to bigClock so that the gotoAndStop statement between the curly braces affects that particular target. Once the with action ends, any subsequent statements refer to the current movie clip.

The with statement can even be nested to simultaneously affect multiple targets at once. For example,

```
with (myFace) {

    with (myEyes) {

        gotoAndStop (2);

    }

    with (myMouth) {

        gotoAndStop (2);

    }

}
```

These nested with statements accomplish the same thing as the following Evaluate statements:

```
myFace.myEyes.gotoAndStop(2);
```

```
myFace.myMouth.gotoAndStop(2);
```

(Figure 5.25).

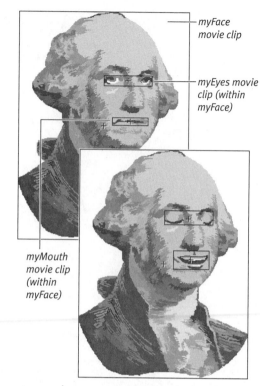

myFace movie clip

myEyes movie clip (within myFace)

myMouth movie clip (within myFace)

Figure 5.25 Nested with statements are an alternative to multiple target paths using the evaluate statement.

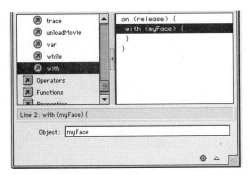

Figure 5.26 The with action in the Actions panel. The Object field contains the target path `myFace`.

Figure 5.27 The action `gotoAndStop(2)` and any other actions between the inner set of curly braces apply to the object "myFace".

Figure 5.28 The action `with (myEyes)` is nested within the action `with (myFace)`.

```
on (release) {
  with (myFace) {
    with (myEyes) {
      gotoAndStop(2);
    }
  }
}
```

Figure 5.29 Selecting the closing curly brace ensures that your next statement will be inserted within the action `with (myFace)` rather than within the action `with (myEyes)`.

```
on (release) {
  with (myFace) {
    with (myEyes) {
      gotoAndStop(2);
    }
    with (myMouth) {
      gotoAndStop(2);
    }
  }
}
```

Figure 5.30 The complete nested with action statements.

To use the with action:

1. Select a button or a frame, and open the Actions panel.

2. Choose Actions > with.
   The Object field appears in the Parameters area.

3. In the Object field, enter the target path or click the Insert Target Path button (**Figure 5.26**).

4. Choose an action for the targeted object.
   The action appears under the with statement between the curly braces (**Figure 5.27**).

To use nested with actions:

1. Select a button or a frame, and open the Actions panel.

2. Choose Actions > with.

3. In the Object field, enter the first target path.

4. Again choose Actions > with.

5. In the Object field, enter the first nested target path (**Figure 5.28**).

6. Choose an action for the first nested object.

7. Select the closing curly brace of the first nested with statement (**Figure 5.29**).
   If you do not select the closing curly brace before proceeding with the next step, the second nested with statement will appear inside the previous one.

8. Again choose Actions > with.

9. In the Object field, enter the second nested target path, then choose an action for this second nested object (**Figure 5.30**).

The Slash Notation and Tell Target

So far, in constructing your target paths, you've been using dots to separate nested movie-clip objects. However, Flash also allows you to insert target paths using slashes instead. The slash syntax is the notation used by previous versions of Flash and may provide a more comfortable way of working for some longtime Flash users. The Insert Target Path dialog box gives you the choice of either Slash notation or Dot notation (**Figure 5.31**).

Slash notation is similar to how computer directories are identified, with slashes separating embedded folders. And as with computer directories, you can drill up or down the Timeline hierarchy by using dots. One dot targets the current Timeline, and two dots target the next Timeline up. A single slash indicates the root Timeline.

Note how Slash notation uses dots to indicate relative paths—you can see how potentially confusing it is to use both Dot and Slash notation together. Fortunately, Flash won't allow mixing the two notations because it wouldn't understand the statements. If you use the evaluate statement to call a Go To method of an object, you write it in Dot notation as:

```
Parent.Child.gotoAndStop(5);
```

In Slash notation, however, the statement breaks down. It doesn't make any sense to say:

```
Parent/Child.gotoAndStop(5);
```

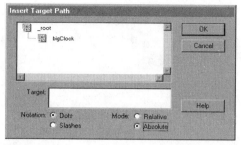

Figure 5.31 The Notation options are at the bottom of the Insert Target Path dialog box.

Table 5.2

Dot and Slash Notation Equivalents	
DOT	SLASH
.	/
_root	/
this	.
_parent	..
.	: (variable separator)

Figure 5.32 Choosing Show Deprecated Syntax in the Options menu of the Actions panel highlights all the actions in the Toolkit window that are remnants of previous versions of Flash and are no longer recommended.

The Slash notation does not work with the evaluate statement, nor does it work with the with statement. The Slash notation should really only be used in conjunction with the action Tell Target, whose use itself is discouraged.

The Tell Target action, like the Slash notation, is a remnant of the previous version of Flash. It was actually a very powerful action, but new capabilities to call methods and evaluate properties of objects using dot syntax make Tell Target obsolete. Although you can access Tell Target from the Actions panel, it is considered a deprecated action. Actions that are deprecated are no longer recommended because of their incompatibilities with newer ActionScript statements and syntax. You can view deprecated syntax in the Actions panel under the Options menu (**Figure 5.32**). It's a good idea to be aware of the Slash notation and the Tell Target action because of their heavy usage in the past, but you should follow evaluate, with, and Dot notation from now on.

Movie Clips as Containers

So far in this chapter, you've learned how to name your movie-clip objects, target each one, and navigate within their Timelines from any other Timeline in your movie. But how does this ability to control movie-clip Timelines translate into meaningful interactivity for your Flash project? The key is to think of movie clips as containers that hold stuff—animation, buttons, sound, even data. By moving the playhead back and forth or playing certain parts of a particular movie-clip Timeline, you can access that stuff whenever you want, independently of what else is going on. In previous versions of Flash, using movie clips in this way was the only way to simulate variables, counters, and other types of placeholders. Though the sophisticated ActionScript in Flash 5 now replaces some of these old techniques, it's still effective to think of movie clips as containers, especially for graphics and animation (**Figure 5.33**).

For example, a common way to use movie clips is to have their Timelines contain different states that toggle from one to the other. In Chapter 4, you built pull-down menus that do exactly that. The pull-down menu is essentially a movie-clip object that toggles between a collapsed state and an expanded state. The buttons inside the movie clip control which of those two states you see, while also providing navigation outside the movie clip's Timeline (**Figure 5.34**).

Another example is the radio button. Building a radio button is a matter of defining two different states that toggle between an on condition and an off condition.

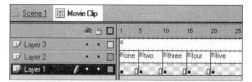

Figure 5.33 The movie clip as a container. This movie clip has a stop action in the first keyframe. The other labeled keyframes can contain buttons, graphics, animations, or any other kind of Flash information, which can be accessed simply by targeting the object and moving the playhead to the appropriate keyframe.

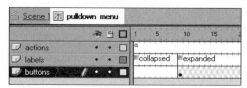

Figure 5.34 The pull-down menu movie clip contains both collapsed and expanded states.

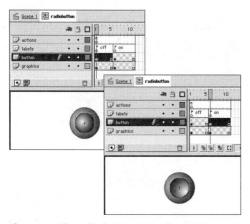

Figure 5.35 The radio-button movie clip contains a stop action in the first keyframe and two different states that toggle. The button in the off state (top) sends the playhead to the on state (bottom), and vice versa.

To create a radio button:

1. Create a movie-clip symbol. Go to editing mode and insert a new keyframe.

2. Label the first keyframe on and the second keyframe off.

3. Insert a new layer. Select a keyframe in the new layer that corresponds to the off label, and open the Actions panel. Select Basic Actions > Stop.

   The stop action prevents this movie clip from cycling endlessly.

4. Insert another new layer. Create a button symbol, and place an instance in a keyframe that corresponds to the off label and another instance in a keyframe that corresponds to the on label of the movie-clip symbol.

5. Select the first button instance, and open the Actions panel. Assign the actions:

   ```
   on (release) {
       gotoAndStop (on);
   }
   ```

6. Select the second button instance, and assign the actions:

   ```
   on (release) {
       gotoAndStop (off);
   }
   ```

7. Create graphics in new layers for both the off and on labels that show their respective states (**Figure 5.35**).

8. Drag an instance of the movie clip from the Library onto the Stage of the root Timeline. Test your movie.

MOVIE CLIPS AS CONTAINERS

You can do the same thing to a movie clip that you do to a button to make it invisible. That is, leave the first keyframe that is visible to the user blank, so the instance is initially invisible on the Stage. If the first keyframe of a movie clip is blank and contains a stop frame action to keep it there, you can control when to expose the other frames inside that movie-clip Timeline. For example, you could create a movie clip of an explosion, but keep the first keyframe blank. Place this movie clip on a graphic of a submarine, and at the appropriate time, advance to the next frame to reveal the explosion.

Note that there are other ways of using ActionScript to hide or reveal the contents of a movie clip, and you'll learn about these possibilities in upcoming chapters. But being aware of both the simple (frame-based, as described here) and sophisticated (purely ActionScript-based) approaches will help you tackle new animation and interactivity challenges.

To create an "invisible" movie clip:

1. Create a movie-clip symbol, and insert a new keyframe.

2. Select the first keyframe, and open the Actions panel. Select Basic Actions > Stop.

3. Leave the first keyframe empty and begin placing graphics, animations, or buttons in the second keyframe (**Figure 5.36**).

4. Drag an instance of the movie clip from the Library onto the Stage in the root Timeline.

   The instance appears on the Stage as an empty circle (**Figure 5.37**). The empty circle represents the registration point of the instance. This allows you to place the instance exactly where you want it.

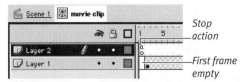

Figure 5.36 A movie clip with an empty first keyframe will be invisible on the Stage. This movie clip has a Stop action in Layer 2, and graphics in Layer 1 starting in frame 2.

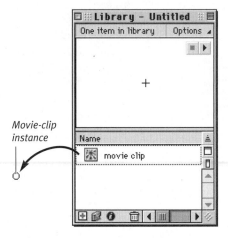

Figure 5.37 An instance of a movie clip with an empty first frame appears as an empty circle.

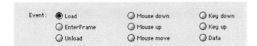

Figure 5.38 The Clip Event options from the onClipEvent action.

Clip Events

One of the ways a movie-clip object communicates within Flash is with its own event handler known as a Clip Event. You have already seen how Mouse Events, Key Events, and the Key Object detect mouse and keyboard responses. The Clip Event is unique in that it handles mouse responses and keyboard responses as well as a few less obvious events such as loading and unloading of the movie clip, playing of movie-clip frames, and loading of external data into a movie clip (**Figure 5.38**). The common thread in these events is that they are all assigned to a movie-clip instance. Actions that follow these Clip Events are scoped to that instance unless specified otherwise.

Clip Events can be used in a variety of generic ways. For example, Mouse up, Mouse down, Key up, and Key down simply detect when those general events occur. Since these events are attached to a movie clip and not a button, there is no Hit area, and the Mouse down and Mouse up events are detected anywhere on the Stage. The Key up and Key down events similarly have no specific information about which keys should be pressed, so any key will trigger the event.

For the most part, however, Clip Events are used in conjunction with a second set of ActionScript statements that refine the event or perform additional manipulation with the event information. The Key up and Key down events combined with a conditional statement that tests which key has been pressed (using the Key Object) provide a better way to detect key presses than either of them could do alone. In the last chapter, for example, you created a conditional statement with the Key Object, but had to create a loop in the root Timeline to have the statement continually tested. With the Key up or

Key down event assigned to a movie clip, you no longer need the loop.

The EnterFrame event is triggered at the FPS of the movie. So if the movie rate is set to 12 frames per second, the EnterFrame event gets triggered 12 times per second. This makes Flash perform the statements assigned to the EnterFrame event continuously. Since movie clips naturally loop, the statements assigned to the EnterFrame event are performed continuously.

The Mouse move event is also used with additional statements allowing you to track the location of the cursor. Any time the mouse moves, you update its new position. You'll learn how to do this and how to use the other Clip Events in upcoming chapters when you learn about controlling the properties of movie clips and loading external assets into Flash.

To detect a general mouse-release event:

1. Create a movie-clip symbol, and drag an instance of it from the Library onto the Stage.

2. Select the movie-clip instance and open the Actions panel.

3. From the Toolkit window, choose Actions > onClipEvent.

4. From the Parameters area, choose Mouse up (**Figure 5.39**).

5. From the Toolkit window, select Actions > evaluate.

6. In the Expression field, enter a target path, then a dot, then a basic action (**Figure 5.40**).

    This action will be executed once the Clip Event is detected.

7. Test your movie.

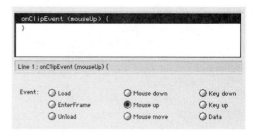

Figure 5.39 The Mouse up Clip Event.

Expression: `_root.nextFrame()`

Figure 5.40 The Expression field for the Evaluate statement.

Table 5.3

Clip Event Descriptions	
CLIP EVENT	INTERACTION
onClipEvent (mouseDown)	When the left mouse button is depressed
onClipEvent (mouseUp)	When the left mouse button is released
onClipEvent (mouseMove)	When the mouse is moved
onClipEvent (keyDown)	When any key is pressed
onClipEvent (keyUp)	When any key is released
onClipEvent (enterFrame)	When each frame of the movie clip is played. Triggered at frame rate of the movie.
onClipEvent (load)	When the movie clip is instantiated and first appears in the Timeline
onClipEvent (unload)	When the first frame after the movie-clip instance is removed from the Timeline
onClipEvent (data)	When either external data or external SWF movies are loaded into the movie clip using the action loadVariables or loadMovie

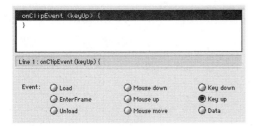

Figure 5.41 The Key up Clip Event.

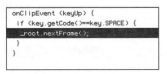

Figure 5.42 The action nextFrame() occurs on the root Timeline when the Key up event happens and the condition in the If statement is true.

As soon as you release your mouse button anywhere on the Stage, the Mouse up Clip Event is detected, and Flash carries out the action in the evaluate statement.

✔ Tip

■ Once the movie clip is selected, you can simply select an action and Flash will automatically insert the Clip Event handler before the action. The default Clip Event is onClipEvent (load). Select the onClipEvent (load) statement, and choose another event to change it.

To use Key up or Key down with the Key Object:

1. Create a movie-clip symbol, and drag an instance of it from the Library onto the Stage.

2. Select the instance, and open the Actions panel.

3. From the Toolkit window, choose Actions > onClipEvent.

4. From the Parameters pane, choose Key up or Key down (**Figure 5.41**).

5. Choose Actions > if.
   The Condition field appears in the Parameters area.

6. In the Condition field, enter the statement
   Key.getCode()==Key.SPACE
   The first part of the statement calls the method getCode() of the Key Object, which retrieves the last key pressed. The last part of the statement is a property of the Key Object specifying the spacebar key. The double equals (=) symbol means compare equality.

7. Choose Actions > evaluate.

8. In the Expression field in the Parameters pane, enter the target path, a dot, and then a basic action (**Figure 5.42**).

CLIP EVENTS

9. Test your movie.

The getCode() method of the Key Object retrieves the last key pressed. However, if you use the Key up Clip Event, Flash only checks the condition of the Key Object when a key is released. The combination gives you the specificity of the Key object with the release behavior of a Key up Event.

To create action loops with EnterFrame:

1. Create a movie-clip symbol, and drag an instance of it from the Library onto the Stage.

2. Select the instance, and open the Actions panel.

3. Choose Actions > onClipEvent.

4. From the Parameters pane, choose EnterFrame (**Figure 5.43**).

5. Choose Actions > if.

The Condition field appears in the Parameters pane.

6. In the Condition field, enter the statement:

Key.getCode()==Key.SPACE

This is the same conditional statement that you constructed in the previous task. In this case, however, Flash does not wait for a Key up or Key down event before testing this condition. Here, Flash tests this condition each time a frame in the movie clip plays.

7. Choose Actions > evaluate.

8. In the Expression field in the Parameters pane, enter the target path, a dot, and then a basic action (**Figure 5.44**).

9. Test your movie.

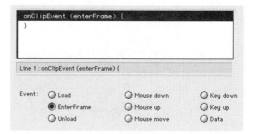

Figure 5.43 The EnterFrame Clip Event.

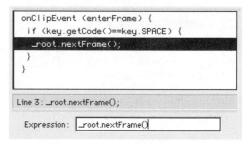

Figure 5.44 The action nextFrame() occurs on the root Timeline when the condition in the if statement is true.

✔ Tip

■ Use the Clip Event onClipEvent (enterFrame) in any situation where you want an ActionScript statement to be performed continuously. In the next section, you'll use this Clip Event to test for for your movie's downloading time over the Web.

Preloaders

All the care you put into creating complex interactivity with multiple Timelines will be wasted if your viewer has to wait too long to download it over the Web and leaves. You can avoid losing viewers by creating short animations that entertain them and trigger the main Flash movie to start when enough data have been delivered over the Web to the viewers' computer. In effect, you hold back the playhead until you know that all the frames are available to play. Only then do you send the playhead to the starting frame of your movie. While you wait for the downloading to be complete, a common diversion is to play a preloader, or a small looping animation, to keep your audience occupied. Preloaders must be small in size since you want them to load almost immediately, and they should be informative, letting your viewers know what they're waiting for or how long they need to wait.

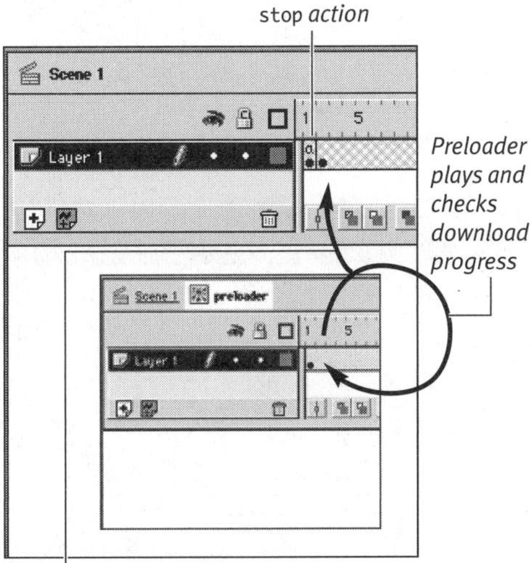

Flash provides two ways of creating the conditional statements inside your preloader that test for downloaded frames. The first is the action ifFrameLoaded. Although considered a deprecated action, it is easy to use because it provides you a way to specify a number of required frames in one simple statement.

The disadvantage of the action ifFrameLoaded is that it doesn't give you information about how many frames have been downloaded in proportion to the total number of frames in your movie. For that kind of specific information, use the properties _framesloaded and _totalframes. When these two properties are compared in a conditional statement using the action if, you can create a preloader that actually measures the proportion of the download and displays a progress bar. In both types of preloaders, the strategy is similar. The preloader is often a movie clip sitting on the first frame of the root Timeline. The first frame of the root Timeline contains a stop action that prevents the movie from playing. An EnterFrame Clip Event tests whether certain frames of the root Timeline have been downloaded. If the condition is true, Flash navigates out of the movie clip and begins playing the root Timeline. If the condition is false, the animation within the movie clip keeps playing (**Figure 5.45**).

stop action

Preloader plays and checks download progress

Once frames are downloaded, main Timeline begins playing and preloader instance is removed from the Timeline.

Figure 5.45 The logic behind a preloader. The movie clip plays until enough downloaded frames are available. Then it tells the root Timeline to begin playing.

To create a simple preloader:

1. Create a movie-clip symbol containing a short animated loop to serve as an entertaining diversion (**Figure 5.46**).

2. Drag an instance of it from the Library onto the Stage.

3. Select the first keyframe of the root Timeline, and assign a `stop` action.

4. Insert a new keyframe at Frame 2, and create your main animation from that point on (**Figure 5.47**).

5. Select the movie clip, and open the Actions panel.

6. Choose Actions > onClipEvent. In the Parameters pane, choose EnterFrame.

7. Choose Actions > ifFrameLoaded. In the Parameters pane, choose a specific frame (**Figure 5.48**).

   As soon as this chosen frame has been downloaded, this condition will hold true, and Flash will carry out the action immediately following the ifFrameLoaded statement.

8. Choose Actions > evaluate. In the Expression field, enter:

   `_root.gotoAndPlay(2)`

   You must specify `_root` because the Clip Event is scoped to the movie clip's Timeline and not to the main movie Timeline.

Figure 5.46 This preloader movie clip contains an animation of a guy tapping his foot and some explanatory text. This animation will loop.

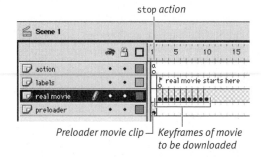

Figure 5.47 The main Timeline contains the preloader movie clip in the first frame and the contents of the rest of the movie following it.

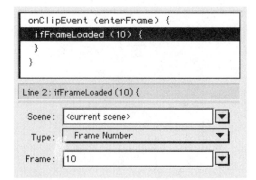

Figure 5.48 Frame 10 must be totally downloaded for the ifFrameLoaded condition to be true. Since Flash downloads frames sequentially, this means that Frames 1 through 9 must be downloaded first.

Data-transfer rate   *Causes delay during playback*

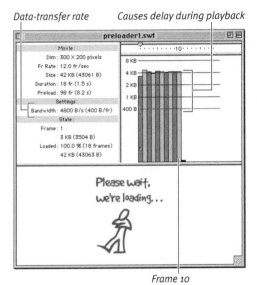

Frame 10

Figure 5.49 The Bandwidth Profiler shows the individual frames that cause pauses during playback because the amount of data exceeds the data-transfer rate. The alternating light and dark bars represent different frames.

Current location of playhead   *Progress of download*

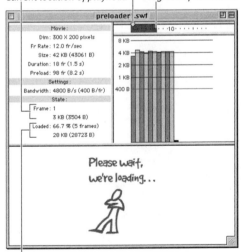

Progress of download

Figure 5.50 The Bandwidth Profiler during Show Streaming.

9. Test your movie. From the View menu, choose Bandwidth Profiler.

   The Bandwidth Profiler is an information window above your movie in the Test Movie mode that displays the number of frames in it and the amount of data in each frame, as vertical bars (**Figure 5.49**). If the vertical bars extend past the bottom red horizontal line, then there is too much data to be downloaded at the bandwidth setting without causing a stutter during playback.

10. From the View menu, choose Show Streaming.

Flash simulates actual download performance (**Figure 5.50**). The green bar at the top shows the download progress. The triangle marks the current location of the playhead. The playhead remains on Frame 1 until the green progress bar passes the frame that you specified in the `ifFrameLoaded` parameter. Only then does the playhead jump to Frame 2 and begin playing the movie.

✔ Tip

■ You won't see your preloader working unless you build an animation with fairly large graphics that require lengthy download times. If your animation is small, you'll see your preloader whiz by, since all the data will download quickly and almost immediately begin playing.

PRELOADERS

125

The Bandwidth Profiler

The Bandwidth Profiler is a handy option to see how data is distributed throughout your Flash movie and how quickly (or slowly) it will download over the Web. In the Test Movie mode, choose View > Bandwidth Profiler (Command-B for Mac, Ctrl-B for Windows) to see this information. The left side of the Bandwidth Profiler shows movie information, such as Stage dimensions, frame rate, file size, total duration, and preload time in frames and seconds. It also shows the Bandwidth setting, which simulates actual download performance at a specified rate. You can change that rate under the Debug menu and choose the rate for a modem that your viewer is likely to have. For example, Flash gives you options for a 28.8 or 56K modems.

The bar graph on the right side of the Bandwidth Profiler shows the amount of data in each frame of your movie. There are two ways you can view the graph: as a Streaming Graph (View > Streaming Graph), or as a Frame By Frame Graph (View > Frame by Frame Graph). The Streaming Graph indicates how the movie downloads over the Web by showing you how data streams from each frame, while the Frame By Frame Graph simply indicates the amount of data in each frame. In Streaming Graph mode, you can tell which frames will cause hang-ups during playback by noting which bar exceeds the given Bandwidth setting.

To watch the actual download performance of your movie, choose View > Show Streaming. Flash simulates playback over the Web at the given Bandwidth setting. A green horizontal bar at the top of the window indicates which frames have been downloaded while the triangular playhead marks the current frame that plays.

To create a complex preloader:

1. Create a movie-clip symbol containing a short animated sequence that has an obvious beginning and end (**Figure 5.51**).

2. Drag an instance of it from the Library onto the Stage.

3. Select the first keyframe of the root Timeline, and assign a `stop` action.

4. Insert a new keyframe at Frame 2, and create your main animation from that point on.

5. Select the movie clip, and open the Actions panel.

6. Choose Actions > onClipEvent. In the Parameters area, choose EnterFrame.

7. Choose Actions > if.

8. In the Condition field, enter the following:

   `_root._framesloaded >= _root._total-frames`

   The first part of the statement retrieves the number of frames already downloaded in the root Timeline. The second part retrieves the total number of frames in the root Timeline. The greater than (>) and equals (=) symbols together mean "greater than or equal to."

9. Choose Actions > evaluate. In the Expression field, enter:

   `_root.gotoAndPlay(2)`

10. Now, choose Actions > else.

    The `else` statement provides an alternative to the first condition in the `if` statement. If the first condition is true, Flash will go to Frame 2 of the root Timeline and play. If the first condition is false, however, Flash will carry out any actions that follow the `else` statement.

11. Choose Actions > evaluate. In the Expression field, enter:

    `this.gotoAndStop`
    `(Math.floor`
    `((_root._framesloaded/`
    `_root._totalframes)*`
    `this._totalframes))`

    This statement looks complicated, but it's simple once you break it down. It calculates the proportion of downloaded frames in the root Timeline and jumps to a corresponding frame in the pre-loader Timeline. Let's analyze the code. First, the inner statement `_root._framesloaded/_root._totalframes` gives the proportion of downloaded frames. This fraction is multiplied by `this._totalframes`, which is the number of frames in the preloader movie clip.

(continued on next page)

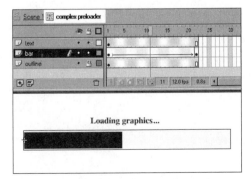

Figure 5.51 This movie clip contains an animation of a bar filling up and some explanatory text above.

Next, you apply the floor method of the Math object, which converts any number to the nearest integer (rounded down). You'll learn much more about the Math object later, but put simply it's an object that provides mathematical calculations. Now that Flash has an integer (a whole number with no decimals or fractions), it is used as the frame number in the statement `this.gotoAndStop` (**Figure 5.52**).

12. Test your movie with the Bandwidth Profiler and with Show Streaming (**Figure 5.53**).

✔ Tips

- The ratio `_framesloaded/_totalframes` isn't really the exact proportion to gauge download progress. The ratio is a percentage of frames and not necessarily the percentage of data. If your movie contains data unevenly spread among the frames, then the ratio `_framesloaded/_totalframes` will not give you an accurate representation of how much data has been loaded and how much is still expected.

- This is just one of many ways to create a proportional preloader. The basic idea is the same for all of them, however. First, test the properties `_framesloaded` and `_totalframes` against each other. Then, make your preloader movie clip respond in some way to the slowly increasing fraction `_framesloaded/_totalframes`. In later chapters you'll learn how to evaluate other properties of movie clips, such as their size or opacity. So, rather than play particular frames based on the download progress, you can increase a movie clip's size or change its opacity based on the download progress.

```
onClipEvent (enterFrame) {
  if (_root._framesloaded>=_root._totalframes) {
    _root.gotoAndPlay(2);
  } else {
    this.gotoAndStop(Math.floor((_root._framesloaded/_root._totalframes)*this._totalframes));
  }
}
```

Figure 5.52 The complete ActionScript code for this more complicated preloader.

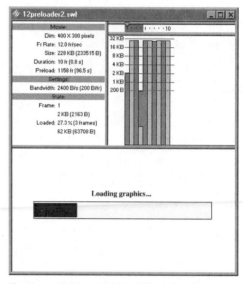

Figure 5.53 The Bandwidth Profiler during Show Streaming. Notice how the progress of the download (5 out of 10 frames have been completely loaded) affects the proportion of the bar in the preloader movie clip (about 50 percent) through its tween.

PRELOADERS

MANAGING OUTSIDE COMMUNICATION

Flash provides powerful tools to communicate with other applications and external data, scripts, and files to extend its functionality. By using Flash to link to the Web, you can build sites that combine Flash animation and interactivity with non-Flash media supported by the browser, and you can develop dynamic interfaces and buttons in Flash that link to PDF documents, QuickTime VR scenes, or even Java applets. Use Flash to link to FTP sites, send e-mail, communicate with JavaScript, or relay information to and from servers with the CGI Get and Post methods. Flash also supports XML, allowing you to create customized code for data-driven e-commerce solutions. This chapter introduces you to some ways Flash can communicate with HTML, JavaScript, CGI, and XML. You can use Flash to communicate with other Flash movies on the Web, loading one or more Flash movies only as they are needed. This lets you create modular projects that are easier to edit and have smaller file sizes. For example, your main Flash movie might simply serve as an interface that loads your portfolio of Flash animations as the viewer selects them. You can also integrate Flash with Macromedia Generator, a tool for delivering visual content over the Web in real time. When you build Generator templates in your Flash documents, it's possible for data to be updated on the fly from a client-side database.

In this chapter you'll also learn about standalone Flash players, called *projectors,* and how specialized commands affect the way they appear, function, and interact with other programs. Since they don't require a browser to play, projectors are ideal for distributing Flash content on CD-ROM or other media.

Finally, you'll see how Flash sends information to the printer. Flash lets the viewer print the text and graphics on all or just a portion of the Stage and even text and graphics that are hidden from the Stage.

With such versatile printing options, sophisticated Web and server-side communication, and content that updates on the fly, Flash can serve as a key component in the development of dynamic, commercial applications.

Communicating Through the Web Browser

Flash links to the Web browser through the basic action getURL in the Actions panel (**Figure 6.1**). This action is very similar to the HTML tag <A HREF>, where the URL of a Web site is specified in the form of http://www.domainname.com/directory. Use an absolute URL (a complete address to a specific file) to link to any Web site, or use a relative URL (a path to a file that's described in relation to the current directory) to link to local files contained on your hard drive or a CD-ROM. The getURL action also provides ways to target different frames you create within the browser window or entirely new browser windows. You can create Flash movies that navigate between these frames and windows and control what loads in each one.

Linking to the Web

Use the action getURL to link to the Web with the standard scheme http:// followed by the rest of the Web address. Use different schemes to request different protocols, such as ftp:// for file transfers or mailto: for e-mail.

If you play your Flash movie using Control > Test Movie or in the Flash Player, the action getURL will automatically launch the default browser and load the specified Web address in a new window.

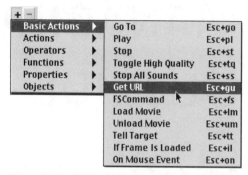

Figure 6.1 The getURL action in the Object Actions panel.

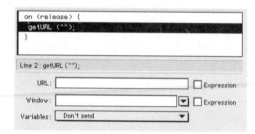

Figure 6.2 The getURL action has parameters for a URL, window name, and methods of sending variables to CGI scripts.

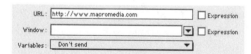

Figure 6.3 Enter a URL in the Parameters pane of the getURL action.

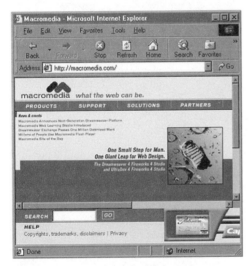

Figure 6.4 The Flash movie (top) links to the Macromedia site in the same browser window (bottom) when the window field is left blank.

Figure 6.5 A Web address in the URL field in the Character tab of the Character panel makes the entire static text field link to the site.

To link to a Web site with the getURL action:

1. Create a button symbol, and drag an instance from the Library onto the Stage.

2. Select the button instance, open the Actions panel, and choose Basic Actions > Get URL (Esc + gu).

   The on (release) event handler is automatically added in front of the getURL action (**Figure 6.2**).

3. In the URL field in the Parameters pane of the Actions panel, enter the full address of a Web site (**Figure 6.3**). Leave the Expression box unchecked.

4. Export your Flash movie, and play it in either the Flash Player or a browser.

   When you click the button you created, the Web site loads in the same window as your Flash movie (**Figure 6.4**). Click the back button on your browser to return to your Flash movie.

✔ Tips

■ You can also link to the Web from a static text block. Create static text with the text tool, and in the Character tab of the Character panel, enter the address of the Web site in the URL field (**Figure 6.5**). When your viewers click the text, the Web site will load in the same browser window as your Flash movie.

■ In addition to button instances, the getURL action can be assigned to a keyframe. If assigned to a keyframe, getURL will link to the URL when the playhead enters that particular frame. This method is effective for automatically loading Web links—perhaps after an introductory splash animation, or maybe as a way to mimic a series of banner ads that load automatically. You don't give your audience control but essentially pull them along for the ride.

To begin a file transfer with FTP:

1. Create a button symbol, and drag an instance from the Library onto the Stage, as you did in the previous task.

2. Select the button instance, open the Actions panel, and choose Basic Actions > Get URL.

   The on (release) event handler is automatically added in front of the getURL action.

3. In the URL field in the Parameters area, enter ftp://, then your user name, a colon, your password, the "@" symbol, and finally the full FTP address of the desired directory or file (**Figure 6.6**). Leave the Expression box unchecked.

4. Export your Flash movie, and play it in either the Flash Player or a browser.

   When you click the button you created, the FTP site loads in the same window as your Flash movie, giving you access to the directory and files on the server (**Figure 6.7**).

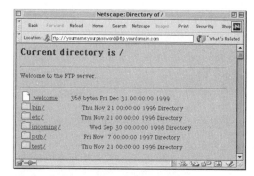

Figure 6.6 An FTP address in the URL field of the getURL action can include user-name and password information, or just the FTP address for anonymous access.

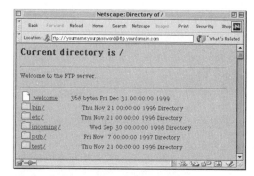

Figure 6.7 A typical FTP directory in a browser window.

Figure 6.8 Enter e-mail recipients after mailto: in the URL field. Separate additional e-mail addresses with commas.

Figure 6.9 A new e-mail message appears in a new window above your Flash movie.

Figure 6.10 This e-mail address is also a button that links to the browser via mailto: .

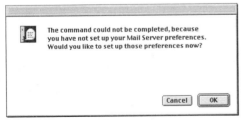

Figure 6.11 Some people use separate programs for e-mail and for Web browsing. In these cases, their browsers will not be configured to send e-mails linked from Flash.

To pre-address an e-mail:

1. Again, create a button symbol, and drag an instance from the Library onto the Stage.

2. Select the button instance, open the Actions panel, and choose Basic Actions > Get URL.

3. In the URL field of the Parameters pane, enter mailto: and the e-mail address of the person who should receive the e-mail (**Figure 6.8**). Leave the Expression box unchecked.

4. Export your Flash movie, and play it in either the Flash Player or a browser.

   When you click the button you created, an e-mail form appears with the recipient's e-mail address already filled in (**Figure 6.9**). The viewer then types in a message, and clicks Send. Use getURL to preaddress e-mail that viewers can then use to contact you on your Web site or to request more information.

✔ Tip

■ It's a good idea to spell out the e-mail address of the getURL mailto: recipient in your Flash movie (**Figure 6.10**). If a person's browser isn't configured to send e-mail, then an error message will appear instead of an e-mail form (**Figure 6.11**). By spelling out the address, you allow users to enter it into their e-mail applications themselves.

Linking to Local Files

Use relative paths rather than complete URLs to specify local files instead of files on the Web. This allows you to distribute your Flash movie on a CD-ROM or floppy disk without requiring an Internet connection. For example, instead of using the complete URL, `http://www.myServer.com/images/photo.jpg`, you can specify just `images/photo.jpg`, and Flash will only have to look inside the images folder to find the file called photo.jpg.

To link to a local file:

1. Create a button symbol, and drag an instance from the Library onto the Stage, as you did in the previous tasks.

2. Select the button instance, open the Actions panel, and choose Basic Actions > Get URL.

   The `on (release)` event handler is automatically added in front of the `getURL` action.

3. In the URL field of the Parameters pane, enter the relative path to the desired file. Use a slash (/) to separate directories, and two dots (..) to move up one directory (**Figure 6.12**). Leave the Expression box unchecked.

4. Export your Flash movie, and place it and your linked file in the correct folder hierarchy (**Figure 6.13**). Play it in either the Flash Player or a browser.

   When you click the button you created, Flash looks for the file using the relative path and loads it into the same browser window (**Figure 6.14**).

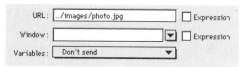

Figure 6.12 This relative URL goes up one directory level and looks for a folder called images, which contains a file called photo.jpg.

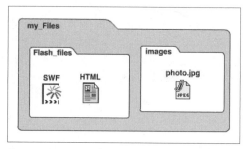

Figure 6.13 Your Flash movie (SWF) and its accompanying HTML file are in a directory that's at the same level as the directory that contains the file photo.jpg.

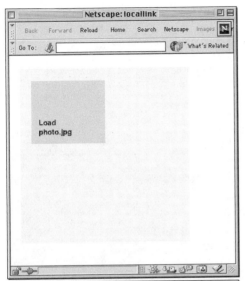

Figure 6.14 The Flash movie (top) links to the local file in the same browser window (bottom).

✔ Tips

- Any file type can be targeted in the URL field of the getURL action. You can load HTML, JPEG, GIF, QuickTime, and PDF files, and even other Flash movies. Just keep in mind that the viewer's browser must have the required plug-ins to display these different media types.

- With Microsoft Internet Explorer 4 and earlier on the Mac, the getURL link is relative to the Flash movie (SWF) and not to its accompanying HTML file. Most of the time, you'll place your exported Flash movie (SWF) and its HTML file in the same folder, but if you separate these two files, know that only Internet Explorer 5 for Mac can retrieve the getURL links properly (**Figure 6.15**).

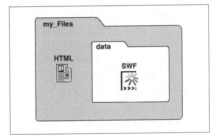

Figure 6.15 Separating the SWF file and its HTML file will cause relative URLs to behave differently with Microsoft Internet Explorer 4 on the Mac. Using the URL photo.jpg, Internet Explorer looks for the file relative to the SWF file and would look inside the data directory. Internet Explorer 4 for Windows and other browsers look for the file relative to the HTML file, so they would look inside the my_Files directory. This problem has been fixed with Internet Explorer 5 for Mac.

Browser Framesets and Windows

When you play your Flash movie in a browser window, the getURL action loads the new Web address in the same window, replacing your Flash movie. In order to make it load into a new window or a different frame of your window so that your original Flash movie isn't replaced, use the Window options in getURL (**Figure 6.16**).

What's the difference between a window and a frame? Browser windows can be divided into separate areas, or *frames,* that contain individual Web pages. The collection of frames is called a *frameset,* and the frameset HTML file defines the frame proportions and the name of each frame (**Figure 6.17**).

The Flash Window parameter can use the name that the frameset HTML file assigns a frame to load a URL directly into that specific frame. This is very similar to using the HTML <A HREF> tag attribute TARGET. For example, if you divide a Web page into two frames, you can call the left frame Navigator and the right frame Contents. Place a Flash movie in the Navigator frame with buttons that are assigned the getURL action. By entering the frame name Contents in the Window parameter of getURL, you target the right-hand frame to load the URL.

The Window parameter also provides reserved target names for you to use (**Figure 6.18**). The following table summarizes what they do.

Figure 6.16 The Window field lets you choose reserved keywords from a pull-down menu.

Figure 6.17 A typical Web site using frames to divide content. The window is divided horizontally into two frames. The bottom frame is divided vertically into two more. Ad banners, navigation bars, and content are usually separated from each other this way.

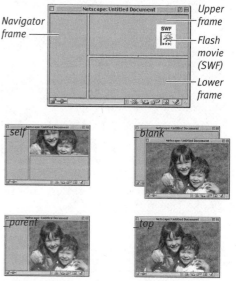

Figure 6.18 At top, a frameset divides a window into a left and a right frame. The right frame contains another frameset that divides itself into upper and lower frames. The Flash movie (SWF) plays in the UPPER frame of the second frameset. The window names specify where the URL loads.

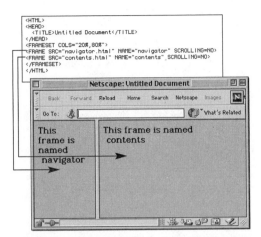

```
<HTML>
<HEAD>
  <TITLE>Untitled Document</TITLE>
</HEAD>
<FRAMESET COLS="20%,80%">
  <FRAME SRC="navigator.html" NAME="navigator" SCROLLING=NO>
  <FRAME SRC="contents.html" NAME="contents" SCROLLING=NO>
</FRAMESET>
</HTML>
```

Figure 6.19 The frameset file (top) divides this window into a left column named navigator, which is 20 percent of the browser width, and a right column named contents, which is 80 percent of the browser width (bottom).

Figure 6.20 The parameters area of the getURL action specifies the Google.com Web site to load in the *contents* frame.

To open a Web site in a named frame:

1. Create an HTML frameset with two frames and unique names for both.

   Your Flash movie will be in one frame, and the Web-site links will be loaded into the other frame (**Figure 6.19**).

2. Create a button symbol, and drag an instance from the Library onto the Stage as you did in the previous tasks.

3. Select the button instance, open the Actions panel, and choose Basic Actions > Get URL.

   The on (release) event handler is automatically added in front of the getURL action.

4. In the URL field of the Parameters pane, enter the address of a Web site, beginning with http://. Leave the Expression box unchecked.

5. In the Window field of the Parameters pane, enter the name of the frame established in the HTML frameset (**Figure 6.20**).

6. Publish your Flash movie with its accompanying HTML file. Create another HTML file for the other frame in the frameset.

Table 6.1

Window Parameters for get URL	
WINDOW NAME	**EXPLANATION**
_self	Specifies the current frame of the current browser window. This is the default behavior when no Window parameter is specified.
_blank	Specifies a new browser window.
_parent	Specifies the frameset that contains the current frame
_top	Specifies the top-level frameset in the current browser window.

COMMUNICATING THROUGH THE WEB BROWSER

137

7. Name both HTML files according to <FRAME SRC> tags in the frameset document, and place all files within the same folder (**Figure 6.21**).

8. Open the frameset document within a browser.

   Your Flash movie plays in one frame. The button loads a Web site in the other frame (**Figure 6.22**).

To open a Web site in a new window:

1. Create a button, and assign the action getURL to the button instance.

2. In the URL field of the Parameters pane of the Actions panel, enter a Web-site address.

3. In the Window field, choose _blank from the pull-down menu (**Figure 6.23**).

4. Export your Flash movie, and play it in the Flash Player or a browser.

   When you click the button you created, a new window appears and the Web site loads in it.

or

1. In the Window field of the getURL action, instead of choosing _blank from the pull-down menu, simply enter a unique name for your new window (**Figure 6.24**).

2. Export your Flash movie, and play it in the Flash Player or a browser.

   When you click your button, Flash looks for the frame or window with the name that you specified in the Window field of the getURL action. Not finding it, Flash creates a new window with that name.

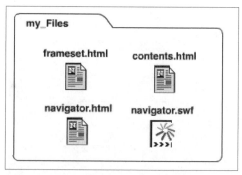

Figure 6.21 The frameset.html file puts the contents.html file in the contents frame and the navigator.html file in the navigator frame. The navigator.html file embeds the Flash movie (navigator.swf).

Figure 6.22 The ActionScript for the button in the navigator frame is shown. The Google site loads in the other frame.

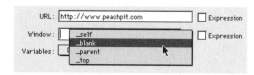

Figure 6.23 When _blank is chosen from the Window pull-down menu, the Peachpit Web site will load in a new, unnamed window.

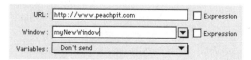

Figure 6.24 The Peachpit Web site will load in a new window called myNewWindow if that name is entered in the Window field.

Figure 6.25 Multiple getURL actions with the Window field set to _blank (top), and set to a unique name (bottom).

✔ Tips

- There is a crucial difference between opening a new window using _blank and using a name that you enter yourself. If you use _blank then each time you click your button to link to a Web site, a new window will be created. If you use a name in the Window field, then the first click will open a new window. Subsequent clicks actually find the newly created window you named, so Flash reloads the Web site into that existing window (**Figure 6.25**). Both methods are useful, depending on whether you want your Web links to be in separate windows or if you want your Web links to replace each other in the first new window.

- Be careful when creating new browser windows, and keep track of where they are. Sometimes they may be hidden behind the active window, loading Web sites that the viewer cannot see.

Using JavaScript to Control New Window Parameters

The Window field in the `getURL` action is useful for directing Web links to new browser windows, but the appearance and location of these new windows are set by the browser's preferences. For example, if you play a Flash movie in a browser that shows the location bar and the toolbar, and you open a new window, the new window will also have a location bar and a toolbar. You can't control these window parameters directly with Flash, but you can indirectly with JavaScript.

In the HTML page that holds your Flash movie, you can define JavaScript functions that control the opening and even closing of new browser windows. In your Flash movie,

you can call on these JavaScript functions using the `getURL` action. Instead of entering a Web address in the URL field, you enter `javascript:` and the name of the function. Flash finds the JavaScript in the HTML page, and the browser calls the function.

You can use JavaScript to control several window properties. These properties specify the way the window looks, how it works, and where it's located on the screen (**Figure 6.26**). These properties can be defined within the JavaScript function in the HTML page with a yes (1) or a no (0), or a number specifying pixel dimensions or coordinates. The following table contains the most common window properties that are compatible with both Internet Explorer and Netscape Navigator (**Table 6.2**).

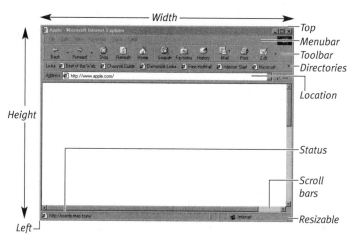

Figure 6.26 The properties of a browser window can be set with JavaScript.

Table 6.2

JavaScript Window Properties

PROPERTY	DESCRIPTION
height	Vertical dimension in pixels.
width	Horizontal dimension in pixels.
left	X-coordinate of left edge.
top	Y-coordinate of top edge.
resizable	Resizable area in the bottom-right corner that allows the window to change dimensions (yes/no or 1/0).
scrollbars	The vertical and horizontal scroll bars (yes/no or 1/0).
directories	Also called the personal bar, where certain bookmarks are accessible (yes/no or 1/0).
location	Location bar, containing URL area (yes/no or 1/0).
menubar	Menu bar, containing drop-down menus such as File and Edit. Only on Windows operating system. (yes/no or 1/0).
status	Status area in the bottom-left corner, containing browser status and security (yes/no or 1/0).
toolbar	Toolbar containing the back and forward buttons and other navigation aides (yes/no or 1/0).

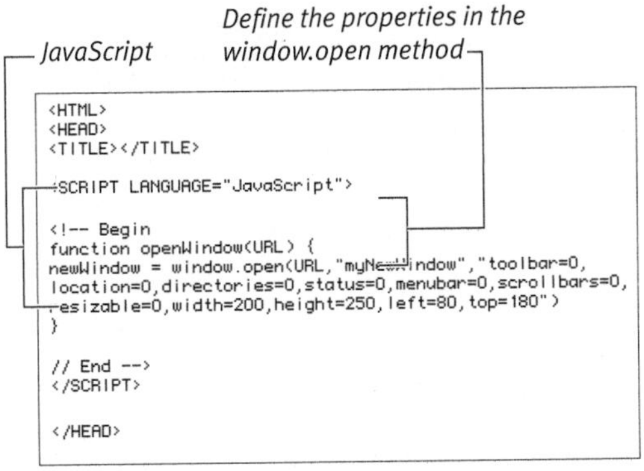

JavaScript — *Define the properties in the window.open method*

```
<HTML>
<HEAD>
<TITLE></TITLE>

<SCRIPT LANGUAGE="JavaScript">

<!-- Begin
function openWindow(URL) {
newWindow = window.open(URL,"myNewWindow","toolbar=0,
location=0,directories=0,status=0,menubar=0,scrollbars=0,
resizable=0,width=200,height=250,left=80,top=180")
}

// End -->
</SCRIPT>

</HEAD>
```

Figure 6.27 JavaScript code in the header of an HTML document. The Flash movie embedded in this HTML document will call on the function openWindow (URL).

To open a new window with JavaScript:

1. First you must define the function in the HTML page that holds your Flash movie. Add the following script to the head of the HTML page.

   ```
   <SCRIPT LANGUAGE="JavaScript">
   function openWindow(URL) {
   newWindow = window.open(URL);
   }
   </SCRIPT>
   ```

   This script defines a function openWindow with the argument URL. When this function is called, the object newWindow is created with the URL being passed as the Web address to load.

2. Now add the window properties to the script within the parentheses of the window.open method:

   ```
   <SCRIPT LANGUAGE="JavaScript">
   function openWindow(URL) {
   newWindow = window.open(URL,
   "myNewWindow", "toolbar=0,
   location=0,directories=0,status=0,
   menubar=0,scrollbars=0,resizable=0,
   width=200,height=250,left=80,top=180")
   }
   </SCRIPT>
   ```

3. Add the following parameter inside the <EMBED> tag after the width and height parameters in the HTML code where your Flash movie (SWF) is referenced.

   ```
   SwLiveConnect=true
   ```

   This is a crucial parameter that enables the browser to begin the interface allowing your Flash movie to communicate with JavaScript. The HTML page should be similar to **Figure 6.27**.

COMMUNICATING THROUGH THE WEB BROWSER

4. Now create the Flash movie that communicates with your newly created JavaScript function. Create a button, and attach the getURL action to an instance on the Stage.

5. In the URL field, enter:

javascript:openWindow
('http://www.peachpit.com')

Leave the Expression box unchecked and the Window field blank. The Web address that you enter in single quotes between the parentheses gets passed to the JavaScript function as the argument URL (**Figure 6.28**).

6. Export your Flash movie, and open the HTML page that holds the SWF file in a browser.

When you click the button that you created, Flash passes the Web address to the JavaScript function called openWindow. JavaScript then creates a new window with the parameters defined in the HTML page (**Figure 6.29**).

Figure 6.28 The javascript: statement calls the openWindow function in the HTML page that embeds the Flash movie.

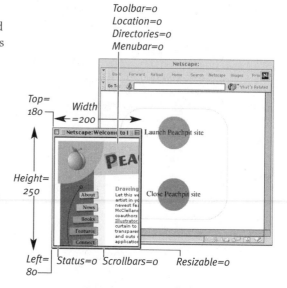

Figure 6.29 The customized window without any features is called "chromeless." "Chrome" refers to all the interface features of a window.

✔ Tips

■ This method of using Flash to talk to JavaScript will not work with older versions of Internet Explorer (version 3 or earlier), nor will it work with Internet Explorer 4.5 or earlier on the Macintosh.

■ There are more JavaScript window properties, but many of them work on only one or the other of the two most popular browsers. For example, the properties `innerHeight` and `innerWidth` define the dimensions of the actual window content area, but these properties are unique to Netscape Navigator. You are safe if you stick to the properties listed in **Table 6.2.**

■ Just as you can pass the argument URL to the JavaScript function from Flash, you can set up your `openWindow` function to accept more arguments. That way, you can define the height, width, and other window properties from inside Flash instead of having them predetermined in the JavaScript portion of your HTML page.

COMMUNICATING THROUGH THE WEB BROWSER

To close a window with JavaScript:

1. Once you open a window with JavaScript, you can close it with the same strategy. First, define a function in JavaScript in the HTML page holding your Flash movie. Then, call that function within the action getURL. Follow the previous task, and add the new function after the openWindow function:

```
function closeWindow()         {
newWindow.close()
}
```

The function closeWindow basically calls the method close() for the object newWindow that you created in the first function.

2. In your Flash movie, create a second button, and attach the getURL action to an instance on the Stage.

3. In the URL field, enter:

```
javascript:closeWindow()
```

Leave the Expression box unchecked and the Window field blank (**Figure 6.30**).

4. Export your Flash movie, and open the HTML page that holds the SWF file in a browser.

When you click the first button, Flash tells JavaScript to create a new window called newWindow. When you click the second button, Flash tells JavaScript to close the object newWindow.

✔ Tip

- Notice that the window object name is different from the window name. The object name is used to close the window. The window name is used to target it to load URLs into it. In these examples, the object is called newWindow, but the name for targeting purposes is myNewWindow.

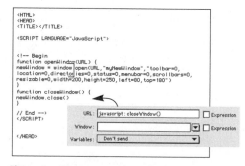

Figure 6.30 The getURL action calls the JavaScript closeWindow function. The window object called newWindow closes.

COMMUNICATING THROUGH THE WEB BROWSER

CGI and the GET and POST Method

The last parameter in the getURL action allows you to send information via the GET and POST methods. These methods send variables you define in your Flash movie to a server-side application—a CGI application, for instance—for processing. These methods are most commonly used to send information such as keywords to a search engine or a login name and password to a enter a Web site.The difference between GET and POST is very simple:

GET appends the variables to the URL in the getURL action and is used only for very few variables, and for variables that contain only a small amount of information. The variables term=CGI, category=All, and pref=all are put at the end of this URL as follows: http://search.domain.com/cgi-bin/ search?term=CGI&category=All&pref=all You've probably seen this type of long URL after you've requested information from a search engine.

POST sends the variables in the HTTP header of the user's browser. Use POST to send long strings of information in the getURL operation. For instance, a message board would do better with a POST method.

Once the variables are sent to the Web server, they are processed by the CGI scripts in the URL or HTTP headers. These server-side scripts are handled by your Internet service provider or your Webmaster, so you should contact them for more information.

To send information using GET:

1. Select the text tool, and drag out a text box on the Stage.

2. Open the Text Options panel by choosing Window > Panels > Text Options (**Figure 6.31**).

3. In the Text Options panel, choose Input Text from the pull-down menu.

   This option lets you use the text box you created to enter information.

4. In the Variable field enter emailStr (**Figure 6.32**).

   Whatever you enter in that text box is assigned to the variable name emailStr.

5. Create a button, and place an instance of it onto the Stage.

6. Select the button, open the Actions panel, and choose Actions > Get URL.

   The getURL statement appears under the on (release) mouse event.

7. In the URL field of the Parameters pane in the Actions panel, enter the address to the server-side script—for example, http://www.myserver.com/cgi-bin/list.cgi.

8. In the Window field, select _self.

9. From the Variables pull-down menu, select Send using GET (**Figure 6.33**).

   Your Action should look as follows:
   ```
   on (release) {
        getURL (
   "http://www.myserver.com/cgi-
   bin/list.cgi", "_self", "GET");
   }
   ```

   When your viewers enter an e-mail address into the text field and then click the button, the e-mail address is added to the end of the URL and is sent to the CGI script.

   You'll learn more about variables and input text in Part V: Working with Information.

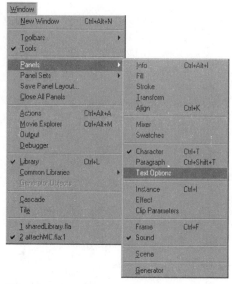

Figure 6.31 Choosing Window > Panels > Text Options brings up a dialog box that lets you choose Input Text for your text field.

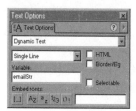

Figure 6.32 Enter emailStr in the Variable field of the Text Options panel.

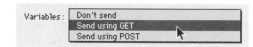

Figure 6.33 You can choose either the GET or POST method from the Variables parameter in the getURL action.

Communicating with XML Objects

In addition to HTML and JavaScript, Flash 5 supports XML. While it's beyond the scope of this book to cover XML in depth, this short discussion will help you understand the exciting possibilities Flash brings to XML.

XML (extensible markup language) is a powerful language currently being ratified by the World Wide Web Consortium (W3C). Its extensible nature allows you to define content according to its meaning and its audience. XML is very different from a traditional markup language like HTML, which tells the browser how to lay out the content—put this text here, set it to this font, and put it next to this image. XML defines data types, which makes it very scalable—the content is not tied to the presentation, and can be customized based on audience requirements. A portion of XML would look something like this:

```
<invoice>
<vendorname>Big Tents</vendorname>
<vendorID>MYBDAY021570</vendorID>
<vendorLogo>03SUIRAUQA.GIF</vendorLogo>
<productdescription>
    <name>All-Weather Tent</name>
    <dimensions>
        <height>7.25"</height>
        <width>7.25"</width>
        <depth>48.5"</depth>
        <weight>8lbs.</weight>
    </dimensions>
        <wholesale>$75.43</wholesale>
        <retail>$135.99</retail>
</productdescription>
</invoice>
```

In Flash 5, the XML and XMLSocket objects let you communicate with other applications and style sheets to manage media-rich content that is unique to each user. Such industries as entertainment, automotive,

banking, and e-commerce have recognized the benefits of combining Flash and XML.

A real-world application for e-commerce would provide an extensible interface between an online retailer and its partners, vendors, and suppliers in a Flash-enabled extranet. Using Flash as the tool for the interface—buttons, scroll bars, text-input fields, etc.—you could supply a merchant with a drag-and-drop interface for ordering products and placing them in a warehouse. The same XML object could identify and enable a vendor to change wholesale and retail prices, while negotiating its product's placement in the retailer's Web site and e-mail campaigns. Done traditionally, all of these different Web-based forms would take enormous amounts of time to create, and more would have to be created when a new user came to the extranet.

XSL is the style sheet that is applied to XML, and you might need only one or two to supply all the different types of users of your Flash content. The style sheet transforms the interface based on the user. The merchant might see some streaming data of what's being purchased and sold daily, and negotiate with a vendor in real-time. A partner, on the other hand, may see how well a promotion with the retailer's customers is going, and can make the decision to extend the promotion through to the following year.

Flash 5 can expose that highly extensible layer between front-end, media-rich content and middle/back-end negotiating and data. XML won't make your animations tween more smoothly, or your audio stream more cleanly, but it can make it easier to create unique and scalable user experiences. To learn more about Flash's XML and XMLSocket objects, refer to the Flash ActionScript Reference that comes with the software.

COMMUNICATING THROUGH THE WEB BROWSER

Communicating with External Movies

You've learned how a Flash movie can use the action getURL to link to any file, including another Flash movie. This loads the new SWF file into either the same browser window, replacing the original movie, or into a new browser window. Another way to communicate with external Flash movies and combine them with the original Flash movie is to use the action loadMovieNum (written as Load Movie in the Basic Actions category) (**Figure 6.34**). LoadMovieNum allows you to bring in another SWF and integrate it with the current content. The original Flash movie establishes the frame rate, the Stage size, and the background color, but you can layer multiple external SWF files and even navigate within their Timelines. In the previous Chapter, you learned to navigate the Timelines of movie clips within a single Flash movie. Imagine now the complexity of navigating multiple Timelines of multiple Flash movies!

One of the benefits of loading external Flash movies is that it allows you to keep the size of your Flash project small and maintain quick download times. For example, if you build a Web site to showcase your Flash animation work, you can keep all your individual animations as separate SWF files. Build the main interface so that your potential clients can load each animation as they request it. That way, your viewers download only the content that's needed, as it's needed. The main interface doesn't become bloated with the inclusion of every one of your Flash animations (**Figure 6.35**).

Figure 6.34 The loadMovieNum action in the Actions panel.

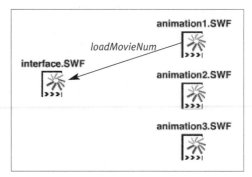

Figure 6.35 A way to keep data-heavy content separate is to maintain external SWF files. Here, the interface.swf movie loads the animation files one by one as they're requested.

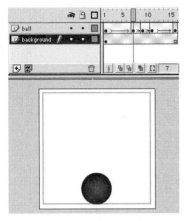

Figure 6.36 An animation of a bouncing ball inside a rectangle.

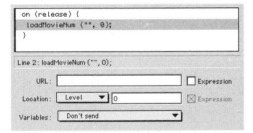

Figure 6.37 The loadMovieNum action has parameters for a URL (its target path), for Location (its destination), and for Variables.

Levels

When you load external SWF files into another Flash movie, you keep track of their locations by using levels. The original Flash movie is always at Level 0, and subsequent Flash movies load at higher levels. Higher-level numbers will overlap lower-level numbers, so loaded movies will always appear above your original movie on the screen. In order to unload a movie, you simply specify the level number, and the movie in that level is purged in the action unloadMovieNum. Another way to remove a movie in a particular level is to replace it with a new movie. If you load a new movie into a level already occupied by another movie, the old one is replaced.

To load an external movie:

1. First create the external movie you want to load. Create a small animation with a few background elements at a relatively small Stage size (**Figure 6.36**).

2. Export your external movie as a SWF file.

3. Open a new Flash document to create the first movie that will load your external movie.

4. Create a button symbol, and drag an instance of it from the Library to the Stage.

5. Select the instance and open the Actions panel. Choose Basic Actions > Load Movie (Esc + lm).

   The loadMovieNum action appears under the on (release) mouse event (**Figure 6.37**).

6. In the URL field , enter the name of your external SWF file. Keep the Expression box unchecked (**Figure 6.38**).

The URL field specifies the path of the target file. Here you enter a relative path, so Flash looks within the same directory for the SWF file. You can also change directories using the slash (/) or double dots (..), or enter an absolute path if your SWF file resides on a Web site on the Internet.

7. For the Location parameters, keep the pull-down menu at Level, and enter a number higher than zero (**Figure 6.39**).

8. Export your movie. Place both this SWF file and the external SWF file in the same directory.

9. Play the movie, that contains the button that you created in the Flash Player or a browser.

When you click the button, Flash loads the external movie, which sits on top of your original movie (**Figure 6.40**).

Figure 6.38 This relative URL means that bouncingball.swf should be in the same directory as the original Flash movie.

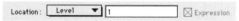

Figure 6.39 One level can hold only one Flash movie, but you can have an unlimited number of levels.

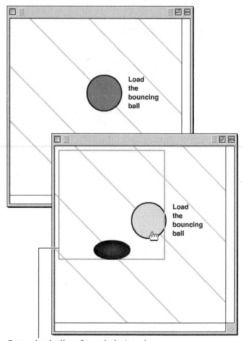

Bouncingball.swf movie in Level 1

Figure 6.40 The original movie in Level 0 (top) and the loaded movie in Level 1 (bottom). The button in Level 0 remains active.

Characteristics of Loaded Movies

◆ Loaded movies in higher levels will overlap loaded movies in lower levels.

◆ Loaded movies have transparent Stages. To have an opaque Stage, create a filled rectangle in the bottom layer of your loaded movie (**Figure 6.41**).

◆ Loaded movies are positioned from their top-left corner at the top-left corner of the original movie. This means that loaded movies with smaller Stage sizes will still show objects that are off their Stage (**Figure 6.42**). Create a mask to block objects that may go beyond the Stage that you don't want your audience to see. Likewise, loaded movies with larger Stage sizes will be cropped at the bottom and right-hand boundaries (**Figure 6.43**).

◆ Movies loaded into Level 0 replace the original movie, but the Stage size, frame rate, and background color are set by the original movie. If the loaded movie has a different Stage size from the original, it is centered and scaled to fit.

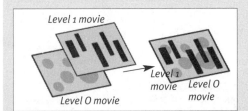

Figure 6.41 The stage of an external SWF becomes transparent when the SWF is loaded on top of the Level 0 movie.

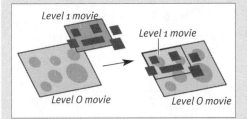

Figure 6.42 Smaller external SWFs are positioned at the top-left corner and display the work area off the Stage. Consider using masks or external SWFs with the same Stage dimensions.

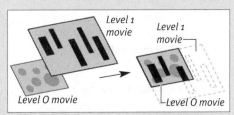

Figure 6.43 Larger external SWFs get cropped when loaded on top of the Level 0 movie.

COMMUNICATING WITH EXTERNAL MOVIES

To unload a movie:

1. Using the same files from the previous task, create another instance of the button in the original movie, and open the Actions panel.

2. Choose Basic Actions > Unload Movie (Esc + um).

   The unloadMovieNum action appears under the on (release) mouse event (**Figure 6.44**).

3. For the Location parameters, choose Level from the pull-down menu, and enter the same number that you entered for the loadMovieNum action (**Figure 6.45**).

4. Export your movie as a SWF file, and place it in the same directory as your external SWF file.

5. Play your movie in the Flash Player or in a browser.

   The first button loads your external movie in the specified level. The second button unloads that movie from that level.

To replace a loaded movie:

1. Open a new Flash document, and create another small Flash animation to serve as a second external movie.

2. Using the same Flash movie you used as the original in the previous task, add a third instance of your button, and open the Actions panel.

3. Choose Basic Actions > Load Movie.

   The loadMovieNum action appears under the on (release) mouse event (**Figure 6.46**).

4. In the URL field, enter the name of the second external movie. Leave the Expression box unchecked (**Figure 6.47**).

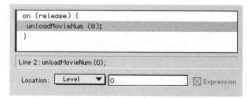

Figure 6.44 The unload MovieNum action has only one parameter for Location.

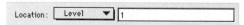

Figure 6.45 The Location parameter for unloadMovieNum. Any movie in Level 1 will be removed.

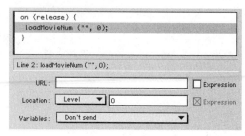

Figure 6.46 The loadMovieNum action assigned to the button.

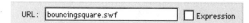

Figure 6.47 The file bouncingsquare.swf is the target path.

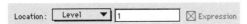

Figure 6.48 The bouncingsquare.swf file will load into Level 1.

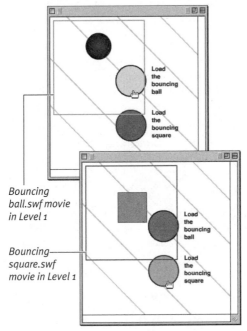

Bouncing ball.swf movie in Level 1

Bouncing square.swf movie in Level 1

Figure 6.49 Initially the bouncingball.swf movie occupies Level 1 (top). Loading another movie in the same level replaces bouncingball.swf.

5. For the Location parameters, keep the pull-down menu at Level, and enter the same number that you use for the first loadMovieNum action (**Figure 6.48**).

6. Export your movie. Place both this SWF file and the two external SWF files in the same directory.

7. Play the original movie that contains the three buttons either in the Flash Player or a browser.

When you click the first button, Flash loads the external movie, which sits on top of your original movie. When you click your newly created third button, Flash loads the second external movie in the same level, which replaces the first (**Figure 6.49**).

Loading Movies into Movie Clips

Loading external movies into levels is somewhat restricting because of the default placement of those movies at the top-left corner of the original Stage. You can work with that positioning by shifting the elements in your external movie relative to where you know it will appear, or you can change all your external movies so that their Stage sizes correspond to the original Stage size.

A better solution is to load those movies into movie clips instead of levels. This places the top-left corner of the loaded movie at the registration point of the targeted movie clip (**Figure 6.50**). Since you can place movie clips anywhere on the Stage, you effectively have a way to place your loaded movie where you want. The loaded movie takes over the movie clip—the Timeline of the movie clip is replaced by the Timeline of the loaded movie. However, the movie clip maintains its instance name, and all the scaling, rotation, skewing, color effects, and alpha effects that have been done to the movie-clip instance are also done to the loaded movie (**Figure 6.51**).

To load an external movie into a movie clip:

1. Create a movie-clip symbol, and drag an instance of it from the Library to the Stage (**Figure 6.52**).

2. Select the instance, and in the Instance panel give it a name.

3. Create a button symbol, and drag an instance of it from the Library to the Stage.

4. Select the button instance, and open the Actions panel.

5. Choose Basic Actions > Load Movie.

   The loadMovieNum action appears after the on (release) mouse event.

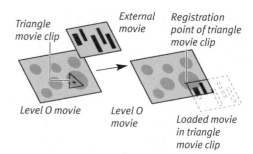

Figure 6.50 A movie loaded into a movie clip is positioned in the top-left corner at the movie's registration point.

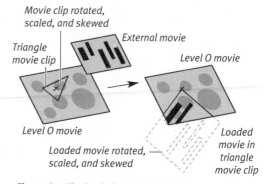

Figure 6.51 The loaded movie inherits the movie-clip instance's name, position, scaling, skewing, rotation, color effects, and alpha effects.

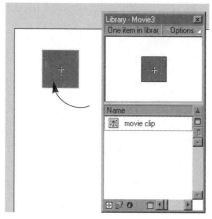

Figure 6.52 A movie-clip instance is the future destination for a loaded movie.

Figure 6.53 The parameters for the loadMovieNum action.

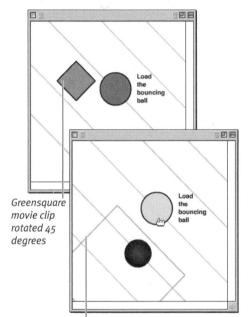

Greensquare movie clip rotated 45 degrees

Bouncingball.swf movie loaded into _root.greensquare

Figure 6.54 The bouncingball.swf movie loads into the greensquare movie clip, which has been rotated.

6. In the URL field, enter the name of an external SWF file. For the Location parameters, choose Target in the pull-down menu, and enter the target path for the movie-clip instance on the Stage (**Figure 6.53**).

7. Export your movie. Place both this SWF file and the external SWF file in the same directory.

8. Play the original movie that contains the button and movie clip either in the Flash Player or a browser.

When you click the button that you created, Flash loads the external movie into the movie clip. The loaded movie inherits all the characteristics of the movie clip, such as position, scale, rotation, instance name, and instance effect, but the Timeline on the Stage is now the Timeline of the loaded movie (**Figure 6.54**).

✔ Tip

■ Make the first keyframe of your movie clip empty so that it acts simply as a container to receive the external movie. Remember that the empty circle that represents the registration point of this movie clip will be the top-left corner of any loaded movie.

Navigating Timelines of Loaded Movies

Once external movies are loaded into your original movie, you can access their Timelines and control when and where the playback head moves. If you thought the navigation between movie-clip Timelines was complex, just think how intricate the navigation can become now with multiple movies, each containing its own movie clips!

Flash provides a straightforward way of targeting loaded movies and their Timelines to minimize confusion. Since loaded movies reside on different levels, Flash uses the term _level1 to refer to the movie in Level 1, _level2 to refer to the movie in Level 2, and so on. Movies that are loaded into movie clips simply take on their instance name, so targeting those loaded movies means just targeting movie clips. If loaded movies have movie clips themselves, use dot syntax to drill down the Timeline hierarchy as you do with movie clips on the root Timeline. For example, _level2.bigCircle.smallCircle is the target path for the movie clip named smallCircle inside the movie clip named bigCircle which resides in the loaded movie on Level 2.

To target a loaded movie:

1. As in the previous tasks, create an animation to serve as an external Flash movie. Export it as a SWF file.

2. Open a new Flash document. Create a button, and drag an instance of it from the Library on to the Stage.

3. Assign the action loadMovieNum to the button, specifying the external SWF file as the URL and a number higher than zero for the Location (**Figure 6.55**).

4. Drag another instance of the button onto the Stage.

Figure 6.55 The loadMovieNum action assigned to a button puts bouncingball.swf in Level 1.

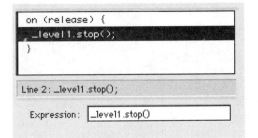

Figure 6.56 The stop method acts on the movie in Level 1.

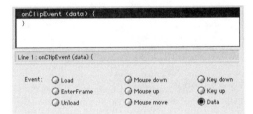

Figure 6.57 The onClipEvent (data) handler in the Actions panel.

This button will control the Timeline of the loaded movie.

5. From the Actions panel, choose Actions > evaluate (Esc + ev).

The evaluate statement appears under the on (release) event handler.

6. In the Expression field, enter _level and the level number, then a dot, and then the method stop() (**Figure 6.56**).

This expression stops the playhead in the movie's Timeline in the specified level.

7. Export your movie as a SWF. Place this file in the same directory as the external SWF file. Play the movie containing the buttons in the Flash Player or a browser.

The first button loads the external SWF in the specified level. The second button targets that level and stops the playback head.

Detecting the Load Movie Event

The actual loading of an external movie constitutes an event that you can detect. External SWF files are considered data, so you can use the clip event, onClipEvent (data), to recognize when the SWF files are fully loaded (**Figure 6.57**).

This event handler is useful when the loadMovieNum action occurs automatically or dynamically. After all, if the loadMovieNum action occurs when you press a button, you can simply use the mouse event as the handler. The onClipEvent(data) handler is also used to detect incoming data in the form of variables. External information can be loaded into Flash just as external SWFs can. You'll learn more about variables in Part V: Working with Information.

To create a load movie event handler:

1. Create a movie-clip symbol, and drag an instance of it from the Library to the Stage.

2. Select the movie-clip instance, and open the Actions panel.

3. Choose Actions > onClipEvent (Esc + oc) (**Figure 6.58**).

4. In the Parameters pane, click the Data radio button.

5. From the Toolkit window, choose an appropriate action to happen as a response to the load movie event (**Figure 6.59**).

   If an external SWF file begins to load into the main movie, the onClipEvent (data) event will hold true, and the following action happens.

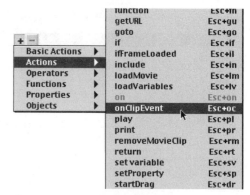

Figure 6.58 The onClipEvent.

Figure 6.59 When an external movie loads, Flash goes to the frame labeled incoming in the display movie clip.

Figure 6.60 Window > Generator Objects.

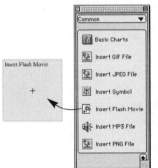

Figure 6.61 Drag an Insert Flash Movie object from the Generator Objects panel to the stage.

Communicating with Generator

While the action `loadMovieNum` is useful for loading external Flash movies, those movies remain static because their graphics and animations have already been created and rendered. If you want to load content on the fly and create Flash graphics and animation with dynamic information, you need to turn to Flash Generator.

There are actually two parts to Generator. First, you create templates, called Shockwave Flash template (SWT) files, in Flash. These templates specify what kind of data to use and what to do with it. Then, when you access those SWT files from a browser, the Generator Dynamic Graphics Server takes those templates, integrates the data, and delivers the newly created media to your audience. Generator is ideal for creating Flash graphics with information that changes continuously. For example, a graphical weather map could be created in run-time with weather information on the server, or a stock-ticker banner could display the latest stock prices.

Since working with Generator involves an entirely separate, server-side application, we'll limit our task to building a simple SWT file that calls up a Flash Movie.

To build a Generator template:

1. Choose Window > Generator Object (**Figure 6.60**).

   The Generator Object palette appears.

2. Place an Insert Flash Movie object on the Stage (**Figure 6.61**).

3. Double-click the Insert Flash Movie object on the Stage, or choose Window > Panels > Generator.

   The Generator panel appears.

COMMUNICATING WITH GENERATOR

4. For File Name, enter the name of another SWF that will be in the same directory (**Figure 6.62**).

5. Choose File > Publish Settings.

The Publish Settings dialog box appears.

6. On the Formats tab, check Flash, Generator Template, and HTML (**Figure 6.63**).

7. On the Generator tab, select a background color, as Generator will be replacing the Flash Movie Settings (**Figure 6.64**).

8. Click Publish.

Flash exports the HTML, SWF, and SWT files.

9. Put all the files (HMTL, SWF, and SWT) in the same directory on your Web server.

10. In a browser, type the SWT file's full URL; for example,

`http://www.myserver.com/intro.swt`

Figure 6.62 myMovie.swf is the relative path of the movie to insert. This file should be in the same directory as the SWT file.

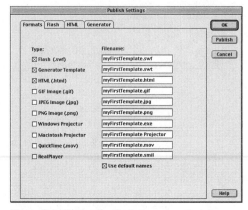

Figure 6.63 Choose the Flash, Generator Template, and HTML file types in the Formats tab in the Publish Settings dialog box.

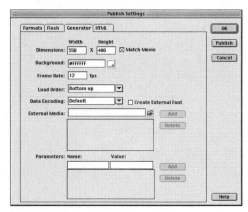

Figure 6.64 Select a background color in the Generator tab of the Publish Settings dialog box.

Projectors and the Fscommand

Most of the time, you'll play your Flash movie in a browser over the Web. Flash was conceived and developed to deliver content this way. However, Flash also provides a way to create projectors, self-executable applications that don't require the browser or the Flash Player for playback. On either Windows or Mac systems, you can publish projectors for either platform. In Windows, the extension to the file is .EXE, and on the Mac, the word *projector* is appended to the filename. These projectors are larger in file size than the normal exported SWF files, but they contain everything you need to play the content you create, including the graphics, animation, sound, and interactivity. Use projectors to deliver your Flash content on transportable media such as floppy disks or CD-ROMs, an ideal scenario for portfolios, presentations, or marketing material.

Playback of Flash content through projectors is different in one respect. Projectors don't use an HTML page that contains tags or "instructions" to tell it how to be displayed. Will playback be full screen? Can the window be scalable? These options are available to you when you publish the HTML page, but not with the projector. In order to set or change these kinds of display parameters, use the fscommand action, which has just a few simple parameters for projectors, as detailed in **Table 6.3.**

Table 6.3

Fscommand Parameters for Projectors	
COMMAND	DESCRIPTION AND ARGUMENT
fullscreen	Allows playback at full screen and prevents resizing (true/false)
allowscale	Makes the graphics scale when the window is resized (true/false)
trapallkeys	Allows the movie to capture key presses rather than the Flash Player (true/false)
showmenu	Shows the control menu when you control-click (Mac) or right-click (Windows) in the movie (true/false)
exec	Opens an executable file (Path to file)
quit	Quits the projector

To publish a projector:

1. Open your Flash file. Select File > Publish Settings (Shift-Command-F12 Mac, Shift-Ctrl-F12 Windows) (**Figure 6.65**). The Publish Settings dialog box appears.

2. Deselect all the checkboxes except for the Macintosh Projector or Windows Projector option (**Figure 6.66**).

3. If you wish to name your projector something other than the default name, deselect the Use default names checkbox, and enter your own filename.

4. Click Publish.

   Your projector file is saved in the same folder as the Flash file.

or

1. Open the Flash Player.

2. Choose File > Open File (Command-O Mac, Ctrl-O Windows). Then select your Flash file.

3. Choose File > Create Projector... (Command-K Mac, Ctrl-K Windows) (**Figure 6.67**).

4. Choose a destination folder and a filename. Click OK.

✔ Tip

■ The getURL action, when used in a projector, launches your default browser to open any Web link.

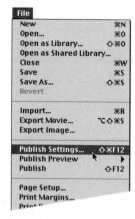

Figure 6.65 The Publish button exports all of your file types selected in the Formats tab.

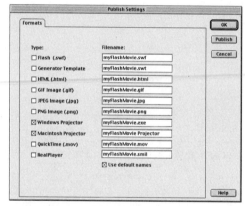

Figure 6.66 The Formats tab of the Publish Settings dialog box. Check the boxes to choose the Windows and the Macintosh projectors.

Figure 6.67 The Create Projector menu command from the Flash Player exports the current file to a Projector.

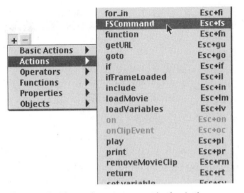

Figure 6.68 The path to fscommand in the Actions panel.

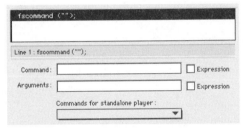

Figure 6.69 fscommand options for projectors appear in the pull-down menu at the bottom of the Parameters area.

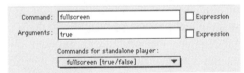

Figure 6.70 When fullscreen is true, playback of the projector fills the entire monitor.

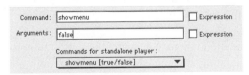

Figure 6.71 When showmenu is false, the menu options (right-click for Windows, control-click for Mac) are disabled.

To use Fscommand actions in the projector:

1. Select the first keyframe of a Flash movie you wish to publish as a projector. Open the Actions panel.

2. Choose Actions > FSCommand (Esc + fs) (**Figure 6.68**).

   The fscommand action appears in the Actions List with the parameters Command and Argument and a pull-down menu specifically for projectors (**Figure 6.69**).

3. From the pull-down menu, select fullscreen.

   The Command field contains fullscreen, and the Argument field contains true (**Figure 6.70**).

4. From the Toolkit window, choose FSCommand again. From the pull-down menu, select showmenu.

   The Command field contains showmenu, and the Argument field contains true.

5. In the Argument field, change true to false (**Figure 6.71**).

6. Create a button, and place an instance of that button on the Stage. Select the instance, and open the Actions panel.

7. Choose Actions > FSCommand.

(continued on next page)

PROJECTORS AND THE FSCOMMAND

8. From the Command pull-down menu in the Parameters pane, select quit (**Figure 6.72**).

9. Publish your movie as a projector. Double-click your projector to play.

The Flash projector plays at full screen. This effectively prevents scaling of the window. The menu options are disabled when you right-click (Windows) or control-click (Mac) in the movie. When you click the button, the projector quits.

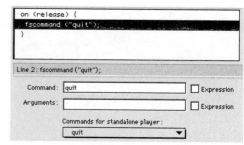

Figure 6.72 The fscommand ("quit") assigned to a button closes the projector.

Communicating with the Printer

Flash can send information directly out to a printer to output text and graphics, circumventing the Web browser's print function. Even during playback with the Flash Player or as a projector, the print command will function. With the actions `print` and `printAsBitmap`, you can specify a single frame or multiple frames to print, and you can also control which areas of those frames should print. The printable areas do not even have to be visible on the Stage. Graphics and text in any frame in the main Timeline of the movie or any frame of a movie clip Timeline are available to the printer, making the print action more than a simple tool for making hard copies of what is on the computer screen.

Imagine, for example, that you have documents in external SWF files. You could easily load a particular movie into a movie clip or in another level with the action `loadMovieNum`, then print selected frames from that loaded movie.

In Chapter 10, you'll learn about input text and dynamic text, with which you can enter information with the keyboard and display text dynamically. You can combine this ability with order forms or receipts, resulting in customized documents that you can then send to the printer.

To print a specific frame of your movie:

1. Create the graphics you wish to be available to the printer in a keyframe. It's a good idea if you can to keep them in a movie clip so they sit in their own Timeline (**Figure 6.73**).

2. Select the keyframe. In the Label field of the Frame panel, enter #P (**Figure 6.74**).

   The #P label designates that keyframe to be printed. If there is no #P label, then all the frames of the movie or targeted movie clip are printed.

3. Return to the main Timeline, and drag an instance of your movie clip onto the Stage. In the Instance panel, give the instance a name.

4. Return to the main Timeline, and create a button. Drag an instance of this button on to the Stage.

5. Select the button, and open the Actions panel. Choose Actions > print (Esc + pr).

   The print action appears under the on (release) mouse event (**Figure 6.75**).

6. In the Parameters area, choose As vectors from the Print pull-down menu, Target from the Location pull-down menu, and Movie from the Bounding box pull-down menu. Enter the target path for your movie-clip instance in the Location field(**Figure 6.76**).

7. Test your movie.

   When you click the button that you created, the graphics in the movie clip in the keyframe #P are sent to the printer. Click OK in the sequence of printer dialog boxes to begin printing (**Figure 6.77**).

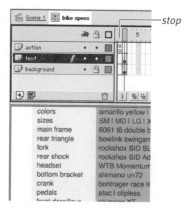

Figure 6.73 A movie clip contains graphics for printing in Keyframe 2. In Keyframe 1, a stop action prevents the clip from playing.

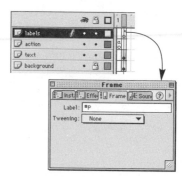

Figure 6.74 In a separate layer, add the #P label to Keyframe 2.

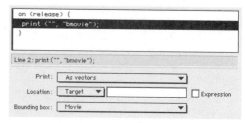

Figure 6.75 The print action is assigned to the button.

Figure 6.76 The movie-clip instance containing the graphics for printing is called bikespecs. This `print` action targets the bikespecs instance.

Figure 6.77 The movie-clip instance on the Stage (top) contains the graphics that print (bottom).

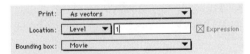

Figure 6.78 The `print` parameters. The movie in Level 1 is targeted to print.

✔ Tips

- Performing the `print` action stops the Flash playhead . Keep this in mind if you're integrating printing with animation. You may have to add a button in your animation to resume playing after the `print` action.

- Printing a keyframe that contains a movie clip will only result in a print of the first frame of that movie clip. If you want to print frames inside a movie clip, target the movie-clip instance itself.

- Don't use the `print` action as a frame action. When Flash prints from a frame action, it becomes caught in an endless loop in that frame and attempts to print an infinite number of times. This will crash your system! Always assign the `print` action to an event handler.

- To calculate how the area of a graphic translates to the size of the printed piece, multiply the pixel dimensions by the screen resolution, which is 72 ppi (pixels per inch). So an 8.5-by-11-inch sheet of paper is equivalent to a Stage size of 612 pixels (8.5 inches x 72 ppi) by 792 pixels (11 inches x 72 ppi). Then you must take into account the margins for the actual printable area.

- Select Level from the Location pull-down menu to target a loaded movie in a specific level **(Figure 6.78)**. All the frames of that loaded movie will print unless specified with the #P labels.

To print multiple frames of your movie:

◆ Mark each keyframe in the target Timeline to print with the label #P.

◆ If you want to print multiple frames that are in separate Timelines, you need to write separate print statements in the Actions panel. Multiple print dialog boxes will appear if you choose this method. Flash can print multiple frames, but only from one target path (**Figure 6.79**).

To control the printable area for your movie:

◆ From the Bounding box pull-down menu in the Actions dialog box, select Movie. Draw a bounding box in a keyframe, and label it #B in the Frame panel.

The last argument in the print action changes to bmovie. The bounding box you draw defines the print area for all the frames designated with the #P label (**Figure 6.80**).

◆ From the Bounding box pull-down menu, select Frame.

The last argument in the print action changes to bframe. Your graphics in each keyframe labeled #P are scaled to fit the maximum printable area (**Figure 6.81**).

Figure 6.79 The frames in the taxforms movie clip and in the receipts movie clip will print. Two separate movie clips require two print statements.

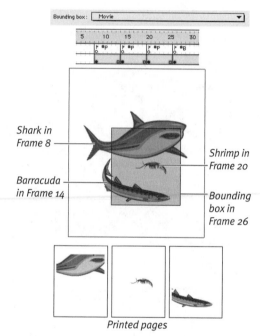

Printed pages

Figure 6.80 The bmovie option. Keyframe 26 contains the bounding box that determines the print area for all three images.

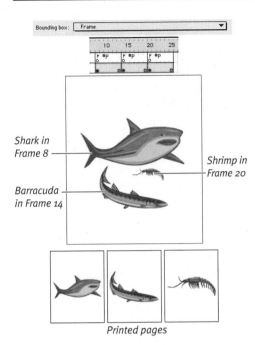

Shark in Frame 8

Shrimp in Frame 20

Barracuda in Frame 14

Printed pages

Figure 6.81 The bframe option. No #B labels are necessary. Each image is scaled to fit the printable area. Note how the shrimp prints as big as the shark.

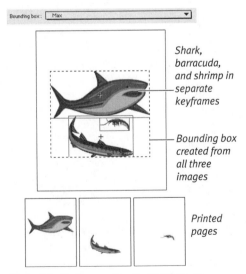

Shark, barracuda, and shrimp in separate keyframes

Bounding box created from all three images

Printed pages

Figure 6.82 The bmax option. No #B labels are necessary. A bounding box is created based on the composite sizes and locations of all three images.

♦ From the Bounding box pull-down menu, select Max.

The last argument in the print action changes to bmax. Flash defines the maximum width and height from all the printable frames, then scales the graphics relative to that printable area (**Figure 6.82**).

✔ Tips

■ The bounding box you define in the keyframe labeled #B can be any shape, but Flash will only recognize the rectangle in which that shape would fit. That rectangle defines the printable area.

■ It's a good idea to copy and paste your bounding-box shape into a guide layer. That way you can see how the printable area relates to the graphics that print.

■ Make sure you don't have other shapes or objects in another layer of the same frame that contains the labeled #B keyframe. If you do, your bounding box will be extended, allowing more of a printable area than you intend (**Figure 6.83**).

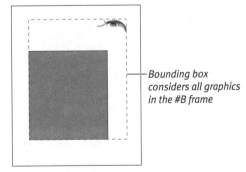

Bounding box considers all graphics in the #B frame

Figure 6.83 These two images in the #B frame force a larger bounding box.

To print graphics containing transparencies or color effects:

◆ From the Print pull-down menu in the Actions dialog box, select As bitmap (**Figure 6.84**).

Graphics that contain alpha or color effects won't print properly unless you choose printAsBitmap as the print statement. However, this option results in lower-quality prints than printing as vectors.

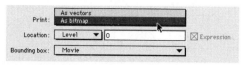

Figure 6.84 The Print As bitmap option in the Actions panel for transparencies and color effects.

Part IV: Transforming Graphics and Sound

CONTROLLING THE MOVIE CLIP

The movie clip is a powerful object. Flash lets you control the way movie clips look and behave. Movie-clip properties such as position, scale, rotation, transparency, color, and even instance name can all be changed with ActionScript. As a result, you can create arcade-style interactivity with characters changing in response to viewer input or conditions. Imagine a game of Tetris created entirely in Flash. Each geometric shape could be a movie clip, and the viewer would control its rotation and position with the keyboard. A game of Asteroids could feature an alien ship that moves in response to the viewer's ship. This kind of animation isn't based on tweens you create while authoring the Flash movie. Rather, this is dynamic animation that is essentially "created" during playback. Learning to control movie-clip properties is the first step in understanding how to animate entirely with ActionScript.

Flash also lets viewers move the movie clip directly with drag-and-drop actions. Use draggable movie clips to create puzzles in which the viewer can actually pick up the pieces and put them in their correct places, or develop a more immersive online shopping experience in which the viewer can grab merchandise and drop it into a shopping cart. You'll learn how to create drag-and-drop movie clips, and create methods to detect where they are dropped on the Stage, as well as control collisions and overlaps with other movie clips. Then you'll deal with duplicating multiple movie clips and even placing movie clips from the Library onto the Stage during playback.

Finally, you'll see how the movie clip lets you customize the pointer. Rather than using the generic arrow or pointing finger, you can create pointers that complement your unique content. For example, build a scope and crosshairs for a hunting game, or a skeletal hand to guide the viewer through a haunted house.

Dragging the Movie Clip

Drag-and-drop behaviors give the viewer one of the most direct interactions with the Flash movie. There's nothing more satisfying than grabbing a graphic on the screen, moving it around, and dropping it somewhere else. It's a natural way of interacting with objects, and it's easy to give your viewers this experience. Creating a drag-and-drop behavior in Flash involves just two basic steps: creating the movie clip, and then creating a button inside it that triggers the drag action.

The usual behavior for drag-and-drop interactivity is for the dragging to begin when the viewer presses the mouse button. Then, when the mouse button is released, the dragging stops. Hence, the action to start dragging is tied to the on (press) mouse event, and the action to stop dragging is tied to the on (release) mouse event.

To start dragging a movie clip:

1. Create a movie-clip symbol, place an instance of it on the Stage, and name it.

2. Create an invisible button as described in Chapter 4, and place an instance of your button inside the movie clip (**Figure 7.1**).

3. Select the button instance, and open the Actions panel.

4. Choose Actions > on (Esc + on)

    The on (release) statement appears in the script window.

5. In the Parameters pane, uncheck the box next to Release, and check the box next to Press (**Figure 7.2**). The on (press) statement changes to on (release).

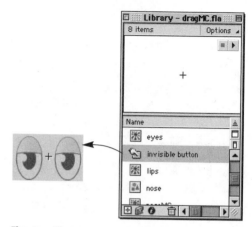

Figure 7.1 These eyes are part of a movie-clip symbol. Drag an invisible button over the eyes in symbol-editing mode to assign a startDrag action to the invisible button.

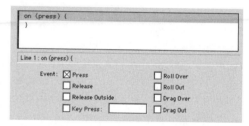

Figure 7.2 Select the Press event for the on handler assigned to the invisible button in your movie clip.

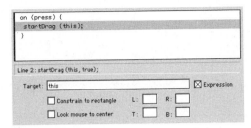

Figure 7.3 The target this makes the startDrag action affect the current movie clip.

6. Choose Actions > startDrag (Esc + dr).

The startDrag action appears under the on (press) mouse event.

7. In the Parameters pane, in the Target field, enter this, and check the Expression box (**Figure 7.3**).

The keyword this refers to the present movie clip. Checking the Expression box removes the quotation marks around this so that Flash recognizes the word as the keyword rather than a string literal.

8. Place an instance of the movie clip from the Library onto the Stage.

Since the button inside the movie clip uses the relative term, this, it wasn't necessary to name your movie clip instance.

9. Test your movie.

When you press your mouse button over the movie clip, you can drag it around.

To stop dragging a movie clip:

1. Using the file created in the previous task, select the closing curly brace in the Actions List.

2. Choose Actions > on.

   The on (release) statement appears.

3. Choose Actions > stopDrag (Esc + sd).

   The stopDrag statement appears with no parameters (**Figure 7.4**).

4. Test your movie.

   When you press your mouse button over the movie clip, you can drag it. When you release your mouse button, the dragging stops (**Figure 7.5**).

✔ Tips

- You can also assign the startDrag action to the movie clip's onClipEvent handler and not bother with the embedded invisible button. Use this approach when you only have one movie clip you want your viewers to drag, and you don't require the specificity that the invisible button provides. For example, when you assign startDrag to onClipEvent (load), Flash automatically makes the movie clip draggable. When you assign startDrag to onClipEvent (mouseDown), Flash makes the movie clip draggable after the user presses the mouse button anywhere on the Stage.

- Only one movie clip can be dragged at any one time. Because of this, the stopDrag action doesn't need any parameters; it will stop the drag action on whichever movie clip is currently draggable.

```
on (press) {
  startDrag (this);
}
on (release) {
  stopDrag ();
}
```

Figure 7.4 Assign the stopDrag action to the on (release) event handler.

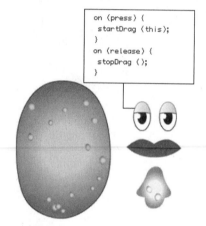

Figure 7.5 Each of the three facial features on the right are movie clips that contain invisible buttons assigned the ActionScript above. The three movie clips can be dragged to the potato face and dropped into position.

Figure 7.6 The Lock mouse to center option forces the viewer to drag the movie clip by its registration point.

In many cases you may want the movie clip to snap to the center of the user's pointer as it is being dragged, rather than wherever the user happens to click.

To center the draggable movie clip:

◆ In the Parameters pane of the Object Actions panel, check the box next to Lock mouse to center (**Figure 7.6**).

After you press the mouse button over the movie clip to begin dragging, the registration point of your movie clip snaps to the mouse pointer.

✔ Tip

■ If you select the Lock mouse to center option, make sure that your invisible button covers the registration point of your movie clip. If it doesn't, then after the movie clip snaps to your mouse pointer, your pointer will no longer be over the invisible button, and Flash won't be able to detect when to stop the drag action.

You may also want to limit the area where viewers can drag movie clips.

To constrain the draggable movie clip:

◆ Check the box next to Constrain to rectangle, and enter pixel coordinates for each of the four fields representing the maximum and minimum limits for the registration point of your draggable movie clip (**Figure 7.7**).

L: This is the leftmost margin (minimum X position) that the registration point of the movie clip can go.

R: This is the rightmost margin (maximum X position) that the registration point of the movie clip can go.

T: This is the topmost margin (minimum Y position) that the registration point of the movie clip can go.

B: This is the bottommost margin (maximum Y position that the registration point of the movie clip can go.

◆ The pixel coordinates are relative to the Timeline in which the movie clip resides. If the draggable movie clip sits on the root Timeline, the pixel coordinates correspond to the Stage, so L=0, T=0 refers to the top-left corner. If the draggable movie clip is within another movie clip, then L=0, T=0 refers to the registration point of the parent movie clip.

✔ Tip

■ You can use the Constrain to rectangle parameters to force a dragging motion along a horizontal or a vertical track, as in a scroll bar. Set the L and R fields to the same number to restrict the motion to just up and down, or set the T and the B fields to the same number to restrict the motion to just left and right.

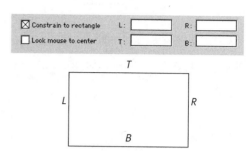

Figure 7.7 The Constrain to rectangle option has settings for the left (L), right (R), top (T), and bottom (B) boundaries.

Setting the Movie-Clip Properties

Many of the movie-clip properties—size, transparency, position, rotation, and quality —define how the movie looks. By using the action `setProperty`, you can target any movie clip and change any of those characteristics during playback. The following table summarizes properties that are available from the action `setProperty`. A few of these properties are global, which means they affect the entire movie and not just a single movie clip.

Table 7.1

Properties Available Through setProperty

PROPERTY	VALUE	DESCRIPTION
_alpha (Alpha)	A number from 0 to 100.	Specifies the alpha transparency, where 0 is totally transparent and 100 is opaque.
_visible (Visibility)	True or false.	Specifies whether a movie clip can be seen or not.
_name (Name)	A name.	Specifies a new instance name of the movie clip.
_rotation (Rotation)	A number.	Specifies the degree of rotation in a clockwise direction. For example, a value of 45 tips the movie clip to the right.
_height (Height)	A number in pixels.	Specifies the vertical dimension.
_width (Width)	A number in pixels.	Specifies the horizontal dimension.
_x (X Position)	A number in pixels.	Specifies the horizontal position of the movie clip's registration point.
_y (Y Position)	A number in pixels.	Specifies the vertical position of the movie clip's registration point.
_xscale (X Scale)	A number.	Specifies the percentage of the original movie-clip symbol's horizontal dimension.
_yscale (Y Scale)	A number.	Specifies the percentage of the original movie-clip symbol's vertical dimension.
_focusrect (Show focus rectangle)	True or false.	Determines whether a yellow rectangle appears around buttons or fields as you use the Tab key to navigate between those buttons or fields. This is a global property that affects the entire movie rather than a single movie clip.
_highquality (High quality)	A number 0, 1, or 2.	Specifies the level of antialiasing for playback of the movie. 2 = best: antialiasing and bitmap smoothing. 1 = high: antialiasing and bitmap smoothing if there is no animation. 0 = low: no antialiasing. This is a global property that affects the entire movie rather than a single movie clip.
_quality (_quality)	LOW, MEDIUM, HIGH, or BEST.	Specifies the level of antialiasing for playback of the movie. BEST = antialiasing and bitmap smoothing. MEDIUM = antialiasing and bitmap smoothing if there is no animation. MEDIUM = lower-quality antialiasing. LOW = no antialiasing. This is a global property that affects the entire movie rather than a single movie clip.
_soundbuftime (Sound buffer time)	A number.	Specifies the number of seconds before the movie begins to stream sound. The default value is 5. This is a global property that affects the entire movie rather than a single movie clip.

✔ Tips

- There is a difference between an Alpha of 0 and a Visibility of false, although the result may look the same. When Visibility is false, then the movie clip literally cannot be seen. Buttons within that movie clip aren't responsive, and any actions that target that movie-clip instance won't work. When the Alpha is 0, on the other hand, buttons within the movie clip still function, and actions can target the movie-clip instance.

- The *x* and *y* coordinate space for the root Timeline is different from movie-clip Timelines. In the root Timeline, the *x*-axis begins at the left edge and increases to the right. The *y*-axis begins at the top edge and increases to the bottom. Thus, $x = 0, y = 0$ corresponds to the upper-left corner of the Stage. For movie clips, the coordinates $x = 0, y = 0$ correspond to the registration point (the crosshair). The value of *x* increases to the right of the registration point, and decreases into negative values to the left of the registration point. The value of *y* increases to the bottom and decreases into negative values to the top (**Figure 7.8**).

- The X Scale and Y Scale properties control the percentage of the original movie-clip symbol, which is different from what may be on the Stage. If, for example, you place an instance of a movie clip on the Stage and shrink it 50 percent, then later during playback you apply an X Scale of 100 and a Y Scale of 100, your movie clip will double in size.

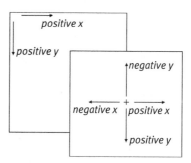

Figure 7.8 The *x, y* coordinates for the root Timeline (top) are centered at the top-left corner of the Stage. The *x, y* coordinates for movie clips (bottom) are centered at the registration point.

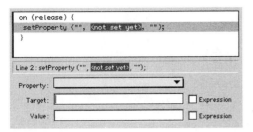

Figure 7.9 Assign the setProperty action to the on (release) event handler. The setProperty action changes movie-clip properties and some global settings.

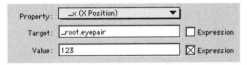

Figure 7.10 The *x* position of the movie clip eyepair on the root Timeline is set to 123.

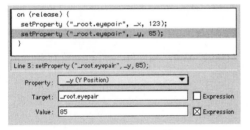

Figure 7.11 The *y* position of the movie clip eyepair on the root Timeline is set to 85.

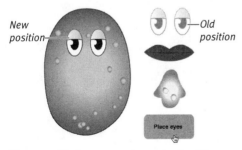

Figure 7.12 The button sets the movie clip of the eyes into its new position on the potato.

To change the position of a movie clip:

1. Create a movie-clip symbol, place an instance of it on the Stage, and name it.

2. Create a button symbol, place an instance of it on the Stage, select it, and open the Actions panel.

3. Choose Actions > setProperty (Esc + sp).

   The setProperty statement appears under the on (release) event handler (**Figure 7.9**).

4. From the Property pull-down menu in the Parameters pane, select _x (X Position).

5. In the Target field, enter the target path of your movie clip, or use the Insert Target Path button at the bottom right corner of the Parameters pane.

6. In the Value field, enter a number for the *x* position, and check the Expression box, since this number represents a value (**Figure 7.10**).

7. Again, choose Actions > setProperty.

   A second setProperty statement appears under the first.

8. For Property, select _y (Y Position); for Target, enter the target path; for Value, enter a number for the *y* position; and check the Expression box (**Figure 7.11**).

9. Test your movie.

   When you click the button that you created, your movie clip jumps to the new position defined by your two setProperty actions (**Figure 7.12**).

An alternative way of setting movie-clip properties is to use dot syntax in this form: _root.movieclip._property=value. Use the set variable or the evaluate action to assign a value to the property of a particular movie clip.

To set movie-clip properties in dot syntax:

◆ In the Actions panel, choose Actions > set variable (Esc + sv). In the Variable field, enter the target path to the movie clip whose property you wish to modify. Enter a dot, and then the property you wish to affect. In the Value field, enter the required argument (**Figure 7.13**).

◆ In the Actions panel, choose Actions > evaluate (Esc + ev). In the Expression field, enter the target path to the movie clip, a dot, and then the property you wish to affect. Enter the equal sign and then the value you wish to assign to the property (**Figure 7.14**).

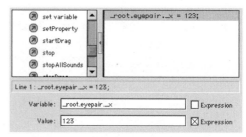

Figure 7.13 Use set variable to enter the property of a movie clip in the Variable field and its new value in the Value field.

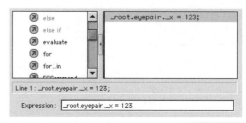

Figure 7.14 Use evaluate to assign the property of a movie clip to its new value all in one parameter field.

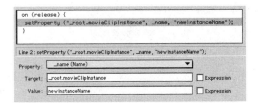

Figure 7.15 This setProperty statement changes the name of the movie-clip instance from movieClipInstance to newInstanceName.

Change the name of a movie clip to make it available or unavailable to other actions that target it. For example, imagine that a button calls the method `_root.myDisplay.gotoAndStop(2)` and then you change `myDisplay` to `yourDisplay`. The button would no longer be able to find the instance.

To change the name of a movie clip:

1. Create a movie-clip symbol, place an instance of it on the Stage, and name it.

2. Create a button symbol, place an instance of it on the Stage, select the button, and open the Actions panel.

3. Choose Actions > setProperty.

   The `setProperty` statement appears under the `on (release)` event handler.

4. From the Property pull-down menu in the Parameters pane, select _name (Name).

5. In the Target area, enter the target path of your movie clip, or use the Insert Target Path button at the bottom right corner of the Parameters pane.

6. In the Value area, enter a new name for the instance. Leave the Expressions box unchecked, since this is an actual name.

   The completed ActionScript statement appears in the Actions List (**Figure 7.15**). When you test your movie and click the button, the instance name of the movie clip changes.

Modifying the Movie-Clip Color

One conspicuous omission from the list of movie-clip properties that setProperty controls is color. However, you can use the Color object, a predefined class, to define and transform the color of movie clips.

The first step to modify a movie clip's color is to instantiate a new color object with the constructor function:

```
nameofColorObject =
new Color(movieClipInstance)
```

where nameofColorObject is the name of your new color object and movieClipInstance is the target path of the movie clip you wish to control.

Next, you can use your new color object to set the RGB values of the movie clip using the method setRGB. To define your new color, use the hexadecimal equivalents of each color component (red, green, and blue) in the form of 0xRRGGBB. You may have seen this six-digit code in HTML to specify the background color of a Web page. You can find these values for a color in the Mixer panel. Choose the Hex color mode in the options pull-down menu (**Figure 7.16**), and the hexadecimal values for each color component appear in the panel. The six-digit code is also displayed next to the color swatch in the pull-down color menu under the fill or stroke color (**Figure 7.17**).

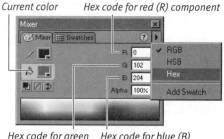

Current color   Hex code for red (R) component

Hex code for green (G) component   Hex code for blue (B) component

Figure 7.16 The options pull-down menu in the Mixer panel has a Hex option to show the RGB components in hexadecimal code.

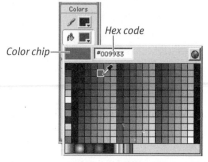

Hex code

Color chip

Figure 7.17 The hex code is shown in the display box next to the color chip.

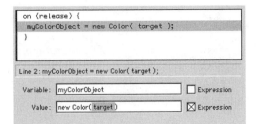

```
on (release) {
    myColorObject = new Color( target );
}
```

```
Line 2: myColorObject = new Color( target );

Variable:  myColorObject                    □ Expression

Value:     new Color( target )              ☒ Expression
```

Figure 7.18 The new Color constructor function is used to create a new color object.

```
Variable:  myColorObject                    □ Expression

Value:     new Color(_root.shirt)           ☒ Expression
```

Figure 7.19 The new color object is called myColorObject and is associated with the movie clip called shirt.

```
Expression:  myColorObject.setRGB( 0xRRGGBB )
```

Figure 7.20 The setRGB method takes the parameter 0xRRGGBB which is the hex code for a color.

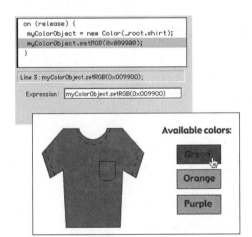

```
on (release) {
    myColorObject = new Color(_root.shirt);
    myColorObject.setRGB(0x009900);
}
```

```
Line 3: myColorObject.setRGB(0x009900);

Expression:  myColorObject.setRGB(0x009900)
```

Available colors:

Green

Orange

Purple

Figure 7.21 Use setRGB with different hex codes to change the color of this movie clip shirt.

To set the color of a movie clip:

1. Create a movie-clip symbol, place an instance of it on the Stage, and name it.

2. Create a button symbol, place an instance of it on the Stage, select the button, and open the Actions panel.

3. Choose Actions > set variable.

4. In the Variable field, enter the name for your new color object.

5. Click in the Value field, and choose Objects > Color > new Color, and check the Expression box next to the Value field.

   The new Color statement appears in the Value field with the target argument highlighted (**Figure 7.18**).

6. Replace the highlighted target word with the target path of your movie clip, or use the Insert Target Path button at the bottom right corner of the Parameters pane.

   Your first ActionScript statement is complete. This instantiates a new color object (**Figure 7.19**).

7. Choose Actions > evaluate. In the Expression field, enter the name of your newly created color object.

8. Choose Objects > Color > setRGB.

   The setRGB method appears in the Expression field of the Parameters pane in front of the name of your color object. The argument 0xRRGGBB is highlighted (**Figure 7.20**).

9. Between the parentheses of the setRGB method, enter 0x, then the six-digit hexadecimal code for the new color (**Figure 7.21**).

10. Test your movie. When you press the button, a color object that calls the setRGB method is instantiated. The movie clip associated with the color object is assigned a new RGB value.

MODIFYING THE MOVIE-CLIP COLOR

185

Using the Color Transform Object

You can also transform the color of any movie clip by using the method setTransform. This method allows you to define both the percentages and the offset values for each of the RGB components as well as the alpha transparency. These parameters appear in the Instance panel under the Advanced pull-down menu (**Figure 7.22**).

To use the setTransform method for your color object, you must first create another object that essentially holds the color transformation information, which is in the parameters ra, rb, ga, gb, ba, bb, aa, ab (**Table 7.2**). The color transform object is created using the generic predefined class called Object. Once you define the color transform object, you use it in the setTransform method of your color object. This may be a little confusing, but the basic idea is this: Where you would normally see numbers or strings as parameters for a method—for example, the number 5 in the method gotoAndStop(5) —you will now use an object such as setTransform(myColorTransformObject).

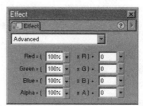

Figure 7.22 The options for instance effects in the Advanced pull-down menu control the RGB and alpha percentages and offset values.

Table 7.2

setTransform Parameters	
PARAMETER	VALUE
ra	Percentage (-100 to 100) of red component
rb	Offset (-255 to 255) of red component
ga	Percentage (-100 to 100) of green component
gb	Offset (-255 to 255) of green component
ba	Percentage (-100 to 100) of blue component
bb	offset (-255 to 255) of blue component
aa	Percentage (-100 to 100) of alpha transparency
ab	Offset (-255 to 255) of alpha transparency

```
on (release) {
  myNewColor = new Color(_root.shirt);
}
```

Line 2: myNewColor = new Color(_root.shirt);

Variable: `myNewColor` ☐ Expression

Value: `new Color(_root.shirt)` ☒ Expression

Figure 7.23 A new color object called myNewColor is created for the shirt movie clip.

```
on (release) {
  myNewColor = new Color(_root.shirt);
  myColorTransform = new Object();
}
```

Line 3: myColorTransform = new Object();

Variable: `myColorTransform` ☐ Expression

Value: `new Object()` ☒ Expression

Figure 7.24 Create a new generic object called myColorTransform with the constructor function new Object. This object will hold the RGB and alpha information.

```
on (release) {
  myNewColor = new Color(_root.shirt);
  myColorTransform = new Object();
  myColorTransform.ra = 100;
  myColorTransform.rb = 75;
  myColorTransform.ga = 100;
  myColorTransform.gb = 90;
  myColorTransform.ba = 100;
  myColorTransform.bb = 255;
  myColorTransform.aa = -50;
  myColorTransform.ab = 255;
}
```

Line 11: myColorTransform.ab = 255;

Variable: `myColorTransform.ab` ☐ Expression

Value: `255` ☒ Expression

Figure 7.25 The red, green, blue, and alpha values are set with a series of set variable statements.

To transform the color and alpha of a movie clip:

1. Create a movie-clip symbol, place an instance of it on the Stage, and name it.

2. Create a button symbol, place an instance of it on the Stage, select the button, and open the Actions panel.

3. Choose Actions > set variable.

4. Instantiate a new color object as in the previous task (**Figure 7.23**).

5. Again, choose Actions > set variable.

6. In the Variable field, enter the name for a color transform object.

7. Click in the Value field, and choose Objects > Object > new Object. Check the Expression box next to the Value field.

   Your new color transform object is instantiated (**Figure 7.24**).

8. Choose Actions > set variable. In the Variable field, enter the name of your color transform object, a dot, then one of the parameters. In the Value field, enter a number. Check the Expression box next to the Value field. Do this for all eight parameters (**Figure 7.25**).

   The parameters for your color transform object are defined.

9. Choose Actions > evaluate. In the Expression field, enter the name of your color object.

(continued on next page)

MODIFYING THE MOVIE-CLIP COLOR

187

10. Choose Objects > Color > setTransform.

The setTransform method appears after your color object in the Expression field with the highlighted target cxform in parentheses. The term cxform stands for "color transform." **(Figure 7.26)**.

11. Replace the highlighted target cxform with the name of your color transform object (**Figure 7.27**).

The full script should look like the one in **Figure 7.28**.

12. Test your movie.

When you press the button that you created, a color object and a color transform object is instantiated. The color object calls the setTransform method, which uses the color transform object as its argument. The movie clip associated with the color object changes color and transparency.

✔ Tip

■ Instead of creating eight separate statements to define the parameters of your color transform object, you can write just one statement that lists them all. You can use the syntax

myColorTransform = { ra: '100', rb: '150', ga: '75', gb: '200', ba: '20', bb: '188', aa: '50', ab: '255'}

where the parameters are separated by their values with colons, and the parameter/value pairs are separated by commas.

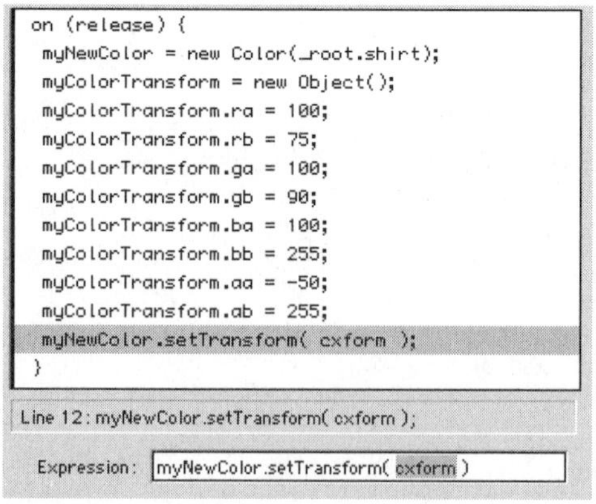

```
on (release) {
    myNewColor = new Color(_root.shirt);
    myColorTransform = new Object();
    myColorTransform.ra = 100;
    myColorTransform.rb = 75;
    myColorTransform.ga = 100;
    myColorTransform.gb = 90;
    myColorTransform.ba = 100;
    myColorTransform.bb = 255;
    myColorTransform.aa = -50;
    myColorTransform.ab = 255;
    myNewColor.setTransform( cxform );
}
```

Line 12: myNewColor.setTransform(cxform);

Expression: myNewColor.setTransform(cxform)

Figure 7.26 The setTransform method requires the argument cxform, where cxform is an object that holds the color transformation information.

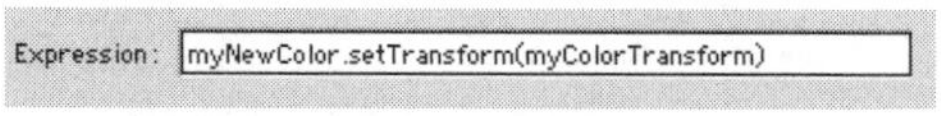

Expression: myNewColor.setTransform(myColorTransform)

Figure 7.27 The setTransform method uses the myColorTransform object to change the myNewColor Color object.

```
on (release) {
    // instantiate a new color object
    myNewColor = new Color(_root.shirt);
    // instantiate a new color transform object
    myColorTransform = new Object();
    // set the parameters for the
    // color transform object
    myColorTransform.ra = 100;
    myColorTransform.rb = 75;
    myColorTransform.ga = 100;
    myColorTransform.gb = 90;
    myColorTransform.ba = 100;
    myColorTransform.bb = 255;
    myColorTransform.aa = -50;
    myColorTransform.ab = 255;
    // call the set transform method with
    // the color transform object
    myNewColor.setTransform(myColorTransform);
}
```

Figure 7.28 The full ActionScript changes the color and alpha of the movie clip shirt with a button click.

Swapping Overlapping Movie Clips

When you have multiple draggable movie clips, you'll notice that the objects maintain their stacking order even while being dragged, which can seem a little odd. You would expect that the one you pick would come to the top. You can make it do so by using the `swapDepths` action to swap the stacking order of movie clips dynamically. `swapDepths` can switch the stacking order of movie clips either by swapping two named movie clips or by swapping a named movie clip with whatever movie clip is in a designated depth level. The *depth level* is a number that refers to a movie clip's stacking order. Higher depth-level numbers will overlap lower ones, much like levels of loaded movies. The amazing thing about `swapDepths` is that it even works across layers, so a movie clip in the bottom layer can swap with a movie clip in the topmost layer.

To swap a movie clip with another movie clip:

1. Create two draggable movie clips as outlined earlier in this chapter. They should be two different symbols.

2. Place instances of both movie clips on the Stage in the same layer. In the Instance panel, name both instances.

3. Go to symbol-editing mode for the first draggable movie clip, and select the movie clip's invisible button.

4. Open the Actions panel and select the startDrag statement. Choose Actions > evaluate. In the Expression field, enter this.

5. Choose Objects > Movie Clip > swapDepths.

   The swapDepths method appears after this in the Expression field with the word target highlighted (**Figure 7.29**).

6. In the Expression field, replace the word target with the target path of the second movie clip (**Figure 7.30**).

7. Go to symbol-editing mode for your other draggable movie clip, and add a similar swapDepths statement to its invisible button. In the target field for this swapDepths statement, choose the target path of the first movie clip.

   The scripts for both buttons in the two different movie clips should look like the script in **Figure 7.31**.

8. Test your movie.

   When you drag the first movie clip, it will swap its stacking order with the second movie clip, and vice versa.

```
on (press) {
  startDrag (this);
  this.swapDepths( target );
}
on (release) {
  stopDrag ();
}
```
Line 3: this.swapDepths(target);

Expression: | this.swapDepths(target)

Figure 7.29 Assign the swapDepths action to the on (press) event handler. SwapDepths changes the stacking order of movie clips.

Expression: | this.swapDepths(_root.puzzle2)

Figure 7.30 The current movie clip and the movie clip puzzle2 swap in the stacking order.

```
on (press) {
  startDrag (this);
  this.swapDepths(_root.puzzle2);
}
on (release) {
  stopDrag ();
}
```

```
on (press) {
  startDrag (this);
  this.swapDepths(_root.puzzle1);
}
on (release) {
  stopDrag ();
}
```

Figure 7.31 The swapDepths method is associated with the startDrag action. The button that is assigned the actions on top is in the movie clip called puzzle1. The button that is assigned the actions on bottom is in the movie clip called puzzle2. Both movie clips switch their stacking orders when dragged.

```
on (press) {
  startDrag (this);
  this.swapDepths(2);
}
on (release) {
  stopDrag ();
}
```

Line 3: this.swapDepths(2);

Expression: this.swapDepths(2)

Figure 7.32 The current movie clip swaps with the one in Depth Level 2.

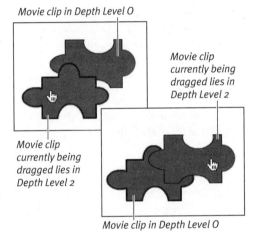

Movie clip in Depth Level 0

Movie clip currently being dragged lies in Depth Level 2

Movie clip currently being dragged lies in Depth Level 2

Movie clip in Depth Level 0

Figure 7.33 Swapping depth levels is ideal for dealing with multiple draggable movie clips such as these puzzle pieces.

To swap the depth level of a movie clip:

1. Continue with the same file created with the previous task.

2. Go to symbol-editing mode for the first draggable movie clip, and select its invisible button.

3. Replace the target path in the swapDepths argument with a number specifying the depth level (**Figure 7.32**).

4. Go to symbol-editing mode for your other draggable movie clip, and replace the target path in its swapDepths argument with the same depth level.

5. Test your movie.

   The first movie clip you drag is put into the specified depth level. The second movie clip you drag is swapped with whatever is currently in that depth level (**Figure 7.33**).

✔ Tip

■ The difference between using a target path and using a depth number in the swapDepths argument depends on your needs. Use a target path to simply swap the two named movie clips, so a movie clip that is overlapping the other movie clip will be sent behind it. To always keep a draggable movie clip above all other movie clips, use depth level to send it to the top of the stacking order.

Detecting Dropped Movie Clips

Now that you can make a movie clip that can be dragged around the Stage, you'll want to know where the user drops it. If the movie clips are puzzle pieces, for example, you need to know whether or not those pieces are dragged and dropped on the correct spots. One of the simplest ways to detect the dropped movie clip's location is to use the movie clip property _droptarget. This property retrieves the absolute target path of another movie clip where the draggable movie clip was dropped. The second movie clip is essentially the destination for the draggable movie clip. Use a conditional statement to compare whether the _droptarget of the draggable movie clip is the same as the target path of the destination movie clip. Perform any actions based on whether the condition is true or false.

A common practice with drag-and-drop movie clips is to create snap-to and bounce-back behaviors. When the user drops a movie clip very near a correct location, you can detect that with _droptarget and adjust, or snap, the movie clip to a more exact position using the setProperty action, which sets its x and y positions. When the user drops a movie clip in an inappropriate location, you can detect that with _droptarget and send, or bounce, it back to its original position using the setProperty action.

A word of caution here: The _droptarget property returns the absolute target path in slash syntax. This property originated in Flash 4, which supported only the slash syntax. So to test whether the _droptarget property matches the target path of a destination movie clip, you construct a conditional statement that looks like the following:

```
_root.draggableMovieClip._droptarget ==
"/destinationMovieClip"
```

```
on (press) {
  startDrag (this, true);
}
on (release) {
  stopDrag ();
  if (this._droptarget == "/destination") {
  }
}
```

Line 6: if (this._droptarget == "/destination") {

Condition: this._droptarget == "/destination"

Figure 7.34 This condition tests if the current movie clip has been dropped on the movie clip called destination. The slash (/) refers to the root Timeline.

```
on (press) {
  // begin dragging this movie clip
  startDrag (this, true);
}
on (release) {
  // stop dragging this movie clip
  stopDrag ();
  // check to see if this movie clip
  // is dropped on the destination movie clip
  if (this._droptarget == "/destination") {
    // if it's true, then make it invisible
    setProperty (this, _visible, false);
  }
}
```

Figure 7.35 If the draggable movie clip is dropped on the movie clip called destination, its visibility is set to false.

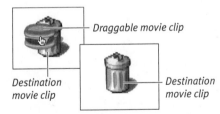

— Draggable movie clip

Destination movie clip

— Destination movie clip

Figure 7.36 This hamburger disappears when it is dropped on the trash can.

To detect a dropped movie clip:

1. Create a draggable movie clip, place an instance of it on the Stage, and name it in the Instance panel.

2. Create another movie clip, place an instance of it on the Stage, and name it.

   This movie clip is the destination for the draggable movie clip.

3. Go to symbol-editing mode for the draggable movie clip, and select the invisible button.

4. Select the stopDrag action and choose Actions > if (Esc + if).

   The if statement appears under the stopDrag statement.

5. In the Condition field, enter this. Next, enter a dot.

6. Choose Properties > _droptarget.

7. Enter two equal signs.

   A pair of equal signs tests whether one value is the same as another. A single equal sign is used to assign one variable to another.

8. Enter the target path of the destination movie clip within quotation marks, using slash syntax.

   The final conditional statement is constructed (**Figure 7.34**).

9. Choose an action to be performed when this condition is met. The final script should look like **Figure 7.35**.

10. Test your movie (**Figure 7.36**).

    When you drop the draggable movie clip, Flash checks if its _droptarget property matches the target path of the second movie clip. If it does, the _visibility property of the draggable movie clip is set to true and it disappears.

DETECTING DROPPED MOVIE CLIPS

To create a bounce-back effect:

1. Continue with the same file created in the previous task.

2. Go to symbol-editing mode for the draggable movie clip, and select its invisible button.

3. Select the last action within the `if` statement, and then choose Actions > else (Esc + el).

   The `else` statement appears. It gives you the opportunity to choose an alternative consequence if the condition in the `if` statement returns false (**Figure 7.37**).

4. Choose Actions > setProperty. Select X Position from the Property pull-down menu, enter `this` in the Target field, and enter the original *x* coordinate in the Value field. Check both Expression boxes (**Figure 7.38**).

   This setProperty statement changes the *x* position of the draggable movie clip when it's not dropped over the destination movie clip.

```
on (press) {
 startDrag (this, true);
}
on (release) {
 stopDrag ();
 if (this._droptarget == "/destination") {
  setProperty (this, _visible, false);
 } else {
 }
}

Line 8 : } else {

No Parameters.
```

Figure 7.37 The `else` action provides an alternative to the `if` condition.

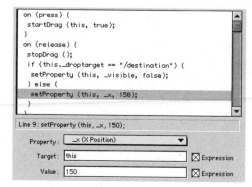

Figure 7.38 The *x* position is set to 150.

```
on (press) {
  // begin dragging this movie clip
  startDrag (this, true);
}
on (release) {
  // stop dragging this movie clip
  stopDrag ();
  // check to see if this movie clip
  // is dropped on the destination movie clip
  if (this._droptarget == "/destination") {
    // if it's true, then make it invisible
    setProperty (this, _visible, false);
  } else {
    // if it's false, send it back
    // to its previous location
    setProperty (this, _x, 150);
    setProperty (this, _y, 100);
  }
}
```

Figure 7.39 The actions for a bounce-back effect are assigned to the `else` condition.

5. Choose Actions > setProperty. Select Y Position from the Property pull-down menu, enter `this` in the Target field, and enter the original *y* coordinate in the Value field. Check both Expression boxes.

This setProperty statement changes the *y* position of the draggable movie clip when it's not dropped over the destination movie clip. The complete script looks like **Figure 7.39**.

6. Test your movie.

When the draggable movie clip isn't dropped over the destination movie clip, Flash sets the *x* and *y* coordinates so that the movie clip bounces back to its original position.

✓ Tips

■ Use the `eval` action to evaluate the `_droptarget` property and convert it from a string in slash syntax to a target path in dot-syntax construction. For example, you could write the conditional statement as,
```
eval(_root.draggableMovieClip.
_droptarget)==_root.
destinationMovieClip
```

■ Flash determines the dropped movie clip's location at its registration point. If the registration point of the dropped movie clip does not land in the graphic area of the destination movie clip, it will not be detected even if parts overlap.

Detecting Movie-Clip Collisions

Another condition you can test for is whether a movie clip intersects another movie clip. For example, the game of Pong simply detects collisions between the ball, the paddles, and the wall, all of which are movie clips. Detecting movie-clip collisions can be useful on sophisticated e-commerce sites, as well. Say you develop an online-shopping site that lets your customers drag merchandise into a shopping cart. You can detect when the object intersects with the shopping cart and provide interaction such as highlighting the shopping cart or displaying the product price before the user drops the object.

Collision detection utilizes the movie-clip method hitTest. There are two ways to use hitTest. One is to check if the *bounding boxes* of any two movie clips intersect. The bounding box of a movie clip is the minimum rectangular area that contains the graphics. This method is ideal for graphics colliding with other graphics, such as a ball with a paddle, a ship with an asteroid, or a book with a shopping cart. In this case, you enter the target path of the movie clip as the hitTest argument—for example, hitTest(_root.target).

The second way is to check if a certain *x-y* coordinate intersects with a graphic. This method is point-specific, which makes it ideal for checking if only the registration point of a graphic or the mouse pointer intersects with a movie clip. In this case, the hitTest arguments are an *x* value, a *y* value, and the shapeflag parameter, as in hitTest(x, y, shapeflag). The shapeflag parameter is true or false. This determines whether the bounding box of a movie clip is considered (false) or just the shape of the graphics are considered (true) (**Figure 7.40**).

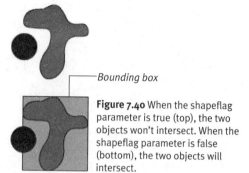

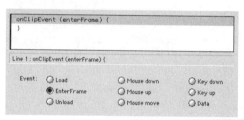

Bounding box

Figure 7.40 When the shapeflag parameter is true (top), the two objects won't intersect. When the shapeflag parameter is false (bottom), the two objects will intersect.

```
onClipEvent (enterFrame) {
}
```

Line 1: onClipEvent (enterFrame) {

Event: ○ Load   ○ Mouse down   ○ Key down
         ● EnterFrame   ○ Mouse up   ○ Key up
         ○ Unload   ○ Mouse move   ○ Data

Figure 7.41 The onClipEvent (enterFrame) is an ideal handler for continuously checking a condition.

```
onClipEvent (enterFrame) {
  if (this.hitTest( _root.asteroid ) == true) {
  }
}
```

Line 2: if (this.hitTest(_root.asteroid) == true) {

Condition :   this.hitTest(_root.asteroid) == true

Figure 7.42 This condition checks if the current movie clip intersects the asteroid movie clip.

```
onClipEvent (enterFrame) {
  if (this.hitTest( _root.asteroid ) == true) {
    this.nextFrame();
  }
}
```

Figure 7.43 The consequence of an intersection is the nextFrame action.

DETECTING MOVIE-CLIP COLLISIONS

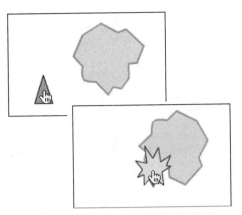

Figure 7.44 Dragging the spaceship movie clip into the bounding box of the asteroid movie clip advances the spaceship movie clip to the next frame, which displays an explosion.

✔ Tips

- For true/false conditions (known as Booleans) like the one in this task, you can also simply state the condition and leave out the last part, `== true`. Flash automatically returns a true or a false when you call the `hitTest` method, and the `if` statement automatically tests whether the condition is true. You'll learn more about conditional statements in Part V: Working with Information.

- It doesn't really matter whether you test the moving movie clip to the target or the target to the moving movie clip. The following two statements detect for the same kind of collision:

  `this.hitTest(_root.target)`

  `_root.target.hitTest(this)`

- If the target of the `hitTest` method is a movie clip that contains moving graphics, then the bounding box of that movie clip will change according to the animation.

To detect an intersection between two movie clips:

1. Create a movie clip, place an instance of it on the Stage, and name it.

2. Create a draggable movie clip, place an instance of it on the Stage, and name it.

3. Select the draggable movie clip, and open the Actions panel.

4. Choose Actions > onClipEvent (Esc + oc). In the Parameters pane, choose EnterFrame as the Event.

   The `onClipEvent (enterFrame)` statement appears. This event occurs at the frame rate of the movie, which makes it ideal for continuously checking the `hitTest` condition (**Figure 7.41**).

5. Choose Actions > if.

6. In the Condition field, enter `this`.

7. Choose Objects > Movie Clip > hitTest.

8. Within the parentheses of the `hitTest` statement, enter the path of the first movie clip.

9. Enter two equal signs, and then the word `true` (**Figure 7.42**).

10. Choose an action to be performed when this condition is met. The final script should look like **Figure 7.43**.

11. Test your movie (**Figure 7.44**).

To detect an intersection between a point and a movie clip:

1. Continue with the same file created in the previous task.

2. Select the draggable movie clip, and open the Actions panel.

3. Select the `if` statement. In the Condition field, change the expression so it reads,

   `_root.asteroid.hitTest(this._x, this._y, true)`

   The `hitTest` now checks whether the x and y positions of the current draggable movie clip intersect with the shape of the movie clip on the root Timeline called asteroid (**Figure 7.45**).

4. Test your movie.

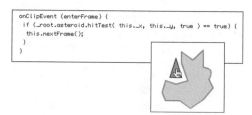

```
onClipEvent (enterFrame) {
  if (_root.asteroid.hitTest( this._x, this._y, true ) == true ) {
    this.nextFrame();
  }
}
```

Figure 7.45 The ActionScript (above) tests whether the registration point of the spaceship movie clip intersects with any shape in the asteroid movie clip. Notice how the spaceship is safe from collision because its registration point is still within the crevice and clear of the asteroid.

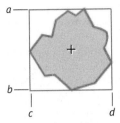

$a = myMovieClip._y - .5*myMovieClip._height$
$b = myMovieClip._y + .5*myMovie Clip._height$
$c = myMovieClip._x - .5*myMovieClip._width$
$d = myMovieClip._x + .5*myMovieClip._width$

Figure 7.46 The bounding box of a centered movie clip can be defined with its Height, Width, and X and Y Position properties.

Getting the Boundaries of Movie Clips

Knowing the boundaries of your movie clip can be useful when you need to constrain a draggable movie clip to the boundaries of another movie clip. Most of the time, the constraining movie clip will be centered, so its left, right, top, and bottom limits can be defined with a combination of its X Position, Y Position, Height, and Width properties (**Figure 7.46**). However, when the movie clip is off-centered, you can't retrieve the limits of its bounding box using the movie clip properties. Instead, you need to use the method `getBounds`. This method gets the minimum and maximum dimensions of the bounding box of a movie clip and puts the information into an object containing the properties xMin, xMax, yMin, and yMax. You can use the values of those properties to constrain your draggable movie clip.

To constrain a movie clip to the bounding box of another:

1. Create a movie-clip symbol, place an instance of it on the Stage, and give it a name.

   This will be the movie clip whose bounding box constrains a draggable movie clip.

2. Create another movie-clip symbol, place an instance of it on the Stage, and give it a name.

   This will be your draggable movie clip.

3. Select the second movie-clip instance and open the Actions panel.

4. Choose Actions > onClipEvent. Select the Load event.

5. Choose Actions > set variable. In the Variable field, enter a name for an object that will hold the boundary information.

(continued on next page)

6. In the Value field, enter the target path to the movie clip whose boundary box you wish to retrieve. Choose Objects > MovieClip > getBounds.

The getBounds method appears in the Value field after the target path to the movie clip. The argument targetCoordinateSpace is highlighted (**Figure 7.47**).

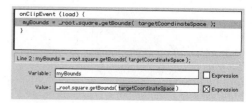

Figure 7.47 The getBounds method requires the argument targetCoordinateSpace.

7. Replace the argument targetCoordinateSpace with a target path to the Timeline whose x-y coordinate space you want the to serve as the reference for the boundary information (**Figure 7.48**).

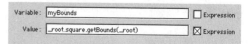

Figure 7.48 getBounds retrieves the minimum x (xMin), minimum y (yMin), maximum x (xMax), and maximum y (xMax) values of the the movie clip called square relative to the _root coordinates, and stores that information in your boundary object called myBounds.

8. Choose Actions > startDrag.

9. In the Target field of the Parameters pane, enter this. Check the Expression box.

10. Check both the Constrain to rectangle and Lock mouse to center boxes.

11. In the L, T, R, and B fields of the Parameters pane, enter the xMin, yMin, xMax, and yMax properties of your boundary object (**Figure 7.49**).

Figure 7.49 The Parameter pane of the startDrag action. The properties of the myBounds object are used in the Constrain to rectangle fields.

12. Test your movie.

The draggable movie clip is constrained to the coordinates that the getBounds method retrieved and put into your boundary object.

Duplicating and Removing Movie Clips

Creating multiple instances from existing movie clips on the fly is possible with the action duplicateMovieClip. Duplicate movie-clip instances are given their own unique names as well as a specific depth level for each instance, which determines stacking order, just as it does with the movie-clip property swapDepths. Once a movie clip is duplicated, you can control any of its properties, navigate within its Timeline, and use it like any other movie clip. Duplicating movie clips can come in handy to dynamically generate graphics. For example, by duplicating short line segments or simple primitive shapes and then controlling their properties (position, scale, rotation), you can create animations or even simulate 3D objects on the fly. (That requires a lot of math, though!) Or, if you want an infinite supply of a certain draggable item such as merchandise pulled off the shelf of an online store, you can duplicate it each time as the viewer drags it away from its original spot. In a game of Asteroids, for example, creating the breakup of a big asteroid into smaller asteroids would be made easier by duplicating the asteroid movie clip.

It's a common practice to duplicate movie clips by using looping functions that append successive numbers to the instance name and automatically assign depth levels. For example, a movie clip named asteroid may be duplicated in this manner, producing asteroid1 in Depth Level 1, asteroid2 in Depth Level 2, asteroid3 in Depth Level 3, and so on. Check out Chapter 9, Controlling Information Flow, to learn about the looping actions that complement the duplication of movie clips.

To duplicate a movie-clip instance:

1. Create a movie-clip symbol, place an instance on the Stage, and name it.

2. Create a button symbol, and place an instance of it on the Stage.

3. Select the button, and open the Actions panel.

4. Choose Actions > duplicateMovieClip (Esc + dm).

   The duplicateMovieClip action appears below the on (release) event in the Actions List (**Figure 7.50**).

5. In the Target field, enter the target path for the movie clip. Check the Expression box.

6. In the New Name field, enter the name for the new duplicate movie clip. Leave the Expression box unchecked.

7. In the Depth field, enter a number greater than 0 to specify the stacking order for your duplicate movie clip (**Figure 7.51**).

   At this point, when you play your movie, the actions assigned to your button duplicate the nerd movie clip, but the new instance appears right above the original, so you can't actually see if anything happened. In order to see the duplicate, you need to move it or change it in some way to make it stand out from the original.

8. Choose Actions > setProperty.

9. From the Property pull-down menu, select X Position.

10. In the Target field, enter the target path of the duplicate movie clip. Check the Expression box.

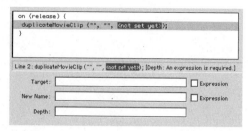

Figure 7.50 Assign the duplicateMovieClip action to the on (release) mouse event of your button.

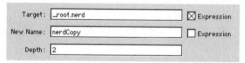

Figure 7.51 The duplicate movie clip called nerdCopy is made in Depth Level 2 from the movie clip called nerd.

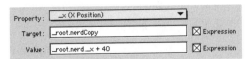

Figure 7.52 The nerdCopy movie clip is shifted 40 pixels to the right of the nerd movie clip.

```
on (release) {
    duplicateMovieClip (_root.nerd, "nerdCopy", 2);
    setProperty (_root.nerdCopy, _x, _root.nerd._x+40);
    setProperty (_root.nerdCopy, _xscale, 75);
    setProperty (_root.nerdCopy, _yscale, 110);
}
```

Figure 7.53 The ActionScript (above) is assigned to the button instance at the bottom of the Stage. When the original movie clip (left) is duplicated, the copy can be targeted and controlled just like any other (right). This movie clip copy, called nerdCopy has its x position, x scale, and y scale properties modified.

11. In the Value field, enter an expression that adds 40 to the x position of the original movie clip (**Figure 7.52**). Check the Expression box.

12. Add more setProperty statements to transform the duplicate movie clip (**Figure 7.53**).

13. Test the movie.

✔ Tips

- There can only be one movie-clip instance per depth level. If you duplicate another instance in a level that's already occupied, it replaces the first one.

- Duplicate movie clips take on the properties of the original instance. If the original instance has an alpha transparency of 50 percent, for example, the duplicate movie-clip instance will also have an alpha transparency of 50 percent. However, duplicate instances will always start on Frame 1, even if the original movie-clip instance is on a different frame when it is duplicated.

- The depth level corresponds to the same depth level in the movie-clip method swapDepths. Use swapDepths to change the stacking order of duplicated movie clips.

DUPLICATING AND REMOVING MOVIE CLIPS

To remove a movie-clip duplicate:

1. Continue with the file created in the previous task. Place a new instance of the button on the Stage.

2. Select the new button instance and open the Actions panel.

3. Choose Actions > removeMovieClip (Esc + rm).

   The `removeMovieClip` statement appears under the `on (release)` event.

4. In the Parameters pane of the Actions panel, in the Target field, enter the target path of the duplicate movie clip. Leave the Expression box unchecked (**Figure 7.54**).

5. Test your movie.

   The first button creates a duplicate. The second button targets the duplicate and removes it from the Stage (**Figure 7.55**).

✔ Tip

■ You can't use `removeMovieClip` to remove the original movie-clip instance on the Stage. You can only do that in authoring mode by inserting a keyframe and deleting the movie-clip instance.

Figure 7.54 removeMovieClip removes the duplicate instance called nerdCopy.

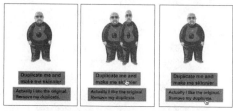

Figure 7.55 The original movie clip (left) is duplicated with the duplicateMovieClip action assigned to the first button (middle). The duplicate instance is called nerdCopy. The removeMovieClip action assigned to the second button removes the duplicate instance (right).

Figure 7.56 The Linkage option in the Library.

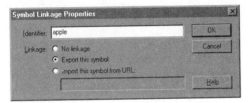

Figure 7.57 The Symbol Linkage Properties dialog box.

Attaching Movie Clips

The technique of duplicating existing movie clips is great, but what if you need to dynamically place a movie clip on the Stage from the Library? In this situation, you would turn to the attachMovie method. It lets you create new instances of movie clips from the Library and attach them to existing movie-clip instances already on the Stage. The attached movie clip doesn't replace the original, but actually becomes part of the movie-clip object in a parent-child relationship. If the original instance on Stage is called parentInstance, then the target path for the attached movie clip would be something like: _root.parentInstance.attachedInstance.

To attach a movie clip from the Library:

1. Create a movie-clip symbol, and place an instance of it from the Library onto the Stage. In the Instance panel, give it a name.

   This instance will be the original, parent instance to which you'll attach another movie clip.

2. Create another movie-clip symbol.

3. From the Library options pull-down menu, choose Linkage (**Figure 7.56**).

   The Symbol Linkage Properties dialog box appears.

4. From the Linkage choices, select Export this symbol, and in the Identifier field enter an identifier for your movie clip. Click OK (**Figure 7.57**).

   This identifier allows you to call on this movie clip by this name from ActionScript and attach it to an instance on the Stage.

5. Create a button, and drag an instance of it to the Stage.

(continued on next page)

6. Select the button, and open the Actions panel.

7. Choose Actions > evaluate. In the Expression field, enter the target path of the movie-clip instance on the Stage.

8. Choose Objects > MovieClip > attachMovie.

The `attachMovie` method appears in the Expression field after the target path of the movie-clip instance (**Figure 7.58**).

9. Between the parentheses of the `attachMovie` method, enter the identifier of the movie clip in the Library, a name for the attached instance, and a depth level (**Figure 7.59**).

10. Test your movie.

When you click the button that you created, the movie clip identified in the Library attaches to the instance on Stage and overlaps it. The registration point of the movie clip lines up with the registration point of the parent instance (**Figure 7.60**).

There are several names you need to keep straight when you use the `attachMovie` method. In this example, the name of the movie clip symbol in the Library is apple movie clip. The name of the identifier is apple. The name of the attached instance is attachedApple.

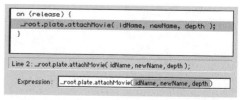

Figure 7.58 The attachMovie method requires the arguments idName, newName, and depth.

Figure 7.59 This `attachMovie` method attaches the movie clip instance called apple to the instance plate in Depth Level 2, and names the attached instance attachedApple.

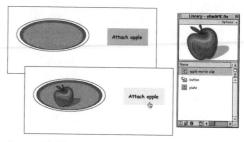

Figure 7.60 The movie clip instance called plate sits on the Stage (top). The actions assigned to the button attach an instance of the apple movie clip from the Library (right) to the plate instance (bottom).

✔ Tips

■ An attached movie clip takes on the same properties of the movie clip instance that it attaches to. If the original movie clip instance is rotated 45 degrees, then the attached movie clip will also be rotated 45 degrees.

■ Attach a movie clip to an instance on the Stage that has an empty first frame. That way, the parent instance acts just as an empty vessel to receive any movie clips from the Library.

■ You can attach multiple movie clips to the same parent instance, as long as you specify different depth levels. But each depth level can hold only one movie clip.

■ You can also attach movie clips to a recently attached movie clip itself. The target path for the first attached movie clip becomes _root.parentInstance. attachedInstance1. The target path for another attached movie clip becomes _root.parentInstance. attachedInstance1.attachedInstance2, and so on.

■ Once a movie clip from the Library is attached to an instance on the Stage, you can modify the parent instance, as in _root.parentInstance._alpha = 50, and any attached movie clips will be affected as well.

To remove an attached movie clip:

◆ Use the action `removeMovieClip`. Choose Actions > removeMovieClip (Esc + rm). In the Target field of the Actions panel, enter the target path of the attached movie clip (**Figure 7.61**).

◆ Use the action `unloadMovie`. Choose Actions > unloadMovie (Esc + um). From the Location pull-down menu in the Actions panel, select Target, and enter the target path of the attached movie clip (**Figure 7.62**).

Figure 7.61 The target path for the attachedApple movie clip must include the movie clip to which it is attached.

Figure 7.62 UnloadMovie, which usually removes external SWF files, can be used to remove attached movie clips.

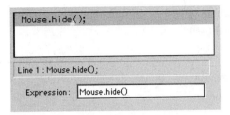

Figure 7.63 The hide method of the Mouse object doesn't require prior instantiation.

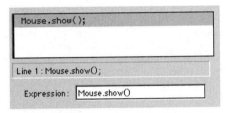

Figure 7.64 The show method of the Mouse object makes a hidden mouse visible again.

Customizing Your Pointer

Once you understand how to control the movie clip, you can build your own, custom pointer. Think of all the different pointers you use in Flash. As you choose different tools from the Tools window—the paint bucket, the eyedropper, the pencil—your pointer changes to help you understand and apply those tools. Similarly, you can tailor the pointer's form to match its function.

Customizing the pointer involves first hiding the default mouse pointer. Then you must match the location of your new graphic to the location of the hidden (but still functional) mouse pointer. To do this, you set the X Position and Y Position properties of a movie clip to the *x* and *y* positions of the mouse pointer. The *x* and *y* positions of the mouse pointer are defined by the properties _xmouse and _ymouse.

To hide the mouse pointer:

◆ Select the first frame, and open the Actions panel. Choose Objects > Mouse > hide (**Figure 7.63**).

When you test your movie, the mouse pointer becomes invisible.

✔ Tip

■ Hiding the mouse pointer is a nice feature for Flash movies that are pure animations with no interactivity. You can eliminate the distraction that the pointer would cause, just as long as your users don't need to click any buttons in the movie.

To show the mouse pointer:

◆ From the Actions panel, choose Objects > Mouse > show (**Figure 7.64**).

To create your own mouse pointer:

1. Create a movie-clip symbol, and place an instance of it on the Stage. In the Instance panel, give it a name.

   This movie clip will become your pointer.

2. Select the movie-clip instance, and open the Actions panel.

3. Choose Actions > onClipEvent (Esc + oc). Select the Load event.

4. Choose Objects > Mouse > hide.

   The `Mouse.hide()` method appears under the `onClipEvent (load)` statement. When this movie clip loads, the mouse pointer disappears (**Figure 7.65**).

5. Select the closing curly brace of the `onClipEvent (load)` handler. Choose Actions > onClipEvent. Select the Mouse move event.

   The `onClipEvent (mouseMove)` handler appears under the `onClipEvent (load)` handler.

6. Choose Actions > setProperty.

7. From the Property pull-down menu, select X Position. In the Target field, enter `this`. In the Value field, enter `_root`, then a dot, and then choose Properties > _xmouse. Check both Expression boxes.

8. Again, choose Actions > setProperty.

9. From the Property pull-down menu, select Y Position. In the Target field, enter `this`. In the Value field, enter `_root`, then a dot, and then choose Properties > _ymouse. Check both Expression boxes (**Figure 7.66**).

10. Test your movie (**Figure 7.67**).

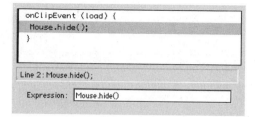

Figure 7.65 The mouse pointer disappears as soon as this movie clip loads.

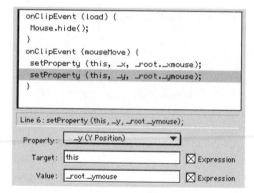

Figure 7.66 The setProperty statements set the x and y positions of the current movie clip to the x and y positions of the mouse pointer whenever it moves.

Figure 7.67 This magnifying glass is a movie clip that matches the x and y positions of the pointer. Create helpful pointers like this whose appearance matches their function.

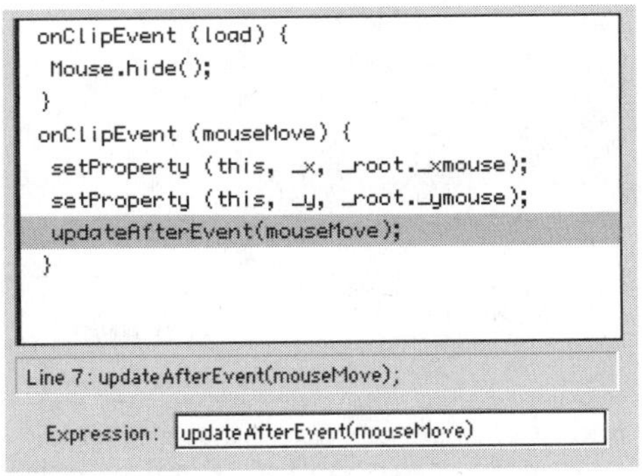

```
onClipEvent (load) {
  Mouse.hide();
}
onClipEvent (mouseMove) {
  setProperty (this, _x, _root._xmouse);
  setProperty (this, _y, _root._ymouse);
  updateAfterEvent(mouseMove);
}
```

Line 7: updateAfterEvent(mouseMove);

Expression: updateAfterEvent(mouseMove)

Figure 7.68 Add the updateAfterEvent action to force Flash to refresh the display and create smoother motion.

Use the function updateAfterEvent to force Flash to redraw the screen independent of the movie's frame rate. This eliminates the flicker associated with graphics moving around the screen faster than Flash can update the display, and is especially important when you use a custom pointer. The action updateAfterEvent can only be used with the following clip events: mouseMove, mouseDown, mouseUp, keyDown, and keyUp. Enter one of these clip events as the argument for the updateAfterEvent method.

To update the graphics on screen:

1. Continue with the previous file created in the previous task. Select the movie clip of the magnifying glass and open the Actions panel.

2. Select the last setProperty statement under the onClipEvent (mouseMove) handler.

3. Choose Actions > evaluate.

   A new statement line appears in the Actions List and an Expression field appears in the Parameters pane.

4. Choose Functions > updateAfterEvent.

   The updateAfterEvent function appears in the Expression field.

5. Enter the event mouseMove within the parentheses of the updateAfterEvent function (**Figure 7.68**).

   Flash updates the graphics on the screen each time the pointer moves, creating smoother motions.

✔ Tip

■ Explore using multiple movie clips that track the location of your pointer. For example, a vertical line that follows _xmouse and a horizontal line that follows _ymouse create moving crosshairs.

Beginning to Animate with ActionScript

The actions discussed so far in this chapter, scripts that let you control and test virtually all aspects of the movie clip—appearance, position, draggability, collisions, depth level, and duplication—are the basic tools for animating entirely using ActionScript. While motion tweens and shape tweens are created before playback, ActionScript animation is generated *during* playback, so it can respond to and change according to your viewer's actions.

The following Flash example is a simple game of tag. It's a good demonstration of how ActionScript can animate objects in response to user events. You create a movie clip that follows your pointer, and if the movie clip catches up to you, you lose the game.

To create a mouse-tracking game:

1. Create a movie-clip symbol with two keyframes. The first keyframe contains a graphic and a stop action, and the second keyframe contains a "You lose" message (**Figure 7.69**).

2. Place an instance of the movie clip on the Stage. In the Instance panel, give it a name. In this example, it's called cat.

3. Select the instance, and open the Actions panel.

4. Choose Actions > onClipEvent. Select Enter frame for the event.

5. Choose Actions > set variable.

6. In the Variable field of the Actions panel, enter the absolute path of the movie clip, a dot, then the X Position property. The statement should look like the following:

```
_root.cat._x
```

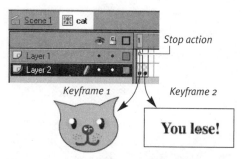

Figure 7.69 This cat movie clip displays a cat graphic in Keyframe 1 when it chases your pointer, and a different graphic in Keyframe 2 when you lose the game.

```
onClipEvent (enterFrame) {
    _root.cat._x = _root.cat._x + (_root._xmouse-_root.cat._x)/10;
    _root.cat._y = _root.cat._y + (_root._ymouse-_root.cat._y)/10;
}
```

Line 3: _root.cat._y = _root.cat._y + (_root._ymouse-_root.cat._y)/10;

Variable: | _root.cat._y | □ Expression

Value: | _root.cat._y + (_root._ymouse-_root.cat._y)/10 | ☒ Expression

Figure 7.70 The *x* and *y* positions of the cat movie-clip instance change according to the position of the pointer.

```
onClipEvent (enterFrame) {
    _root.cat._x = _root.cat._x + (_root._xmouse-_root.cat._x)/10;
    _root.cat._y = _root.cat._y + (_root._ymouse-_root.cat._y)/10;
    if (_root.cat.hitTest(_root._xmouse, _root._ymouse, True )) {
    }
}
```

Line 4: if (_root.cat.hitTest(_root._xmouse, _root._ymouse, True)) {

Condition: | _root.cat.hitTest(_root._xmouse, _root._ymouse, True)

Figure 7.71 The condition checks if the pointer intersects the cat movie-clip instance.

```
onClipEvent (enterFrame) {
    _root.cat._x = _root.cat._x + (_root._xmouse-_root.cat._x)/10;
    _root.cat._y = _root.cat._y + (_root._ymouse-_root.cat._y)/10;
    if (_root.cat.hitTest(_root._xmouse, _root._ymouse, True )) {
        _root.cat.nextFrame();
    }
}
```

Line 5: _root.cat.nextFrame();

Expression: | _root.cat.nextFrame()

Figure 7.72 The cat movie clip advances to the next frame in its Timeline.

7. In the Value field, enter the following:

`_root.cat._x + (_root._xmouse - _root.cat._x)/10`

Check the Expression box next to the Value field.

This statement starts with the *x* position of the cat movie clip and adds the difference between the mouse position and the cat position. If the mouse is to the right of the cat, it adds a positive value. If the mouse is to the left of the cat, it adds a negative value. In either case, the cat gets closer to the mouse. The division by 10 makes sure the cat doesn't immediately jump on the mouse. The increment is small (one-tenth of the distance), so the cat lags behind the position of the mouse.

8. Choose Actions > set variable. In the Variable field and Value field, enter the same information for the *y* coordinates as for the *x* coordinates (**Figure 7.70**).

9. Choose Actions > if.

10. In the Condition field, enter the following:

`_root.cat.hitTest(_root._xmouse, _root._ymouse, true)`

This statement uses the `hitTest` method to test whether the *x* and *y* positions of the mouse intersect the cat movie clip. The `shapeflag` argument is set to `true` so that only the graphics of the cat movie clip are considered, rather than the entire bounding box (**Figure 7.71**).

11. Choose Actions > evaluate. Enter the target path for the cat movie clip, a dot, and the `nextFrame()` method.

When the `hitTest` returns true, the cat movie clip goes to the next frame, displaying the "You lose" message (**Figure 7.72**).

(continued on next page)

12. Chose Actions > setProperty.

13. From the Property pull-down menu, select Name. In the Target field, enter the absolute path of the cat movie clip. Check the Expression box. In the Value field, enter a new name (**Figure 7.73**).

The instance name of the cat movie clip changes, preventing the first set of action statements from moving the cat movie clip around any more.

14. Test your movie (**Figure 7.74**).

```
onClipEvent (enterFrame) {
    _root.cat._x = _root.cat._x + (_root._xmouse-_root.cat._x)/10;
    _root.cat._y = _root.cat._y + (_root._ymouse-_root.cat._y)/10;
    if (_root.cat.hitTest(_root._xmouse, _root._ymouse, True )) {
        _root.cat.nextFrame();
        setProperty (_root.cat, _name, "youLoseMessage");
    }
}
```

Line 6: setProperty (_root.cat, _name, "youLoseMessage");

Property: _name (Name)
Target: _root.cat ☒ Expression
Value: youLoseMessage ☐ Expression

Figure 7.73 These parameters for setProperty change the instance name of the cat movie clip to youLoseMessage.

```
onClipEvent (enterFrame) {
    // set x,y for cat closer to x,y of mouse
    _root.cat._x = _root.cat._x + (_root._xmouse-_root.cat._x)/10;
    _root.cat._y = _root.cat._y + (_root._ymouse-_root.cat._y)/10;
    // test if x,y of mouse intersects cat
    if (_root.cat.hitTest(_root._xmouse, _root._ymouse, True )) {
        // if it does, display a you lose message
        _root.cat.nextFrame();
        // and change the name of the cat instance so
        // it no longer follows the mouse
        setProperty (_root.cat, _name, "youLoseMessage");
    }
}
```

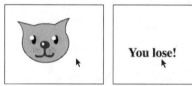

Figure 7.74 The ActionScript assigned to the cat movie clip instance (top) provides all the interactivity for the mouse-chasing game. The cat movie clip chases the pointer (left) and displays a message that was hidden on frame 2 of its Timeline when it intersects with the pointer (right).

CONTROLLING SOUND

Incorporating sound into your Flash movie can enhance the animation and interactivity and give even the simplest project a boost by engaging more of the user's senses. You can play background music to establish the mood of your movie, use narration to accompany a story, or give audible feedback to interactions such as button clicks and drag-and-drop actions. Flash's support for MP3—a highly compressed yet high-quality audio format—enables you to work with a much broader spectrum of sounds and still keep your Flash file size to a minimum.

This chapter begins with an exploration of the Sound object—the Flash object that lets you control sound with ActionScript. You should already be familiar with basic sound handling in Flash, such as importing sounds and assigning them to keyframes with the Event, Start, Stop, and Stream Sync options. If you are unsure of some of these methods, review the tutorials and the manual that accompany Flash for additional information. Moving forward, you'll learn how to use the Sound object to play sounds directly from the Library without having to assign them to keyframes. You can adjust the sound volume and its stereo effect, giving you dynamic control based on user interactions or movie conditions, and you can let the user change the sound volume or left-right balance. You'll also learn a way to manage sounds by keeping them outside of your Flash project as external movies. For example, you can build a jukebox that plays tunes that are kept separately from the main interface.

The Sound Object

Attaching a sound file to a keyframe in the Timeline is an easy way to incorporate sounds into your movie. Two valid ways to integrate sound are to use the Event Sync option to play a clicking sound in the down state of a button symbol, and to use the Stream Sync option to synchronize dialogue with an animation. But if you need to control when a sound plays, or to dynamically change its volume and playback through the left and right speakers, turn to the Sound object.

The Sound object is a Flash-defined class whose methods control sound files imported and stored in the Library. You need to instantiate the Sound object using a constructor function to give it a name, just as you've done with the Color object in the previous chapter. Once the Sound object is named, you'll be able to use it to play and modify sound files in your Library.

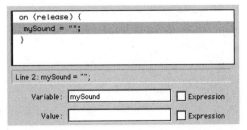

```
on (release) {
  mySound = "";
}
```

Line 2: mySound = "";

Variable: `mySound` ☐ Expression

Value: `_____` ☐ Expression

Figure 8.1 Enter mySound for the name of your sound object, and leave the Expression box unchecked.

```
on (release) {
  mySound = new Sound( target );
}
```

Line 2: mySound = new Sound(target);

Variable: `mySound` ☐ Expression

Value: `new Sound( target )` ☒ Expression

Figure 8.2 The new Sound constructor function instantiates a new sound object.

```
on (release) {
  mySound = new Sound( );
}
```

Figure 8.3 When the viewer releases the button, Flash creates the sound object called mySound.

To create a global Sound object:

1. Import a sound file by choosing File > Import (Command-R for Mac, Control-R for Windows).

   Your selected sound file appears in the Library.

2. Create a button symbol, and place an instance of it on the Stage.

3. Select the button, and open the Actions panel.

4. Choose Actions > set variable (Esc + sv).

   A new statement appears in the Actions List under the on (release) mouse event handler.

5. In the Variable field, enter the name of your new Sound object (**Figure 8.1**).

6. Click in the Value field, and choose Objects > Sound > new Sound. Check the Expression box.

   The new Sound constructor function appears in the Value field with the target argument highlighted (**Figure 8.2**).

7. Delete the highlighted word target.

   The target argument specifies a movie clip containing the sounds that would be controlled by the sound object. By not specifying a target, you create a sound object that controls all of the sounds in the Timeline (**Figure 8.3**).

THE SOUND OBJECT

Attaching Sounds

When you have multiple imported sounds in your Library, you have to convey to the sound object which sound to play and control. You identify sounds in the Library using the Linkage option, just as you did in Chapter 7 when you attached a movie clip from the Library to a movie-clip instance on the Stage. In addition to identifying your sound, the Linkage option exports it with the SWF file so it will be available when called by the sound object. Once the sound is identified with the Linkage option, you attach it to the sound object using the method attachSound.

To attach a sound to the sound object:

1. Continuing with the previous task, select your sound file in the Library.

2. From the Options menu, choose Linkage (**Figure 8.4**).

   The Symbol Linkage Properties dialog box appears.

3. From the Linkage radio buttons, select Export this symbol. In the Identifier field, enter a name to identify your sound. Click OK (**Figure 8.5**).

   Flash exports the selected sound in the SWF file with the unique identifier so that it is available to play when called by the sound object.

4. Select your button on the Stage, and open the Actions panel.

5. Select the new Sound statement in the Actions List.

   By selecting the new Sound statement, you make sure that your next ActionScript statement appears under it.

6. Choose Actions > evaluate.

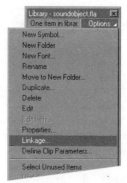

Figure 8.4 Choose the Linkage option from the Library for each sound you want to attach.

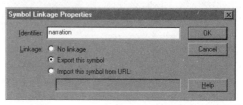

Figure 8.5 This sound is called narration and will be included in the exported SWF file.

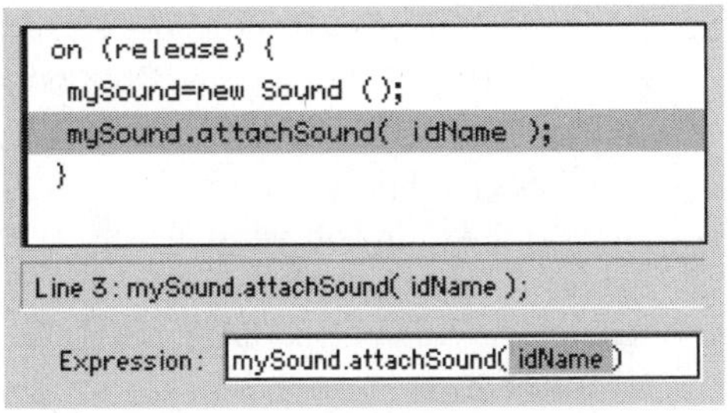

```
on (release) {
  mySound=new Sound ();
  mySound.attachSound( idName );
}
```

Line 3 : mySound.attachSound(idName);

Expression : mySound.attachSound(idName)

Figure 8.6 The attachSound method requires the argument idName, which is the identifer of your sound in the Library.

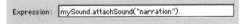

Expression : mySound.attachSound("narration")

Figure 8.7 The method attachSound attaches the sound identified as narration to the mySound sound object.

7. In the Expression field, enter the name of your sound object, and then choose Objects > Sound > attachSound.

The attachSound method appears in the Expression field in the Parameters pane with the argument idName highlighted (**Figure 8.6**).

8. In the Expression field, replace the argument idName with the identifier of your sound file within quotation marks (**Figure 8.7**).

It's very important that you specify the sound file identifier within quotation marks. They tell Flash that the word is the literal name of the identifier and not an expression that it must evaluate to determine the name of the identifier.

✔ Tip

■ You can specify an expression for the argument of the attachSound method. For example, instead of putting the identifier within quotation marks, you can insert a random number generator. Then, in the Library, identify several sounds in the Symbol Linkage Properties dialog box using numbers. Flash will attach sounds randomly. You'll learn more about random numbers in upcoming chapters.

Playing Sounds

Once you have created a new sound object and attached a sound to it from the Library, you can finally play that sound. Use the start method to play a sound from your sound object. The start method has two parameters, secondOffset and loops.

The secondOffset parameter is a number that determines how many seconds into the sound it should begin playing. You can set the sound to start from the beginning or at some later point. For example, if you have a 20-second sound attached to your sound object, a secondOffset of 10 makes the sound play from the middle. It doesn't delay the sound for 10 seconds, but rather begins immediately at the 10-second mark.

The loops parameter is a number that determines how many times the sound will play. A loops of 2 plays the entire sound two times with no delay in between. The loops parameter is optional.

To play a sound:

1. Continuing with the previous task, select your button, and open the Actions panel.

2. Select the attachSound statement in the Actions List.

    By selecting the attachSound statement, you make sure that your next ActionScript statement appears under it.

3. Choose Actions > evaluate.

    A new statement appears in the Actions List.

4. In the Expression field, enter the name of your sound object.

5. After the name of your sound object, add the start method by choosing Objects > Sound > start.

    The start method appears after the name of the sound object in the Expression field with the two parameters, secondOffset and loops, highlighted (**Figure 8.8**).

6. Replace the secondOffset parameter with 0, and replace the loops parameter with 5.

7. Test your movie.

    When your viewer releases the button, the sound begins to play from the beginning and loops five times.

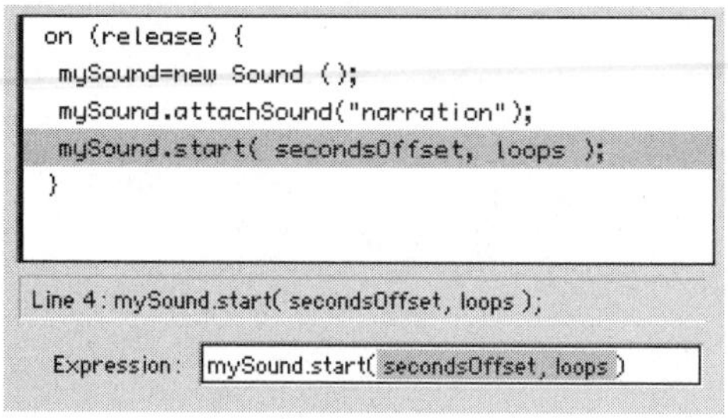

```
on (release) {
    mySound=new Sound ();
    mySound.attachSound("narration");
    mySound.start( secondsOffset, loops );
}
```

Line 4: mySound.start(secondsOffset, loops);

Expression: mySound.start(secondsOffset, loops)

Figure 8.8 The start method is placed after the mySound object is created and after the narration sound is attached. The start method requires the arguments secondOffset and loops.

✔ Tips

■ The start method plays the attached sound whenever it's called, even when the sound is already playing. This can produce multiple, overlapping sounds. In the above task, for example, when the viewer releases the button multiple times, the sounds play over each other. To prevent overlaps like this, insert a stop method, as outlined in the next task, right before the start method. This ensures that a sound always stops before it plays again.

■ The start method plays the latest sound attached to the sound object. This means a different button could attach another sound from the Library to the same sound object, and the start method would play that other sound. You could separate these statements into three buttons assigned the following actions:

First frame (instantiate mySound):

```
mySound = new Sound ();
```

First button:

```
on (release) {
mySound.attachSound("Hawaiian");
}
```

Second button:

```
on (release) {
mySound.attachSound("Jazz");
}
```

Third button:

```
on (release) {
mySound.start(0,1)
}
```

When you click the first button, then the third button, you'll hear the Hawaiian sound. When you click the second button, then the third button, you'll hear the Jazz sound. If you begin playing the Jazz sound before the Hawaiian sound finishes, you'll hear overlapping sounds.

PLAYING SOUNDS

To stop a sound:

1. Continuing with the previous task, place another instance of the button symbol on the Stage.

2. Select the button, and open the Actions panel.

3. Choose Actions > evaluate.

   A new statement appears under the on (release) mouse event handler, and the Parameters pane contains an empty Expression field.

4. In the Expression field, enter the name of your sound object.

5. Choose Objects > Sound > stop.

   The stop method appears after the sound object (**Figure 8.9**).

6. Test your movie.

   When your viewer releases this button, any sound attached to the sound object currently playing stops.

You can have all sounds stop indiscriminately by using the basic action stopAllSounds.

To stop all sounds:

◆ Choose Basic Actions > Stop All Sounds (Esc + ss).

   You can assign this action to a button, as in the previous task, or to a keyframe, and Flash stops all sounds, whether attached to a Sound object or playing from the Timeline with Event, Start, or Stream.

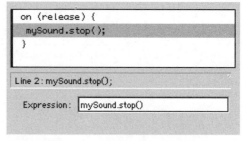

```
on (release) {
    mySound.stop( );
}
```

Line 2 : mySound.stop();

Expression : mySound.stop()

Figure 8.9 This stop method stops playing any sounds attached to the mySound sound object. There are no arguments for the stop method.

Modifying Sounds

When you use the Sound object, Flash gives you full control over the volume of sound and its output through either the left or right speaker, known as pan control. With this level of sound control, you can let your users set the volume to their own preference, and you can create more realistic environments. For example, in a car game, you can vary the volume of cars as they approach or pass you. Playing with the pan controls, you can embellish the classic Pong game by making the sounds of the ball hitting the paddles and the walls play from the appropriate sides.

The two methods for modifying sounds are setVolume and setPan. SetVolume takes a number between 0 and 100 as its argument, where 100 is the loudest and 0 is silence. setPan takes a number between –100 and 100, where –100 plays the sound completely through the left speaker, 100 plays the sound completely through the right speaker, and 0 plays the sound through both speakers equally.

To set the volume of a sound:

1. Continuing with the previous task, place another instance of the button symbol on the Stage.

2. Select the button, and open the Actions panel.

3. Choose Actions > evaluate.

   A new statement appears under the on (release) mouse event handler in the Actions List, and the Parameters pane contains an empty Expression field.

4. In the Expression field, enter the name of your sound object.

(continued on next page)

5. Choose Objects > Sound > setVolume.

The setVolume method appears in the Expression field after your sound object, with the volume parameter highlighted (**Figure 8.10**).

6. In the Expression field, replace the volume parameter with a number between 0 and 100 (**Figure 8.11**).

7. Test your movie.

When you play your sound, then release this button, the volume changes according to the volume parameter.

✔ Tip

■ The default value of the setVolume method is 100, so you would change it only to decrease the volume. Think of your parameter as a percentage of full volume.

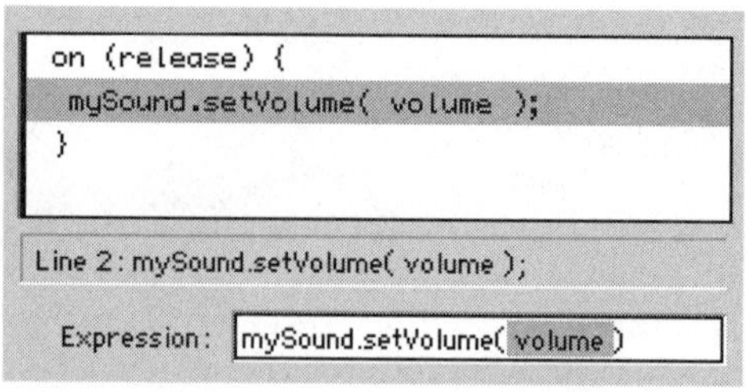

```
on (release) {
    mySound.setVolume( volume );
}
```

Line 2: mySound.setVolume(volume);

Expression: mySound.setVolume(volume)

Figure 8.10 The setVolume method requires a volume parameter.

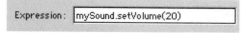

Expression: mySound.setVolume(20)

Figure 8.11 The volume for the mySound sound object is set at 20 percent.

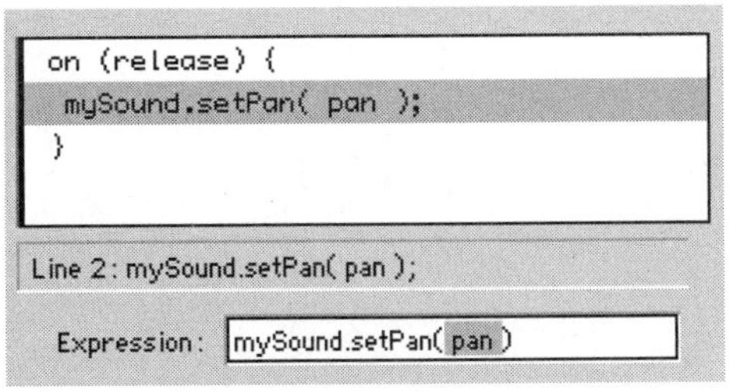

```
on (release) {
   mySound.setPan( pan );
}
```

Line 2: mySound.setPan(pan);

Expression: mySound.setPan(pan)

Figure 8.12 The setPan method requires the pan parameter, a number between –100 and 100.

Expression: mySound.setPan(100)

Figure 8.13 The pan for the mySound sound object is set at 100, so all of its sounds play out of the right speaker.

To set the right and left balance of a sound:

1. Continuing with the previous task, place another instance of the button symbol on the Stage.

2. Select the button, and open the Actions panel.

3. Choose Actions > evaluate.

   A new statement appears under the on (release) mouse event handler, and the Parameters pane contains an empty Expression field.

4. In the Expression field, enter the name of your sound object.

5. Choose Objects > Sound > setPan.

   The setPan method appears in the Expression field after your sound object, with the pan parameter highlighted (**Figure 8.12**).

6. In the Expression field, replace the pan parameter with a number between -100 and 100 (**Figure 8.13**). (This single number controls the balance between left and right speakers.)

7. Test your movie.

   When you play your sound, then release this button, the right-left balance changes according to the pan parameter.

MODIFYING SOUNDS

Modifying Independent Sounds

When you instantiate your sound object and do not specify a target parameter, such as mySound = new Sound (), then the setVolume and setPan methods will have a global effect, controlling all the sounds in the root Timeline. Even if you create two separate Sound objects like the following,

mySound1 = new Sound ();

mySound2 = new Sound ();

you cannot use the setPan method to play mySound1 through the left speaker and mySound2 through the right speaker.

In order to modify sounds independently, you must create your sound objects with specific target movie clips. The sound objects will thereafter be applied to different movie clips, and the setVolume and setPan methods can be used to control the two sounds separately.

To modify two sounds independently:

1. Import two sound files into Flash.

2. From the Options menu in the Library choose Linkage, and give both sounds unique Identifiers in the Symbol Linkage Properties dialog box (**Figure 8.14**).

3. Create a movie-clip symbol, place an instance of it on the Stage, and name it.

4. Place a second instance of the movie-clip symbol on the Stage, and name it (**Figure 8.15**).

5. Create a button symbol, place an instance of it on the Stage, select it, and open the Actions panel.

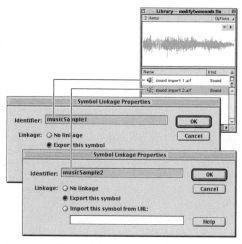

Figure 8.14 Give each imported sound a different identifier in the Symbol Linkage Properties dialog box.

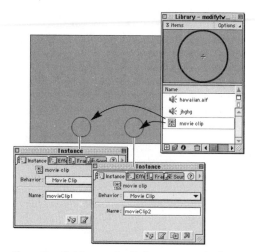

Figure 8.15 Put two movie-clip instances on the Stage to act as targets for the new sound objects. The two movie-clip instances here are called movieClip1 and movieClip2.

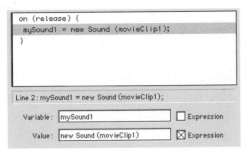

```
on (release) {
    mySound1 = new Sound (movieClip1);
}

Line 2: mySound1 = new Sound (movieClip1);

Variable:  [mySound1]            ☐ Expression

Value:  [new Sound (movieClip1)]  ☒ Expression
```

Figure 8.16 The mySound1 sound object is created and targets movieClip1.

```
on (release) {
    mySound1 = new Sound (movieClip1);
    mySound1 .attachSound("musicSample1");
    mySound1 .start(0,1);
}

Line 4: mySound1 .start(0,1);

Expression:  [mySound1 .start(0,1)]
```

Figure 8.17 This start method plays musicSample1. Notice that although mySound1 targets movieClip1, movieClip1 need not be referenced in the target path to call the methods attachSound or start. The methods attachSound and start refer to the sound object, and not to the targeted movie-clip instance.

```
on (release) {
    mySound2=new Sound (movieClip2);
    mySound2 .attachSound("musicSample2");
    mySound2 .start(0,1);
}

Line 4: mySound2.start(0,1);

Expression:  [mySound2.start(0,1)]
```

Figure 8.18 The mySound2 sound object targets movieClip2 and plays musicSample2.

6. Choose the set variable action to instantiate a new sound object, as you did earlier in this chapter. For the target parameter, enter the name of your first movie-clip instance (**Figure 8.16**).

7. Choose the evaluate action, and attach the first sound to this first sound object.

8. Choose the evaluate action again, and assign the start method (**Figure 8.17**).

   The actions assigned to this button create a new sound object, attach a sound from the Library to the object, and then begin playing the sound.

9. Place another instance of the button symbol on the Stage.

10. In a similar fashion, instantiate another sound object, attach the second sound from the Library to the object, and assign the start method (**Figure 8.18**).

11. Place two more instances of button symbols on the Stage.

(continued on next page)

MODIFYING INDEPENDENT SOUNDS

12. For the first button instance, assign the setPan method to the first sound object with a pan parameter of –100 (**Figure 8.19**).

This button plays the first sound object in the left speaker.

13. In the second button instance, assign the setPan method to the second sound object with a pan parameter of 100 (**Figure 8.20**).

This button plays the second sound object in the right speaker.

14. Test your movie.

✔ Tip

■ The movie-clip instances on the Stage act as placeholders, or empty vessels, for the separate sound objects. You can either place them off the Stage so they're not visible to the user or delete any graphics in their first keyframe.

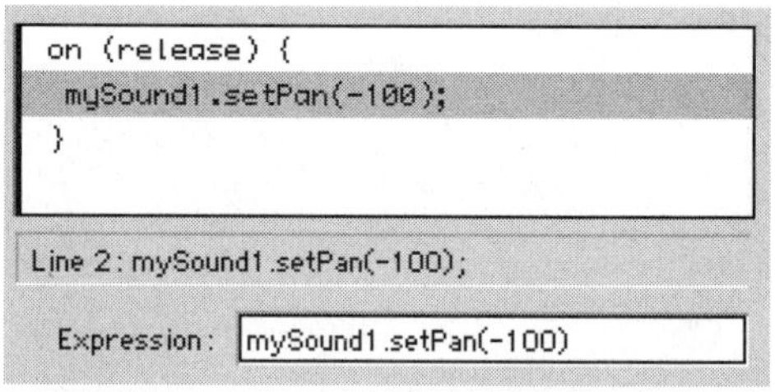

```
on (release) {
    mySound1.setPan(-100);
}
```

Line 2: mySound1.setPan(-100);

Expression: mySound1.setPan(-100)

Figure 8.19 The setPan method for mySound1 plays musicSample1 in the left speaker.

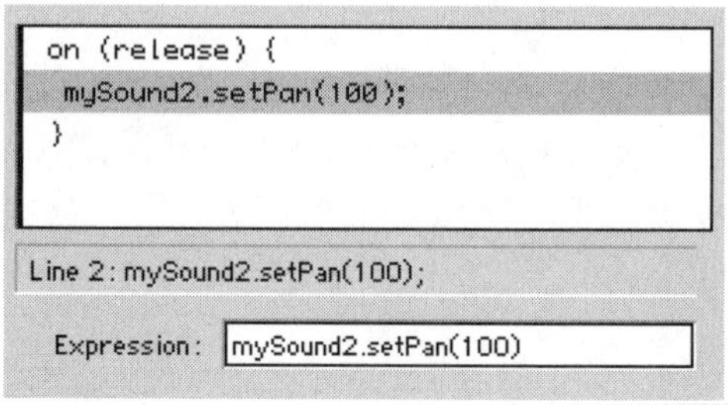

```
on (release) {
    mySound2.setPan(100);
}
```

Line 2: mySound2.setPan(100);

Expression: mySound2.setPan(100)

Figure 8.20 The setPan method for mySound2 plays musicSample2 in the right speaker.

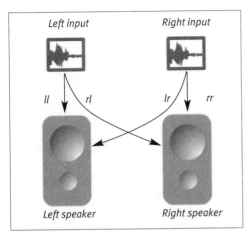

Left input   *Right input*

ll   *rl*   *lr*   *rr*

Left speaker   *Right speaker*

Figure 8.21 The parameters for setTransform determine distribution of sounds between the left and right speakers. The first letter refers to the output speaker; the second letter refers to the input sound.

Transforming Sounds

For advanced users who want more precise control over how a sound is playing through the left and right speakers, Flash provides the method setTransform. This method allows you to set percentages that determine how much of the right or left channel plays through the right and left speakers. Using this method, your sound can dynamically switch speakers from left to right or switch from stereo to mono.

The setTransform method of the Sound object is very similar to the setTransform method of the Color object discussed in Chapter 7. As with the Color object, using setTransform with the Sound object requires that you create a generic object to hold the information specifying the distribution of left and right sounds. The parameters for the sound transformation object are ll, lr, rr, and rl (**Figure 8.21**). A summary of their functions appears in **Table 8.1**.

Table 8.1

setTransform Parameters for the Sound Object	
PARAMETER	VALUE
ll	Percentage value specifying how much of the left input plays in the left speaker.
lr	Percentage value specifying how much of the right input plays in the left speaker.
rr	Percentage value specifying how much of the right input plays in the right speaker.
rl	Percentage value specifying how much of the left input plays in the right speaker.

TRANSFORMING SOUNDS

To switch the left and right speakers:

1. Import a sound file into Flash.

2. From the Options menu in the Library choose Linkage, and give the sound an Identifier in the Symbol Linkage Properties dialog box (**Figure 8.22**).

3. Create a button symbol, and place an instance of it on the Stage. Select it, and open the Actions panel.

4. Choose the set variable action to instantiate a new sound object as you did earlier in this chapter. Don't specify a target parameter (**Figure 8.23**).

5. Choose the evaluate action, and attach the first sound to this first sound object.

6. Choose the evaluate action again, and assign the start method (**Figure 8.24**). This button plays your sound.

7. Place another instance of the button symbol on the Stage.

8. In the Actions panel, choose Actions > set variable.

9. In the Variable field of the Actions panel, enter the name of your new sound transform object.

10. Click inside the Value field, and choose Objects > Object > new Object. Check the Expression box next to the Value field (**Figure 8.25**).

    Your new sound transform object is instantiated.

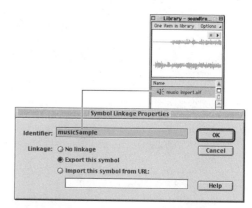

Figure 8.22 This sound is identified as musicSample in the Linkage options in the Library.

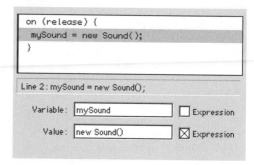

Figure 8.23 The mySound sound object is created.

```
on (release) {
  mySound = new Sound( );
  mySound.attachSound("musicSample" );
  mySound.start(0, 1 );
}
```

Line 4 : mySound.start(0,1);

Expression : mySound.start(0,1)

Figure 8.24 The sound musicSample plays from the mySound sound object.

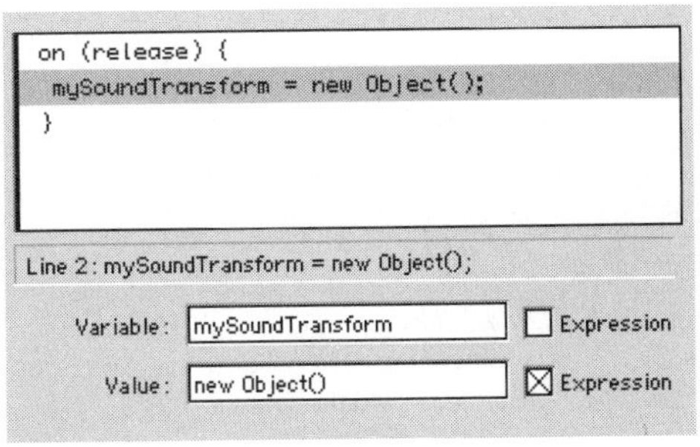

```
on (release) {
    mySoundTransform = new Object();
}
```

```
Line 2 : mySoundTransform = new Object();

    Variable :  mySoundTransform          ☐ Expression

    Value :  new Object()                 ☒ Expression
```

Figure 8.25 The mySoundTransform object is created from the generic object class.

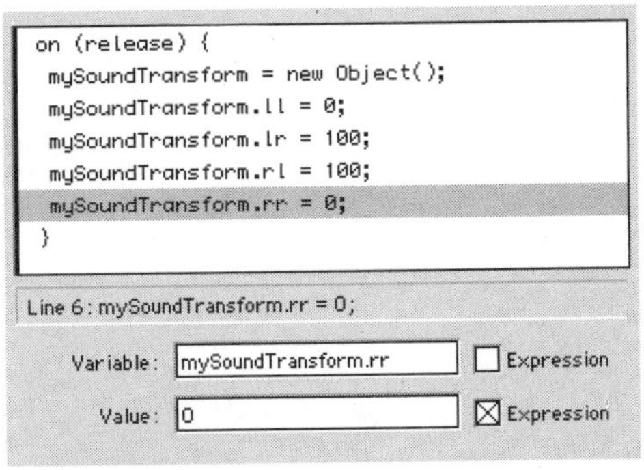

```
on (release) {
    mySoundTransform = new Object();
    mySoundTransform.ll = 0;
    mySoundTransform.lr = 100;
    mySoundTransform.rl = 100;
    mySoundTransform.rr = 0;
}
```

```
Line 6 : mySoundTransform.rr = 0;

    Variable :  mySoundTransform.rr         ☐ Expression

    Value :  0                              ☒ Expression
```

Figure 8.26 The four parameters of the setTransform method are defined as properties of the mySoundTransform object.

```
on (release) {
    mySoundTransform = new Object();
    mySoundTransform.ll = 0;
    mySoundTransform.lr = 100;
    mySoundTransform.rl = 100;
    mySoundTransform.rr = 0;
    mySound.setTransform( sxform );
}
```

```
Line 7 : mySound.setTransform( sxform );

    Expression :  mySound.setTransform( sxform )
```

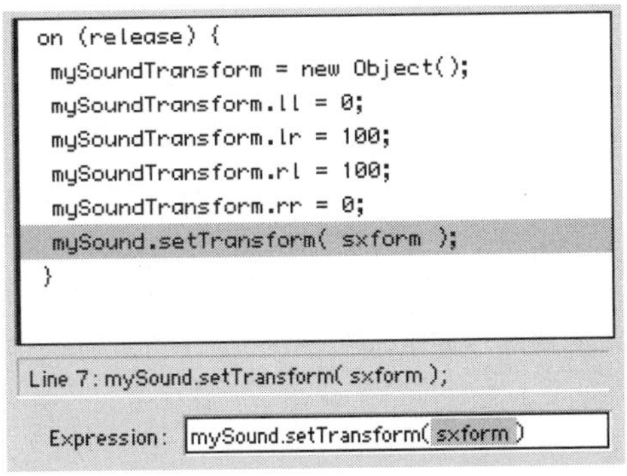

Figure 8.27 The setTransform method requires the parameter sxform, or a sound transform object.

11. Choose Actions > set variable. In the Variable field of the Actions panel, enter the name of your sound transform object, a dot, then one of the parameters. In the Value field, enter a percentage number. Check the Expression box. Do this for all four parameters (**Figure 8.26**).

    The parameters for your sound transform object are defined.

12. Choose Actions > evaluate.

13. In the Expression field of the Actions panel, enter the name of your sound object.

14. Choose Objects > Sound > setTransform.

    The setTransform method appears in the Expression box after your sound object, with the highlighted target sxform in parentheses. sxform stands for "sound transform" (**Figure 8.27**).

15. Replace the highlighted target with the name of your sound transform object (**Figure 8.28**).

    This button creates a generic object that holds the sound transform information. The information is then passed to the sound object using the setTransform method.

16. Test your movie.

    When you release the second button, the distribution of sound in the left and right speakers changes.

```
    Expression :  mySound.setTransform(mySoundTransform)
```

Figure 8.28 The four setTransform parameters defined in the mySoundTransform object supply the method with the required information.

Creating Dynamic Sound Controls

One of the most effective uses of the Sound object and its methods is to create dynamic controls so that the user can set the desired volume level or speaker balance. The basic strategy is to create a draggable movie clip that acts as a sliding controller. By correlating the position of the draggable movie clip to the volume parameter in the setVolume method, you can make the volume change dynamically as the viewer moves the movie clip.

For a vertical slider bar that controls volume there are two elements: the actual handle or slider, and the track or groove that it runs along (**Figure 8.29**). You would first create a movie clip called groove. To make things easy, make the groove movie clip 100 pixels high with its center point at the bottom of the rectangle. Making the groove 100 pixels high will make it simpler to correlate the position of the slider on the groove to the setVolume parameter. To create the draggable slider, place an invisible button inside the slider movie clip that assigns the startDrag action and constrains the motion relative to the groove movie clip.

Figure 8.29 The components of a volume control are the slider that moves up and down and the groove.

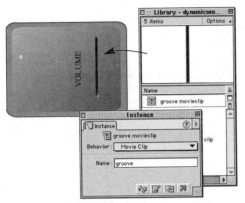

Figure 8.30 This movie-clip instance is called groove and will limit the motion of the draggable movie clip.

Figure 8.31 The constrain to rectangle parameters constrain this slider movie clip from the center point to 100 pixels above the center point of the groove movie clip.

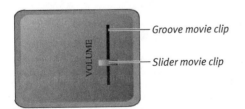

Groove movie clip

Slider movie clip

Figure 8.32 The slider movie clip can be dragged along the groove movie clip.

To constrain a slider over a groove for a volume control interface:

1. Create a movie clip of a tall rectangle that is 100 pixels high and whose center point lies at the bottom edge. Place an instance of it on the Stage and name it groove **(Figure 8.30)**.

2. Create another movie clip of a slider. Enter symbol-editing mode for this movie clip.

3. Create an invisible button and place an instance of it inside of the slider movie clip. Select the button and open the Actions panel.

4. Choose Actions > on. Select only the Press event.

5. Choose Actions > startDrag. In the Target field, enter this. Check the Expression box next to the Target field. Check the Lock mouse to center and Constrain to rectangle box.

    In the L field, enter _root.groove._x
    In the R field, enter _root.groove._x
    In the T field, enter _root.groove._y-100
    In the B field, enter _root.groove._y
    The actions assigned to the slider movie clip constrain the left and right sides to the center of the groove movie clip. The top is constrained to 100 pixels above the lower edge of the groove movie clip and the bottom is constrained to the lower edge of the groove movie clip **(Figure 8.31)**.

6. Choose Actions > on. Select the Release event.

7. Choose Actions > stopDrag.

8. Return to the main Timeline and drag an instance of your slider movie clip on to the Stage and name it slider. Test your movie **(Figure 8.32)**.

CREATING DYNAMIC SOUND CONTROLS

233

The GlobaltoLocal Movie-Clip Method

The second part of creating a dynamic sound control for volume is to correlate the *y* position of the slider bar with the parameter for the setVolume method. You want the top of the groove to correspond to a volume of 100 and the bottom of the groove to correspond to a volume of 0 (**Figure 8.33**). But how do you get the *y* coordinates of the moving slider to match up with a number from 0 to 100? One way is to use the movie clip method globaltoLocal, which can convert the coordinates of the slider bar to coordinates that are relative to the groove movie clip. Since the groove movie clip is 100 pixels high and the slider bar is constrained to the groove movie clip's height, the groove movie clip's local coordinates gives an easier correlation to the volume settings (**Figure 8.34**).

To transform global coordinates to local coordinates:

1. Continuing with the previous task, select the slider movie clip, and open the Actions panel.

2. Choose Actions > onClipEvent.

3. In the Actions panel, select the mouseMove event, and choose Actions > set variable.

4. In the Variable field, enter a name for the object that will hold the *x, y* information to be transformed from global to local coordinates. This is your point object.

5. In the Value field, choose Objects > Object > new Object. Check the Expression box (**Figure 8.35**).

6. Again, choose Actions > set variable.

setVolume(100)

Figure 8.33 The setVolume parameters need to correspond to the position of the slider movie clip on top of the groove movie clip.

setVolume(0)

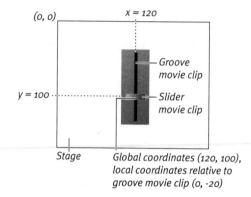

Figure 8.34 The global coordinates of slider are determined by the root Timeline Stage. The local coordinates are relative to the groove movie clip.

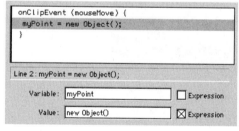

Figure 8.35 The myPoint object is created from the generic Object class.

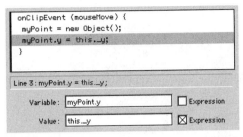

```
onClipEvent (mouseMove) {
  myPoint = new Object();
  myPoint.y = this._y;
}
```

Line 3: myPoint.y = this._y;

| Variable: | myPoint.y | ☐ Expression |
| Value: | this._y | ☒ Expression |

Figure 8.36 myPoint.y is assigned to the y position of the slider movie clip.

```
onClipEvent (mouseMove) {
  myPoint = new Object();
  myPoint.y = this._y;
  myPoint.x = this._x;
  _root.groove.globalToLocal( myPoint );
}
```

Line 5: _root.groove.globalToLocal(myPoint);

Expression: [_root.groove.globalToLocal(myPoint)]

Figure 8.37 The global coordinates of myPoint (myPoint.x and myPoint.y) change to the local coordinates of the groove movie clip.

7. In the Variable field, enter the name of your point object, a dot, then the property y. In the Value field, enter this._y Check the Expression box. (**Figure 8.36**).

This sets the y property of your point object to the y position of the draggable movie clip.

8. Again, choose Actions > set variable.

9. In the Variable field, enter the name of your point object, a dot, then the property x. In the Value field, enter this._x. Check the Expression box.

This sets the X property of your point object to the x position of the draggable movie clip.

10. Choose Actions > evaluate.

11. In the Expression field, enter the target path of the movie clip whose coordinate system you wish to use. Then choose Objects > Movie Clip > globaltoLocal. In between the parentheses of the globaltoLocal method, enter the name of your point object (**Figure 8.37**).

Flash transforms the coordinates of your point object (relative to the root Timeline) to the coordinates of the targeted movie clip (relative to the groove movie clip Timeline).

CREATING DYNAMIC SOUND CONTROLS

To link the slider position to the volume setting:

1. Continuing with the previous task, import a sound file into Flash.

2. From the Options menu in the Library, choose Linkage, and give the sound an Identifier.

3. Create a button symbol, and place an instance of it on the Stage. Select it, and open the Actions panel.

4. Assign actions as you did in the previous tasks to create a new sound object, attach the sound from the Library to the sound object, and then assign the method that starts the sound (**Figure 8.38**).

5. Select your draggable movie clip.

6. Add to the end of the actions within the onClipEvent (mouseMove) event handler by choosing Actions > evaluate.

7. Enter the target path for your sound object, then choose Objects > Sound > setVolume.

8. Replace the volume parameter by entering
   -1*myPoint.y

   The y position for your slider moves from –100 to 0. By multiplying the point object by –1, you convert the range of values from 100 to 0 (**Figure 8.39**).

9. Choose Actions > evaluate. In the Expression field, enter updateAfterEvent (mouseMove);

10. Test your movie.

    When you drag the slider up or down on the groove, you dynamically change the sound volume.

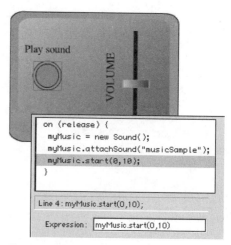

Figure 8.38 Another button starts the musicSample sound.

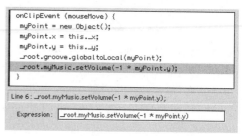

Figure 8.39 The groove movie-clip symbol is 100 pixels tall with its center point at the bottom edge. Hence, the local coordinates of the groove movie clip range from –100 to 0. In order to change this range, multiply by (-1). The result is a range from 100 at the top to 0 at the bottom that can feed into the setVolume parameter.

Managing Sounds as External Files

Each time you use the Symbol Linkage Properties dialog box to identify a sound in the Library and mark it for export, that sound is added to your SWF, increasing its size. Sounds take up an enormous amount of space, even with MP3 compression, so you have to be judicious with your inclusion of sounds. One way to manage sounds so that your file size stays small is to keep sounds in external Flash movies. Use the action loadMovieNum to bring sounds into Flash only when you need them. This also allows you to change the sound in the external Flash movie easily without tinkering with the main Flash movie. For example, you can maintain several background music tracks that users can choose from. To turn the music on, you use the action loadMovieNum, and to turn the music off, you use the action unloadMovieNum. You could even have one external SWF trigger the loading of another external SWF or trigger the loading of a randomly selected SWF. This would add variety by playing a random medley from a collection of external music files.

To play a sound in an external movie:

1. Import a sound into Flash.

2. Place an instance of the sound on the Timeline. From the Sound panel, select the Stream Sync option, and add frames to the Timeline to accommodate the entire sound (**Figure 8.40**).

3. Export the file as a SWF.

4. Open a new Flash file.

5. Create a button symbol, and place an instance of it on the Stage.

6. Select the button, and open the Actions panel.

7. Choose Actions > loadMovie (Esc + lm).

8. In the URL field of the Actions panel, enter the name of your exported SWF file. In the Location pull-down menu, select Level, and enter a number higher than 0 (**Figure 8.41**).

9. Export this movie as a SWF, and keep both SWF files in the same directory.

   When you release this button, the music in the first SWF file loads and plays.

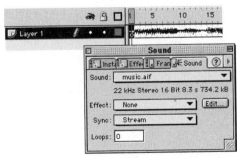

Figure 8.40 A sound set to the Stream Sync option is tied to individual frames of the Timeline.

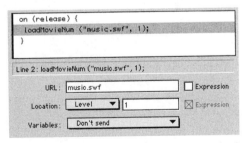

Figure 8.41 These actions assigned to the button load the file music.swf.

To stop a sound in an external movie:

1. Continuing with the previous task, add a second button instance to the file that already has the loadMovieNum action assigned to one button.

2. Choose Actions > unloadMovie (Esc + um).

3. In the Location pull-down menu in the Actions panel, select Level, and enter the same level number you entered for the loadMovieNum action (**Figure 8.42**).

4. Export this movie as a SWF, and keep both SWF files in the same directory.

5. When you release the second button, the music in the first SWF file stops playing because the file is removed from that level.

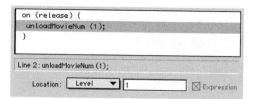

Figure 8.42 These actions assigned to the button remove any file in Level 1.

✔ Tips

■ Play multiple sounds at the same time by loading different SWF files in separate levels, or by loading them in specific movie-clip instances.

■ Assign a frame action to the last keyframe of the external SWF that loads another SWF into the same level. The second SWF automatically replaces the first SWF after the sound ends.

Part V: Working with Information

CONTROLLING INFORMATION FLOW

As your Flash movie displays graphics and animation and plays sounds, there can be a lot happening behind the scenes, unapparent to the viewer. Your Flash document may be tracking many bits of information, such as the number of lives a player has left in a game, a user's log-in name and password, or the items a customer has placed in a shopping cart. Getting and storing this information requires variables, which are containers for information. Variables are essential in any Flash movie that involves complex interactivity because they let you create scenarios based on information that changes. You can modify variables and use them in expressions—formulas that can combine variables with other variables and values—and then test the information against certain conditions to determine how the Flash movie will unfold. This testing is done in conditional statements, which control the flow of information. Conditional statements evaluate information that comes in, and then tell Flash what to do based on that information. For example, you would use conditional statements to make a ball bounce back if it collides with a wall, or increase the speed of the ball if the game time exceeds one minute.

This chapter is about managing information using variables, expressions, and conditional statements. You've dealt with all three in limited ways in earlier chapters, but here you'll learn how to work with them in more detail. Understanding how to get, modify, and evaluate information lets you truly direct your Flash movie and change the graphics, animation, and sound in dynamic fashion.

Initializing Information

Variables hold information. You can create, change the contents of, and discard variables at any time. The first time you put information into a variable is called *initialization*. Initializing and changing a variable involves the `set variable` action. You've initialized variables before; we just didn't call it that. When you create new objects using `set variable`, as in the statement `myColor = new Color (myMovieClip)`, you initialize the variable myColor. In this case, the variable contains the color object, but a variable can hold any kind of information, such as a number, letters, a true or false value, or even a reference to another variable. The different kinds of information that variables can contain are known as *data types*.

Variables and Data Types

Examples of typical types of variables are a user's score (number data type), an Internet address (string data type), a sound object (object data type), and the on/off state of a radio button (Boolean data type). You can easily change the data type that a variable holds. A variable that was initialized with a number data type can be changed later on in the movie to hold a string data type with a new `set variable` action. However, it's a good practice to keep the data type of variables constant so that when you manipulate them, you don't get unexpected results (for example, trying to multiply a string by a string). The different data types that variables can hold are listed in **Table 9.1**.

Variable names should be descriptive of the information that they hold. For example, playerScore and spaceshipVelocity are appropriate variable names and will cause fewer headaches than something like xyz or myVariable. It's a common practice to name variables without spaces between words and to capitalize the first letter of each word except the first word.

Table 9.1

DATA TYPE	DESCRIPTION	EXAMPLE
Variable Data Types		
Number	A numeric value.	`myScore = 24`
String	A sequence of characters, numbers, or symbols. A string is always contained within quotation marks.	`yourEmail = "johndoe@domain.com"`
Boolean	A value of either **true** or **false**. The words are not enclosed in quotation marks. Alternatively, you can use **1** for **true** and **0** for **false**.	`radioButton = true`
Object	The name of an object that you create from a constructor function.	`myColor = new Color(myMovie)`

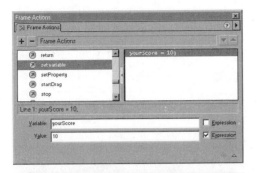

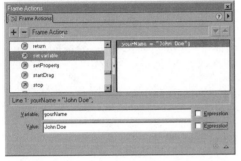

Figure 9.1 Variables can be initialized to hold different kinds of information. A number (top) needs the Value Expression box checked. A string (bottom) doesn't need the Value Expression box checked.

To initialize a variable:

1. Select the first keyframe of the root Timeline, and open the Actions panel.

2. Choose Actions > set variable (Esc + sv).

3. In the Variable field of the Actions panel, enter the name of your variable. Leave the Expression box unchecked.

4. In the Value field, enter the information that the variable holds. This can be a number, a new object, a string, or a Boolean value. Leave the Expression box unchecked for a string data type (**Figure 9.1**).

✔ Tips

■ There are certain words you cannot use for variable names because they are reserved for special functions or for use as keywords in ActionScript. You will just confuse Flash by trying to use them as variables. They are: `break`, `for`, `new`, `var`, `continue`, `function`, `return`, `void`, `delete`, `if`, `this`, `while`, `else`, `in`, `typeof`, `with`, `true`, and `false`.

■ It's a good practice to initialize your variables on the first frame of your Timeline. That way you keep them all in the same place and can edit their initial values easily.

INITIALIZING INFORMATION

Often, you will want to retrieve a certain property of an object and put it into a variable to store for use at a later time. For example, you may want to store a movie clip's *x* and *y* coordinates so that when the user drags the clip somewhere, you can make Flash return it to its original position. To retrieve a property, you can either construct a target path with the property, using dot syntax, or you can use the function getProperty.

To assign a property to a variable with dot syntax:

1. Select the first keyframe on the Timeline, and open the Actions panel.

2. Choose Actions > set variable.

3. In the Variable field of the Actions panel, enter the name of your variable. Leave the Expression box unchecked.

4. In the Value field, enter the target path and the desired property, separated by dots. Check the Expression box (**Figure 9.2**).

To assign a property to a variable with getProperty:

1. Select the first keyframe on the Timeline, and open the Actions panel. Choose Actions > set variable.

2. In the Variable field of the Actions panel, enter the name of your variable.

3. In the Value field, choose Functions > getProperty.

   The getProperty action appears in the Value field with the arguments target and property (**Figure 9.3**).

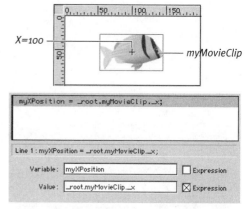

Figure 9.2 Use dot syntax to put an object's property into a variable. The variable myXPosition is set to the *x* position of the myMovieClip object on the root Timeline. The variable myXPosition currently holds the value of 100.

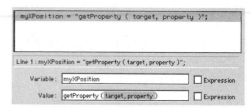

Figure 9.3 The getProperty action requires the arguments target and property.

INITIALIZING INFORMATION

Figure 9.4 The target is `_root.myMovieClip`, and the property is its *x* position. This value is assigned to the variable `myXPosition`.

4. Replace target with the target path, and replace property with the desired property. Check the Expression box (**Figure 9.4**).

✔ Tip

■ When you assign a variable to a property or to reference another variable, Flash determines the value and puts it into your variable at that moment. If the property or the referenced variable subsequently changes, the value of your variable will not change unless you reassign it. For example:

`xPosition = _xmouse`

When you initialize this variable xPosition in the first frame of your movie, it holds the *x* coordinate of the pointer. As you move the pointer around the screen, the property `_xmouse` changes, but the variable xPosition does not. The variable xPosition still holds the original *x* coordinate from when the `set variable` statement was executed. To have the variable continually updated, you must put it within a loop, such as the clip events EnterFrame or Mouse move.

Strings vs Expressions

When you use the action set variable to put information into a variable, you have the option of checking an Expression box in the Parameters pane for the Variable and for the Value (**Figure 9.5**). Checking the Expression box next to the Value field removes the quotation marks around the entry and makes it an expression rather than a string. An expression is a statement that may include variables, properties, and objects that must be evaluated before Flash can determine its value. Think of an expression as an algebraic formula, like $a^2 + b^2$. The value of the expression has to be calculated before it can be assigned to the variable name (**Figure 9.6**). A string, on the other hand, is a statement that Flash uses as is and considers simply as a collection of characters. The string $a^2 + b^2$ is literally a sequence of seven characters (counting the spaces). When you initialize a variable with a string data type, you must leave the Expression box unchecked. On all other data types, you must check the Expression box. Checking the Expression box next to the Variable field changes the entire statement in the Actions List to the form set (variable, value). This syntax lets you enter an expression for the variable as well as for its value. For example, you could have variable names player1, player2, and player3 dynamically created by using the expression "player" + counter, where counter itself is a variable that contains a number (**Figure 9.7**). This kind of expression is discussed later in this Chapter.

Table 9.2

Common Escape Sequences	
SEQUENCE	CHARACTER
\b	Backspace
\r	Return
\t	Tab
\"	Quotation mark
\'	Single quotation mark
\\	Backslash

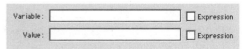

Figure 9.5 The Variable and Value fields in the Parameters pane of set variable both have Expression options.

```
myVolume = myLength*myWidth;
dogYears = 7*Age;
downloadProgress = _root._framesloaded/_root._totalframes;
```

Figure 9.6 Some examples of expressions. The variable names are on the left of the equal symbols, and the expressions are on the right.

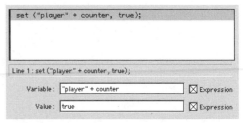

Figure 9.7 The set action (available only through the set variable action) lets you use an expression for a variable name.

✔ Tip

■ If quotation marks always surround a string, how do you include quotation marks in the actual string? You do this by using the backslash (\) character before including a quotation mark. This is called *escaping a character*. For example, the string "The line, \"Call me Shane\" is from a 1953 movie Western" produces the following result: The line, "Call me Shane" is from a 1953 movie Western. A few common escape sequences for special characters are listed in **Table 9.2**.

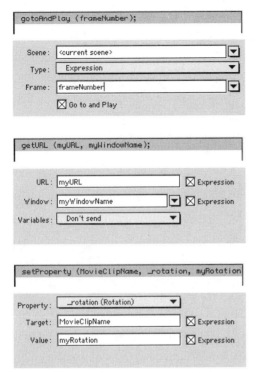

Figure 9.8 Examples of using variables and expressions in parameters fields of actions: The variable frameNumber in gotoAndPlay (top), the variables myURL and myWindowName in getURL (middle), and the variables MovieClipName and myRotation in setProperty (bottom).

Using Variables and Expressions

Use variables and expressions as placeholders for parameters within your ActionScript. In virtually every action that requires you to enter a parameter, you can place a variable or an expression instead. For example, the basic action gotoAndStop gives you the option to enter an expression instead of a frame number in the Frame field. This expression might be a variable called myCard that holds a number between 1 and 52. Frames 1 through 52 on the Timeline could contain graphics of the 52 playing cards, so changing the variable myCard in the gotoAndStop action would make Flash display different cards. In the action getURL, the URL field can be an expression rather than the actual name of an Internet address. For example, the expression might be a string concatenated with a variable such as "http://"+yourWebSite. Changing the variable called yourWebSite makes Flash load different URLs with the getURL action. Values for the properties of objects and target paths for objects can be replaced with expressions in the setProperty action (**Figure 9.8**).

The other common use of a variable is as a simple counter. Rather than taking the place of a parameter, a counter variable just keeps track of the number of a certain kind of occurrence for later retrieval and testing. A player's score can be stored in a variable so that Flash knows when the player reaches enough points to win the game.

To use a variable in a parameter field:

1. In the first keyframe of the root Timeline, choose Actions > set variable. In the Variable field of the Actions panel, enter the name of your variable. In the Value field, enter a number. Check the Expression box next to the Value field (**Figure 9.9**).

2. Create a button symbol, and drag an instance of it to the Stage.

3. Select the button, and in the Actions panel choose Basic Actions > Go To (**Figure 9.10**).

4. In the Parameters pane, in the Type pull-down menu, select Expression. In the Frame field, enter the name of your variable you initialized on the root Timeline (**Figure 9.10**).

5. Provide additional frames so that the playhead has somewhere to go. Test your movie (**Figure 9.11**).

   Your variable contains a number. When Flash performs the `gotoAndPlay` action, it uses the information contained in your variable as the frame to go to.

✔ Tip

■ In the previous task, if you define a string data type for your variable, you can have the `gotoAndPlay` action go to a frame label instead of a frame number. For example, assign the string "Conclusion" to the variable myFrameLabel. By using myFrameLabel as the parameter in the `gotoAndPlay` action, you can have Flash go to the frame labeled Conclusion. Create several labels such as Title, Introduction, and Body. By changing the contents of the variable myFrameLabel, the `gotoAndPlay` action will send the playhead to different frame labels.

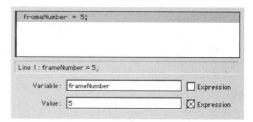

Figure 9.9 The variable frameNumber is initialized to 5.

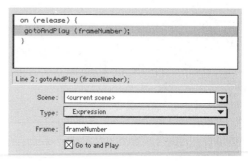

Figure 9.10 By choosing Expression in the Type pull-down menu you can put the variable frameNumber in the Frame field.

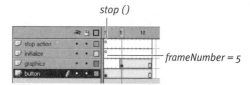

Figure 9.11 When the user releases the button in the bottom layer, Flash goes to the value of frameNumber, which is 5.

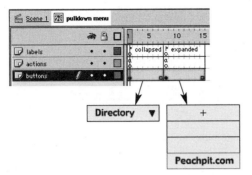

Figure 9.12 A movie clip of a pull-down menu has two states—collapsed and expanded—which toggle back and forth.

The Scope of Variables

When you initialize variables, they belong to a particular Timeline. This is known as the *scope* of a variable. If you initialize a variable from the root Timeline, the variable is scoped to the root Timeline. If you initialize a variable inside a movie clip, then the variable is scoped to that movie clip. Think of a variable's scope as its home. Variables live on certain Timelines, and if you want to use the information inside of a variable, you must first find it with a target path. This is similar to targeting movie clips. In order to access either a movie clip or a variable, you identify it with a target path. When you construct a target path for a variable, you can use the relative and absolute terms _root, this, and _parent.

In the following task, you will build a pull-down menu that loads a Web site using the getURL action. The URL for the action is stored in a variable that is initialized and scoped to the main Timeline. Since the getURL action resides in the movie clip of the pull-down menu, the variable and the action that uses the variable have different scopes. Use a target path to identify the variable on the main Timeline from the movie clip's Timeline.

To target a variable with a different scope:

1. Create a movie clip of a pull-down menu as demonstrated in Chapter 4. Place an instance of the movie clip from the Library onto the Stage (**Figure 9.12**).

2. In the Instance panel, give the movie clip a name.

3. Select the first keyframe of the root Timeline, and open the Actions panel.

4. Choose Actions > set variable.

(continued on next page)

5. In the Variable field, enter a name. In the Value field, enter an Internet address. Leave both Expression boxes unchecked (**Figure 9.13**).

This variable is initialized in the root Timeline and holds a string data type.

6. Enter symbol-editing mode for your movie clip. Select one of the buttons in the expanded pull-down menu.

7. Add to the on (release) event handler by choosing Actions > getURL.

8. In the URL field, enter _root, then a dot, and then the variable name you initialized on the root Timeline. Check the Expression box (**Figure 9.14**).

9. Test your movie.

When you release the button inside your movie clip, Flash retrieves the information stored in the variable on the root Timeline. If you had not specified the root Timeline in the URL field of the getURL action, Flash would look within the movie clip for that variable and would not be able to find it.

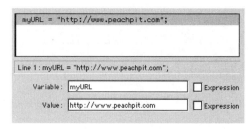

Figure 9.13 Initialize myURL to the Peachpit Press Web site.

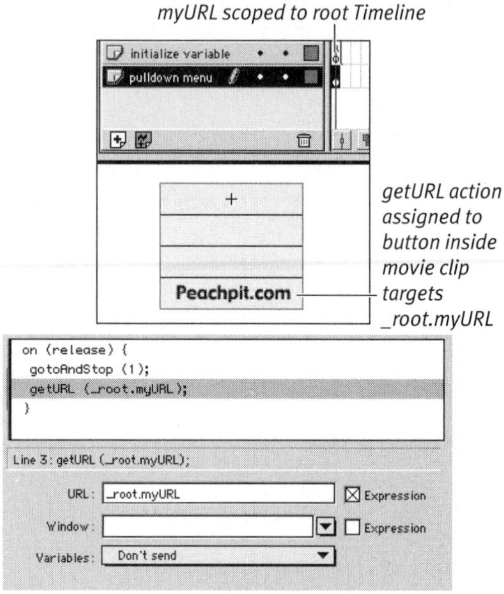

myURL scoped to root Timeline

getURL action assigned to button inside movie clip targets _root.myURL

Figure 9.14 On the last button of the pull-down menu, assign _root.myURL to the URL field. Since this action is inside the movie clip of the pull-down menu, _root is necessary to target the variable myURL on the root Timeline.

Figure 9.15 The target path menu.myURL initializes myURL in the menu movie clip.

myURL scoped to movie clip's Timeline

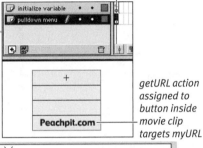

getURL action assigned to button inside movie clip targets myURL

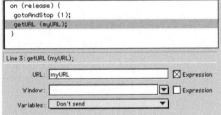

Figure 9.16 The last button in the movie clip of the pull-down menu needs only the variable name myURL, since the variable is scoped to the menu movie clip.

Variables can be initialized to belong to a different Timeline from which they are created. You have the option of setting a variable with a different scope by specifying the target path of the variable in the set variable action.

To set a variable with a different scope:

1. Continuing with the previous task, select the first keyframe of the root Timeline, and open the Actions panel.

2. In the Variable field, replace the contents with the name of the movie-clip instance to which you want the variable scoped, a dot, and then the name of your variable (**Figure 9.15**).

   Your variable is scoped to the movie-clip instance instead of the root Timeline.

3. Enter symbol-editing mode for your movie clip. Select one of the buttons in the expanded pull-down menu.

4. Select the getURL statement.

5. In the URL field, replace the contents with just the variable name you initialized on the root Timeline. Check the Expression box (**Figure 9.16**).

6. Test your movie.

   When you release the button inside your movie clip, Flash retrieves the information stored in the variable in the movie clip. Because the variable was scoped to the movie clip when it was initialized, Flash is able to find it and use its contents as the URL.

Loading External Variables

You don't actually have to initialize variables inside your movie. Flash lets you keep variables outside your Flash movie in a text document you can load whenever you need them. This way, you can easily change the variables in the text document, and thereby change the Flash movie, without even having to edit the movie. For example, build a quiz with variables holding the questions and answers. Keep the variables in a text document, so when you want to change the quiz, simply edit the text document. You can also set up the variables in the text document to be generated automatically with server-side scripts based on other external data. Then your Flash movie can read the variables in the text document with only the most recent or user-customized values. The external text document can contain as many variables as you want, but it needs to be in MIME format, which is a standard format that CGI scripts use. The variables are written in the following form:

```
variable1=value1&variable2=
value2&variable3=value3
```

where the variable/value pairs are separated from one another by a single ampersand symbol.

Variables can be loaded into either a specified level or a specified movie clip. In both cases, you must remember their scope when you want to retrieve their values.

`myRotation=45&mySize=150`

Figure 9.17 Two variables and their values written in MIME format. In this example, these variables are saved in a text document called data.txt.

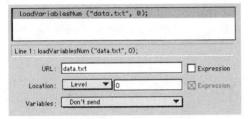

Figure 9.18 The LoadVariablesNum action loads the variables from the data.txt file into Level 0.

To load external variables:

1. Launch a simple text editor, and open a new document. On the Mac, SimpleText is a good application, and on Windows, Notepad works well.

2. Write your variable names and their values in the standard MIME format (**Figure 9.17**).

3. Save your text document in the same directory where your Flash movie will be saved. It doesn't matter what you name your file, but it helps to keep it simple and to stick to a standard 3-letter extension.

4. In Flash, open a new movie. Select the first keyframe of the root Timeline, and open the Actions panel.

5. Choose Actions > loadVariables (Esc + lv).

6. In the URL field, enter the path to your text file. Since your SWF file and the text file will be in the same directory, you can just enter the text file's filename. Leave the Expression box unchecked.

7. In the Location pull-down menu, select Level, and keep the 0 in the field (**Figure 9.18**).

   Flash loads the variables in your text file in Level 0, or the root Timeline.

8. Create a movie-clip symbol, and drag an instance of it on to the Stage.

9. Select the movie clip. In the Actions panel, choose Actions > onClipEvent. Select the Key Down event in the Parameters pane.

10. Choose Actions > setProperty. Select Rotation from the Property pull-down menu.

(continued on next page)

LOADING EXTERNAL VARIABLES

11. In the Target field of the Parameters pane, enter `this`. In the Value field, enter the path to the loaded variable. Since the variables are loaded into Level 0, you need to enter `_root` or `_level0` before the variable name. Check both Expression boxes (**Figure 9.19**).

When you press a key, Flash uses the externally loaded variable as the value of this movie clip's rotation.

12. Add another `setProperty` action in order to use the second externally loaded variable (**Figure 9.20**).

13. Export your movie as a SWF, and save it in the same directory as your text file.

✔ Tips

■ If you want to load external variables into a movie clip, it's a good idea always to use the same movie-clip target. Call it something like loadedVariables and you'll know where to retrieve your variables, since they'll all be scoped to the same place.

■ The variables you specify in an external text file are loaded into Flash as strings, making quotation marks around string values unnecessary.

■ Write your variable and value pairs in an external text file without any line breaks, spaces, or other punctuation except the ampersand sign. Although you may have a harder time reading it, Flash will have an easier time understanding it.

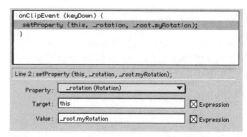

Figure 9.19 The value of myRotation from the text file is used as the rotation of this movie clip.

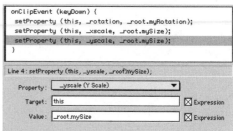

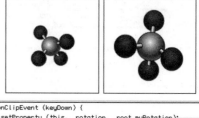

Figure 9.20 Two additional setProperty actions change the scale of the movie clip using the mySize variable from the text file. The movie clip before the Key Down event (top left), and after the Key Down event (top right).

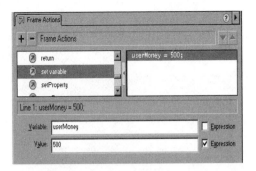

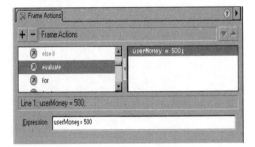

Figure 9.21 The set variable action (top) and the evaluate action (bottom) create equivalent scripts. In the evaluate action, you must enter your own assignment operator.

Table 9.3

Common Operators	
SYMBOL	**DESCRIPTION**
+	Addition
-	Subtraction
*	Multiplication
/	Division
++	Increases the value by one increment. x ++ is equivalent to x = x + 1
--	Decreases the value by one increment. x -- is equivalent to x = x - 1
+=	Adds a value and assigns it to the variable. x += 5 is equivalent to x = x + 5
-=	Subtracts a value and assigns it to the variable. x -= 5 is equivalent to x = x - 5
*=	Multiplies by a value and assigns it to the variable. x *= 5 is equivalent to x = x * 5
/=	Divides by a value and assigns it to the variable. x /= 5 is equivalent to x = x / 5

Modifying Variables

Variables are useful because you can change their contents with updated information about the status of the movie or your viewer. Sometimes this just involves assigning a new value to the variable. Other times, this means adding, subtracting, multiplying, or dividing its numeric values, or changing a Boolean true value to a false value, or modifying a string by adding characters. For example, the variable myScore could be initialized at 0. Then, for every goal a player makes, the myScore variable changes in increments of 1. The job of modifying information contained in variables falls upon operators—symbols that "operate" on data.

Assignment and Arithmetic Operators

The *assignment operator* (=) is a single equal symbol that assigns a value to a variable. You've already been using this operator in the action set variable, which automatically puts the assignment operator between the entries of the Variable field and the Value field. You can also use the evaluate action, which gives you an empty Expression field in the Parameters pane; in that field you enter your variable name, a value, and the assignment operator between the two (**Figure 9.21**). The other common operators appear in **Table 9.3**.

Operators are the workhorses of Flash interactivity. You will use them often to perform calculations behind the scenes, add the value of one variable to another, or change the property of one object by adding or subtracting the value of a variable, for example. The following task is a simple example of how operators can be used to modify a variable that affects the graphics in a movie. You will create a button that increases the value of a variable each time the button is pressed. That variable is used to set the rotation of a movie clip.

To incrementally change a variable affecting a movie-clip property:

1. Create a movie clip, and place an instance of it on the Stage. In the Instance panel, give it a name.

2. In the first keyframe of the root Timeline, initialize a rotation variable to 0.

3. Create a button symbol, and place an instance of it on the Stage.

4. Select the button, and in the Actions panel choose Actions > evaluate. In the Expression field, enter `rotation += 10` (**Figure 9.22**).

    The statement adds 10 to the current value and reassigns the sum to the variable called rotation.

5. Select the movie clip, and in the Actions panel choose Actions > onClipEvent. Select the EnterFrame event in the Parameters pane.

6. Choose Actions > setProperty.

7. From the Property pull-down menu select Rotation. In the Target field, enter `this`. In the Value field, enter `_root.rotation`. Check both Expression boxes (**Figure 9.23**).

    The EnterFrame event makes the `setProperty` action run continuously. This assigns the rotation of the movie clip to the value of the rotation variable, which the user can increase by releasing the button.

8. Place another instance of the button on the Stage. Assign a decrement operator (`--`) to the rotation variable to have it decrease its value each time the button is pressed. This will control the rotation of the movie clip in the opposite direction (**Figure 9.24**).

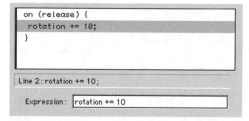

Figure 9.22 Each time the button is released, its actions increase the rotation variable by 10.

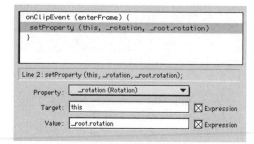

Figure 9.23 The rotation of the current movie clip is continually updated to the value of the rotation variable on the root Timeline.

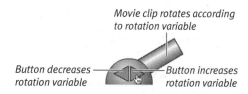

Movie clip rotates according to rotation variable

Button decreases rotation variable — *Button increases rotation variable*

Figure 9.24 The turret of this cannon is the movie clip whose rotation property changes according to the rotation variable.

✔ **Tips**

■ In order to perform more complicated mathematical calculations (such as square root, sine, and cosine) or string manipulations on your variables and values, you must use the Math object or the String object. You'll learn about these objects in Chapters 10 and 11.

■ The same arithmetic rules of associativity (remember them from math class?) apply when Flash evaluates expressions. This means that certain operators take precedence over others. For example, multiplication and division will be performed before addition and subtraction. For example, 3 + 4 * 2 gives a very different result from 3 * 4 + 2.

■ Use parentheses to group variables and operators together so that they are calculated before other parts of the expression are evaluated. For example (3+2)*4 will return a value of 20, but without the parentheses, 3+2*4 will return a value of 11.

Concatenating Variables and the Eval Function

The addition operator (+) adds the values of numeric data types. But it can also be used to put together strings and variables holding string data types. This is called *concatenation*. Concatenation of variables and strings lets you create target paths and complicated expressions. For example, a common practice for naming duplicate movie-clip instances is to concatenate a variable with the name of the original movie clip. The variable is simply a counter that increases by one each time a duplicate is made. If the movie clip name is mushroom and the variable name is counter, then you can concatenate a new name with the following expression:

```
"mushroom" + counter
```

and the result will be something like mushroom1 or mushroom2.

To concatenate a string and a variable:

1. Create a movie-clip symbol, and place an instance of it on the Stage. In the Instance panel, give it a name.

2. Create a button symbol, and place an instance of it on the Stage.

3. In the first keyframe of the root Timeline, use the set variable action to initialize a variable to 1.

4. Select the button, open the Actions panel, and choose Actions > duplicateMovieClip.

5. In the Target field, enter the name of the movie clip. Leave the Expression box unchecked. In the New Name field, enter the name of your movie clip in quotes, then a + symbol, then the name of your variable. Check the Expression box. In the Depth field, enter the name of your variable (**Figure 9.25**).

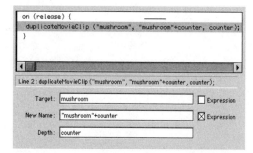

Figure 9.25 The mushroom movie clip is duplicated each time the button is released. Its new name and depth depend on the value of the variable counter.

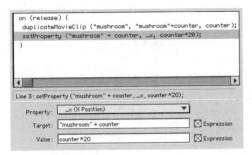

```
on (release) {
  duplicateMovieClip ("mushroom", "mushroom"+counter, counter);
  setProperty ("mushroom" + counter, _x, counter*20);
}
```

Line 3: setProperty ("mushroom" + counter, _x, counter*20);

Property: _x (X Position)
Target: "mushroom" + counter   ☒ Expression
Value: counter*20   ☒ Expression

Figure 9.26 The mushroom duplicate moves to a different position.

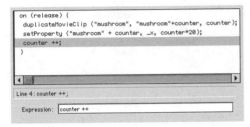

```
on (release) {
  duplicateMovieClip ("mushroom", "mushroom"+counter, counter);
  setProperty ("mushroom" + counter, _x, counter*20);
  counter ++;
}
```

Line 4: counter ++;

Expression: counter ++

Figure 9.27 The counter variable increases by one.

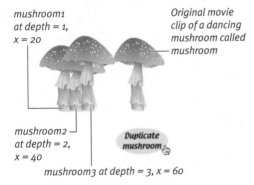

mushroom1
at depth = 1,
x = 20

Original movie
clip of a dancing
mushroom called
mushroom

mushroom2
at depth = 2,
x = 40

Duplicate
mushroom

mushroom3 at depth = 3, x = 60

Figure 9.28 Duplicate dancing mushrooms have names resulting from concatenating the string "mushroom" with the counter variable.

A duplicate movie clip is created with the value of the variable concatenated to the name of the movie clip. The duplicate is put in a depth level that corresponds to the value of the variable.

6. Choose Actions > setProperty. From the Property pull-down menu, select X Position.

7. In the Target field, enter the name of your movie clip in quotes, then a + symbol, and then the name of your variable. Check the Expression box. In the Value field, enter the name of your variable, then the * symbol, and then 20. Check the Expression box (**Figure 9.26**).

The setProperty action puts the duplicate movie clip at a new *x* position based on the value of the variable. This allows you to see the duplicate.

7. Choose Actions > evaluate. In the Expression field, enter the name of your variable, then ++ (**Figure 9.27**).

Each time you release the button and create a duplicate, your variable increases by an increment of one. Hence, new duplicates always have unique names based on the concatenation of the movie-clip string and the variable, as well as unique depth levels and *x* positions (**Figure 9.28**).

CONCATENATING VARIABLES & EVAL FUNCTION

259

Once you've created new variables or new objects by concatenation, you can use them in other expressions. However, in order to evaluate the contents of those expressions, you need to use the **eval** function. The **eval** function reads an expression and returns the value as a single string. For example, let's say you wanted to retrieve the alpha transparency of your duplicated mushroom2 movie clip. You might try to use the following expression:

```
"mushroom" + counter + "._alpha"
```

but Flash reads that expression as a literal string and won't recognize the _alpha as the property of mushroom2. The trick is to group the first part of the expression with **eval**, and then append the property, as in the following:

```
eval ("mushroom" + counter)._alpha
```

You can use the **eval** function wherever you might use concatenated expressions, such as in target paths or in the arguments of methods.

To use eval in a target path:

1. Continue with the previous task. Select the button, and open the Actions panel.

2. Add a statement before the variable increment by first choosing Actions > evaluate.

3. In the Expression field of the Actions panel, choose Functions > eval.

    The **eval** statement appears with the variable argument highlighted.

4. Replace the variable argument with the name of your movie clip in quotes, then a + symbol, and then the variable name.

5. After the **eval** statement, add a dot, then a method that you wish to call (**Figure 9.29**).

    The **eval** statement evaluates the concatenation, then applies the method to that target (**Figure 9.30**).

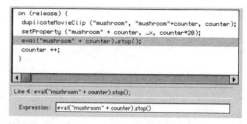

Figure 9.29 The `stop` method applies to each new mushroom duplicate.

mushroom1 stopped at Frame 1

Original dancing mushroom movie clip called mushroom

mushroom2 stopped at Frame 1

Duplicate mushroom

mushroom3 stopped at Frame 1

Figure 9.30 Each new mushroom duplicate is stopped.

Testing Information with Conditional Statements

Variables and expressions go hand in hand with conditional statements. The information you retrieve, store in variables, and modify in expressions will only be useful to you when you can compare it with other pieces of information. Conditional statements let you do this kind of comparison and carry out instructions based on the results. The logic of conditional statements is like the sentence "If *abc* is true, then do *xyz*," and in Flash you define *abc* (the condition) and *xyz* (the consequence). Conditional statements are similar to event handlers in that they both respond to particular situations. In the case of event handlers, the situation is usually a movement of the mouse or a button click. In conditional statements, the situation is the current status of a variable or of a property of an object.

Conditional statements begin with the statement if (). The argument that goes between the parentheses is the *condition*—an expression that compares one thing with another. Is the variable myScore greater than the variable alltimeHighScore? Is the _droptarget property for my draggable movie clip unequal to the target path for the garbageCan movie clip? Does the _currentFrame property of the root Timeline equal 10? These are all typical examples of conditions. How do you construct these conditions? You use comparison operators within expressions.

Comparison Operators

A comparison operator evaluates the expressions on both sides of the symbol and returns a value of true or false. The comparison operators are summarized in **Table 9.4**.

When the condition is evaluated and the condition holds true, then Flash performs the consequences within the if statement curly braces (**Figure 9.31**). If the condition turns out to be false, then all of the actions within the curly braces are ignored.

In the following task, you will use the same file that you created to rotate a cannon turret in the "Modifying Variables" section. We want to constrain the rotation of the turret to a maximum of 90 degrees, so you will construct a conditional statement to have Flash test whether the value of its rotation is greater than 90. If it is, you will keep its rotation at 90, preventing the turret from rotating past the horizontal plane.

To create a conditional statement:

1. Continue with the task demonstrating the rotation of a movie clip in the "Modifying Variables" section above. Select the button, and open the Actions panel.

2. After the variable incrementally increases by 10, add a conditional statement by choosing Actions > if (Esc + if).

3. In the Condition field of the Actions panel, enter the variable name, then the > symbol, and then 90 (**Figure 9.32**). Flash tests to see if the variable is greater than 90.

Table 9.4

Comparison Operators	
SYMBOL	**DESCRIPTION**
==	Equal to
<	Less than
>	Greater than
<=	Less than or equal to
>=	Greater than or equal to
!=	Not equal to

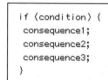

Figure 9.31 If and only if the condition within the parentheses is true, then consequence1, consequence2, and consequence3 are all performed.

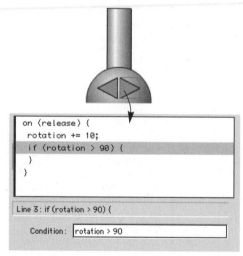

Figure 9.32 Add a condition to the actions assigned to the right button that tests the rotation variable.

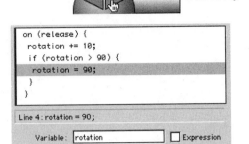

Movie-clip rotation at 90

```
on (release) {
  rotation += 10;
  if (rotation > 90) {
    rotation = 90;
  }
}
```

Line 4 : rotation = 90;

Variable: rotation   ☐ Expression

Value: 90   ☒ Expression

Figure 9.33 The cannon turret can't rotate past 90 degrees because the `if` statement won't allow the variable rotation to increase beyond 90.

4. Choose Actions > set variable. In the Variable field, enter your variable name. In the Value field, enter 90. Check the Expression box (**Figure 9.33**).

When the variable exceeds 90, Flash resets the variable to 90. This prevents the cannon turret from rotating past the horizontal plane.

5. Choose the other button that decreases the rotation variable and create a similar conditional statement to test if the variable is less than −90. If the condition is true, set the variable to −90.

✔ Tip

■ Any action residing outside of the `if` statement will be performed regardless of whether the condition in the `if` statement is true or false. Consider the following script, for example:

```
If (myVariable == 10) {
    myVariable = 20;
    }
myVariable = 30;
```

After Flash runs this statement, `myVariable` will always be set to 30, even if the condition `myVariable == 10` is true. The last statement is executed no matter what.

Providing Alternatives to Conditions

In many cases you'll need to provide an alternative response to the conditional statement. The else statement lets you create consequences when the condition in the if statement is false. The else statement was discussed in Chapter 7 as the way to detect dropped movie clips. In that example, the if statement tested whether a movie clip was dropped on another movie clip; when true, the dropped movie clip disappeared, and when false, the else statement made the dropped movie clip bounce back to its original position. The else statement takes care of any condition that the if statement doesn't cover.

The else statement has to be used in conjunction with the if statement and follows the following syntax:

```
If (condition) {

        consequence1;

} else {

        consequence2;

}
```

Use else for either-or conditions—something that can be just one of two options—for example, collision detection, true/false or right/wrong answer checking, or password verification.

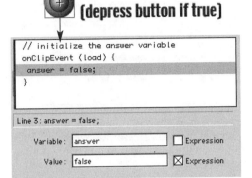

```
// initialize the answer variable
onClipEvent (load) {
  answer = false;
}
```

Line 3: answer = false;	
Variable: answer	☐ Expression
Value: false	☒ Expression

Figure 9.34 The radio-button movie clip initializes the answer variable to the Boolean value false.

```
Scene 1    radiobutton
                        👁 🔒 ☐  1    5    10
  actions       • • ■
  labels        • • ■      ▸ off   ▸ on
  button        / • • ■
  graphics      • 🔒 ☐
```

```
on (release) {
  gotoAndStop ("on");
  answer = true;
}
```

Line 3: answer = true;	
Variable: answer	☐ Expression
Value: true	☒ Expression

Figure 9.35 The button in the off state changes the answer variable to true.

To use else for the false condition:

1. Create a radio-button movie clip as demonstrated in Chapter 5. The movie clip should have buttons that toggle between an on and an off state. Place an instance of the movie clip on the Stage. In the Instance panel, give it a name.

2. Select the movie clip, and open the Actions panel.

3. Choose Actions > onClipEvent. Keep the Load event.

4. Choose Actions > set variable. In the Variable field, enter a variable name. In the Value field, enter false. Check the Expression box next to the Value field (**Figure 9.34**).

   When this movie clip loads, the variable is initialized to false. Note that the Value field is an expression, so false is considered a Boolean data type and not a string data type.

5. Enter symbol-editing mode for the radio-button movie clip.

6. Select the button in the off state that sends the playhead to the on state. Add another statement under the gotoAndStop action by choosing Actions > set variable. In the Variable field enter the name of your variable you initialized in the clip event handler. In the Value field, enter true. Check the Expression box next to the Value field (**Figure 9.35**).

   When you depress the radio button, your variable is set to true.

(continued on next page)

PROVIDING ALTERNATIVES TO CONDITIONS

7. Select the button in the on state that sends the playhead to the off state. Add another statement under the gotoAndStop action by choosing Actions > set variable. In the Variable field enter the name of your variable you initialized in the clip event handler. In the Value field, enter false. Check the Expression box next to the Value field (**Figure 9.36**). Pressing the radio button again to turn it off sets your variable to false.

8. Create a button symbol, and place an instance of it on the Stage.

9. Select the button, and in the Actions panel choose Actions > if.

10. In the Condition field, enter the target path and variable name, and test if the variable is true.

   Remember that your variable is scoped to the movie clip, and not to the root Timeline.

11. Choose an action as a response to the true condition (**Figure 9.37**).

12. Choose Actions > else (Esc + el).

13. Choose another action as a response to the false condition (**Figure 9.38**).

✔ Tip

■ Don't confuse the true or false condition with the true or false value of a Boolean variable. In this example, when the variable is true, the condition is true. However, it's possible to have the opposite scenario, where the condition is true when the variable is false.

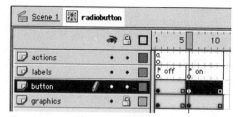

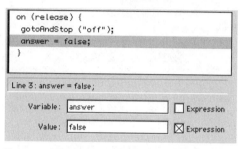

Figure 9.36 The button in the on state changes the answer variable to false.

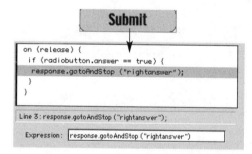

Figure 9.37 The button tests the answer variable, which is scoped to the radio button movie clip. If the condition is true, another movie clip, called response, goes to another frame to display a message.

```
on (release) {
  if (radiobutton.answer == true) {
    response.gotoAndStop ("rightanswer");
  } else {
    response.gotoAndStop ("wronganswer");
  }
}
```
Line 5: response.gotoAndStop ("wronganswer");
Expression: response.gotoAndStop ("wronganswer")

Figure 9.38 The else statement makes the response movie clip go to a different frame when the answer variable is false.

Branching Conditional Statements

If you have multiple possible conditions and just as many consequences, then you need to use more complicated branching conditional statements that a single `else` statement can't provide. For example, if you create an interface to a Web site or a game that requires keyboard input, you would want to test which keys are pressed and respond appropriately to each of them. Flash gives you the `else if` statement, lets you construct multiple conditions and responses in the following syntax:

```
If (condition1) {

        consequence1;

} else if (condition2) {

        consequence2;

} else if (condition3) {

        consequence3;

}
```

Each `else if` statement has its own condition that it evaluates, and its own set of consequences to perform if that condition returns true. The following example uses the Key object and branching conditional statements to move and rotate a movie clip according to different key presses.

To use else if for branching alternatives:

1. Create a movie-clip symbol, and place an instance of it on the Stage. In the Instance panel, give it a name.

2. Select the movie clip, and open the Actions panel.

3. Choose Actions > onClipEvent. Select the EnterFrame event.

4. Choose Actions > if. In the Condition field, enter `Key.isDown(Key.UP)`.

   The first condition uses the `isDown` method of the Key object to test whether the up-arrow key is depressed.

5. Choose Actions > setProperty. From the Property pull-down menu, select Rotation. In the Target field, enter `this`. In the Value field, enter 0. Check both Expression boxes.

6. Again, choose Actions > setProperty. From the Property pull-down menu, select Y Position. In the Target field, enter `this`.
   In the Value field, enter `this._y - 30`.

   The two `setProperty` actions rotate the movie clip so that the head faces the top, and subtract 30 pixels from its *y* position, making it move up the Stage. Check both Expression boxes (**Figure 9.39**).

7. Choose Actions > else if (Esc + ei). In the Condition field, enter `Key.isDown(Key.RIGHT)`.

8. Choose two `setProperty` actions to set the rotation of the movie clip to 90 and add 30 pixels to its *x* position.

9. Choose Actions > else if. In the Condition field, enter `Key.isDown(Key.DOWN)`.

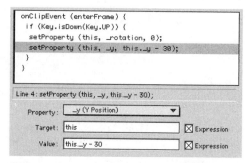

Figure 9.39 If the up-arrow key is depressed, this movie clip is rotated to 0 degrees and is repositioned 30 pixels up the Stage.

```
onClipEvent (enterFrame) {
 if (Key.isDown(Key.UP)) {
  setProperty (this, _rotation, 0);
  setProperty (this, _y, this._y - 30);
 } else if (Key.isDown(Key.RIGHT)) {
  setProperty (this, _rotation, 90);
  setProperty (this, _x, this._x + 30);
 } else if (Key.isDown(Key.DOWN)) {
  setProperty (this, _rotation, 180);
  setProperty (this, _y, this._y + 30);
 } else if (Key.isDown(Key.LEFT)) {
  setProperty (this, _rotation, -90);
  setProperty (this, _x, this._x -30);
 }
}
```

Figure 9.40 The complete script (bottom) has four conditions using if and else if to test whether the up-, left-, right-, or down-arrow key is depressed. The rotation and position of the movie clip (this beetle, top) change depending on which condition holds true.

10. Choose two setProperty actions to set the rotation of the movie clip to 180 and add 30 pixels to its y position.

11. Choose Actions > else if. In the Condition field, enter Key.isDown(Key.LEFT).

12. Choose two setProperty actions to set the rotation of the movie clip to 270 and subtract 30 pixels from its x position.

13. Test your movie.

Your series of if and else if statements tests whether or not the user presses the arrow keys, and moves the movie clip accordingly (**Figure 9.40**). Now you have the beginnings of a game of Frogger!

✔ **Tip**

■ The conditions for this task did not include an equality comparison operator (==). For Boolean data types and methods that return Boolean values, you don't need to explicitly compare them to the value true. So, the following two conditions are equivalent:

if (Key.isDown(Key.LEFT))

if (Key.isDown(Key.LEFT)==true)

Combining Conditions with Logical Operators

You can create compound conditions with the logical operators && (AND), || (OR), and ! (NOT). The operators combine two or more conditions in one `if` statement to test for more complicated scenarios. For example, you could test whether the up-arrow key and the right-arrow key are pressed together to make a movie clip move diagonally. Or you could test whether a draggable movie clip is dropped on one target or another valid target. You could use the NOT operator to test whether a variable contains a valid e-mail address, but one whose domain is not restricted.

The following task uses the same file that you created previously to move a movie clip from the keyboard. You will combine conditions to have Flash test for combination key strokes to move the movie clip diagonally.

To combine conditions:

1. Continue with the previous task. Select the movie-clip symbol, and open the Actions panel.

2. Select the first `if` statement.

3. In the Condition field, place your pointer at the end of the existing condition.

4. Choose Operators > &&.

5. Enter your second condition after the two ampersands (**Figure 9.41**).

   Both conditions appear in the Condition field separated by the && operator.

6. Change the `setProperty` actions to rotate and move the movie clip diagonally (**Figure 9.42**).

Condition: `Key.isDown(Key.UP) && Key.isDown(Key.RIGHT)`

Figure 9.41 The logical && operator joins these two expressions so that both the up- and right-arrow keys must be depressed in order for the whole condition to be true.

```
if (Key.isDown(Key.UP) && Key.isDown(Key.RIGHT)) {
    setProperty (this, _rotation, 45);
    setProperty (this, _y, this._y - 15);
    setProperty (this, _x, this._x + 15);
```

Figure 9.42 The first portion of the script shows that when both up- and right-arrow keys are depressed, the beetle rotates 45 degrees and moves diagonally to the upper right.

```
onClipEvent (enterFrame) {
    if (Key.isDown(Key.UP) && Key.isDown(Key.RIGHT)) {
        setProperty (this, _rotation, 45);
        setProperty (this, _y, this._y - 15);
        setProperty (this, _x, this._x + 15);
    } else if (Key.isDown(Key.RIGHT) && Key.isDown(Key.DOWN)) {
        setProperty (this, _rotation, 135);
        setProperty (this, _y, this._y + 15);
        setProperty (this, _x, this._x + 15);
    } else if (Key.isDown(Key.DOWN) && Key.isDown(Key.LEFT)) {
        setProperty (this, _rotation, -135);
        setProperty (this, _y, this._y + 15);
        setProperty (this, _x, this._x - 15);
    } else if (Key.isDown(Key.LEFT) && Key.isDown(Key.UP)) {
        setProperty (this, _rotation, -45);
        setProperty (this, _y, this._y - 15);
        setProperty (this, _x, this._x - 15);
    } else if (Key.isDown(Key.UP)) {
        setProperty (this, _rotation, 0);
        setProperty (this, _y, this._y - 30);
    } else if (Key.isDown(Key.RIGHT)) {
        setProperty (this, _rotation, 90);
        setProperty (this, _x, this._x + 30);
    } else if (Key.isDown(Key.DOWN)) {
        setProperty (this, _rotation, 180);
        setProperty (this, _y, this._y + 30);
    } else if (Key.isDown(Key.LEFT)) {
        setProperty (this, _rotation, -90);
        setProperty (this, _x, this._x -30);
    }
}
```

Figure 9.43 The complete script contains combined conditions for two key presses as well as conditions for a single key press.

7. Continue to add else if statements with combined conditions for the other three diagonal key presses while still keeping the four conditions for the cardinal directions (**Figure 9.43**).

Using the && logical operator to combine two conditions, Flash checks whether the user presses two key combinations.

✔ Tip

■ You can nest if statements within other if statements, which is equivalent to using the logical && operator in a single if statement. For example, these two scripts test whether both conditions are true before setting a new variable:

```
If (yourAge >= 12) {
  If (yourAge <=20) {
      status = "teenager";
  }
}


If (yourAge >= 12 && yourAge <=20) {
      status = "teenager";
}
```

Looping Statements

With looping statements, you can create an action or set of actions that repeat a certain number of times or while a certain condition holds true. Repeating actions are often used to build arrays, which are special kinds of variables that hold data in a structured, easily accessible way. The looping action makes sure that each piece of data is put into a particular order or retrieved in a particular order. You'll learn more about arrays in Chapter 11. In general, use looping statements to automatically execute actions a specific number of times using an incremental variable. That incremental variable modifies the arguments of each successive method in the loop, or modifies certain properties of objects that are created. For example, you can generate graphics dynamically entirely with ActionScript by duplicating movie clips using looping statements and the `duplicateMovieClip` action. Use looping statements to change the properties of a whole series of movie clips, modify multiple sound settings, or alter the values of a set of variables.

There are three kinds of looping statements—the `while`, `do while`, and `for` actions—but they all accomplish the same type of task. The first two perform loops while a certain condition holds true. The third statement performs loops using a built-in counter.

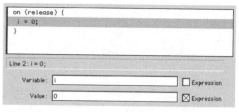

Figure 9.44 Initialize the variable i within the `on (release)` handler.

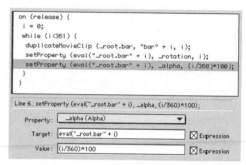

Figure 9.45 The bar movie clip is duplicated, rotated, and changed in transparency as long as the variable i is less than 361.

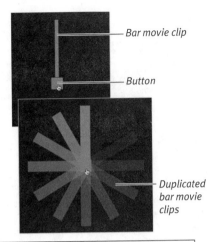

— *Bar movie clip*

— *Button*

— *Duplicated bar movie clips*

```
on (release) {
  i = 0;
  while (i<361) {
    duplicateMovieClip (_root.bar, "bar"+i, i);
    setProperty (eval("_root.bar"+i), _rotation, i);
    setProperty (eval("_root.bar"+i), _alpha, (i/360)*100);
    i += 30;
  }
  bar._visible = 0;
}
```

Figure 9.46 The bar movie clip (top) is the basis for the pattern (middle) made with a looping statement (bottom).

To use the while statement to duplicate movie clips:

1. Create a movie-clip symbol, and place an instance of it on the Stage. In the Instance panel, give it a name.

2. Create a button symbol, and place an instance of it on the Stage.

3. Select the button, and open the Actions panel. Choose Actions > set variable. In the Variable field, enter i. In the Value field, enter 0. Check the Expression box next to the Value field (**Figure 9.44**). The variable i or j is often used as a loop counter.

4. Choose Actions > while (Esc + wh). In the Condition field, enter i < 361.

5. Assign any actions that you want to run while the condition still remains true (i is less than 361). In this example, add a duplicateMovieClip statement and two setProperty statements that rotate and modify the transparency of the duplicates (**Figure 9.45**).

6. Choose Actions > evaluate. In the Expression field, enter i += 30. Or use setVariable to enter the equivalent statement, i = i + 30.

   Each time the loop runs, the variable i increases by an increment of 30. When it exceeds 361, the condition that the while statement checks at each pass becomes false. Flash ends the loop and proceeds with the next statement (**Figure 9.46**).

LOOPING STATEMENTS

The Do While Statement

The do while (Esc + do) statement is similar to the while statement except that the condition is checked at the end of the loop rather than the beginning. This means that the actions in the loop are executed at least once. The same script in the previous task could be written with the do while statement, as shown in **Figure 9.47**.

```
on (release) {
    // initialize variable at 0
    i = 0;
    do {
        // make copies of the movie clip
        duplicateMovieClip (_root.bar, "bar" + i, i);
        // rotate the copies i degrees
        setProperty (eval("_root.bar" + i), _rotation, i);
        // make the copies gradually opaque
        setProperty (eval("_root.bar" + i), _alpha, (i/360)*100);
        // increment the counter by 30
        i = i+30;
        // check the condition
    } while (i<361);
    // make the original movie clip invisible
    bar._visible = 0;
}
```

Figure 9.47 The equivalent do while statement.

The For Statement

The for (Esc + fr) statement provides a built-in counter and parameters for increments or decrements to the counter so you don't have to write separate statements. The parameter fields for the for statement are: Init, which initializes the counter variable; Condition, which is the expression that is tested; and Next, which determines the amount of increment or decrement of the counter variable. The previous task could be written with the for statement, as shown in **Figure 9.48**.

```
on (release) {
    for (i=0; i<361; i+=30) {
        duplicateMovieClip (_root.bar, "bar" + i, i);
        setProperty (eval("_root.bar" + i), _rotation, i);
        setProperty (eval("_root.bar" + i), _alpha, (i/360)*100);
    }
    bar._visible = 0;
}
```

Figure 9.48 The equivalent for statement.

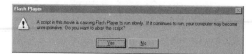

Figure 9.49 This warning dialog box appears when you inadvertently run an infinite loop.

✔ Tips

- Do not use looping statements to build continuous routines to check a certain condition. Real-time testing should be done with the if statement in an EnterFrame or a Mouse move clip event. When Flash executes looping statements, the display remains frozen, and no mouse or keyboard events can be detected.

- Make sure that the increments to your variables are inside the curly braces of the while or do while statements. If they aren't, the condition will never be met, and Flash will be stuck executing the loop infinitely. Fortunately, Flash warns you of this problem when an infinite loop slows the computer processor down (**Figure 9.49**).

CONTROLLING TEXT

Of course you know that Flash lets you create visually engaging text elements, such as titles, labels, and descriptions, to accompany your graphics, animation, and sound. But did you know that you can do more with text than just set the style, color, and size? Flash text can be live, meaning your viewers can enter text into the Flash movie as it plays, as well as select and edit the text. And Flash text can be dynamic, so it can update during playback. The text that viewers can enter is called *input text*, and the text that you can update during playback is called *dynamic text*. Input and dynamic text provide a way to receive complex information from the viewer and tailor your Flash movie using that information. For example, you can use input text to let your viewers enter their names, and then use that information to personalize the messages that appear throughout the movie. Or you can develop online tutorials using input text for short-answer responses and dynamic text for customized feedback.

Using the Text Options panel, you define input text boxes, in which your viewers enter text, and dynamic text boxes that display text that changes based on criteria you specify. You assign a variable to input text so that you can store and modify the information your viewers enter, and test it with conditional statements. This text can then be used in other ActionScripts. Two objects that control the information within input and dynamic text—the Selection object and the String object—let you analyze and manipulate the text or the placement of the cursor within the text. For example, you can catch misspellings or incorrectly entered information before using it in your Flash movie or passing it on to an outside application for processing. This chapter explores some of the many possibilities of input and dynamic text and introduces you to the tools you can use to control the information exchange between your Flash movie and your audience.

Input Text

You can build your Flash project to gather information directly from the viewer—information such as a log-in name and password, personal information for a survey, answers to quiz questions, requests for an online purchase, or responses in an Internet chat room. You assign these user inputs, which Flash calls *input text,* to a variable so that they can then be passed along to other parts of the Flash movie for further processing, or sent to a server-side application through the CGI GET or POST method.

The following task demonstrates how you can use input text to let your user control the parameters of an action. In this case, you will accept information from the viewer in an input text box and use that information to load a URL.

To use input text to request a URL:

1. Choose the text tool from the Tools window, and drag out a text box onto the Stage (**Figure 10.1**).

2. In the Text Options panel, select Input Text from the top pull-down menu (**Figure 10.2**).

   Your currently selected text box becomes input text, allowing text entry during playback.

3. In the Variable field of the Text Options panel, enter the name of your variable.

   Any text entered into the input text during playback is assigned and stored in this variable.

4. Check the Border/Bg box.

   Your text box is drawn with a black border and a white background (**Figure 10.3**).

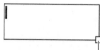

Figure 10.1 A text box is created with the text tool. You can resize the text box with the handle at the bottom-right corner.

Text-box handle ─

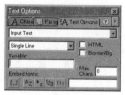

Figure 10.2 This Text Options panel defines a text box as an input text box.

Figure 10.3 The text box without a border or background (left) shows up on your Stage in authoring mode with a dotted border. The text box with a border and background (right) has a solid black border and a white background.

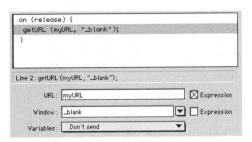

```
on (release) {
  getURL (myURL, "_blank");
}
```

Line 2: getURL (myURL, "_blank");

URL : myURL   ☒ Expression
Window : _blank   ▼   ☐ Expression
Variables : Don't send   ▼

Figure 10.4 The actions assigned to your button load the URL with the variable myURL in a new browser window.

Figure 10.5 The variable in the input text box is used as the URL for the getURL action. Note that the protocol "http://" must be included in the input text.

5. Create a button symbol, and place an instance of the button on the Stage under the text box. Select the button, and open the Actions panel.

6. Choose Actions > on. In the Parameters pane, select the Release event.

7. Choose Actions > getURL. In the URL field of the Parameters pane, enter your input text box variable name. Check the Expression box next to the URL field. In the Window field, choose _blank (**Figure 10.4**).

8. Test your movie.

When your viewer enters a URL in the text box, the address is stored in the variable. Then, when the viewer presses the button, Flash opens a new browser window and loads the specified Web site (**Figure 10.5**).

✔ Tips

■ The options you select in the Character and Paragraph panels, such as font, color, and alignment, will apply to the text that is input by the viewer.

■ You can put text in an input text box to instruct viewers on what to enter. For example, put Enter Web site address here in your text box so that viewers know to replace that phrase with their Web site address. Or, you could start them off by putting http:// in the text box so that it's there already.

Selecting Input Text Options

There are many different options in the Text Options panel for Input Text (**Figure 10.6**). Although the most important field to fill in is the Variable field, the others let you modify the way viewers enter text.

◆ **Single Line** forces entered text to stay on one row in the text box. If text goes beyond the limits of the text box, the text begins to scroll horizontally.

◆ **Multiline** allows entered text to appear on more than one row in the text box if the viewer presses the Return key for a carriage return.

◆ **Password** disguises the letters entered in the text box with asterisks. Use this option to hide sensitive information such as a password from people looking over your viewer's shoulder.

◆ **HTML** allows text formatted with HTML 1.0 tags to be displayed correctly.

◆ **Border/Bg** draws a black border and white background on your text box. Uncheck this option to leave the text box invisible, but be sure to draw your own background or border so viewers can find your text box on the Stage.

◆ **Word wrap**, which appears only for the Multiline selection, automatically puts line breaks in text that goes beyond the text box.

◆ **Max. Chars** puts a limit on the amount of text your viewer can enter. For example, if you want the viewer to enter his or her home state using only the two-digit abbreviation, enter 2 in this field.

◆ **Embed fonts** includes font outlines with your exported SWF, so your text box displays antialiased type in the font of your choice, rather than in whatever is available on the viewer's computer. Keep in mind that this increases your file size.

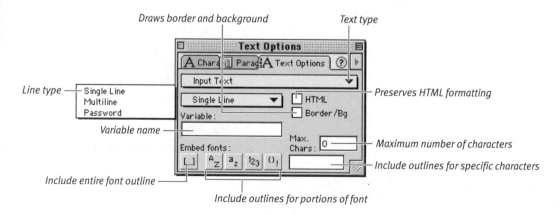

Figure 10.6 The options in the Text Options panel define your text-box properties.

More on Embedding Fonts and Device Fonts

Embedding font outlines ensures that the font you use in the authoring environment is the same one your viewer sees during playback. This is done by default for static text, but you must choose the option when you create input text or a dynamic text. When you don't embed fonts in your movie, Flash uses the closest font available on your viewer's computer and displays it as aliased text (**Figure 10.7**).

Why wouldn't you choose to embed font outlines all the time? Embedding fonts dramatically increases the file size of your exported SWF because the information to render that font is included. However, you can keep the file size down by embedding only the characters that your viewers will use in the input text field. For example, if you ask them to enter numeric information, you can embed just the numbers of the font outline. All the numbers would be available during movie playback, while the other characters would be disabled and not display at all.

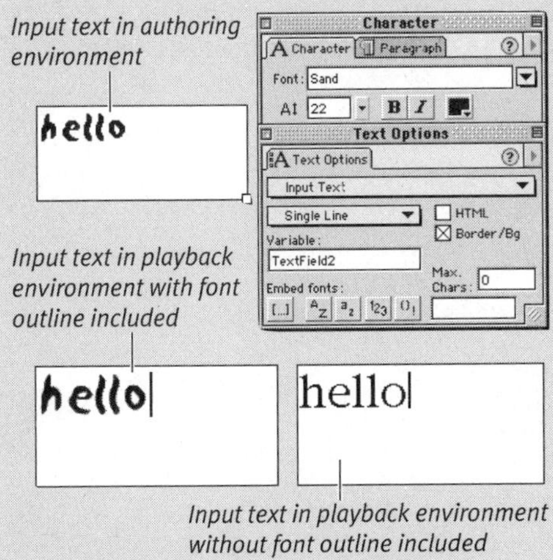

Another way to maintain small file sizes and eliminate the problem caused by your viewer not having the matching font is to use device fonts. Device fonts appear at the end of your font-style pull-down menu. The three device fonts are _sans, _serif, and _typewriter. This option finds the fonts on a viewer's system that most closely resemble the specified device font. The following are the corresponding fonts for the device fonts:

On the Mac:

◆ _sans maps to Helvetica

◆ _serif maps to Times

◆ _typewriter maps to Courier

On Windows,

◆ _sans maps to Arial

◆ _serif maps to Times New Roman

◆ _typewriter maps to Courier New

When you use device fonts, you can be assured that your viewer sees text that is very similar to the text in the authoring environment. However, two warnings about device fonts: They do not display antialiased, and they cannot be tweened or masked.

Input text in authoring environment

Input text in playback environment with font outline included

Input text in playback environment without font outline included

Figure 10.7 Input text using a font in authoring mode (top) displays differently during playback on a viewer's computer that doesn't have the font depending on whether the font outlines are included (bottom).

Dynamic Text

For text that you control, such as scores for an arcade game, results of a calculation, or the actual percentage of frames in your Flash movie that have been downloaded over the Web, take advantage of Flash's Dynamic Text option. Whereas input text boxes accept information from the viewer, dynamic text boxes output information to the viewer. As with input text, a variable is assigned to dynamic text, and the contents of this variable are displayed in the text box. In addition, the options for dynamic text are similar to input text except for one addition, the Selectable checkbox. Checking this option makes it possible for the viewer to select and copy text in the dynamic text box but not change it.

In the following task, you will create an input text box and a dynamic text box. When viewers enter the temperature in Celsius in the input text box, Flash will convert the value into Fahrenheit and display it in the dynamic text box.

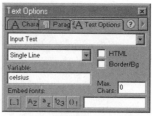

Figure 10.8
Name your input text box celsius.

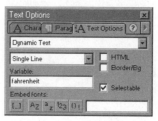

Figure 10.9
Name your dynamic text box fahrenheit.

To use dynamic text to output expressions:

1. Choose your text tool from the Tools window, and drag out a text box onto the Stage.

2. In the Text Options panel, select Input Text from the first pull-down menu. In the Variable field, enter the name of the input text variable (**Figure 10.8**).

   Your currently selected text box becomes input text, allowing text entry during playback.

3. Again choose your text tool from the Tools window, and drag out another text box onto the Stage.

4. In the Text Options panel, this time select Dynamic Text from the first pull-down menu.

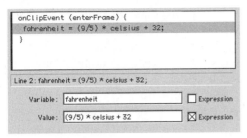

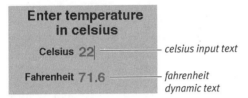

Figure 10.10 This statement calculates the value of fahrenheit from the expression in the Value field.

Enter temperature in celsius

Celsius 22| ——————— *celsius input text*

Fahrenheit 71.6 ——————— *fahrenheit dynamic text*

Figure 10.11 The dynamic text (fahrenheit) updates when new input text (celsius) is entered.

✔ Tips

■ In this task, the dynamic text variable is updated constantly because it is inside the `onClipEvent (enterFrame)` event handler. Instead, you can assign the `set variable` action on a mouse event handler so that the dynamic text is only updated when the user clicks a button.

■ Use dynamic text to show the contents of variables as a debugging tool. If you are developing a complicated Flash movie involving multiple variables, you can create a dynamic text box to display their current values so that you know how Flash is processing the information. In Chapter 12 you'll learn other ways to track variables, but this way you can actually integrate the display of variables in your movie.

Your currently selected text box becomes dynamic text, allowing you to display and update text in that field.

5. In the Variable field of the Text Options panel, enter the name of the variable for the dynamic text (**Figure 10.9**).

6. Select both text boxes, and choose Insert > Convert to Symbol from the top menu. Enter a name for your symbol, and choose Movie Clip Behavior. Click OK.

Flash puts both text boxes into a movie-clip symbol, and an instance of the movie clip remains on Stage.

7. Select the newly converted movie-clip instance that contains your input text box and dynamic text box, and open the Actions panel.

8. Choose Actions > onClipEvent. In the Parameters pane, select the EnterFrame event.

9. Choose Actions > set variable. In the Variable field, enter the name of your dynamic text variable. In the Value field, enter a formula that incorporates the input text variable. Check the Expression box next to the Value field (**Figure 10.10**).

10. Test your movie.

Flash displays the value of the dynamic text variable based on the information that the viewer enters in the input text box (**Figure 10.11**). The calculation is done in real time, and the display is updated anytime the input text changes.

Concatenating Text

Using dynamic text to concatenate, or connect, input text with other variables and strings lets you work with expressions in more flexible ways and can also create more personalized Flash interactions with your viewers. For example, you can have them first enter their names in an input text box called yourName. In a dynamic text box, you can set its variable to

```
"Hello, "+yourName+", welcome to Flash!"
```

and your viewers will see their own names concatenated with your message.

In an earlier task in this chapter, you created a Flash movie that loaded a URL based on input text. By concatenating the input text variable called myURL in the expression

```
"http://"+myURL
```

you eliminate the requirement that your viewer type in the Internet protocol scheme before the actual Web site address.

Use this strategy in combination with other Flash actions to develop flexible and customizable functions and interfaces. In the following example, you concatenate input text boxes from a customer to automatically compile the information in the correct layout, and then use the print action to print out a complete receipt or order form.

To concatenate text boxes for custom printing:

1. Choose the text tool in the Tools window, and create several input text boxes. In the Text Options panel, give each of them a unique variable name (**Figure 10.12**).

2. Create a movie-clip symbol, and enter symbol-editing mode for that movie clip.

3. In the first keyframe of the movie clip, assign a stop action. Leave this first keyframe empty of any graphics.

   The stop action prevents this movie clip from playing and cycling endlessly.

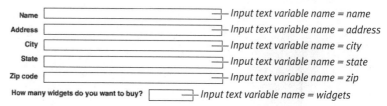

Figure 10.12 Define six input text boxes with unique variable names.

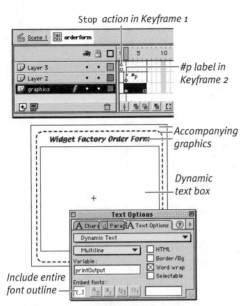

Stop *action in Keyframe 1*

#p label in Keyframe 2

Accompanying graphics

Dynamic text box

Include entire font outline

Figure 10.13 The dynamic text box is laid out in Keyframe 2 with graphics ready to print.

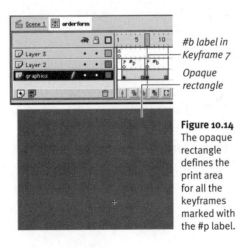

#b label in Keyframe 7

Opaque rectangle

Figure 10.14 The opaque rectangle defines the print area for all the keyframes marked with the #p label.

```
on (release) {
    orderform.printOutput =
"Hello, " + name + " thanks for your order! \rDelivery to: \r" +
name + "\r"+ address + "\r" + city + ", " + state + " " +
zip + "\r\rWidgets: " + widgets + "\rTOTAL COST: $ " + widgets*5;
}
```

Figure 10.15 The target path to the dynamic text box called printOutput includes the movie clip called orderform. The dynamic text box displays a string that concatenates the input text variables and totals the cost of ordered widgets by multiplying the variable by 5.

4. Label the next keyframe #p, and create a large dynamic text box in it. In the Text Options panel, choose Multiline from the pull-down menu, enter a variable name, check the Word wrap option, and select the Embed fonts option to include the entire font outline. Add graphics you wish to include in the printed piece (**Figure 10.13**).

The dynamic text box will display concatenated information, and the #p label marks this keyframe to print.

5. Label another keyframe #b, and draw a large opaque rectangle that covers the same area covered by the dynamic text box in the previous keyframe (**Figure 10.14**).

The #b label marks this keyframe as the print area.

6. Return to the root Timeline, and drag an instance of the three-keyframe movie clip you just created onto the Stage. In the Instance panel, give the instance a name.

7. Create a button symbol, and drag an instance of the button onto the Stage.

8. Select the button instance, and in the Actions panel choose Actions > set variable.

9. In the Variable field, enter the target path to the dynamic text variable. In the Value field, enter a combination of strings and the input text variables to concatenate the user-entered information into a compact, printable form. Use escape sequences such as \r for carriage returns. Check the Expression box next to the Value field (**Figure 10.15**).

(continued on next page)

10. In the Actions panel choose Actions > print. In the Print pull-down menu select As vectors, select Target as the Location, and enter the name of your movie-clip instance. Check the Expression box next to the Location fields. Select Movie for the Bounding box (**Figure 10.16**).

11. Test your movie.

When your viewer enters information into the input text boxes and then clicks the button, the dynamic text in the movie clip concatenates the input text variables and displays the information in the keyframe labeled #p. The `print` action then prints this keyframe (**Figure 10.17**).

✔ Tips

■ Make sure that the movie clip containing the frame to print is named in the Instance panel. Even if you didn't need a name to target it from your print button, Flash requires a named movie clip to print.

■ You can also hide a movie clip that's on the Stage from the viewer but still have it available for printing by setting the `_visible` property to false. Changing the visibility property of a movie clip doesn't affect how it prints.

■ It's important that you embed fonts for dynamic text boxes sent to the printer. Embedding fonts for a text box results in a much better quality print.

Figure 10.16 The print statement sends the information in the #p frame to the printer.

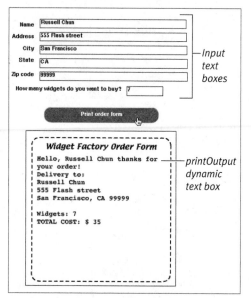

Figure 10.17 The Flash movie (top) provides input text boxes, which are compiled in a dynamic text box and printed (bottom).

Displaying HTML

Flash can display HTML 1.0–formatted text in dynamic text boxes. When you mark up text with HTML tags and assign the text to a dynamic text variable, Flash will interpret the tags and preserve the formatting. This means you can actually integrate HTML pages inside your Flash movie, maintaining the styles and functional HREF anchors.

HTML Tags Supported by Text Boxes

◆ <A HREF> Anchor tag to create hot links

◆ <B> Bold style

◆ <FONT COLOR> Font-color style

◆ <FONT FACE> Font-face style

◆ <FONT SIZE> Font-size style

◆ <I> Italics style

◆ <P> Paragraph

◆ <U> Underline style

A powerful combination is to load HTML-formatted text into dynamic text boxes with the action loadVariablesNum. By simply changing the HTML that resides outside the Flash file, you can update the information that displays during playback of your movie. This can be very convenient because you don't have to open the Flash file to make periodic edits, and a server-side script or even a user unfamiliar with Flash can make the necessary updates.

To load and display HTML in a dynamic text box:

1. Open a text-editing application or a WYSIWYG HTML editor, and create your HTML document. At the very beginning of the HTML text, add a variable name and the assignment operator (the equal symbol [=]). Save the text file (**Figure 10.18**).

2. In Flash, select the first keyframe on the root Timeline, and open the Actions panel.

3. Choose Actions > loadVariables. In the URL field, enter the name of the text file you just created. Keep the Location on Level and at 0 (**Figure 10.19**).

   Flash loads the text file that contains the variable.

4. Choose the text tool, and drag out a large text box that nearly covers the Stage.

5. In the Text Options panel, select Dynamic Text, select Multiline, and check the HTML and Word wrap boxes. Give the text box a variable name (**Figure 10.20**).

6. Create a button symbol, and place an instance of it on the Stage. Select the button, and open the Actions panel.

7. Choose Actions > set variable. In the Variable field, enter the name of your dynamic text variable. In the Value field, enter the variable you assigned in the text file (**Figure 10.21**).

Figure 10.18 The HTML text is assigned to the variable called HTMLpage and saved as a separate document.

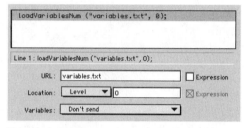

Figure 10.19 This frame action loads the file variables.txt, which contains the variable holding HTML text.

Figure 10.20 Name your dynamic text box displayMyPage.

Figure 10.21 The dynamic-text variable called displayMyPage shows the contents of the variable HTMLpage.

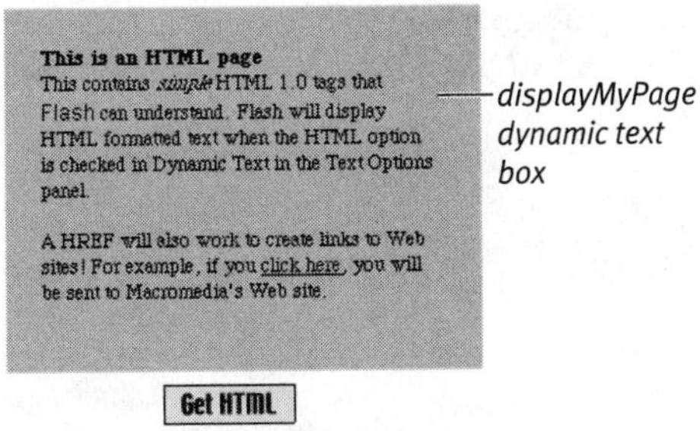

displayMyPage dynamic text box

Figure 10.22 The dynamic text box displays the HTML-formatted text.

8. Export a SWF file to the same directory that contains your text file. Play the SWF in either the Flash Player or a browser.

When your viewer clicks the button, Flash sets the dynamic text variable to the external variable in the text file, which holds HTML-formatted text. The dynamic text box displays the information, preserving all the style and format tags (**Figure 10.22**).

✔ **Tips**

■ Since only a limited number of HTML tags are supported by dynamic text, you should do a fair amount of testing to see how the information displays. When Flash doesn't understand a tag, it simply ignores it.

■ The anchor tag <A> normally appears underlined and in a different color in browser environments. However, in Flash the hot link is only indicated by the pointer's changing to a finger. To manually create the underline and color style for hot links, apply the underline tag <U> and the font color tag <FONT COLOR="#0000FF>.

■ The HTML tags override any style settings you assign in the Character or Paragraph panels for your dynamic text. For example, if you choose a red color for your dynamic rext box, when you display HTML text in the field, the <FONT COLOR> tag would modify the text to a different color.

DISPLAYING HTML

Tweening Dynamic Text

If you convert dynamic text boxes into symbols, you can apply motion tweens to them, just as you can with other symbol instances. This lets you create titles and banners that not only can be dynamically updated, but that can move across the screen, rotate, and shrink or grow in size. For example, imagine a blimp traveling across the Stage with a giant scoreboard attached to its side. By having the dynamic text box as the scoreboard on the blimp graphic, you can update scores or have messages appear as the blimp floats. A stock ticker-tape monitor could be created this way as well, with the stock prices moving across the screen. Or you could create a game that displays the current status of an individual player right next to the player's icon, even as it moves around the Stage.

To create a moving dynamic text box:

1. Select the text tool, and drag out a text box.

2. In the Text Options panel, choose Dynamic Text and Single Line in the two pull-down menus. Give this text box a variable name, and embed the entire font outline (**Figure 10.23**).

3. Choose Insert > Convert to Symbol from the main toolbar menu. Name your symbol, and select Graphic Behavior in the dialog box that appears. Click OK.

   Flash puts your Dynamic Text box inside a graphic symbol and places an instance of it on the Stage.

4. Select your graphic instance, and choose Insert > Convert to Symbol. Name your symbol, and select Movie Clip Behavior in the dialog box that appears. Click OK.

   Flash puts your graphic symbol inside a movie-clip symbol and places an instance of it on the Stage.

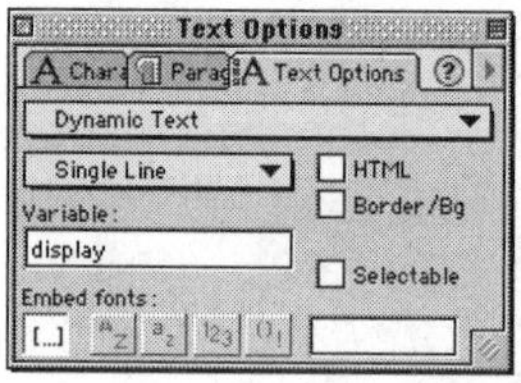

Figure 10.23 Name your dynamic text variable display, and embed all font outlines.

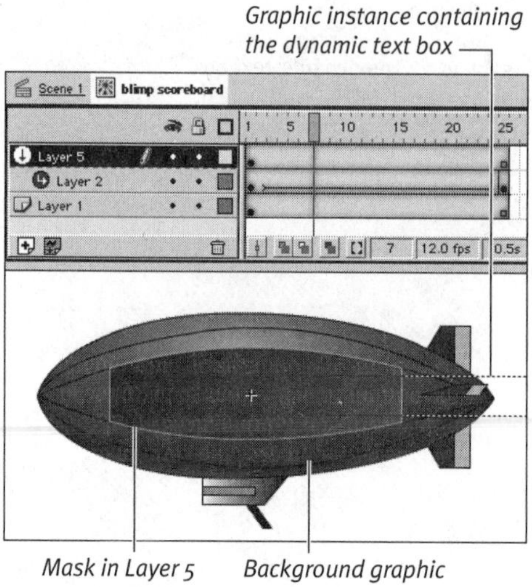

Figure 10.24 On the blimp scoreboard movie-clip Timeline, tween the graphic instance that contains the dynamic text. This graphic moves across the Stage behind a mask of the scoreboard.

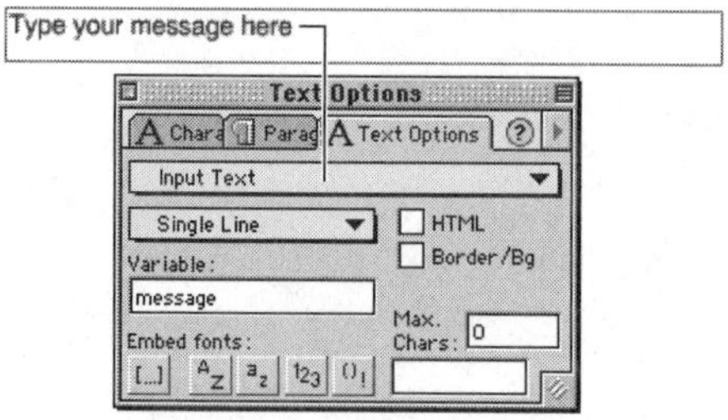

Figure 10.25 Name the input text box message.

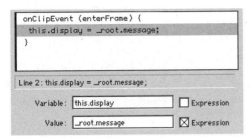

Figure 10.26 Assign the dynamic text variable called display to the input text variable called message.

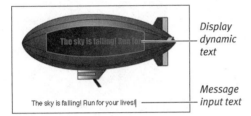

Display dynamic text

Message input text

Figure 10.27 The dynamic text box (top) tweens any message your viewer enters in the input text box (bottom).

✔ **Tips**

■ Put a dynamic text box in a movie clip, and control its appearance with ActionScript. Use the `setProperty` action to modify the properties of the movie clip—such as its rotation, transparency, or position—and the text in your dynamic text box changes accordingly.

■ It's important to include the entire font outline in a dynamic text box when you tween it or if it's part of a masked layer. If the font outline is not included, the text box won't tween properly or show up behind the mask.

5. In the Instance panel, name the movie-clip instance.

6. Enter symbol-editing mode for your movie-clip symbol.

   Your movie-clip symbol contains a graphic instance that contains your dynamic text box.

7. Create a motion tween of the graphic instance moving across the Stage (**Figure 10.24**).

8. Return to the root Timeline. Select the text tool, and drag out another text box below the movie-clip instance.

9. In the Text Options panel, choose Input Text and Single Line. Give this text box a variable name (**Figure 10.25**).

10. Select the movie-clip instance, and open the Actions panel. Choose Actions > onClipEvent. Select the enterFrame event.

11. Choose Actions > set variable. In the Variable field, enter the target path to the dynamic text variable. In the Value field, enter the target path to the input-text variable. Check the Expression box next to the Value field (**Figure 10.26**).

    The dynamic text box is continuously updated with the contents of the input text box.

12. Test your movie.

    When your viewer enters information in the input text box, it is assigned to the dynamic text box in the movie-clip animation, and the updated text moves across the screen (**Figure 10.27**).

Tweening Dynamic Text

Controlling Text Box Scrolling

When the information in multiline input text or dynamic text exceeds the defined boundaries of the text box, Flash automatically scrolls the text so that the currently input text remains visible. Rows of text that can't fit within the text box are hidden from view but still accessible by the viewer by clicking inside the text box and dragging the cursor up or down . You can dynamically display different rows of text, whether they are hidden or not, by controlling the position of the first visible row of text in a text box. This property is called scroll. The top row has the value of 0, and as new lines of text scroll up or down, that value changes (**Figure 10.28**).

Flash lets you retrieve the value of the scroll property so you know exactly which text row your viewer is currently looking at. You can also modify the value of the scroll property to force your viewer to look at a particular text row. It is common to provide interface controls so that viewers themselves can control the scrolling of text, just as they control the scroll bars in a Web browser or any window on the computer screen. In the following task, you'll create interface controls of this kind.

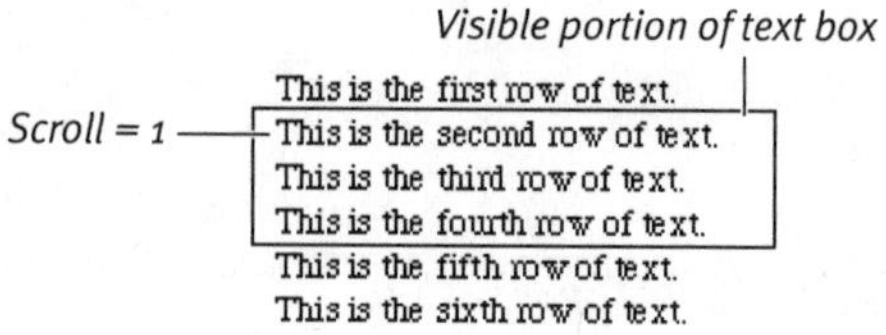

Figure 10.28 The scroll property is the first visible row of text.

Figure 10.29 Name the input text box scrollwindow.

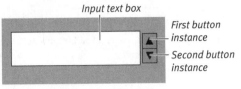

Input text box

First button instance

Second button instance

Figure 10.30 Place two buttons next to the input text box.

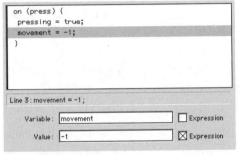

```
on (press) {
  pressing = true;
  movement = -1;
}
```

Line 3 : movement = -1 ;

Variable : movement   ☐ Expression

Value : -1   ☒ Expression

Figure 10.31 Pressing the up-arrow button sets the variable pressing to true and the variable movement to -1.

To create a scrolling input text box:

1. Select the text tool from the Tools window, and drag out a text box onto the Stage.

2. In the Text Options panel, select Input Text and Multiline in the pull-down menus. Check the Border/Bg box and the Word wrap box. In the Variable field, enter a name for the input text box (**Figure 10.29**).

3. Create a button symbol of an upward pointing arrow. Place an instance of the button on the Stage.

4. Place a second instance of the button on the Stage, and choose Modify > Transform > Flip Vertical to make the second button point down. Align both buttons vertically next to the input text box (**Figure 10.30**).

5. Select the up-arrow button, and open the Actions panel. Choose Actions > on. Select the Press event.

6. Choose Actions > set variable. In the Variable field, enter the variable name pressing. In the Value field, enter the Boolean value true. Check the Expression box next to the Value field.

7. Again, choose Actions > set variable. In the Variable field, enter the variable name movement. In the Value field, enter the number –1 and check the Expression box (**Figure 10.31**).

    When the mouse is pressed, the variable pressing is set to true and the variable movement is set to –1.

8. Choose Actions > on. Select the Release event.

   (continued on next page)

9. Choose Actions > set variable. In the Variable field, enter the variable name `pressing`. In the Value field, enter the Boolean value `false` and check the Expression box.

When the mouse is released, the variable `pressing` is set to `false` (**Figure 10.32**).

10. Select the down-arrow button, and enter the same statements in the Actions List of the Actions panel, except assign the variable `movement` to 1 when the mouse is pressed (**Figure 10.33**).

11. Select both buttons, and choose Insert > Convert to Symbol. Enter a symbol name, and choose Movie Clip Behavior. Click OK.

Your up- and down-arrow buttons are put inside a movie-clip symbol. An instance of the movie clip remains on the Stage.

12. Select the movie-clip instance that contains your two buttons, and in the Actions panel choose Actions > onClipEvent. Select the enterFrame event.

13. Choose Actions > if. In the Condition field, enter:

```
this.pressing == true
```

14. Choose Actions > set variable. In the Variable field, enter the full target path of the input text variable, then a dot, and then the property `scroll`. In the Value field, enter the full target path of the input text variable, then a dot, and then the property `scroll`, and add the value of the variable `this.movement`. Check the Expression box (**Figure 10.34**).

Flash checks to see if one of the buttons is depressed. If it is, Flash adds the value of `movement` to the current `scroll` index. If the up arrow is pressed, the `scroll` index is decreased by 1. If the down arrow is pressed, the `scroll` index is increased by 1 (**Figure 10.35**).

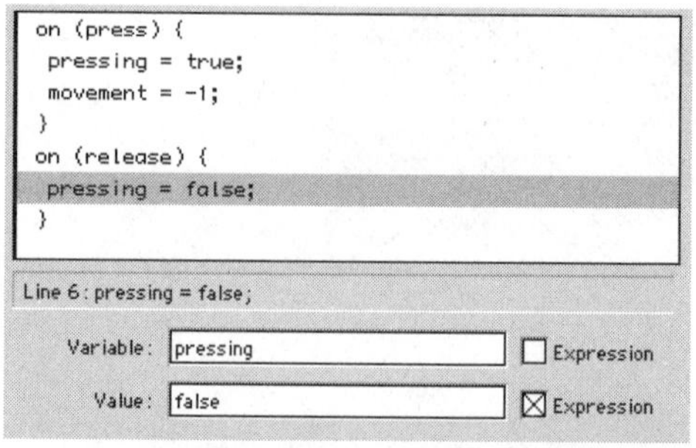

Figure 10.32 Releasing the up-arrow button sets the variable pressing to false.

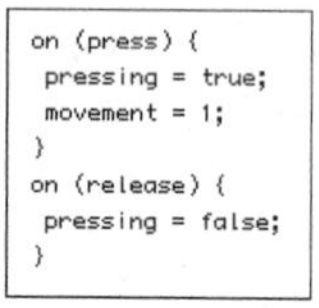

Figure 10.33 The complete down-arrow button script as seen in the Actions List of the Actions panel.

Figure 10.34 The actions assigned to the movie clip add the value of the variable movement to the `scroll` property of scrollwindow when pressing is true.

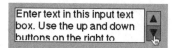

Figure 10.35 The buttons on the right increase or decrease the value of the scroll property of the input text box.

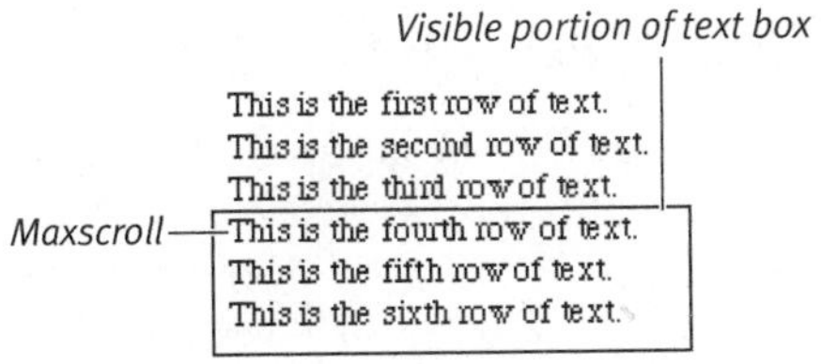

Visible portion of text box

This is the first row of text.
This is the second row of text.
This is the third row of text.
Maxscroll — This is the fourth row of text.
This is the fifth row of text.
This is the sixth row of text.

Figure 10.36 In this example, maxscroll = 4.

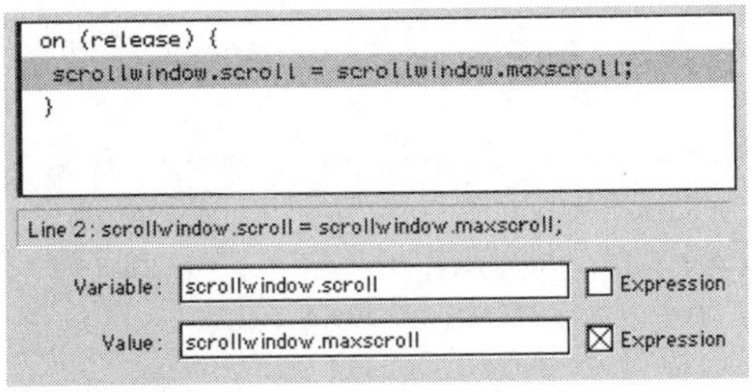

```
on (release) {
    scrollwindow.scroll = scrollwindow.maxscroll;
}
```

Line 2: scrollwindow.scroll = scrollwindow.maxscroll;

Variable: scrollwindow.scroll   ☐ Expression
Value: scrollwindow.maxscroll   ☒ Expression

Figure 10.37 Maxscroll is assigned to the scroll property of scrollwindow.

While the scroll property defines the first visible text row in a text box, the maxscroll property defines the maximum allowable value for scroll in that text box. This is the row that appears at the top of the text box when the last line of text is visible (**Figure 10.36**). You can't change the value of maxscroll since it's defined by the amount of text and size of the text box itself, but you can read its value. Assign the value of maxscroll to scroll, and you can automatically scroll the text to the bottom of the text box. Or you can calculate the value of scroll proportional to maxscroll and build a draggable scrollbar that reflects and controls the text's position within the text box.

To scroll to the end of a text box:

1. Continuing with the previous task, create a new button symbol, and drag an instance of it to the Stage.

2. Select the button, and open the Actions panel. Choose Actions > set variable.

3. In the Variable field, enter the name of the input-text variable, then a dot, and then the property scroll. In the Value field, enter the name of the input-text variable, then a dot, and then the property maxscroll. Check the Expression box next to the Value field (**Figure 10.37**).

   When the viewer clicks this button, the current value of maxscroll for the input text box is assigned to scroll for the input text box. The text automatically moves so that the last line is visible.

Manipulating Strings

When you define a text box as Input Text, you give your viewers the freedom to enter and edit information. You've seen how this information can then be used in expressions with other actions, or concatenated and displayed in dynamic text boxes. However, it's often necessary to analyze the text entered by the viewer before using it. You may want to tease out certain words, or identify the location of a particular character or sequence of characters. For example, if you require viewers to enter an e-mail address in an input field, you can check to see if that address is in the correct format by looking for the @ symbol. Or you could check a customer's telephone number, find out the area code based on the first three digits, and personalize a directory or news listing with local interests.

This kind of parsing, manipulation, and control of the information within an input text box is done with a combination of the Selection object and the String object. The Selection object lets you control which text box is currently selected and the position of the cursor within that text box. The String object lets you retrieve and change the properties of the information inside the text box.

The Selection Object

The Selection object controls the selection of text in input text boxes. Unlike most objects, the Selection object doesn't need a constructor function to be instantiated before you can use it. This is because there can be only one cursor position or selection in a Flash movie at a time. So the Selection object will always refer to that one cursor position or selection.

The methods of the Selection object affect two properties of a text box: where the cursor is positioned, and which text box is currently active, or *focused*. The methods of the Selection object are summarized in **Table 10.1**.

Table 10.1

Methods of the Selection Object	
METHOD	**DESCRIPTION**
getBeginIndex()	Retrieves the index at the beginning of the selection.
getEndIndex()	Retrieves the index at the end of the selection.
getCaretIndex()	Retrieves the index of the cursor position.
setSelection (beginIndex, endIndex)	Positions the selection at a specified beginIndex and endIndex.
getFocus()	Retrieves the variable name of the currently active text box.
setFocus (variableName)	Sets the focus of the text box specified by the variable name so you can get or retrieve information about the text in that particular text box when multiple text boxes are present.

Figure 10.38 Name your input text box mySelection.

Figure 10.39 Name your dynamic text box myIndex.

Controlling the Selection Within Text Boxes

You can control the selection or cursor position inside editable text boxes. This lets you direct your viewers' attention to particular characters or words they've entered, perhaps to point out errors or misspellings. It also lets you keep track of the cursor position, much like the way the _xmouse and _ymouse properties let you keep track of the location of the viewer's mouse pointer.

The position of each character in a string is numbered and used as the index for the methods of the Selection object. The first character is assigned the index of 0, the second character is 1, and so on. If a cursor isn't positioned within a text box when Flash retrieves the selection index, it returns a value of −1.

To identify the position of the cursor in a text box:

1. Select the text tool, and drag out a text box onto the Stage. In the Text Options panel, select Input Text and Multiline from the pull-down menus. Give the input text box a variable name. Check the Border/Bg and Word wrap boxes (**Figure 10.38**).

2. Select the text tool, and drag out a second text box onto the Stage. In the Text Options panel, select Dynamic Text and Multiline in the pull-down menus. Give the Dynamic Text box a variable name. Check the Border/Bg box (**Figure 10.39**).

3. Select both text boxes, and choose Insert > Convert to Symbol. Give the symbol a name, and choose Movie Clip Behavior. Click OK.

(continued on next page)

Your two text boxes are put into a movie-clip symbol, and an instance of the movie clip remains on the Stage.

4. Select the movie-clip instance on the Stage, and open the Actions panel. Choose Actions > onClipEvent. Select the enterFrame event.

5. Choose Actions > set variable. In the Variable field, enter the name of the dynamic text variable. Put your cursor in the Value field, and choose Objects > Selection > getCaretIndex (**Figure 10.40**).

   The getCaretIndex method appears in the Value field. Check the Expression box.

6. Test your movie.

   Initially the dynamic text box displays −1 because the input text box is not currently focused. When your viewer begins to type in the input text box, Flash updates the dynamic text box to display the cursor's position (**Figure 10.41**).

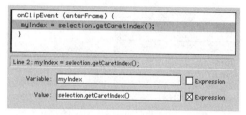

Figure 10.40 Flash assigns the position of the cursor, or *caret*, to the variable myIndex.

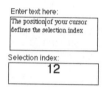

Figure 10.41 The current index of cursor is 12. The first letter "T" is 0. The space between "position" and "of" is 12.

To change the selection in a text box:

1. Continuing with the previous task, select the movie-clip instance, and open the Actions panel.

2. Add a statement after the set variable action by choosing Actions > if.

3. In the Condition field, enter:

   Key.isDown(Key.ENTER)

   Flash checks to see if the Enter key or the Return key is depressed.

4. Choose Actions > evaluate.

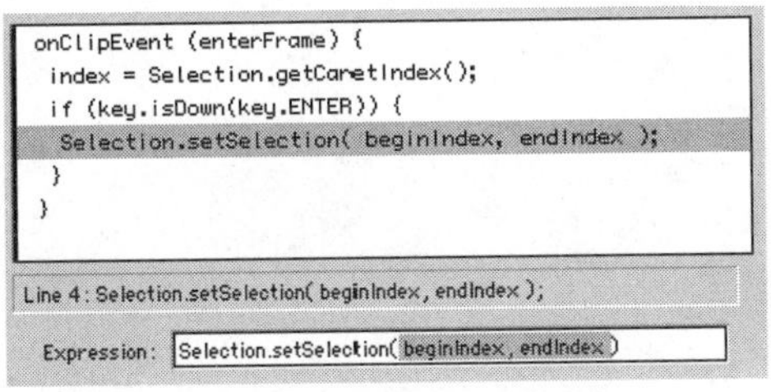

```
onClipEvent (enterFrame) {
  index = Selection.getCaretIndex();
  if (key.isDown(key.ENTER)) {
    Selection.setSelection( beginIndex, endIndex );
  }
}
```

Line 4 : Selection.setSelection(beginIndex, endIndex);

Expression : Selection.setSelection(beginIndex, endIndex)

Figure 10.42 The setSelection method selects the substring between the parameters beginIndex and endIndex.

Expression : Selection.setSelection(0,Selection.getCaretIndex())

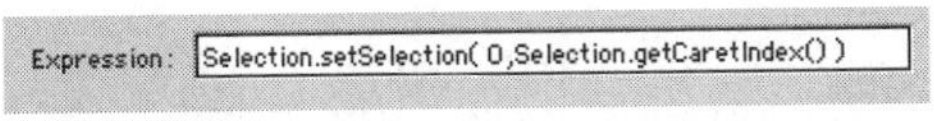

Figure 10.43 This setSelection method selects the substring between the first character and the current cursor position.

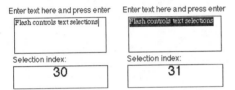

Enter text here and press enter

Flash controls text selections

Selection index:

30

Enter text here and press enter

Flash controls text selections

Selection index:

31

Figure 10.44 The viewer types in the input text box (left). When the viewer presses the Enter or Return key, Flash selects the text automatically (right). The index at the bottom changes from 30 to 31 because the Enter or Return key counts as an index number.

5. Put your cursor in the Expression field, and choose Objects > Selection > setSelection.

The setSelection method appears in the Expression field with the parameters beginIndex and endIndex highlighted (**Figure 10.42**).

6. Replace the beginIndex parameter with 0. Replace the endIndex parameter by choosing Objects > Selection > getCaretIndex (**Figure 10.43**).

7. Test your movie.

When your viewer begins to type in the input text box, the dynamic text box displays the index of the cursor. When the viewer presses the Enter or Return key, the setSelection method is called; this method selects the characters between index 0 (the first character) and the current cursor position, so everything the viewer typed is selected (**Figure 10.44**).

Controlling the Focus of Text Boxes

If you have multiple text boxes on the Stage, you need to be able to control which one is currently active, or focused, before you can retrieve or assign the cursor location or selection. The getFocus and setFocus methods of the Selection object let you do this.

The method getFocus returns a string containing the absolute path to the text box using the _level0 term. For example, if the currently selected text box called yourName is on the root Timeline and you call the getFocus method, the returned value is:

"_level0.yourName"

It's important to remember that the returned value is a string and that the _level0 term is used. If you compare the getFocus value with a path name using _root or this or forget the quotation marks, then Flash won't recognize the path. The getFocus method returns a value of null if there is no currently focused text box on the Stage.

Like getFocus, the method setFocus requires that you use a string and an absolute path to the text box. However, you can use either the _level0 term or _root.

In the following task, you will create multiple input text boxes. Depending on which text box your viewer selects, you will display a different message in a dynamic text box.

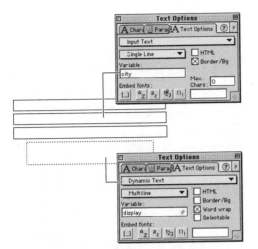

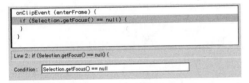

Figure 10.45 Create three input text boxes (the Text Option panel for the middle input text box is shown) (top) and one dynamic text box (bottom).

```
onClipEvent (enterFrame) {
    if (Selection.getFocus() == null) {
    )
    )
)
```

Line 2: if (Selection.getFocus() == null) {

Condition: Selection.getFocus() == null

Figure 10.46 When getFocus returns null, there is no focused text box.

To get the focus of a text box:

1. Select the text tool, and drag out a text box onto the Stage. In the Text Options panel, select Input Text and Single Line from the pull-down menus. Enter a variable name for this input text box.

2. Select the text tool again, and create two more input text boxes. Enter unique variable names for them.

3. Select the text tool, and drag out a fourth text box on the Stage. In the Text Options panel, select Dynamic Text and Multiline from the pull-down menus. Check the Word wrap box. Enter a variable name for this dynamic text box (**Figure 10.45**).

4. Select all the text boxes, and choose Insert > Convert to Symbol. Enter a symbol name, and choose Movie Clip Behavior. Click OK.

   Your text boxes are put inside a movie-clip symbol. An instance of the movie clip remains on the Stage.

5. In the Instance panel, give the movie clip a name.

6. With the movie-clip instance selected, open the Actions panel. Choose Actions > onClipEvent. Select the enterFrame event.

7. Choose Actions > if.

8. With the cursor in the Condition field, choose Objects > Selection > getFocus.

   The getFocus method appears in the Condition field.

9. Add to the Condition field == null (**Figure 10.46**).

   Flash checks to see if the viewer has not selected any of the text boxes.

   (continued on next page)

10. Choose Actions > set variable. In the Variable field, enter the name of your dynamic text variable. In the Value field, enter a message that instructs the viewer to select a text box (**Figure 10.47**).

11. Choose Actions > else if. In the Condition field, choose the `getFocus` method, and compare its returned value to the target path of the first input text variable (**Figure 10.48**).

12. Choose Actions > set variable. Assign a message to the dynamic text variable that gives instructions to the viewer (**Figure 10.49**).

13. Add two more `else if` conditions, and have the dynamic text box change when each condition holds true. The final script should look like the one in **Figure 10.50**.

14. Test your movie.

When your viewer first sees your Flash movie, none of the text boxes are focused, but the message in the dynamic text box tells the viewer what to do. When the viewer selects a text box, Flash recognizes which one it is (**Figure 10.51**).

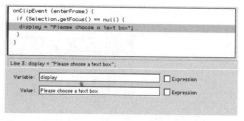

Figure 10.47 The message in the Value field appears in the dynamic text box called display.

Figure 10.48 Flash checks to see if the input text box called name that lies inside myMovieClip is currently selected.

Figure 10.49 The message in the Value field appears in the dynamic text field called display.

```
onClipEvent (enterFrame) {
    // check if no text box is selected
    if (Selection.getFocus() == null) {
        display = "Please choose a text box";
    // check if the name text box is selected
    } else if (Selection.getFocus() == "_level0.myMovieClip.name") {
        // give directions for the name text box
        display = "Please enter your name";
    // check if the address text box is selected
    } else if (Selection.getFocus() == "_level0.myMovieClip.address") {
        display = "Please enter your address";
    // check if the city text box is selected
    } else if (Selection.getFocus() == "_level0.myMovieClip.city") {
        display = "Please enter your city";
    }
}
```

Figure 10.50 The full script contains conditions for each focused text box.

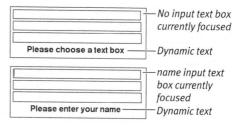

Figure 10.51 A different message appears for each focused input text box. This example shows when no box is focused (top) and when the top box is focused (bottom).

```
onClipEvent (enterFrame) {
  // check if no text box is selected
  if (Selection.getFocus() == null) {
    display = "Please choose a text box";
    // check if the name text box is selected
  } else if (Selection.getFocus() == "_level0.myMovieClip.name") {
    // also check if the enter key is pressed
    if (key.isDown(key.ENTER)) {
    }
    // give directions for the name text box
    display = "Please enter your name";
    // check if the address text box is selected
  } else if (Selection.getFocus() == "_level0.myMovieClip.address") {
    display = "Please enter your address";
    // check if the city text box is selected
  } else if (Selection.getFocus() == "_level0.myMovieClip.city") {
    display = "Please enter your city";
  }
}
```

```
Line 8: if (key.isDown(key.ENTER)) {

Condition:  key.isDown(key.ENTER)
```

Figure 10.52 Add a condition to check if the Enter or Return key is pressed under the first else if condition.

```
Expression:  Selection.setFocus("_level0.myMovieClip.address")
```

Figure 10.53 This setFocus method focuses the input text called address that sits inside myMovieClip.

```
onClipEvent (enterFrame) {
  // check if no text box is selected
  if (Selection.getFocus() == null) {
    display = "Please choose a text box";
    // check if the name text box is selected
  } else if (Selection.getFocus() == "_level0.myMovieClip.name") {
    // also check if the enter key is pressed
    if (key.isDown(key.ENTER)) {
      // if so, focus the next text box
      Selection.setFocus("_level0.myMovieClip.address");
    }
    // give directions for the name text box
    display = "Please enter your name";
    // check if the address text box is selected
  } else if (Selection.getFocus() == "_level0.myMovieClip.address") {
    // also check if the enter key is pressed
    if (key.isDown(key.ENTER)) {
      // if so, focus the next text box
      Selection.setFocus("_level0.myMovieClip.city");
    }
    display = "Please enter your address";
    // check if the city text box is selected
  } else if (Selection.getFocus() == "_level0.myMovieClip.city") {
    display = "Please enter your city";
  }
}
```

Figure 10.54 The full script contains conditions to focus the next input text box if the Enter or Return key is pressed.

To set the focus of a text box:

1. Continuing with the previous task, select the movie-clip instance, and open the Actions panel.

2. Select the first else if statement. Add an if statement under it. In the Condition field, enter

   `Key.isDown (Key.ENTER)`

   This instructs Flash to check if the viewer presses the Enter or Return key while the first text box is focused (**Figure 10.52**).

3. Choose Actions > evaluate. With your cursor in the Expression field, choose Objects > Selection > setFocus.

   The setFocus method appears in the Expression field with the parameter variableName highlighted.

4. Replace the parameter variableName with the absolute path of the second input text variable within quotation marks (**Figure 10.53**).

   Flash changes the focus to the next input text box.

5. Continue adding conditional statements and setFocus methods to the other two else if scripts (**Figure 10.54**).

6. Test your movie.

   When your viewer enters information in the first input text box and then presses the Enter or Return key, Flash focuses the next input text box so that users can continue entering information without having to click to select a text box. Use this kind of control over text box focus to customize how the Tab key automatically cycles through text box selections.

The String Object

You can apply the methods and properties of the String object to analyze and manipulate string data types. For example, the String object can tell you the position of a certain character, or what character occupies a certain position. You can also dissect just a portion of the string and put that part, called a *substring*, into a new string, or concatenate substrings and strings. You can even change the lowercase and uppercase style of different parts of the string. Several methods and properties of the String object are summarized in **Table 10.2**.

You can perform all this parsing and shuffling of strings without first having to create an instance of the String object. Flash does this automatically by creating a temporary String object that it discards after the work of the method is completed.

As with the Selection object, the indices of the String object are based on the positions of the characters in the string. The first character is assigned an index of 0, the second character had an index of 1, and so on.

✔ Tip

- You can use the String function to convert the value of any variable, expression, or object into a string before applying the methods of the String object. For example, if your variable radioButton is a Boolean data type, the statement

  String (radioButton)

  returns the string "true" or "false." Now the actual characters can be manipulated with the methods of the String object.

Table 10.2

Methods and Properties of the String Object

METHOD OR PROPERTY	DESCRIPTION
indexOf(searchString, fromIndex)	Searches the string and returns the index of the first occurrence of a susbstring specified in the parameter searchString. The optional fromIndex parameter sets the starting position of the search.
lastIndexOf(searchString, fromIndex)	Searches the string and returns the index of the last occurrence of a substring specified in the parameter searchString. The optional fromIndex parameter sets the starting position of the search.
charAt(index)	Returns the character at the specified index position.
substring(indexA, indexB)	Returns the string between the indexA and the indexB parameters.
substr(start, length)	Returns the string from the start index with the specified length.
concat(string1,…,stringN)	Concatenates the specified strings.
toLowerCase()	Converts the characters in the string to lowercase.
toUpperCase()	Converts the characters in the string to uppercase.
length	A property that returns the length of the string.

Figure 10.55 Name your input text box myString.

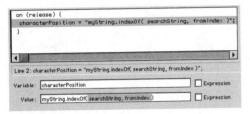

Figure 10.56 Assign the indexOf method to myString.

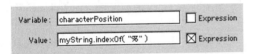

Figure 10.57 This indexOf method searches myString for the % sign and puts the index into the variable characterPosition.

Analyzing Strings with the String Object

Use the methods of the String object to identify a character or characters in a string. The following tasks analyze input text boxes to verify that the viewer has entered the required information.

To identify the position of a character:

1. Select the text tool from the Tools window, and drag out a text box onto the Stage. In the Text Options panel, select Input Text and Single Line from the pull-down menus. Enter a variable name for this input text box (**Figure 10.55**).

2. Create a button symbol, and place an instance of it on the Stage. Select it, and open the Actions panel.

3. Choose Actions > set variable.

4. In the Variable field, enter a variable name. In the Value field, enter the variable name of your input text box. Then, with the cursor still in the Value field, choose Objects > String > indexOf.

   The indexOf method appears after your input text variable. The arguments searchString and fromIndex are highlighted. The parameter searchString is the specific character you want to identify in the string. The parameter fromIndex is the starting position in the string. The parameter fromIndex is optional (**Figure 10.56**).

5. Replace the parameter searchString with the character you want to find. Make sure you include quotation marks around the character. Delete the fromIndex parameter. Check the Expression box next to the Value field (**Figure 10.57**).

(continued on next page)

303

When your viewer enters information in the input text box and clicks the button you created, Flash searches the information for the specified character and assigns its position to your variable. Use this variable in the methods of the Selection object or the String object to further modify the information.

✔ Tips

- The flip side of the method `indexOf` is `charAt`. This method returns the character that occupies the index position you specify for a string. For example, you could use this method to verify that the first, second, and third character corresponds to numbers for a certain area code of a telephone number.

- If the character you search for with `indexOf` occurs more than once in the string, Flash returns the index of only the first occurrence. Use the method `lastIndexOf` to retrieve the last occurrence of the character.

- If you want to retrieve all the occurrences of a certain character, you must use several iterations of the method `indexOf`. Use its optional second parameter fromIndex, which begins the search at a specific index. For example, imagine that the variable input contains the string "home/images/vacation." Then assign the script

```
slash1 = input.indexOf ("/")
slash2 = input.indexOf ("/",
slash1+1)
```

The first statement assigns the variable slash1 to the first occurrence of the slash symbol in the string input (slash1 = 4). The second statement searches for the slash symbol again, but starts the search at the next character after the first slash (at index 5 or the "i" in "images"). By constructing a `while` or a `do while` loop, you can make Flash march down the string, starting new searches as it finds occurrences of the character. Do this until the returned value of the `indexOf` method equals the value of the `lastIndexOf` method.

Figure 10.58 Name your input Text box yourEmail.

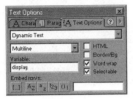

Figure 10.59 Name your dynamic text box display.

If Flash searches a string with the `indexOf` or `lastIndexOf` method and doesn't find the specified character, it returns a value of –1. You can use this fact to check for missing characters within a string. For example, if `indexOf("%") == -1`, then you know that the percentage symbol is missing from the string. In the next task, we search an input text variable for the @ symbol and the period to check if an e-mail address has been entered correctly.

To check for a missing character:

1. Select the text tool, and drag out a text box onto the Stage. In the Text Options panel, select Input Text and Single Line from the pull-down menus. Enter a variable name for this input text box (**Figure 10.58**).

2. Select the text tool again, and drag out another text box onto the Stage. In the Text Options panel, select Dynamic Text and Multiline from the pull-down menus. Check the Word wrap box. Enter a variable name for this dynamic text box (**Figure 10.59**).

3. Create a button symbol, and place an instance of the button on the Stage between the input text box and the dynamic text box. Select the button, and open the Actions panel.

4. From the Actions panel, choose Actions > if.

5. In the Condition field, enter the name of the input text variable. With your cursor still in the Condition field, choose Objects > Objects > String > indexOf. The `indexOf` method appears after your input text variable. The arguments searchString and fromIndex are highlighted.

(continued on next page)

ANALYZING STRINGS WITH THE STRING OBJECT

6. Replace the parameter searchString with "@". Make sure you include the quotation marks. Delete the fromIndex parameter.

Flash searches the input text box for the @ symbol.

7. Complete the rest of the condition so that the whole statement looks like the following:

`yourEmail.indexOf ("@") == -1`

This condition checks to see if the @ symbol in the variable yourEmail is not present (**Figure 10.60**).

8. In the same Condition field, enter the logical OR operator, ||.

9. Add a second condition that checks if a period (.) is not present in the variable.

`yourEmail.indexOf (".") == -1`

10. Choose Actions > set variable. In the Variable field, enter the name of your dynamic text variable. In the Value field, enter a message that notifies your viewer of a problem with the input (**Figure 10.61**).

11. Choose Actions > else. Then choose Actions > set variable. Assign an alternate message to the dynamic text variable that thanks your viewer for submitting an e-mail address (**Figure 10.62**).

12. Test your movie.

When the viewer clicks the button after entering an e-mail address in the Input Text box, Flash checks the string for both the @ symbol and a period, and returns the indexes of those symbols. If either index is –1, the viewer receives a message that the input is incorrect. Otherwise, the viewer receives a thank-you message (**Figure 10.63**).

Figure 10.60 If the @ symbol is missing from the variable yourEmail, this condition will hold true.

Figure 10.61 The message in the Value field appears in the dynamic text box called display.

Figure 10.62 This message appears in the dynamic text box called display when the condition is false.

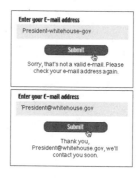

Figure 10.63 Entering an incorrect e-mail address into the input text box results in a warning displayed in the dynamic text box (top). Entering an e-mail address with an @ sign and a period results in a thank you message displayed in the dynamic text box (bottom).

✔ Tip

■ Use the `indexOf` or `lastIndexOf` method to check for a character or sequence of characters. If you specify a string in the argument, for example `indexOf (".org")`, Flash returns the index of the first occurrence of the sequence `.org` that appears in the string.

Condition: `yourEmail.indexOf( "@") == -1 || yourEmail.indexOf(".") == -1 || yourEmail.length == 0`

Figure 10.64 Flash checks if the @ symbol is missing, if the period is missing, or if the input text box called yourEmail is empty.

The String object has one property, `length`, that contains the value of the number of characters in a string. This is a read-only property that is useful for checking the relative positions of characters. For example, if you are building an online purchasing interface with input text boxes for prices, you can check the input text to see if a period character is three positions before the length of the input string in the following expression:

```
input.indexOf (".") == input.length - 3
```

If this condition is true, you could treat the last two digits as a decimal.

The following task refines the previous example of verifying an e-mail address. You will have Flash check to make sure the length of the input isn't 0 (meaning the viewer hasn't entered anything at all).

To check the length of a string:

1. Continue with the previous task to verify an e-mail address. Select the button, and open the Actions panel.

2. Select the `if` statement.

3. In the Condition field, add another logical || operator.

4. Add a third condition that checks the length of the string. The expression should look like the following:

   `yourEmail.length == 0`

   When your viewer clicks the button, Flash checks the length of the input text box to see if anything has been entered (**Figure 10.64**).

Rearranging Strings with the String Object

Once you have information about the position of certain characters and the length of a string, you can select a portion of the string and put it in a new variable. Flash provides tools to get specific selections from a string and put them together with other strings using methods such as concat, fromCharCode, slice, split, substr, or substring. Many of these methods are similar. Here we will discuss only substring to get a specific portion of a string, and concat, to put several separate strings together. You can use a combination of these two methods to control the information that flows from input text boxes into the rest of your Flash movie and back out into dynamic text boxes.

Figure 10.65 Name your input text box inputBox.

Figure 10.66 Name your dynamic text box outputBox.

The following task copies the current selection that the viewer has made and pastes it into a dynamic text box.

To get selected portions of strings:

1. Select the text tool, and drag out a text box onto the Stage. In the Text Options panel, select Input Text and Multiline from the pull-down menus. Enter a variable name for this input text box. Check the Word wrap box (**Figure 10.65**).

2. Drag out another text box onto the Stage. In the Text Options panel, select Dynamic Text and Multiline from the pull-down menus. Check the Word wrap box. Enter a variable name for this dynamic text box (**Figure 10.66**).

3. Create a button symbol, and place an instance of it on the Stage between the input text box and the dynamic text box. Select the button, and open the Actions panel.

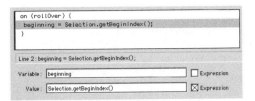

Figure 10.67 The variable called beginning contains the position of the start of the selection.

Figure 10.68 The variable called ending contains the position of the end of the selection.

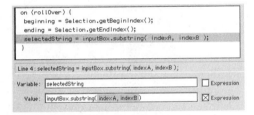

Figure 10.69 The substring method creates a substring out of the variable called inputBox between indexes indexA and indexB.

Figure 10.70 The variable called beginning marks the start of the substring, and the variable called ending marks the end of the substring.

4. Choose Actions > on. Select the Roll Over event.

5. Choose Actions > set variable. In the Variable field, enter a variable name. In the Value field, choose Objects > Selection > getBeginIndex. Check the Expression box next to the Value field (**Figure 10.67**).

    The position of the start of the selection is assigned to this variable.

6. Choose Actions > set variable. In the Variable field, enter another variable name. Place your cursor in the Value field, and choose Objects > Selection > getEndIndex. Check the Expression box next to the Value field (**Figure 10.68**).

    The position of the end of the selection is assigned to this variable.

7. Choose Actions > set variable. In the Variable field, enter another variable name. In the Value field, enter the input-text variable. Then choose Objects > String > substring.

    The substring method appears after your input text variable with the parameters indexA and indexB highlighted. IndexA defines the start of the sequence of characters you want to grab, and indexB defines the end of the sequence (**Figure 10.69**).

8. Replace indexA with your variable for the beginning of the selection. Replace indexB with your variable for the end of the selection. Check the Expression box next to the Value field (**Figure 10.70**).

9. Create a new event handler by choosing Actions > on. Select the Release event.

(continued on next page)

Rearranging Strings with String Object

10. Choose Actions > set variable, and assign the variable holding the selected substring to the dynamic text box (**Figure 10.71**).

Your viewer can enter information into the input text box and select portions of the text. When the viewer's mouse rolls over the button that you created, Flash captures the position of the selection and puts the substring into another variable. When your viewer clicks the button, the substring appears in the dynamic text box (**Figure 10.72**).

✔ Tip

■ You might wonder why the Selection methods are assigned to the Roll Over event rather than the Release event. That's because Flash must maintain the focus of a text box in order to capture information about the position of the cursor or the selection. If the viewer clicks a button, the text box loses focus and the selection disappears. Assigning the information about the selections in the Roll Over event ensures that you have it before it is lost.

```
on (rollOver) {
    beginning = Selection.getBeginIndex( );
    ending = Selection.getEndIndex( );
    selectedString = inputBox.substring( beginning, ending );
}
on (release) {
    outputBox = selectedString;
}
```

Line 7: outputBox = selectedString;

Variable: outputBox   ☐ Expression

Value: selectedString   ☒ Expression

Figure 10.71 The variable called outputBox displays the contents of the variable called selectedString.

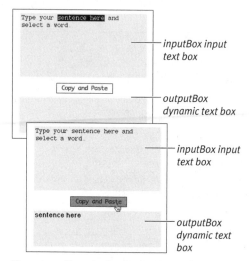

Figure 10.72 The selection "sentence here" (top) is put in a substring and displayed in the dynamic text box under the button (bottom).

Refining E-mail Verification with the Substring Method

You can apply the substring method to the previous task to refine the feedback message. For example, instead of displaying a thank-you message directed at the full e-mail address, you can personalize it somewhat by stripping out everything that comes after the @ symbol. That way, your thank-you message is just directed at the user name, which is often the user's actual name, or close to it. Set the dynamic text box variable to:

```
"Thank you, " + yourEmail.substring (0,
(yourEmail.indexOf("@"))) + ", we'll
contact you soon."
```

The substring returns the selection from the first character (index 0) to the @ character.

REARRANGING STRINGS WITH STRING OBJECT

With the method concat, you can put together strings you've dissected in an order that's more useful. The parameters of the concat method are individual expressions, separated by commas, that you want to combine. The concat method accomplishes the same thing as the addition operator (+), which was discussed earlier in this chapter. For example, the following two statements are equivalent:

```
"Hello, ".concat (firstName, " ",
lastName);

"Hello, " + firstName + " " + lastName;
```

To combine two separate strings:

1. Select the text tool, and drag out a text box onto the Stage. In the Text Options panel, select Input Text and Multiline from the pull-down menus. Enter a variable name for this input text box. Check the Word wrap box.

2. Select the text tool again, and drag out two more input text boxes with the same settings as the first. Give these input text boxes different variable names (**Figure 10.73**).

3. Select the text tool, and drag a fourth text box onto the Stage. In the Text Options panel, select Dynamic Text and Multiline from the pull-down menus. Check the Word wrap box. Enter a variable name for this dynamic text box (**Figure 10.74**).

4. Create a button symbol, and place an instance of it on the Stage. Select it, and open the Actions panel.

(continued on next page)

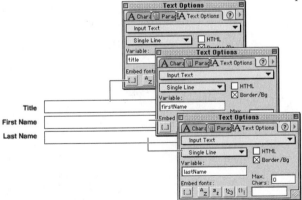

Figure 10.73 Create three input text boxes.

Figure 10.74 Name your dynamic text box display.

5. Choose Actions > set variable. In the Variable field, enter the name of your dynamic text variable. In the Value field, enter the name of the first input text variable. Then choose Objects > String > concat.

The concat method appears in the Value field after your first input text variable. The parameters string1 and stringN are highlighted. These parameters are values that will be concatenated (**Figure 10.75**).

6. Replace the highlighted parameters with the names of the second and third input text variables and spaces, separated by commas. Check the Expression box (**Figure 10.76**).

7. Test your movie.

When the viewer enters information into the input text boxes and then clicks the button, Flash concatenates the three input text variables and displays them in the dynamic text box (**Figure 10.77**).

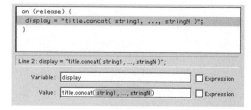

Figure 10.75 The concat method combines the values specified in its parameters with the variable called title.

Figure 10.76 This concat method is equivalent to title + " " + firstName + " " + lastName.

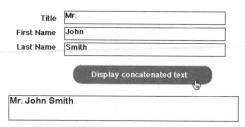

Figure 10.77 Flash concatenates the top three input text fields into one string in the bottom dynamic text field.

Modifying Strings with the String Object

There are two simple methods you can perform on a string to modify its characters: toUpperCase and toLowerCase. Both methods change the entire string to all uppercase letters or all lowercase letters. If you want to modify only certain letters to upper- or lowercase, you'll need to first create substrings of those specific characters as discussed in the previous section. Modify the substrings to upper- or lowercase, and then put the string back together with concat.

To change the case of characters in strings:

1. Select the text tool, and drag a text box onto the Stage. In the Text Options panel, select Input Text and Single Line in the pull-down menus. Enter a variable name for this input text box.

2. Select the text tool, and drag out another text box onto the Stage. In the Text Options panel, select Dynamic Text and Single Line in the pull-down menus. Enter a variable name for this dynamic text box.

3. Create a button symbol, and place an instance of it on the Stage. Select it, and open the Actions panel.

(continued on next page)

MODIFYING STRINGS WITH THE STRING OBJECT

4. Choose Actions > set variable. In the Variable field, enter the name of your dynamic-text variable. In the Value field enter the name of your input-text variable. Then choose Objects > String > toUpperCase. Check the Expression box.

The **toUpperCase** method appears in the Value field after your input-text variable. No parameters are required for this method because it will convert the entire string to uppercase characters (**Figure 10.78**).

5. Test your movie.

When your viewer enters text into the input text box and clicks the button you created, Flash modifies the entire string to uppercase and displays the results in the dynamic text box (**Figure 10.79**).

✔ **Tip**

■ To modify a string to display in different styles, such as bold type or italics, you must define those styles in the Character and Paragraph options for a dynamic text box. Uppercase and lowercase are actually different characters rather than a different style, which is why you need to modify the string.

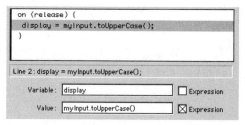

Figure 10.78 The toUpperCase method converts the characters in the variable called myInput to uppercase.

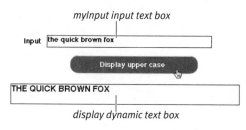

Figure 10.79 The results of the toUpperCase method show in the dynamic text box called display.

MANIPULATING INFORMATION

The information that you store in variables, modify in expressions, and test with conditional statements often needs to be processed and manipulated using mathematical functions such as square roots, sines, cosines, or exponents. Flash can perform these calculations with the Math object, which lets you create formulas for complicated interactions between the objects in your movie and your viewer or for sophisticated geometry in your graphics. For example, the Math object allows you to model the correct trajectory of colliding objects or the effects of gravity for a physics tutorial, calculate probabilities for a card game, or generate random numbers to add unpredictable elements in your movie. Much of this information you manipulate sometimes needs to be stored in arrays to give you better control over your data and a more efficient way to retrieve it. You can use arrays to keep track of ordered data such as shopping lists, color tables, or scorecards.

When the information you need depends on the time or the date, you can use the Date object to retrieve the current year, month, or even millisecond. Build clocks and timers to use inside your Flash movie, or send the time information along with a viewer's profile to a server-side script.

All of this information handling and processing is made easier with the use of functions. You'll learn how to build functions that string together separate action statements and objects to extend their predefined capabilities. Build a single function, for example, that automatically attaches a sound, plays it, and adjusts the volume level and pan settings based on the parameters you provide. You can even build functions to customize your own objects. Extend the capabilities of predefined Flash objects by creating your own methods and properties for your customized objects. This chapter explores the variety of ways you can manipulate information with added complexity and flexibility and shows how to integrate the objects you've learned about in previous chapters.

Calculations with the Math Object

The Math object lets you access trigonometric functions such as sine, cosine, and tangent; logarithmic functions; rounding functions; and mathematical constants such as *pi* or *e*. The methods and properties of the Math object are summarized in **Table 11.1**. As with the Key object, you don't need to instantiate the Math object in order to call on its methods or properties, and all of the Math object's properties are read-only values and written in all capital letters. You precede the method with the object Math. For example, to calculate the square root of 10, you write:

```
myAnswer = Math.sqrt (10)
```

and the calculated value is put into the variable myAnswer. To use a constant, use a similar syntax:

```
myCircum = Math.PI * 2 * myRadius
```

The mathematical constant *pi* is multiplied by 2 and the variable myRadius, and the result is put into the variable myCircum.

Table 11.1

Methods and Properties of the Math Object	
METHOD OR PROPERTY	DESCRIPTION
abs(number)	Calculates the absolute value. Math.abs(-4) returns 4.
acos(number)	Calculates the arc cosine.
asin(number)	Calculates the arc sine.
atan(number)	Calculates the arc tangent.
atan2(y, x)	Calculates the angle (in radians) from the *x*-axis to a point on the *y*-axis.
ceil(number)	Rounds the number up to the nearest integer. Math.ceil (2.34) returns 3.
cos(number)	Calculates the cosine of an angle in radians.
exp(number)	Calculates the exponent of the constant e.
floor(number)	Rounds the number down to the nearest integer. Math.floor (2.34) returns 2.
log(number)	Calculates the natural logarithm.
max(x, y)	Returns the larger of two values. Math.max (2, 7) returns 7.
min(x, y)	Returns the smaller of two values. Math.min (2, 7) returns 2.
pow(base, exponent)	Calculates the exponent of a number.
random()	Returns a random number between 0.0 and 1.0.
round(number)	Rounds the number to the nearest integer. Math.round (2.34) returns 2.
sin(number)	Calculates the sine of an angle in radians.
sqrt(number)	Calculates the square root.
tan(number)	Calculates the tangent of an angle in radians.
E	Euler's constant; the base of natural logarithms.
LN2	The natural logarithm of 2.
LOG2E	The base 2 logarithm of *e*.
LN10	The natural logarithm of 10.
LOG10E	The base 10 logarithm of *e*.
PI	The circumference of a circle divided by its diameter.
SQRT1_2	The square root of 1/2.
SQRT2	The square root of 2.

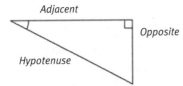

Sin theta = opposite/hypotenuse
Cos theta = adjacent/hypotenuse
Tan theta = opposite/adjacent

Figure 11.1 The angle, theta, of a right triangle is defined by sin, cos, and tan, and the length of the three sides.

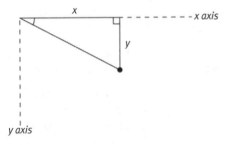

Figure 11.2 A point on the Stage makes a right triangle with x (adjacent side) and y (opposite side).

Calculating Angles with the Math Object

The angle that an object makes relative to the Stage or to another object is useful information for many game interactions, as well as for when you want to create dynamic animations and interfaces based purely in ActionScript. For example, to create a dial that controls the sound volume, you need to compute the angle at which your viewer drags the dial relative to the horizontal or vertical axis, and change the dial's rotation and sound's volume accordingly. Calculating the angle also requires that you brush up on some of your high school trigonometry, so a review of some basic principles related to sine, cosine, and tangent is in order.

The mnemonic device SOH CAH TOA can help you keep the trigonometric functions straight. These are acronyms that stand for Sine = Opposite over Hypotenuse, Cosine = Adjacent over Hypotenuse, and Tangent = Opposite over Adjacent (**Figure 11.1**). Knowing the length of any two sides of a right triangle is enough information for you to calculate the other two angles. You will most likely know the lengths of the opposite and adjacent sides of the triangle because they represent the y and x coordinates of a point (**Figure 11.2**). When you have the x and y coordinates, you can calculate the angle (theta) using the following mathematical formulas:

Tan theta = opposite/adjacent

or

Tan theta = y/x

or

theta = ArcTan (y/x)

In Flash, you can write this expression using the Math object this way:

```
myTheta = Math.atan(this._y/this._x)
```

Alternatively, Flash provides an even easier method that lets you define the *y* and *x* positions without having to do the division. The atan2 method accepts the *y* and *x* positions as two arguments, so you can write the equivalent statement:

```
myTheta = Math.atan2(this._y, this._x)
```

Unfortunately, the trigonometric methods of the Math object require and return values in radians, which describe angles in terms of the constant *pi*—easier mathematically, but not so convenient if you want to use the values to modify the _rotation property of a movie clip. You can convert an angle from radians to degrees and vice versa using the following formulas:

```
Radian = Math.PI/180 * degrees
```

```
Degrees = Radian * 180/Math.PI
```

The following tasks calculate the angles of a draggable movie clip and display the angles in degrees in a dynamic text box.

To calculate the angle relative to the Stage:

1. Create a movie-clip symbol, and place an instance of it on the Stage. In the Instance panel, give the movie-clip instance a name.

2. Create a dynamic text box on the Stage, as discussed in Chapter 10. In the Text Options panel, choose Single Line, and give the dynamic text box a variable name.

3. Select the movie-clip instance, and open the Actions panel.

4. Choose Actions > onClipEvent. Select the Load event.

5. Choose Actions > startDrag. In the Target field, enter this. Check the Expression box. Check the Constrain to rectangle box and the Lock mouse to center box. Enter 0 in the L field, 0 in the T field, the Stage width in the R field, and the Stage height in the B field (**Figure 11.3**).

   As a result, the center of the movie clip follows your viewer's pointer and is constrained to the boundaries of the Stage.

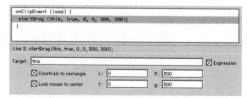

Figure 11.3 This startDrag action makes the movie clip follow the pointer and constrains it within a 300-by-300-pixel rectangle.

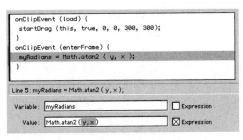

```
onClipEvent (load) {
  startDrag (this, true, 0, 0, 300, 300);
}
onClipEvent (enterFrame) {
  myRadians = Math.atan2 ( y, x );
}
```

Line 5: myRadians = Math.atan2 (y, x);

| Variable: | myRadians | ☐ Expression |
| Value: | Math.atan2 (y, x) | ☒ Expression |

Figure 11.4 The Math.atan2 method in the Value field requires the arguments y and x.

| Variable: | myRadians | ☐ Expression |
| Value: | Math.atan2 (this._y, this._x) | ☒ Expression |

Figure 11.5 The Math.atan2 method calculates the angle that the movie clip makes with the origin (top-left corner of the Stage).

```
onClipEvent (load) {
  startDrag (this, true, 0, 0, 300, 300);
}
onClipEvent (enterFrame) {
  myRadians = Math.atan2 ( this._y, this._x );
  _root.myDegrees = myRadians * 180/Math.PI + " degrees";
}
```

Line 6: _root.myDegrees = myRadians * 180/Math.PI + " degrees";

| Variable: | _root.myDegrees | ☐ Expression |
| Value: | myRadians * 180/Math.PI + " degrees" | ☒ Expression |

Figure 11.6 The dynamic text box called myDegrees displays the angle in degrees.

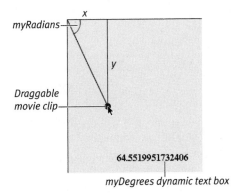

Figure 11.7 The movie clip makes an angle of approximately 65 degrees below the x axis.

6. Choose Actions > onClipEvent. Select the enterFrame event.

7. Choose Actions > set variable. In the Variable field, enter a name for your variable that will hold the angle in radians. Place your cursor in the Value field, and choose Objects > Math > atan2. Check the Expression box (**Figure 11.4**).

8. In the Value field, replace the y argument with this._y, and replace the x argument with this._x (**Figure 11.5**).

   Flash calculates the arc tangent of the *y* position of the pointer divided by the *x* position of the pointer and returns the value in radians.

9. Choose Actions > set variable. In the Variable field, enter the full target path to your dynamic text box on the root Timeline.

10. In the Value field, enter the expression that multiplies your variable that holds the radian angle by 180 and divides it by the constant pi:

    `myRadians * 180/Math.PI`

    Check the Expression box, and concatenate the string `"degrees"` to the end of the expression.

    The angle is converted from radians to degrees and assigned to the dynamic text variable (**Figure 11.6**).

11. Test your movie.

    As the viewer moves the pointer around the Stage, the movie clip follows the pointer. Flash calculates the angle that the movie clip makes with the axis of the root Timeline and displays the angle (in degrees) in the dynamic text box (**Figure 11.7**).

To calculate the angle relative to another point:

1. Continuing with the previous task, create another movie-clip symbol, and place an instance of it on the Stage. In the Instance panel, give it a name.

2. Select the first movie-clip instance (the draggable one), and open the Actions panel.

3. Select the statement that calculates the angle from the atan2 method. Change the expression to read:

   ```
   Math.atan2((this._y-
   _root.myReferencePoint._y),
   (this._x-_root.myReferencePoint._x))
   ```

   where myReferencePoint is the name of the second movie clip, which remains stationary.

   By subtracting the *y* and *x* positions of the reference point from the draggable movie clip's position, Flash calculates the *y* and *x* distances between the two points (**Figure 11.8**).

4. Test your movie.

   As the viewer moves the pointer around the Stage, the movie clip follows the pointer. Flash calculates the angle that the draggable movie clip makes with the stationary movie clip, and displays the angle (in degrees) in the dynamic text box.

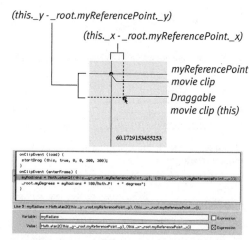

Figure 11.8 The difference between the *y* positions of the draggable movie clip and the myReferencePoint movie clip is the y parameter for Math.atan2. The difference between the *x* positions of the draggable movie clip and the myReferencePoint movie clip is the x parameter for Math.atan2.

Figure 11.9 The expression within the parentheses is rounded to the nearest integer and displayed in the dynamic text box called myDegrees.

So far, the returned values for your angles have had many decimal places. Often, you will need to round those values to the nearest whole number (or integer) so you can use those values as parameters in methods and properties. Use `Math.round` to round values to the nearest integer, use `Math.ceil` to round to the closest integer greater than or equal to the value, and use `Math.floor` to round to the closest integer less than or equal to the value.

To round a number to an integer:

1. Continuing with the previous task, select the draggable movie clip and open the Actions panel.

2. Select the statement that converts the angle from radians to degrees.

3. Place your cursor in the Value field in front of the expression, and enter the method `Math.round`. Use parentheses to group the expression that converts radians to degrees (**Figure 11.9**).

   Flash converts the angle from radians to degrees, and then applies the `Math.round` method to that value, returning an integer.

You can apply the methods that calculate angles and round values to create a draggable rotating dial. The approach is to calculate the angle of the mouse's position to the center point of the dial. Then, set the `_rotation` property of the dial to the angle.

To create a draggable rotating dial:

1. Create a movie-clip symbol of a dial. Create a button symbol, and place an instance of the button inside the movie-clip symbol.

2. Select the button instance that's inside the movie clip, and open the Actions panel.

(continued on next page)

3. Choose Actions > on. Select the Press event and deselect the Release event.

4. Choose Actions > set variable. In the Variable field, enter the variable name pressing. In the Value field, enter true. Check the Expression box next to the Value field (**Figure 11.10**).

5. Choose Actions > on. Select both the Release and the Release Outside events.

6. Choose Actions > set variable. In the Variable field, enter the variable name pressing. In the Value field, enter false. Check the Expression box next to the Value field (**Figure 11.11**).

   The button instance keeps track of whether your viewer is pressing or not pressing this button.

7. Return to the root Timeline, and place an instance of your movie clip (that contains the button) on the Stage.

8. Select the movie-clip instance, and open the Actions panel.

9. Choose Actions > onClipEvent. Select the enterFrame event.

10. Choose Actions > if. In the Condition field, enter pressing == true.

11. Choose Actions > set variable. In the Variable field, enter a variable name. In the Value field, enter:

    Math.atan2((_root._ymouse-this._y), (_root._xmouse-this._x))

    Check the Expression box next to the Value field.

    Flash calculates the angle between the viewer's pointer and the center of the movie clip (**Figure 11.12**).

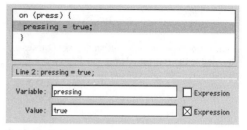

Figure 11.10 Set pressing to be true when the button is depressed.

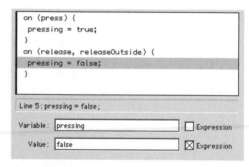

Figure 11.11 Set pressing to be false when the button is either released or released outside the button's hit area.

Figure 11.12 The variable myRadians contains the calculated angle between the pointer and the movie clip.

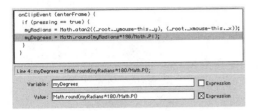

Figure 11.13 The angle is converted from radians to degrees, rounded to the nearest integer, and assigned to the variable myDegrees.

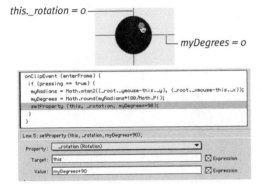

Figure 11.14 The rotation of the movie-clip dial is set at myDegrees + 90 to account for the difference between the calculated angle (myDegrees) and the rotation property.

12. Choose Actions > set variable. In the Variable field, enter a variable name. In the Value field, enter the expression to convert radians into degrees and round the result to an integer. Check the Expression box next to the Value field (**Figure 11.13**).

13. Choose Actions > setProperty. Select Rotation from the Property pull-down menu. In the Target field, enter this. Check the Expression box. In the Value field, enter your variable that holds the angle in degrees, and add 90. Check the Expression box.

The rotation of the movie clip is assigned to the calculated angle. The 90 is added to compensate for the difference between the calculated angle and the movie-clip rotation property. A value of 0 for _rotation corresponds to the 12 o'clock position of a movie clip, but a value of 0 corresponds to the 3 o'clock position of the calculated arcTangent angle, so adding 90 equalizes them (**Figure 11.14**).

14. Test your movie.

When viewers press the button in the dial, they can rotate it by dragging it around its center point. When they release the button, the dial stops rotating.

CALCULATING ANGLES WITH THE MATH OBJECT

Using Sine and Cosine for Directional Movement

When you want to control how far an object on the Stage travels based on its angle, you can use the sine and cosine trigonometric functions to help you do the calculations. For example, say that you want to create a racing game that features a car that your viewer moves around a track. The car travels at a certain speed, and it moves according to where the front of the car is pointed. If the car is pointed up, it'll move forward. If the car is pointed to the right, it'll move to the right, and if the car is pointed at 75 degrees, it'll move in that direction. Calculating just how far the car moves in any direction requires the `Math.sin` and `Math.cos` methods of the Math object. The new location of the car is determined by both the *x* and *y* components of the triangle that is formed by the angle of the car. When the car is angled up, the *y* component is 1 and the *x* component is 0. When the car is angled to the right, the *y* component is 0 and the *x* component is 1. When the car is angled somewhere in the middle, the sine and cosine of the angle give you the *x* and *y* contributions (**Figure 11.15**). The sine of the angle determines the magnitude of the *y* component, and the cosine of the angle determines the magnitude of the *x* component. However, sine and cosine are based on angles that begin at 0 degrees from the horizontal axis. The rotation property, on the other hand, is based on angles that begin at 0 degrees from the vertical axis. Hence, you need to use cosine for the *y* component and sine for the *x* component (**Figure 11.16**).

```
myCar._y = myCar_y —Math.cos(angle);

myCar._x = myCar_x +Math.sin(angle);
```

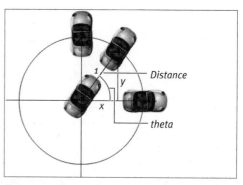

Figure 11.15 The x and y components of this car, which moves a certain distance, is determined by the cosine and sine of its angle, theta.

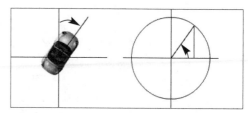

Figure 11.16 The rotation of a movie clip begins from the vertical axis and increases in the clockwise direction (left). Values for sine and cosine angles begin from the horizontal axis and increase in the counterclockwise direction (right).

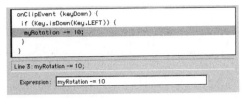

```
onClipEvent (keyDown) {
  if (Key.isDown(Key.LEFT)) {
    myRotation -= 10;
  }
}
```

Line 3 : myRotation -= 10;

Expression : myRotation -= 10

Figure 11.17 The variable myRotation decreases when the left arrow key is depressed.

```
onClipEvent (keyDown) {
  if (Key.isDown(Key.LEFT)) {
    myRotation -= 10;
  } else if (Key.isDown(Key.RIGHT)) {
    myRotation += 10;
  }
}
```

Line 5 : myRotation += 10;

Expression : myRotation += 10

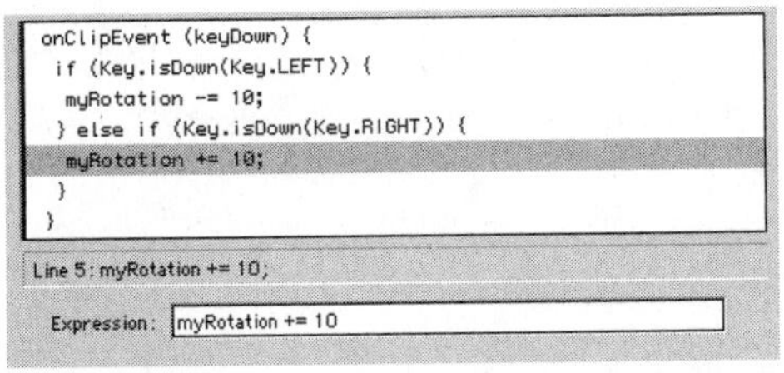

Figure 11.18 The variable myRotation increases when the right arrow key is depressed.

In the following task, you will create a movie clip whose rotation can be controlled by the viewer. The movie clip has a constant velocity, so it will travel in the direction of where it is pointed, just as a car moves according to where it is steered.

To create a controllable object with directional movement:

1. Create a movie-clip symbol, place an instance of it on the Stage, and name it.

2. Select the movie-clip instance, and open the Actions panel.

3. Choose Actions > onClipEvent. Select the Key Down event.

4. Choose Actions > if. In the Condition field, enter:

   `Key.isDown (Key.LEFT)`

   Flash checks to see if the left arrow key is depressed.

5. Choose Actions > evaluate. In the Expression field, enter myRotation as the variable for the rotation of your movie clip, then the -= operator, and then 10. Flash subtracts 10 from the current value of myRotation if the left arrow key is depressed (**Figure 11.17**).

6. Choose Actions > else if. In the Condition field, enter:

   `Key.isDown (Key.RIGHT)`

   Flash checks if the right arrow key is depressed.

7. Choose Actions > evaluate. In the Expression field, enter myRotation, then the += operator, and then 10. Flash adds 10 from the current value of myRotation if the right arrow key is depressed (**Figure 11.18**).

(continued on next page)

SINE, COSINE FOR DIRECTIONAL MOVEMENT

8. Choose Actions > onClipEvent. Select the EnterFrame event.

9. Choose Actions > set variable. In the Variable field, enter the variable name ychange. Put your pointer in the Value field, and choose Objects > Math > cos.

The Math.cos method appears in the Value field with the argument highlighted.

10. Replace the highlighted argument with an expression to convert the value in myRotation from degrees to radians. Multiply the entire expression by 3, and check the Expression box next to the Value field (**Figure 11.19**).

The variable ychange represents the magnitude of the *y* component. Multiplying by 3 increases the magnitude of the change so that the movie clip moves a little faster in the *y* direction.

11. Choose Actions > set variable. In the Variable field, enter the variable name xchange. Put your pointer in the Value field, and choose Objects > Math > cos.

The Math.sin method appears in the Value field with the argument highlighted.

12. Replace the highlighted argument with an expression to convert the value in myRotation from degrees to radians. Multiply the entire expression by 3, and check the Expression box next to the Value field (**Figure 11.20**).

The variable xchange represents the magnitude of the *x* component. Multiplying by 3 increases the magnitude of the change so that the movie clip moves a little faster in the *x* direction.

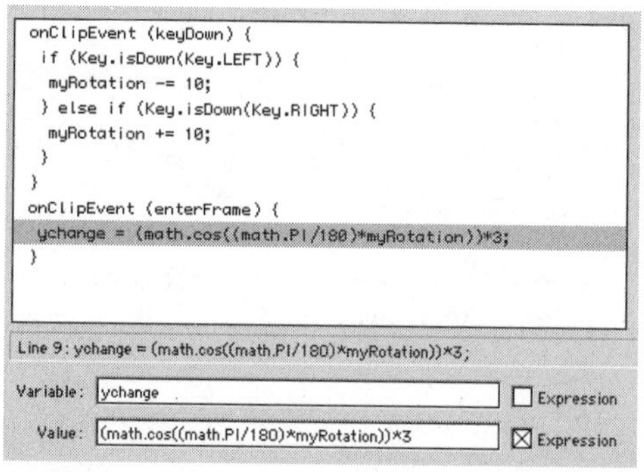

```
onClipEvent (keyDown) {
  if (Key.isDown(Key.LEFT)) {
    myRotation -= 10;
  } else if (Key.isDown(Key.RIGHT)) {
    myRotation += 10;
  }
}
onClipEvent (enterFrame) {
  ychange = (math.cos((math.PI/180)*myRotation))*3;
}
```

Line 9: ychange = (math.cos((math.PI/180)*myRotation))*3;

Variable: ychange   ☐ Expression

Value: (math.cos((math.PI/180)*myRotation))*3   ☒ Expression

Figure 11.19 The cosine of the movie clip's rotation is calculated and assigned to ychange.

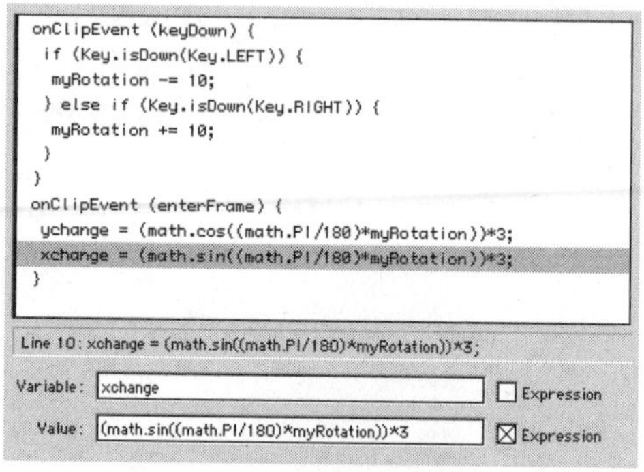

```
onClipEvent (keyDown) {
  if (Key.isDown(Key.LEFT)) {
    myRotation -= 10;
  } else if (Key.isDown(Key.RIGHT)) {
    myRotation += 10;
  }
}
onClipEvent (enterFrame) {
  ychange = (math.cos((math.PI/180)*myRotation))*3;
  xchange = (math.sin((math.PI/180)*myRotation))*3;
}
```

Line 10: xchange = (math.sin((math.PI/180)*myRotation))*3;

Variable: xchange   ☐ Expression

Value: (math.sin((math.PI/180)*myRotation))*3   ☒ Expression

Figure 11.20 The sine of the movie clip's rotation is calculated and assigned to xchange.

```
onClipEvent (keyDown) {
  if (Key.isDown(Key.LEFT)) {
    myRotation -= 10;
  } else if (Key.isDown(Key.RIGHT)) {
    myRotation += 10;
  }
}
onClipEvent (enterFrame) {
  ychange = (math.cos((math.PI/180)*myRotation))*3;
  xchange = (math.sin((math.PI/180)*myRotation))*3;
  setProperty (this, _y, this._y - ychange);
  setProperty (this, _x, this._x + xchange);
  setProperty (this, _rotation, myRotation);
}
```

Line 13: setProperty (this, _rotation, myRotation);

Property: _rotation (Rotation)

Target: this ☒ Expression

Value: myRotation ☒ Expression

Figure 11.21 The last three setProperty statements in the Actions List modify the x and y positions on the variables xchange and ychange and also change the rotation of the movie clip based on the variable myRotation.

Figure 11.22 As the movie clip of the car rotates, the x and y components are calculated from cosine and sine, and the car's new position is defined.

13. Choose Actions > setProperty. From the Property pull-down menu, select Y Position. In the Target field, enter this. In the Value field, enter

this._y - ychange

Check both Expression boxes.

14. Choose Actions > setProperty. From the Property pull-down menu, select X Position. In the Target field, enter this. In the Value field, enter

this._x + xchange

Check both Expression boxes.

15. Choose Actions > setProperty. From the Property pull-down menu, select Rotation. In the Target field, enter this. In the Value field, enter the variable myRotation. Check both Expression boxes (**Figure 11.21**).

16. Test your movie.

When your viewer presses the left or right arrow key, the rotation of the movie clip changes. The x and y positions change as well, calculated from the angle of the movie clip. The movie clip moves according to where its nose is pointed (**Figure 11.22**).

Calculating Distances with the Math Object

Figure 11.23 This right triangle has sides *a, b,* and *c.*

Using the Pythagorean theorem, Flash makes it possible for you to calculate the distance between two objects. This technique can be useful for creating novel interactions between interface elements—for example, graphics, buttons, or sounds that react in proportion to their distance from the viewer's pointer. You can also create games that have interaction based on the distance between objects and the player. For example, a game where the player uses a net to catch goldfish in an aquarium can use the distance between the goldfish and the net to model the behavior of the goldfish. Perhaps the closer the net comes to one, the quicker it swims away.

The distance between any two points is defined by the equation

$a^2 + b^2 = c^2$

or

c = square root $(a^2 + b^2)$

The variables *a* and *b* are the lengths of the sides of a right triangle, and *c* is the length of the hypotenuse (**Figure 11.23**). Using Flash's `Math.sqrt` and `Math.pow` methods, the distance between the points on the hypotenuse can be calculated with the following:

```
c = Math.sqrt ((Math.pow (a, 2)) +
(Math.pow (b, 2)))
```

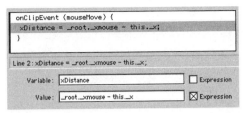

Figure 11.24 The difference between the *x* position of the pointer and the *x* position of the movie clip is the distance between them on the *x* axis.

```
onClipEvent (mouseMove) {
    xDistance = _root._xmouse - this._x;
    yDistance = _root._ymouse - this._y;
}
```

Line 3: yDistance = _root._ymouse - this._y;

Variable: yDistance ☐ Expression

Value: _root._ymouse - this._y ☒ Expression

Figure 11.25 The difference between the *y* position of the pointer and the *y* position of the movie clip is the distance between them on the *y* axis.

To calculate the distance between the pointer and another point:

1. Create a movie clip, and place an instance of it on the Stage. In the Instance panel, give it a name.

2. Select the movie-clip instance, and open the Actions panel.

3. Choose Actions > onClipEvent. Select the Mouse move event.

4. Choose Actions > set variable. In the Variable field, enter xDistance. In the Value field, enter:

   `_root._xmouse - this._x`

   Check the Expression box next to the Value field.

   The distance between the *x* position of the pointer and the *x* position of the movie clip is assigned to the variable xDistance (**Figure 11.24**).

5. Choose Actions > set variable. In the Variable field, enter yDistance. In the Value field, enter:

   `_root._ymouse - this._y`

   Check the Expression box next to the Value field.

   The distance between the *y* position of the pointer and the *y* position of the movie clip is assigned to the variable yDistance (**Figure 11.25**).

6. Choose Actions > set variable. In the Variable field, enter the name myDistance. Put your pointer in the Value field, and choose Objects > Math > sqrt.

   The Math.sqrt method appears in the Value field with the argument high- lighted.

(continued on next page)

7. Replace the highlighted argument by choosing Objects > Math > pow and entering xDistance and 2 for the Math.pow method. Add another Math.pow method with the arguments yDistance and 2 (**Figure 11.26**).

Flash calculates the square of the xDistance and adds it to the square of the yDistance. Then it calculates the square root of that sum.

8. Choose Actions > set variable. Assign the value of myDistance to a dynamic text box on the Stage (**Figure 11.27**).

9. Test your movie.

As the pointer moves around the movie clip, Flash calculates the distance between them in pixels.

Figure 11.26 The distance between the two points is calculated from the variables xDistance and yDistance.

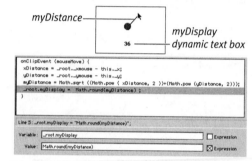

Figure 11.27 The dynamic text box myDisplay shows an integer of myDistance.

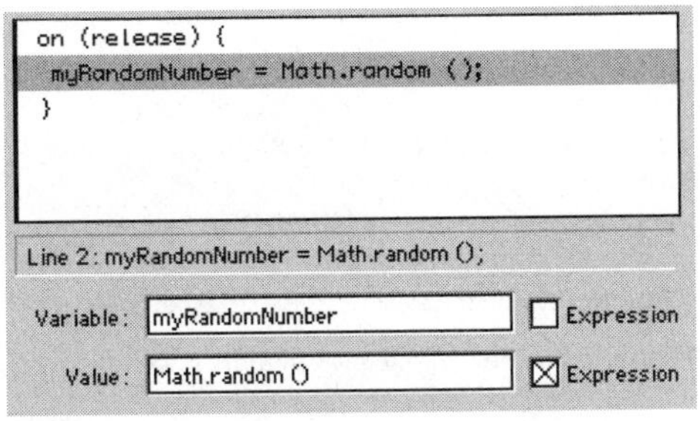

```
on (release) {
    myRandomNumber = Math.random ();
}
```

Line 2: myRandomNumber = Math.random ();

| Variable: | myRandomNumber | ☐ Expression |
| Value: | Math.random () | ☒ Expression |

Figure 11.28 A random number between 0 and 1 is assigned to the variable myRandomNumber.

Generating Random Numbers

When you need to incorporate random elements into your Flash movie, either for a design effect or for game play, you can use the Math object's `Math.random` method. The `Math.random` method generates random numbers between 0 and 1 with up to 15 decimal places in between. For example, typical return values are:

0.242343544598273

0.043628738493829

0.7567833408654

You can modify the random number by multiplying it or adding to it in order to get the span of numbers you need. For example, if you need random numbers between 1 and 10, multiply the return value of `Math.random` by 9, and then add 1, as in the following statement:

`Math.random () * 9 + 1`

If you need an integer, apply the `Math.round` method to round the number to the nearest integer.

To generate a random number:

1. Create a button symbol, and place an instance of it on the Stage. Select the instance, and open the Actions panel.

2. Choose Actions > set variable.

3. In the Variable field, enter a variable name. Place your pointer in the Value field, and choose Objects > Math > random. Check the Expression box.

   The `Math.random` method appears in the Variable field (**Figure 11.28**).

4. Create a dynamic text box on the Stage with the same variable name you assigned in your button instance actions.

(continued on next page)

When the button is clicked, a new random number between 0 and 1 is generated and displayed in the dynamic text box.

Use randomly generated numbers to add unpredictable animated elements to your movie. Enemy ships in an arcade game could appear anywhere to attack the player. You can make Flash deal random cards from a deck of cards so every hand is different. Or for a test, you can shuffle the order in which the questions appear. The following task demonstrates how random numbers can modify property values by setting the *x* and *y* properties of a movie clip.

To use random numbers as property values:

1. Create a movie-clip symbol, and place an instance of it on the Stage. In the Instance panel, give it a name.

2. Select the movie-clip instance, and open the Actions panel.

3. Choose Actions > onClipEvent. Select the enterFrame event.

4. Choose Actions > set variable. In the Variable field, enter a variable name. In the Value field, enter

   `Math.random () * 299 + 1`

   Check the Expression box.

   Flash generates a random number between 1 and 300 (**Figure 11.29**).

5. Again, choose Actions > set variable. Assign a second variable to a random number between 1 and 300.

6. Choose Actions > setProperty. Select X Position in the Property pull-down menu. In the Target field, enter this. In the Value field, apply the `Math.round` method to the first of your randomly generated numbers. Check both Expression boxes (**Figure 11.30**).

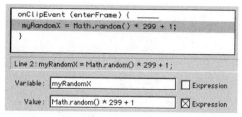

Figure 11.29 The variable myRandomX is assigned a number between 1 and 300.

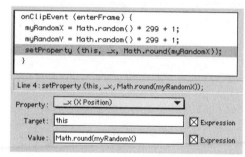

Figure 11.30 The *x* position of the movie clip is set to an integer of myRandomX.

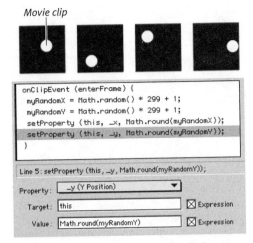

Movie clip

```
onClipEvent (enterFrame) {
  myRandomX = Math.random() * 299 + 1;
  myRandomY = Math.random() * 299 + 1;
  setProperty (this, _x, Math.round(myRandomX));
  setProperty (this, _y, Math.round(myRandomY));
}
```

Line 5: setProperty (this, _y, Math.round(myRandomY));

Property: _y (Y Position)

Target: this   ☒ Expression

Value: Math.round(myRandomY)   ☒ Expression

Figure 11.31 The *y* position of the movie clip is set to an integer of myRandomY. The movie clip changes its position on the Stage randomly (top).

The movie clip's *x* position is set to the first random number.

7. Choose Actions > setProperty. Select Y Position in the Property pull-down menu. In the Target field, enter this. In the Value field, apply the Math.round method to the second of your randomly generated numbers. Check both Expression boxes.

   The movie clip's *y* position is set to the second random number (**Figure 11.31**).

8. Set your Stage size to 300 x 300. Test your movie.

   The *x* and *y* positions of your movie clip are set randomly, making your movie clip jump around the stage.

✔ **Tip**

■ The Math.random method replaces the random action used in earlier versions of Flash. While the random action still works, it is deprecated, so you should stick to using the Math object to generate your random numbers.

Ordering Information with Arrays

When you have many pieces of related information that you want to store, you may need to use the Array object to help you arrange that information. Arrays are containers that hold data, just as variables do, except arrays hold data in a specific sequence, called an index. The index begins at 0 and is numbered sequentially so that each piece of data corresponds to an index, as in a two-column table (**Figure 11.32**). Since each piece of data is ordered numerically, the information can be retrieved and modified easily, and most importantly, automatically, by just referencing its index. For example, let's say you're building a foreign-language tutorial and want to search the content of a viewer's text input for important vocabulary words. You can store those words in an array, so that index 0 holds the first vocabulary word, index 1 holds the second word, and so on. By using a looping statement you can check the input text against each entry in the array automatically.

The indexes of an array are referenced with the square bracket, as in the following:

```
myArray[4]
```

The square brackets are known as *array access operators*. This statement accesses the data in index 4 of the array called myArray. The number of entries defines the length of an array, so the length of the array in **Figure 11.32** is 6. You can think of an array as a sequence of ordered variables. For example, the variables myScores0, myScores1, myScores2, and myScores3 could be a single array called myScores of length 4 with indices between 0 and 3. Since you only have to handle one array object instead of four separate variables, using arrays makes information easier to manage.

Index	Value
0	"monitor"
1	"mouse"
2	"keyboard"
3	"CPU"
4	"modem"
5	"speakers"

Figure 11.32 An array is like a two-column table with an index column and a corresponding value column.

The data that arrays hold can be mixed. So you could have a number in index 0, a string in index 1, and a Boolean value in index 2. You can change the data in any index in an array at any time, just as you can with variables. The length of arrays is not fixed, either, so arrays can grow or shrink to accommodate new information as needed.

Creating an array involves two steps. The first is to use a constructor function to instantiate a new array from the Array object. For example,

```
myArray = new Array ()
```

The second step is to fill, or *populate*, your array with data. One way to populate your array is to assign the data to each index in separate statements like this:

```
myArray [0] = "Russell";

myArray [1] = "Rebecca";

myArray [2] = "Elissa";

myArray [3] = "Marjorie";
```

Another way to assign the data is to put the information within the constructor function like so:

```
myArray = new Array ("Russell",
"Rebecca", "Elissa", "Marjorie")
```

The second way is a more compact way of populating your array, but you are restricted to entering data in sequence.

To create an array:

1. Select the first keyframe of the Timeline, and open the Actions panel.

2. Choose Actions > set variable.

3. In the Variable field, enter the name of your array. Put your cursor in the Value field, and choose Objects > Array > new Array. Check the Expression box next to the Value field.

   The new Array constructor function appears in the Value field. Flash instantiates a new array (**Figure 11.33**).

4. Choose Actions > set variable.

5. In the Variable field, enter the name of your new array, then an index within square brackets. In the Value field, enter the data you want to store in the array at that index position (**Figure 11.34**).

6. Continue choosing Actions > set variable to assign more data to the array.

✔ Tip

■ You can predefine the length of your new array by putting a number in the parentheses of the constructor function. For example,

   myArray = new Array (4)

   creates a new array of four entries. Even if you don't fill all the positions of the array, myArray will still have a length of 4.

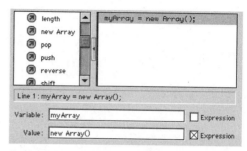

Figure 11.33 A new object called myArray is instantiated.

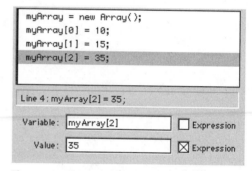

Figure 11.34 This array contains three entries.

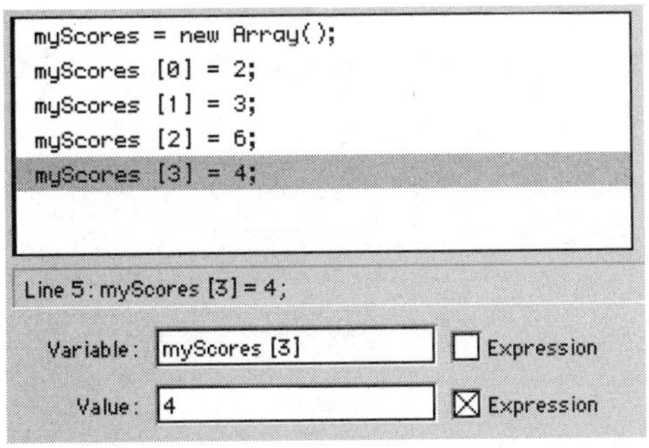

```
myScores = new Array();
myScores [0] = 2;
myScores [1] = 3;
myScores [2] = 6;
myScores [3] = 4;
```

Line 5: myScores [3] = 4;

Variable: myScores [3]   ☐ Expression

Value: 4   ☒ Expression

Figure 11.35 This array, called myScores, has four entries.

Since the entries contained in arrays are indexed numerically, they lend themselves nicely to looping actions. By using looping actions such as `while`, `do while`, and `for`, you can have Flash go through each index value and retrieve or assign new data quickly and automatically. For example, to average the scores of many players in an array without a looping action, you would have to total all their scores and divide by the number of players, like this:

```
mySum = myScores [0] + myScores [1] +
myScores [2] + ...
```

```
myAverage = mySum/myScores.length;
```

The property `length` defines the number of entries in the array.

Using a looping action, however, you can calculate the mySum value this way:

```
For (i=0; i<myScores.length; i++) {

mySum = mySum + myScores[i];

}
```

```
myAverage = mySum/myScores.length;
```

Flash starts at index 0 and adds each indexed entry in the array to the variable mySum until it reaches the end of the array.

To loop through an array:

1. Select the first keyframe of the Timeline, and open the Actions panel.

2. Choose Actions > set variable, and define a new array called myScores, as you did in the previous task.

3. Choose Actions > set variable, and populate your myScores array with numbers representing scores (**Figure 11.35**).

4. Create a button symbol, and place an instance of the button on the Stage. Select the button instance, and open the Actions panel.

(continued on next page)

5. Choose Actions > for. In the Init field, enter i=0. In the Condition field, enter i<myScores.length. In the Next field, enter i++.

   Flash begins with the counter variable i set at the value 0. It increases the variable by increments of one until the variable reaches the length of the array called myScores (**Figure 11.36**).

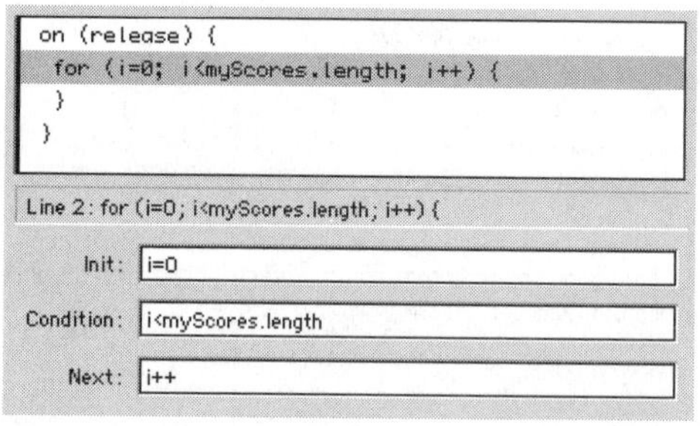

Figure 11.36 This for action loops the same number of times as there are entries in the array myScore.

6. Choose Actions > set variable. In the Variable field, enter mySum. In the Value field, enter mySum + myScores[i]. Check the Expression box next to the Value field.

   At each index of the myScore array, Flash adds the value in that index to mySum. When the value of i reaches the value of myScores.length, Flash jumps out of the for loop and stops adding any more index values. Therefore, the last addition is myScores [myScores.length-1], which corresponds to the last index of the array (**Figure 11.37**).

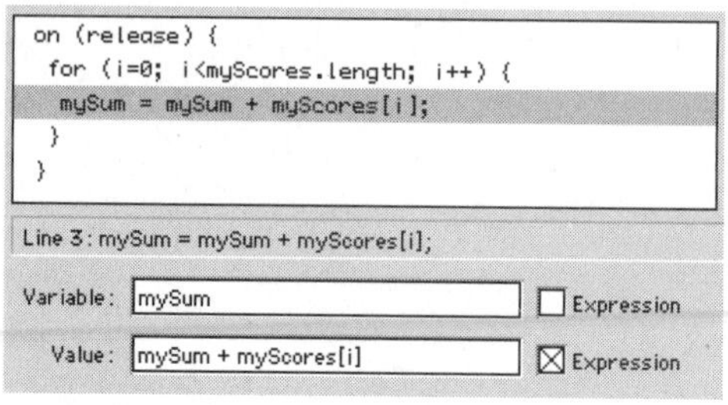

Figure 11.37 The variable mySum adds the value of each entry in the array.

7. Select the ending curly brace of the for statement. Choose Actions > set variable.

   The next statement appears after the curly brace outside the **for** statement.

8. In the Variable field, enter myAverage. In the Value field, enter the expression mySum/myScores.length. Check the Expression box next to the Value field (**Figure 11.38**).

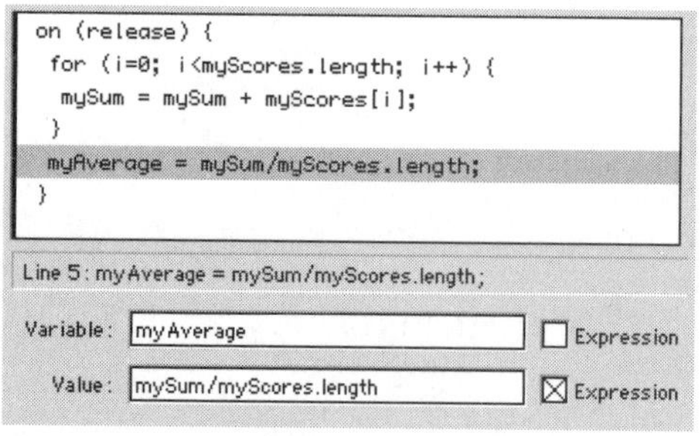

Figure 11.38 Outside the for loop, the variable myAverage calculates the average value of the entries in the array.

9. Create a dynamic text box on the Stage with the variable name myAverage.

10. Test your movie.

    When the button on the Stage is clicked, Flash loops through the myScores array to add all the data entries, and divides the total by the number of entries. The average is displayed in the dynamic text box on the Stage.

The methods of the Array object let you sort, delete, add, and manipulate the data in an array. A summary of the methods of the Array object is listed in **Table 11.2**. It's convenient to think of the methods in pairs. For example, `shift` and `unshift` both modify the beginning of an array, `push` and `pop` both modify the end of an array, and `slice` and `splice` modify the middle of an array.

Table 11.2

Methods of the Array Object

METHOD	DESCRIPTION
concat(array1,…,arrayN)	Concatenates the specified values and returns a new array.
join(separator)	Concatenates the elements of the array, inserts the separator between the elements, and returns a string. The default separator is a comma.
pop()	Removes the last element in the array and returns the value of that element.
push(value)	Adds elements to the end of the array and returns the new length.
shift()	Removes the first element in the array and returns the value of that element.
unshift(value)	Adds elements to the beginning of the array and returns the new length.
slice(indexA,indexB)	Returns a new array beginning with indexA and ending with the (indexB-1).
splice(index,count,elem1,…,elemN)	Inserts or deletes elements. Set count to o to insert specified values starting at index. Set count > o to delete the number of elements starting at and including index.
reverse()	Reverses the order of elements in the array.
sort()	Sorts an array using the < operator. Numbers are sorted in ascending order, and strings are sorted alphabetically.
toString()	Returns a string with every element concatenated and separated by a comma.

The following is an example of how some of these methods operate:

STATEMENT	VALUE OF MYARRAY
myArray = new Array (2, 4, 6, 8)	2, 4, 6, 8
myArray.pop()	2, 4, 6
myArray.push(1,3)	2, 4, 6, 1, 3
myArray.shift()	4, 6, 1, 3
myArray.unshift(5,7)	5, 7, 4, 6, 1, 3
myArray.splice(2,0,8,9)	5, 7, 8, 9, 4, 6, 1, 3
myArray.splice(3,2)	5, 7, 8, 6, 1, 3
myArray.reverse()	3, 1, 6, 8, 7, 5
myArray.sort()	1, 3, 5, 6, 7, 8

✔ Tips

- It's important to note which methods of the Array object modify the actual array and which ones return a new array. Concat, join, slice, and toString return new arrays or strings and require that you assign their values to a variable. For example, myNewArray = myArray.con-cat(8) puts 8 at the end of myArray and assigns the resulting array to myNewArray.

- Also note that some methods modify the array as well as return a specific value. These two things are not the same. For example, the statement myArray.pop() modifies myArray by removing the last element and it also returns the value of that last element. So in the following example:

```
myArray = new Array (2, 4, 6, 8);
myPop = myArray.pop();
```

The value of myPop is 8 and the value of myArray is now 2, 4, 6.

Using the Date and Time

The Date object lets you retrieve the local or universal (GMT) date and time information from the clock in your viewer's computer system. Using the Date object, you can retrieve the year, month, date, day of the week, hour, minute, second, and millisecond. Use the Date object and its methods to create accurate clocks in your movie or to find information about certain days and dates in the past. For example, you can create a date object for your birthday by specifying the month, date, and year. Using methods of the Date object, you can retrieve the day of the week for your date object that tells you what day you were born.

The Date object first needs to be instantiated with the constructor function new Date. Then you can call on its methods to retrieve specific time information. The common methods for retrieving the dates and times are summarized in **Table 11.3**.

To create a clock:

1. Create a dynamic text box on the Stage. Give the dynamic text box a variable name.

2. Select the dynamic text box, and choose Insert > Convert to Symbol. Give the symbol a name, and select Movie Clip Behavior. Click OK.

    Your dynamic text box is put into a movie-clip symbol. An instance of your movie clip remains on the Stage.

3. Select the movie-clip instance, and open the Actions panel.

4. Choose Actions > onClipEvent. Select the EnterFrame event.

(continued on next page)

Table 11.3

Methods of the Date Object	
METHOD	**DESCRIPTION**
getDate	Returns the day of the month as a number between 1 and 31.
getDay	Returns the day of the week as a number between 0 (Sunday) and 6 (Saturday).
getFullYear	Returns the year as a four-digit number.
getHours	Returns the hour of the day as a number between 0 and 23.
getMilliseconds	Returns the milliseconds.
getMinutes	Returns the minutes as a number between 0 and 59.
getMonth	Returns the month as a number between 0 (January) and 11 (December).
getSeconds	Returns the seconds as a number between 0 and 59.

5. Choose Actions > set variable. In the Variable field, enter the name of your new date object. Place your cursor in the Value field, and choose Objects > Date > new Date. Check the Expression box next to the Value field.

The new Date constructor function appears in the Value field with high-lighted arguments (**Figure 11.39**).

6. Delete all the highlighted arguments of the new Date constructor function.

When you don't specify the arguments of the Date object, you create a generic date object that you can use to retrieve current date and time information. When you specify the arguments of the Date object, you create an object that references a specific date or time.

7. Choose Actions > set variable. In the Variable field, enter currentHour. In the Value field, enter the name of your date object. With your cursor still in the Value field, choose Objects > Date > getHours. Check the Expression box.

The getHours method appears after the name of your date object. Flash retrieves the current hour and puts the returned value in your variable called currentHour (**Figure 11.40**).

8. Repeat the previous step to retrieve the current minute with the getMinutes method and the current second with the getSeconds method, and assign the returned values to variables (**Figure 11.41**).

9. Choose Actions > if. In the Condition field, enter

currentHour > 12

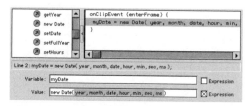

Figure 11.39 The arguments of the new Date constructor function are optional.

Figure 11.40 The current hour is assigned to the variable currentHour.

```
onClipEvent (enterFrame) {
    myDate = new Date();
    currentHour = myDate.getHours();
    currentMinute = myDate.getMinutes();
    currentSecond = myDate.getSeconds();
}
```

Figure 11.41 The current hour, minute, and second are assigned to different variables.

```
onClipEvent (enterFrame) {
  myDate = new Date();
  currentHour = myDate.getHours();
  currentMinute = myDate.getMinutes();
  currentSecond = myDate.getSeconds();
  if (currentHour>12) {
    currentHour = currentHour-12;
  }
}
```

Line 7: currentHour = currentHour-12;

Variable: currentHour ☐ Expression

Value: currentHour-12 ☒ Expression

Figure 11.42 The returned value for the method getHours is a number from 0 to 23. To convert the hour to the standard 12-hour cycle, subtract 12 from values greater than 12.

```
onClipEvent (enterFrame) {
  myDate = new Date();
  currentHour = myDate.getHours();
  currentMinute = myDate.getMinutes();
  currentSecond = myDate.getSeconds();
  if (currentHour>12) {
    currentHour = currentHour-12;
  } else if (currentHour == 0) {
    currentHour = 12;
  }
}
```

Line 9: currentHour = 12;

Variable: currentHour ☐ Expression

Value: 12 ☒ Expression

Figure 11.43 Since there is no "0" on our clocks, have Flash assign a 12 to any hour that has the value 0.

myDisplay dynamic text

Variable: myDisplay ☐ Expression

Value: "The time is now: \r" + currentHour + ":" + currentMinute+ ":" + currentSecond ☒ Expression

Figure 11.44 The dynamic text box (top) displays the concatenated values.

10. Choose Actions > set variable. In the Variable field, enter currentHour. In the Value field enter currentHour-12 (**Figure 11.42**).

11. Choose Actions > else if. In the Condition field, enter currentHour == 0

12. Choose Actions > set variable. In the Variable field enter currentHour. In the Value field enter 12. Check the Expression box next to the Value field (**Figure 11.43**).

13. Select the closing brace of the else statement, and choose Actions > set variable. In the Variable field, enter the name of your dynamic text box. In the Value field, concatenate the variable names for the hour, the minute, and the second with appropriate spacers in between. Check the Expression box next to the Value field (**Figure 11.44**).

14. Test your movie.

    The dynamic text box displays the current hour, minute, and second in the 12-hour format.

✔ Tip

- Note that minutes and seconds that are less than 10 display as single digits like 1 and 2, rather than as 01 and 02. Refine your clock by adding conditional statements to check the value of the current minutes and seconds, and add the appropriate 0 digit.

USING THE DATE AND TIME

The returned values for the getMonth and getDays methods of the Date object are numbers instead of string data types. The getMonth method returns values from 0 to 11 (0 = January), and the getDays method returns values from 0 to 6 (0 = Sunday). In order to correlate these numeric values to the names of the months or days of the week, you can create arrays that contain this information. For example, an array that contains the days of the week can be created with the following statements:

```
daysofWeek = new Array ();

daysofWeek[0] = "Sunday";

daysofWeek[1] = "Monday";

daysofWeek[2] = "Tuesday";

daysofWeek[3] = "Wednesday";

daysofWeek[4] = "Thursday";

daysofWeek[5] = "Friday";

daysofWeek[6] = "Saturday";
```

```
daysofWeek = new Array();
daysofWeek[0] = "Sunday";
daysofWeek[1] = "Monday";
daysofWeek[2] = "Tuesday";
daysofWeek[3] = "Wednesday";
daysofWeek[4] = "Thursday";
daysofWeek[5] = "Friday";
daysofWeek[6] = "Saturday";
```

Figure 11.45 The array daysofWeek contains strings of the days of the week.

To create a calendar:

1. Select the first keyframe of the Timeline, and open the Actions panel.

2. Choose Actions > set variable. In the Variable field, enter a name for a new array that will hold the days of the week. In the Value field, enter the constructor function new Array. Check the Expression box next to the Value field.

3. In a series of statements, assign to each index of your new array a string representing the names of the days of the week (**Figure 11.45**).

4. Choose Actions > set variable. In the Variable field, enter a name for a second new array, which will hold the months of the year. In the Value field, enter the constructor function new Array. Check the Expression box next to the Value field.

```
daysofMonth = new Array ();
daysofMonth[0] = "January";
daysofMonth[1] = "February";
daysofMonth[2] = "March";
daysofMonth[3] = "April";
daysofMonth[4] = "May";
daysofMonth[5] = "June";
daysofMonth[6] = "July";
daysofMonth[7] = "August";
daysofMonth[8] = "September";
daysofMonth[9] = "October";
daysofMonth[10] = "November";
daysofMonth[11] = "December";
```

Figure 11.46
The array daysofMonth contains strings of the months.

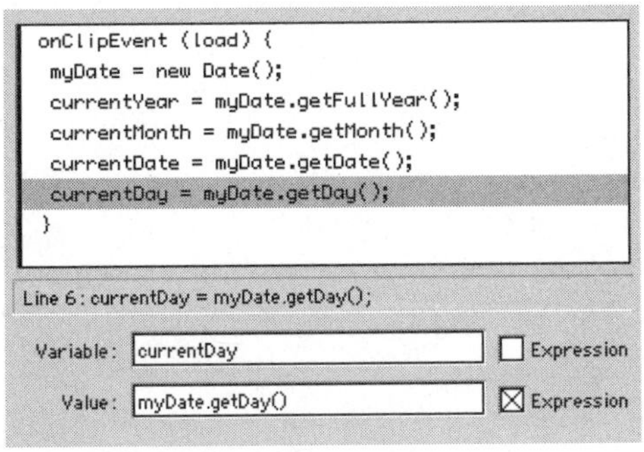

```
onClipEvent (load) {
  myDate = new Date();
  currentYear = myDate.getFullYear();
  currentMonth = myDate.getMonth();
  currentDate = myDate.getDate();
  currentDay = myDate.getDay();
}
```

Line 6: currentDay = myDate.getDay();

Variable: currentDay   ☐ Expression

Value: myDate.getDay()   ☒ Expression

Figure 11.47 The current year, month, date, and day are assigned to new variables.

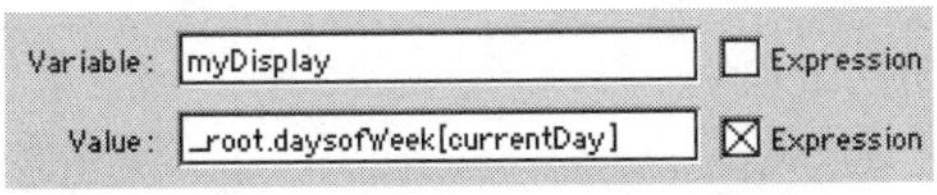

Variable: myDisplay   ☐ Expression

Value: _root.daysofWeek[currentDay]   ☒ Expression

Figure 11.48 The value of the variable currentDay is a number between 0 and 6. The expression in the Value field retrieves the correct string in the array corresponding to the current day.

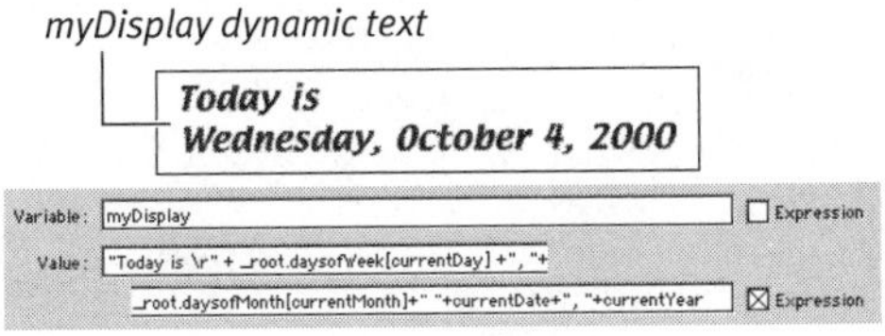

myDisplay dynamic text

> **Today is**
> **Wednesday, October 4, 2000**

Variable: myDisplay   ☐ Expression

Value: "Today is \r" + _root.daysofWeek[currentDay]+", "+
_root.daysofMonth[currentMonth]+" "+currentDate+", "+currentYear   ☒ Expression

Figure 11.49 The day, month, date, and year information is concatenated and displayed in myDisplay (top).

5. In a series of statements, assign to each index of your second new array a string representing the names of the months of the year (**Figure 11.46**).

6. Create a dynamic text box on the Stage. Give the dynamic text box a variable name.

7. Select the dynamic text box, and choose Insert > Convert to Symbol. Give the symbol a name, and select Movie Clip Behavior. Click OK.

   Your dynamic text box is put into a movie-clip symbol. An instance of your movie clip remains on the Stage.

8. Select the movie-clip instance, and open the Actions panel.

9. Choose Actions > onClipEvent. Select the Load event.

10. Choose Actions > set variable. In the Variable field, enter the name of your new date object. In the Value field enter the constructor function new Date without any arguments. Check the Expression box.

11. In a series of statements, call the getFullYear, getMonth, getDate, and getDay methods, and assign their values to new variables (**Figure 11.47**).

12. Choose Actions > set variable. In the Variable field, enter the name of your dynamic text box. In the Value field, enter the target path to your array that contains the days of the week. Put in the variable containing the getDay returned value as its index (**Figure 11.48**).

13. Concatenate the array that contains the days of the month. Put the variable containing the getMonth returned value as its index. Concatenate the other variables holding the current date and year (**Figure 11.49**).

(continued on next page)

14. Test your movie.

Flash gets the day, month, date, and year from the system clock. The names of the specific day and month are retrieved from the array objects you initialize in the first keyframe, and the information is displayed in the dynamic text box.

Another way to provide time information to your viewer is to use the Flash function `getTimer`. This function returns the number of milliseconds that have elapsed since the Flash movie started playing. You can compare the returned value of `getTimer` at one instant to the returned value of it at another instant, and the difference gives you the elapsed time between those two instances. Use the elapsed time to create timers for games and activities in your Flash movie. For example, time how long it takes for your viewer to correctly answer questions in a test, or only give your viewer a certain amount of time to complete the test. Or you can award more points in a game if the player successfully completes a mission within an allotted time.

Since `getTimer` is a function and not an object, you don't need to use a constructor function to instantiate it, which makes it a very simple and convenient way to get elapsed times.

To create a timer:

1. Create a dynamic text box on the Stage, and give it a variable name.

2. Select the dynamic text box, and choose Insert > Convert to Symbol. Enter a name for your symbol, and choose Movie Clip Behavior. Click OK.

The dynamic text box is put into a movie-clip symbol. An instance of that movie clip remains on the Stage.

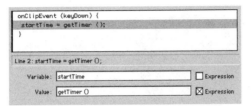

```
onClipEvent (keyDown) {
  startTime = getTimer ();
}
```

Line 2 : startTime = getTimer ();

Variable : startTime   ☐ Expression

Value : getTimer ()   ☒ Expression

Figure 11.50 When this movie clip loads, the getTimer function retrieves the time elapsed since the start of the Flash movie. That time is put in the variable startTime.

```
onClipEvent (keyDown) {
  startTime = getTimer ();
}
onClipEvent (enterFrame) {
  currentTime = getTimer ();
}
```

Line 5 : currentTime = getTimer ();

Variable : currentTime   ☐ Expression

Value : getTimer ()   ☒ Expression

Figure 11.51 On an ongoing basis, the getTimer function retrieves the time elapsed since the start of the Flash movie. That time is put in the variable currentTime.

```
onClipEvent (keyDown) {
  startTime = getTimer ();
}
onClipEvent (enterFrame) {
  currentTime = getTimer ();
  elapsedTime = Math.round( (currentTime - startTime)/1000);
}
```

Line 6 : elapsedTime = Math.round((currentTime - startTime)/1000);

Variable : elapsedTime   ☐ Expression

Value : Math.round((currentTime - startTime)/1000)   ☒ Expression

Figure 11.52 The variable elapsedTime is the time between the two instances of time recorded in the variables startTime and currentTime.

3. Select your movie-clip instance, and give it a name in the Instance panel. Open the Actions panel.

4. Choose Actions > onClipEvent. Select the Key down event.

5. Choose Actions > set variable. In the Variable field, enter startTime. Put your cursor in the Value field, and choose Functions > getTimer.

   The getTimer function appears in the Value field. Check the Expression box (**Figure 11.50**).

6. Choose Actions > onClipEvent. Select the enterFrame event.

7. Choose Actions > set variable. In the Variable field enter currentTime. Put your cursor in the Value field, and choose Functions > getTimer.

   The getTimer function appears in the Value field. Check the Expression box. (**Figure 11.51**).

8. Choose Actions > set variable. In the Variable field, enter elapsedTime. In the Value field, enter

   Math.round ((currentTime-startTime)/1000)

   Check the Expression box next to the Value field.

   Flash calculates the difference between the current timer and the timer at the instant a key on the keyboard was pressed. The result is divided by 1000 to give seconds, then rounded to the nearest integer (**Figure 11.52**).

(continued on next page)

9. Choose Actions > set variable. Assign the variable elapsedTime to display in the dynamic text box (**Figure 11.53**).

10. Test your movie.

    Flash displays the time elapsed since the last instant the viewer pressed a key. Experiment with different event handlers to build a stopwatch with start, stop, and lap buttons.

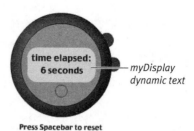

Press Spacebar to reset

Figure 11.53 The value of elapsedTime is displayed in myDisplay (top).

Using the Timeline as a Timer

Another common method of creating timers is to count the number of actual frames on a Timeline that have played. If the frame rate of a movie is set at 12 frames per second (fps), then you know that every 12 frames that play are equivalent to 1 second. You can either use the property _currentframe to retrieve the number of the current frame, or you can assign actions to the keyframe corresponding to the specific time you wish to measure. For example, place the statement i = i + 1 on keyframe 60 of a movie-clip Timeline in a movie set at 12 fps. Every 5 seconds (60 frames / 12 fps = 5 seconds), the variable i increases by 1.

Although simple to implement, creating timers this way isn't as accurate as using the getTimer function or the Date object. Frame rates are notoriously unstable, frequently dropping as the amount of graphics and animation in a movie increases. Because frame rates are tied to the performance of the movie and the CPU of your viewer's computer, stick to the getTimer function or the Date object if time measurements are critical to your movie.

Building Reusable Scripts

When you need to perform the same kind of manipulation of information multiple times, you can save time by building your own functions. The functions you've learned about so far, the `getTimer`, `updateAfterEvent`, and `getProperty` functions, are created and provided by Flash. Now with the action `function`, you can customize your own functions to perform specific tasks. Functions are pieces of reusable ActionScript statements that you put together and mix and match as needed. For example, in a task earlier in this chapter, you calculated the angle that a draggable movie clip makes with another movie-clip reference point. The ActionScript that computes the angle resides with the draggable movie clip. If you wanted to have multiple draggable movie clips the viewer could choose from, you would have to put the same ActionScript code in each of those movie clips. With functions, you would write the ActionScript that calculates the angle just once and put it on the root Timeline. Then each draggable movie clip could invoke, or *call*, that function whenever it needed to.

The following task builds a function that creates a sound object, attaches a sound, starts it, and sets the volume. By consolidating all these methods, you can play the sound with just one call to a single function, and do so multiple times from different places in your movie.

To build and call a sound function:

1. Select the first keyframe of the main Timeline, and open the Actions panel.

2. Choose Actions > function (Esc + fn).

3. In the Name field, enter the name of your function. Leave the Parameters field empty.

(continued on next page)

The function statement appears in the Actions List with a set of curly braces. All statements included within the curly braces become part of the function. They will be performed when the function is called (**Figure 11.54**).

4. Choose Actions > set variable. In the Variable field, enter the name of a new sound object. In the Value field, enter the constructor function new Sound. Check the Expression box next to the Value field (**Figure 11.55**).

5. Choose Actions > with. In the Object field, enter the name of your new sound object.

6. Using the evaluate action, add the attachSound, start, and setVolume methods with appropriate parameters (**Figure 11.56**).

    The with action associates all three methods with your new sound object. The equivalent statements would be:

    mySound.attachSound ("musicID")

    mySound.start (0,2)

    mySound.setVolume (50)

7. Create a button symbol, and place an instance of the button on the Stage. Select the button, and open the Actions panel.

8. Choose Actions > evaluate. In the Expression field, enter the name of your function with parentheses.

    The function is called when this button is released (**Figure 11.57**).

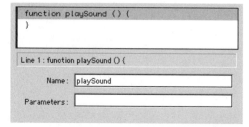

```
function playSound () {
}
```

Line 1 : function playSound () {

Name : playSound

Parameters :

Figure 11.54 This function is called playSound and contains no parameters.

```
function playSound () {
    mySound = new Sound ();
}
```

Line 2 : mySound = new Sound ();

Variable : mySound ☐ Expression

Value : new Sound () ☒ Expression

Figure 11.55 The new object mySound is instantiated.

```
function playSound () {
    mySound = new Sound ();
    with (mySound) {
    attachSound ("musicID");
    start (0, 2);
    setVolume (50);
    }
}
```

Line 6 : setVolume (50);

Expression : setVolume (50)

Figure 11.56 The three methods of the Sound object will be called when the function playSound is called.

```
on (release) {
    playSound ();
}
```

Line 2 : playSound ();

Expression : playSound ()

Figure 11.57 The function playSound is called.

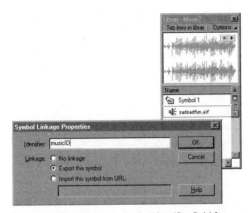

Figure 11.58 Enter a name in the Identifier field for your imported sound.

9. Import a sound clip, and define the Identifier in the Symbol Linkage Properties dialog box (**Figure 11.58**).

10. Test your movie.

Your function is defined in the first keyframe of the main Timeline. When your viewer clicks the button on the Stage, Flash calls the function that creates a new sound object, attaches a sound, and starts playing it at a specified volume level.

✔ Tips

■ Functions, like variables and objects, reside on particular Timelines. When you call a function, you need to be aware of its target path. For example, to call a function named `myFunction` that has been defined on the main Timeline, you can use the target path `_root.myFunction.` or `_level0.myFunction.`

■ You can initialize variables that are called local variables, which are only scoped within the function. Local variables expire at the end of the function and won't conflict with variables you've initialized elsewhere. Local variables are initialized in the Actions panel by choosing Actions > var (Esc + vr). Use local variables to keep your functions independent and self-contained. That way, you can easily copy and paste functions from one project to another without having to worry about conflicts with duplicate variable names.

Parameters and Returned Values

When you define a function, you can tell it to perform a certain task based on parameters that you provide, or *pass*, to the function at the time you call on it. This makes functions more flexible because the work they do is tailored to particular contexts. For example, in the previous task, you can define the function to accept a parameter for the sound volume. When you call the function, you also provide a value for the sound volume, and the function incorporates that value in the setVolume method.

To build a function that accepts parameters:

1. Continuing with the previous task, select the first keyframe, and open the Actions panel.

2. Select the function statement. In the Parameters field, enter sndLoop and sndVolume, separated by a comma.

   These names are the parameters for your function (**Figure 11.59**).

3. Select the start method within your function. Replace the loop parameter with sndLoop. Select the setVolume method, and replace the volume parameter with sndVolume (**Figure 11.60**).

4. Select the button instance on the Stage.

5. In the Actions panel, select your function call. In between the parentheses, enter a value for the sndLoop parameter and a value for the sndVolume parameter. Separate the two values with a comma (**Figure 11.61**).

6. Test your movie.

   The actual values of the parameters that pass to the function are defined when you call the function. Another button may call the function with different values for the parameters.

```
function playSound (sndLoop, sndVolume) {
  mySound = new Sound ();
  with (mySound) {
    attachSound ("musicID");
    start (0, 2);
    setVolume (50);
  }
}
```

```
Line 1 : function playSound (sndLoop, sndVolume) {
```

```
Name :  playSound
```

```
Parameters :  sndLoop, sndVolume
```

Figure 11.59 The function playSound has the parameters sndLoop and sndVolume.

```
function playSound (sndLoop, sndVolume) {
  mySound = new Sound ();
  with (mySound) {
    attachSound ("musicID");
    start (0, sndLoop);
    setVolume (sndVolume);
  }
}
```

```
Line 6 : setVolume (sndVolume);
```

```
Expression :  setVolume (sndVolume)
```

Figure 11.60 The parameters of the function playSound modify the start method and the setVolume method.

```
on (release) {
  playSound (2, 50);
}
```

```
Line 2 : playSound (2, 50);
```

```
Expression :  playSound (2, 50)
```

Figure 11.61 The function playSound is called, passing the parameters 2 and 50. The sound "musicID" starts playing and loops twice at a volume of 50.

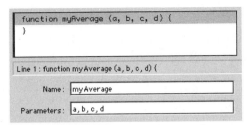

```
function myAverage (a, b, c, d) {
}
```

Line 1 : function myAverage (a, b, c, d) {

Name : myAverage

Parameters : a, b, c, d

Figure 11.62 The function myAverage has the parameters a, b, c, and d.

```
function myAverage (a, b, c, d) {
    return (a + b + c + d)/4;
}
```

Line 2 : return (a + b + c + d)/4;

Value : (a + b + c + d)/4

Figure 11.63 The return action evaluates the expression and makes the result available to the statement that called the function.

```
on (release) {
    myDisplay = myAverage (3, 54, 4, 6);
}
```

Line 2 : myDisplay = myAverage (3, 54, 4, 6);

Variable : myDisplay   ☐ Expression

Value : myAverage (3, 54, 4, 6)   ☒ Expression

Figure 11.64 The function myAverage is called, and the returned value appears in the myDisplay dynamic text box.

✔ **Tip**

■ The function action replaces the call action used in previous versions of Flash. While the call action still works, it can't pass parameters or receive returned values as easily as the function action.

When you pass parameters to a function, you will often want to know the results of a particular calculation. In order to make your function report a resulting calculation, use the return action. The return action is defined in your function statement and returns the value of any expression.

To build a function that returns values:

1. Select the first keyframe of the main Timeline, and open the Actions panel.

2. Choose Actions > function.

3. In the Name field, enter the name of your function. In the Parameters field, enter a, b, c, d (**Figure 11.62**).

4. Choose Actions > return (Esc + rt). In the Value field, enter an expression to average the four parameters.

    This function returns the value of the expression (**Figure 11.63**).

5. Select the text tool from the Tools window, and create a dynamic text box. Name the box.

6. Create a button symbol, and place an instance of it on the Stage. Select the instance, and in the Actions panel choose Actions > set variable.

7. In the Variable field, enter the name of your dynamic text box. In the Value field, enter the name of your function and four values for its parameters. Separate the values with commas. Check the Expression box next to the Value field (**Figure 11.64**).

    The four values pass to the function, where it is processed. The returned value is assigned to the dynamic text box, where it is displayed.

8. Test your movie.

BUILDING REUSABLE SCRIPTS

Building Custom Classes with Functions

You can use functions not only to perform certain tasks, such as those in the previous examples, but also to define the properties and methods of new classes. This lets you organize and customize information in your scripts for easier access and storage and to save memory by consolidating your scripts. Using a constructor function (the operator new plus the name of your function) lets you instantiate an object of a custom class. For example, consider the function:

```
function Scores (player1, player2) {

this.player1Score = player1;

this.player2Score = player2;

}
```

This function defines a class called Scores that has the properties player1Score and player2Score. You instantiate an object from this class by using the constructor function, as in the following:

```
myScores  = new Scores (4, 6);
```

This statement creates a new object called myScores out of the Scores class. This new object has the properties player1Score with a value of 4, and player2Score with a value of 6.

If you now want to create a method for your Scores class that lets you change the scores to either the player1Score property or the player2Score property, you need to define another function, as in the following:

```
function setScores (player, newScore) {

set ("this.player" + player + "Score",
newScore);

}
```

```
function Scores (player1, player2) {
}
```

Line 1 : function Scores (player1, player2) {

Name : Scores

Parameters : player1, player2

Figure 11.65 The function called Scores has the parameters this.player1 and this.player2.

```
function Scores (player1, player2) {
  this.player1Score = player1;
  this.player2Score = player2;
}
```

Line 3 : this.player2Score = player2;

Variable : this.player2Score   ☐ Expression

Value : player2   ☒ Expression

Figure 11.66 The Scores class contain two properties, which are called player1Score and player2Score.

This function changes the value of player1Score or player2Score depending on the parameters that are passed to it. However, this function is not yet associated with the Scores class that you defined in the first function. You want this function to belong to the Scores class, so that any new object created from it will have access to this function called setScores. You can associate the setScores function with the Scores class by using its *prototype* property. The prototype property affects all new objects made from the Scores class, so that all new objects *inherit* the setScores function. You assign the prototype property of the Scores class to the setScores function with the following statement:

```
Scores.prototype.setScoresMethod =
setScores;
```

In order to call this method from your object, you would write the statement

```
myScores.setScoresMethod (2,3)
```

By using functions to create your own classes, properties, and methods, you have a powerful and flexible way to go beyond the classes that Flash provides.

To create a custom class:

1. Select the first keyframe of the main Timeline, and open the Actions panel.

2. Choose Actions > function. In the Name field, enter Scores. In the Parameters field, enter the parameter names player1 and player2, separated by a comma (**Figure 11.65**).

3. Choose Actions > set variable. Assign property names to the parameters.
   This function defines the class called Scores with two properties (**Figure 11.66**).

BUILDING CUSTOM CLASSES WITH FUNCTIONS

To define a method of a custom class:

1. Continuing with the previous task, select the first keyframe of the main Timeline, and open the Actions panel.

2. Select the closing curly brace of the function. The next action you add will appear outside the function.

3. Choose Actions > function. In the Name field, enter setScores. In the Parameters field, enter the parameter names player and newScore, separated by a comma.

   A second function, called setScores, is defined (**Figure 11.67**).

4. Choose Actions > set variable. Assign the appropriate property name using the set variable action (concatenate the player parameter) to the newScore parameter.

   This function assigns a new value to either this.player1Score or this.player2Score (**Figure 11.68**).

5. Select the closing curly brace of the second function. The next action you add will appear outside the function.

6. Choose Actions > set variable. In the Variable field, enter

   Scores.prototype.setScoresMethod

   In the Value field, enter setScores. Check the Expression box.

   The second function, called setScores, is attached to the first function, called Scores. All new instances of the scores class inherit the setScores function. You call this function with setScoresMethod (**Figure 11.69**).

Figure 11.67 The function called setScores has the parameters player and newScore.

Figure 11.68 The function called setScores assigns the value of newScore to the property this.player1Score if player = 1, or to this.player2Score if player = 2.

Figure 11.69 The prototype property of the Scores class is assigned to the function called setScores. All instances of the Scores class inherit the setScores method, which can be called using the syntax instanceName.setScoresMethod(player, newScore).

```
function Scores (player1, player2) {
  this.player1Score = player1;
  this.player2Score = player2;
}
function setScores (player, newScore) {
  set ("this.player"+player+"Score", newScore)
}
Scores.prototype.setScoresMethod = setScores;
firstGame = new Scores(4, 6);
```

Line 9: firstGame = new Scores(4, 6);

Variable: `firstGame`   ☐ Expression

Value: `new Scores(4, 6)`   ☒ Expression

Figure 11.70 The object firstGame is instantiated from the Scores class. The object firstGame has the properties player1Score=4 and player2Score=6.

```
on (release) {
  firstGame.setScoresMethod(2, 8);
}
```

Line 2: firstGame.setScoresMethod(2, 8);

Expression: `firstGame.setScoresMethod(2, 8)`

Figure 11.71 When this button is pressed, the firstGame object calls the setScoresMethod method. Its property player2Score is set to 8.

```
// create a class called Scores with 2 parameters
function Scores (player1, player2) {
  // define two properties based on parameters
  this.player1Score = player1;
  this.player2Score = player2;
}
// create a method for the Scores class
function setScores (player, newScore) {
  set ("this.player"+player+"Score", newScore);
}
// attach the method to the Scores class
Scores.prototype.setScoresMethod = setScores;
// instantiate an object from the Scores class
firstGame = new Scores(4, 6);
```

```
on (release) {
  // call a method to change the score of player 2
  firstGame.setScoresMethod(2, 8);
}
```

Figure 11.72 This is the full ActionScript, which is assigned to the first frame of the Timeline (top), to create a new class, attach a method, and instantiate a new object. The script, which is attached to a button (bottom) calls the setScoresMethod method for the new object.

To instantiate an object from a custom class:

1. Continuing with the previous task, select the first keyframe of the Timeline, and open the Actions panel.

2. Select the last statement in the Actions List.

3. Choose Actions > set variable. In the Variable field, enter the name of your new object. In the Value field, enter new Scores() and enter two numeric values within the parentheses, separated by a comma. Check the Expression box next to the Value field (**Figure 11.70**).

    A new object is instantiated from the Scores class, with its properties defined by the values passed to the function. This new object inherits the method setScoresMethod.

To call a method of a custom class:

1. Continuing with the previous task, drag another instance of your button symbol onto the Stage. Select the button, and open the Actions panel.

2. Choose Actions > evaluate. In the Expression field, enter your object name, a dot, then setScoresMethod(). In between the parentheses, enter values for the parameters of the method. Separate the parameters with commas (**Figure 11.71**).

    When this button is pressed, the setScoresMethod method is called, and the properties of your object change.

The complete script that creates the custom class and method is shown in (**Figure 11.72**).

MANAGING CONTENT AND TROUBLE-SHOOTING

As the complexity of your Flash movie increases with the addition of bitmaps, sounds, and animations, and the ActionScripts that integrate them, you'll need to keep close track of these elements so you can make necessary revisions and bug fixes. After all, the most elaborate Flash movie is useless if you can't pinpoint the one variable that's keeping the whole thing from working. Fortunately, Flash provides several tools for trouble-shooting and managing Library symbols.

This chapter shows you how to create shared Libraries and external ActionScripts that supply common elements—symbols and code—to a team of Flash developers working on a project. This chapter also delves into the Movie Explorer, Output window, and Debugger panel, which offer information about the organization and status of your movie. These three windows let you review your ActionScript in context with the other components in your movie, receive error and warning messages, and monitor the changing values of variables and properties as your movie plays.

Finally, you'll learn some strategies for making your Flash movie leaner and faster— optimizing graphics, organizing your work environment, and avoiding some common mistakes—guidelines to help you become a better Flash animator and developer.

Creating Shared Libraries

Flash makes it possible for teams of animators and developers to share common components of a complex project. Each animator might be working on a separate movie that uses the same symbol—the main character in an animated comic book, for example. An identical symbol of this main character needs to reside in the Library of each movie, and if the art director decides to change this character's face, a new symbol has to be copied to all the Libraries—that is, unless you create a shared Library. Shared Libraries store symbols that are commonly used among many movies. You can store the main-character symbol in a shared Library for all the movies to use. This simplifies the editing process and ensures consistency throughout a Flash project (**Figure 12.1**).

Your viewers also benefit from the shared Library since they only have to download it once. For example, the main character would be downloaded just once for the first movie and all subsequent movies using that character.

To create a shared Library, you mark the symbols you want to share with a linkage identifier in the same way that you identified sounds and movies for the methods attachSound and attachMovie. When you export the SWF file, the symbols you identified will be available as shared symbols.

To create a shared library:

1. In a new Flash document, create a symbol you want to share. The symbol can be a graphic, button, movie clip, sound, or bitmap.

2. In the Library, select your symbol. From the Options pull-down menu, choose Linkage (**Figure 12.2**).

   The Symbol Linkage Properties dialog box appears.

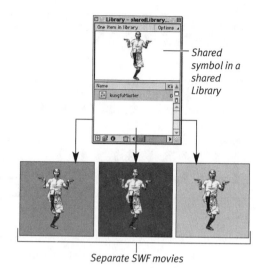

Shared symbol in a shared Library

Separate SWF movies

Figure 12.1 A shared Library (top) lets multiple SWF files use the same symbol.

Figure 12.2 Choose Options > Linkage from the Library.

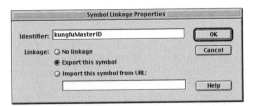

Figure 12.3 To mark a symbol as shared, it is given an identifier in the Symbol Linkage Properties dialog box and selected for export.

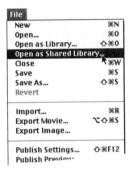

Figure 12.4 Choose File > Open as Shared Library to access the shared symbols in the Library of another movie.

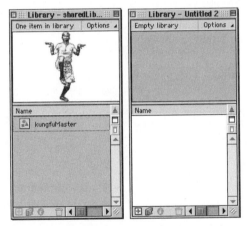

Figure 12.5 The Library at left contains the symbol that was marked to be shared. The Library at right is your current Library.

3. From the Linkage choices, select Export this symbol. In the Identifier field, enter a unique name for your symbol. Click OK (**Figure 12.3**).

   Your selected symbol is now marked for export and available to be shared by other movies.

4. Export your Flash movie as a SWF file.

   Your selected symbol resides in the SWF file, which provides the shared assets to other movies.

Once you create a shared Library, you can use the shared assets in other movies. You do this by opening the shared Library in a new Flash document and dragging the shared symbol into the new document. A link is created between the SWF using the shared symbol and the SWF containing the shared symbol (the shared Library). The original source file (FLA) that contains the shared Library is the master file, the only place where you can edit the shared symbols.

To use a shared symbol:

1. Open a new Flash document. Choose File > Open as Shared Library (**Figure 12.4**).

2. In the dialog box that appears, select the FLA file that contains the symbols you marked for export to be shared. Click Open.

   A new Library window opens, showing all the symbols from the selected FLA file. The background of the window is gray, indicating that the Library does not belong to the Flash file that is currently open. You cannot modify, add, or delete the symbols in this Library from the current Flash file (**Figure 12.5**).

(continued on next page)

CREATING SHARED LIBRARIES

3. Select the symbol in the shared Library that you marked for export in the previous task, and drag it into the current Library or onto the Stage.

The shared symbol is added to the current Library and is now available for you to use in the movie. Choose Options > Linkage to verify that the symbol is linked to the shared Library (**Figure 12.6**).

4. Use the shared symbol in your movie. Export a SWF, and place it and the shared Library SWF file in the same directory (**Figure 12.7**).

When you play the SWF that uses a shared symbol, it accesses the symbol by downloading the shared Library from the SWF that contains it.

✔ Tip

■ When you make changes and revisions to the symbols in the shared Library, all the SWF movies that use the shared symbol will be automatically updated to reflect the change. However, when you open the FLA file that uses the shared symbol, you'll notice that the shared symbol in the Library has not been updated. You need to import the shared symbol from the shared Library again in order to update its appearance in the current Library.

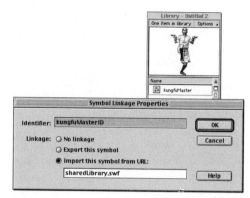

Figure 12.6 The Symbol Linkage Properties dialog box shows that this symbol is imported from the file called sharedLibrary.swf.

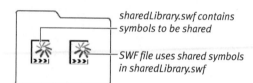

sharedLibrary.swf contains symbols to be shared

SWF file uses shared symbols in sharedLibrary.swf

Figure 12.7 The two SWF files are in the same directory.

CREATING SHARED LIBRARIES

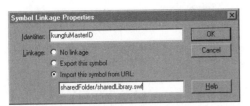

Figure 12.8 The Symbol Linkage Properties dialog box shows that this symbol is imported from the file called sharedLibrary.swf, which is inside a folder called sharedFolder.

SWF file uses shared symbols in sharedFolder/sharedLibrary.swf

sharedLibrary.swf contains symbols to be shared

sharedFolder

Figure 12.9 The two SWF files are in different directories.

Figure 12.10 Choose Options > Shared Library Properties from the shared Library.

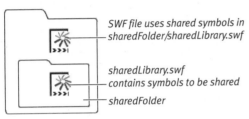

Figure 12.11 The path name in the URL field determines where the shared symbols will be referenced. Place your shared Library where this URL specifies.

The default location of a shared Library is in the same directory as the SWF file that uses it. You can put the shared Library in a different location by specifying an absolute or relative path name to the shared Library file. You can do this either in the shared Library file or in the file that uses the shared Library.

To specify a different location for a shared Library:

1. In the file that uses a shared Library, select the shared symbol in the Library and choose Linkage in the Options pull-down menu.

   The Symbol Linkage Properties dialog box appears. The Import this symbol from URL option is selected, and the current path name to the shared Library appears in the bottom field.

2. Enter a new path name to the shared Library. Click OK (**Figure 12.8**).

3. Repeat this process for every shared symbol.

4. Export a SWF. Place it and the shared Library in the correct directories so that Flash can find the shared symbols (**Figure 12.9**).

or

1. From the file that contains the shared Library, select Shared Library Properties from the Options pull-down menu (**Figure 12.10**).

   The Shared Library Properties dialog box appears.

2. In the URL field, enter the path name to the shared Library. Click OK (**Figure 12.11**).

3. In a new Flash document, open the shared Library and drag the shared symbols onto the Stage or into the current Library.

   The shared symbols will be linked to the shared Library specified in the URL field of the Shared Library Properties dialog box.

Sharing Fonts

Just as you can identify shared symbols, you can create symbols that let you share fonts. After creating a font symbol, you identify it to be exported using the Linkage identifier, in a process identical to the one used to create shared symbols. When multiple movies share a common font from a shared Library, the font only has to be downloaded once for the first movie, reducing file size and download times for the subsequent movies.

To create a font symbol to share:

1. Open the Library window. From the Options pull-down menu, choose New Font (**Figure 12.12**).

   The Font Symbol Properties dialog box appears.

2. Enter a name for your new font symbol in the Name field. In the Font field, select the font you wish to convert to a font symbol. Check the optional boxes for Style. Click OK (**Figure 12.13**).

   The font symbol appears in your Library.

3. Select your font symbol. From the Library Options pull-down menu, choose Linkage.

   The Symbol Linkage Properties dialog box appears.

4. From the Linkage choices, select Export this symbol. In the Identifier field, enter a unique name for your symbol. Click OK (**Figure 12.14**).

   Your selected font symbol is now marked for export and available to be shared by other movies.

5. Export your Flash movie as a SWF file.

   Your selected font symbol resides in the SWF file. This SWF file provides the shared font to other movies.

Figure 12.12 Choose Options > New Font in the Library.

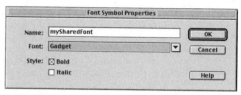

Figure 12.13 Create a font symbol by choosing a font and giving it a name in the Font Symbol Properties dialog box.

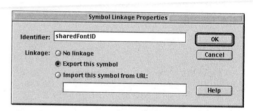

Figure 12.14 In the Symbol Linkage Properties dialog box, mark your symbol font to be shared.

Figure 12.15 Shared fonts are available in the Character panel and are distinguished by an asterisk after their names.

To use a shared font symbol:

1. Follow the same process as described in the previous section, "Creating Shared Libraries," to open the Library containing the shared font symbol.

2. Drag the shared font symbol from the shared Library to the Library of a new Flash file.

   The shared font symbol will appear in the list of available fonts in the Character panel.

3. Select the text tool, and choose the shared font symbol from the Character panel (**Figure 12.15**).

Editing ActionScript

When the script in the Actions List of the Actions panel becomes long and complex, you can check, edit, and manage it using the options pull-down menu of the Actions panel. In addition to the choices for Normal and Expert mode, the menu options include searching and replacing words, importing and exporting scripts, and printing your scripts, as well as different ways to display your script (**Figure 12.16**). All these functions work in both Normal and Expert modes.

To check the syntax in the Actions List:

◆ In the Actions panel, choose Check Syntax from the options pull-down menu (Command-T for Mac, Control-T for Windows).

Flash checks the script in the Actions List for errors in syntax. If it finds an error, it displays a warning dialog box and reports any errors in an Output window (**Figure 12.17**). Use the information provided in the Output window to locate the error and correct the syntax.

✔ Tip

■ Check Syntax reports just the errors in the current Actions List. If no errors are found, you will see a dialog box indicating that there are no errors in the script (**Figure 12.18**).

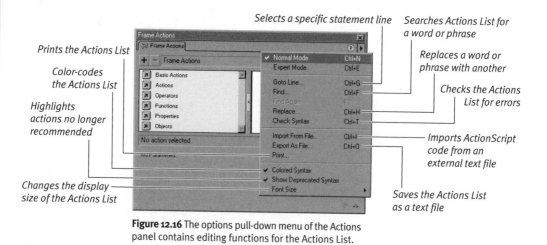

Selects a specific statement line

Searches Actions List for a word or phrase

Prints the Actions List

Color-codes the Actions List

Highlights actions no longer recommended

Replaces a word or phrase with another

Checks the Actions List for errors

Imports ActionScript code from an external text file

Changes the display size of the Actions List

Saves the Actions List as a text file

Figure 12.16 The options pull-down menu of the Actions panel contains editing functions for the Actions List.

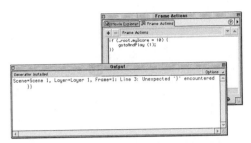

Figure 12.17 The Actions List (above) contains an extra closing curly brace. Flash notifies you of the nature and location of the error in the Output window (below).

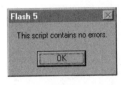

Figure 12.18 Flash notifies you when your Actions List is clear of syntax errors.

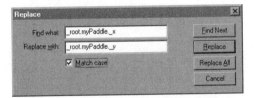

Figure 12.19 Every occurrence of _root.myPaddle._x will be replaced with _root.myPaddle._y.

Use the Find and Replace functions in the Actions panel to quickly change variable names, properties, or even actions. For example, if you created a lengthy script involving the variable redTeamStatus, you can copy and paste the script, and replace all instances of redTeamStatus with blueTeamStatus. You could find all the occurrences of the property _x and replace them with _y, or you could find all the occurrences of the action gotoAndStop and replace them with gotoAndPlay.

To find and replace ActionScript terms in the Actions List:

1. In the Actions panel, choose Replace from the options pull-down menu (Command-H for Mac, Control-H for Windows).
   The Replace dialog box appears.

2. In the Find what field, enter a word or words that you want Flash to find. In the Replace field, enter a word or words that you want the found words to be replaced with. Check the Match case box to make Flash recognize upper- and lowercase letters (**Figure 12.19**).

3. Click Replace to replace the first instance of the found word, or click Replace All to replace all instances of the found word.

✔ Tips

- The Replace dialog box replaces all the occurrences of a particular word or phrase only in the current Actions List of the Actions panel. In order to replace every occurrence of a certain word in the whole movie, you need to open the Actions panel for each individual script and repeat this process.

- The Actions panel must be in Expert mode to search for and replace actions.

EDITING ACTIONSCRIPT

367

The import, export, and print functions of the Actions panel let you work with external text editors or print the contents of the Actions List.

To import an ActionScript:

◆ Select Import From File from the options pull-down menu (Command-I for Mac, Control-I for Windows). From the dialog box that appears, choose the text file that contains the ActionScript you wish to import. Click Open.

   Flash replaces the contents of the current Actions List with the ActionScript contained in the text file.

To export an ActionScript:

◆ Select Export As File from the options pull-down menu (Command-O for Mac, Control-O for Windows). Enter a filename for the text file that will hold the exported ActionScript. Click Save.

   Flash saves a text file that contains the entire contents of the current Actions List. The recommended extension for external ActionScript files is .as, as in myCode.as.

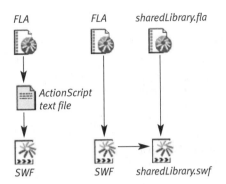

FLA   FLA   sharedLibrary.fla

ActionScript text file

SWF   SWF   sharedLibrary.swf

Figure 12.20 Flash incorporates external ActionScript with the #include action when the SWF is exported (left). A shared Library, however, is incorporated in the SWF during playback (right).

```
startDrag (this, true);
```

Figure 12.21 This is the ActionScript in a text file saved as myCode.as.

Including External ActionScript

You can create external ActionScript files to share common code among multiple movies. Create the ActionScript code that appears many times in different movies, and keep that code in a text file outside the Flash movies. If you need to change the code, you only need to change it in one place.

External code can be incorporated into a Flash movie with the action #include. This action pulls in an external text file containing ActionScript and includes it in the existing script in the Actions List.

However, there is a critical difference between using #include to share external ActionScript code and using shared Libraries to share symbols. External ActionScript code is not compiled dynamically during playback, so you must re-export your Flash movie in order for Flash to include the most current ActionScript. This means that the #include action, although useful, is limited to authoring mode (**Figure 12.20**).

In the following task, the #include action is assigned to a movie clip. A text document contains the ActionScript action startDrag. When you export the SWF file, the code in the external text document is incorporated in the actions assigned to the movie clip.

To include external ActionScript with the #include action:

1. Open a text-editing application, such as SimpleText for Mac or Notepad for Windows.

2. Write your ActionScript code, and save it as a text document. Do not include any quotation marks around your script. Use the extension .as to identify it as an ActionScript file (**Figure 12.21**).

(continued on next page)

INCLUDING EXTERNAL ACTIONSCRIPT

3. Open a new document in Flash. Create a movie-clip symbol, and place an instance of it on the Stage. Select the instance, and open the Actions panel.

4. Choose Actions > onClipEvent. Select the Load event from the Parameters pane.

5. Choose Actions > include (Esc + in).

6. In the Path field, enter the name of your text file that contains ActionScript. Do not include quotation marks, as they are included automatically in the Actions List (**Figure 12.22**).

7. Save your FLA file in the same directory as your ActionScript text file.

8. Export a SWF from your FLA file.

Flash integrates into the movie clip the code contained in the text document. If you change the code in the text file, you must re-export the SWF so that Flash can include the latest changes.

✔ Tip

- If you are using the Actions panel in Expert mode to write out your ActionScript manually, do not include a semicolon at the end of a #include statement. Although semicolons usually separate ActionScript statements, the #include statement is an exception.

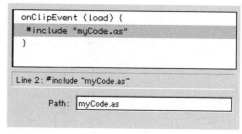

Figure 12.22 When this movie clip loads into memory, the external text file called myCode.as is included in this block of ActionScript.

INCLUDING EXTERNAL ACTIONSCRIPT

Using the Movie Explorer

Click to collapse or expand *Find field* *Display* *Filtering buttons*

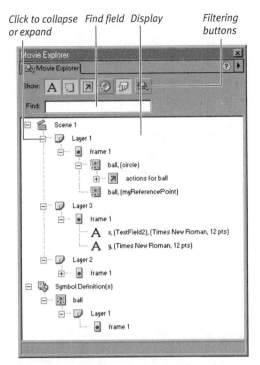

Figure 12.23 A typical display in the Movie Explorer shows various elements of the movie in an expandable hierarchy.

In order to get a bird's-eye view of your whole Flash movie, you can use the Movie Explorer panel (Option-Command-M for Mac, Control-Alt-M for Windows). The Movie Explorer is a powerful tool for tracking all the elements of your movie, and it will take you directly to a particular ActionScript, graphic, or frame you want to modify. The Movie Explorer panel can selectively represent the graphical components of a movie and provide information about frames and layers, as well as show ActionScripts assigned to buttons, movie clips, and keyframes. The display list is organized hierarchically, letting you see the relationships between various elements (**Figure 12.23**).

The Movie Explorer even updates itself in real time, so as you're authoring a Flash movie, the panel displays the latest modifications. Use the Movie Explorer to find particular elements in your movie. For example, if you want to find all the instances of a movie clip, you can search for them and have Flash display the exact scene, layer, and frame where each instance resides. You can then quickly go to those spots on the Timeline to edit the instances. You can also edit various elements within the Movie Explorer panel itself, such as the names of symbols or the contents of a text selection. The Movie Explorer makes it much easier to find your way around a complex movie because of its customized display and quick navigation to the selected element.

To display different categories of elements:

From the options pull-down menu at the right of the Movie Explorer panel, select one or more of the following (**Figure 12.24**):

◆ Show Movie Elements displays all the elements in your movie and organizes them by scene. Only the current scene is displayed.

◆ Show Symbol Definitions displays all the elements associated with symbol instances that are on the Stage.

◆ Show All Scenes displays all the elements in your movie in all scenes.

To filter the categories of elements that are displayed:

From the row of filtering buttons at the top of the panel, click one or more to add categories of elements to display (**Figure 12.25**).

◆ Show Text displays the actual string in a text selection, the font name and font size, and the name of the variables for input and dynamic text.

◆ Show Buttons, Movie Clips, and Graphics displays the symbol names of buttons, movie clips, and graphics on the Stage, as well as the instance names of movie clips.

◆ Show ActionScripts displays the actions assigned to buttons, movie clips, and frames.

◆ Show Video, Sounds, and Bitmaps displays the symbol names of imported video, sounds, and bitmaps on the Stage.

◆ Show Frames and Layers displays the names of layers, keyframes, and frame labels in the movie.

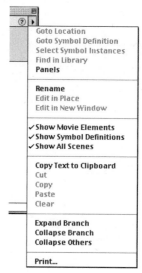

Figure 12.24 The options pull-down menu of the Movie Explorer panel.

Show Buttons, Movie Clips, and Graphics

Show Text · ┌─ Show ActionScripts

Show Video, ─── Show Frames   Customize
Sounds, and Bitmaps   and Layers   which Items
to Show

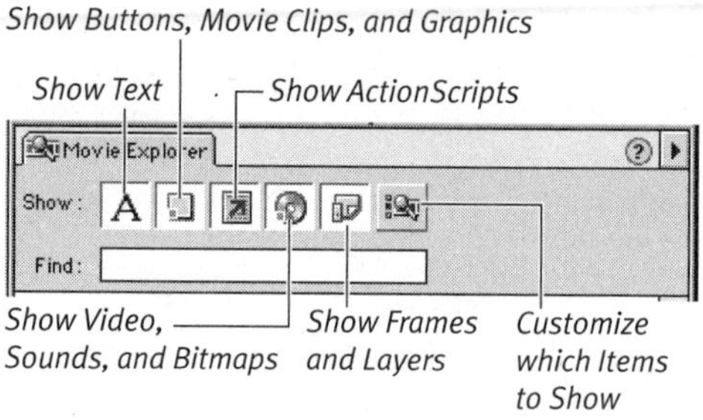

Figure 12.25 The filtering buttons let you selectively display elements.

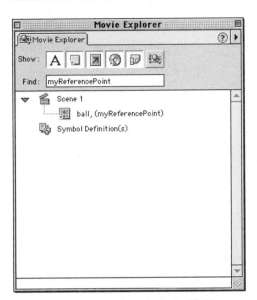

Figure 12.26 Entering a phrase in the Find field displays all occurrences of that phrase in the Display window. Here, the instance name myReferencePoint of the movie-clip symbol called ball has been found.

◆ Customize which Items to Show displays a dialog box from which you can choose individual elements to display.

To find and edit elements in the display:

1. Enter the name of the element you wish to find in the Find field at the top of the Movie Explorer panel (**Figure 12.26**).

   All the elements of the movie that contain that name appear in the display list automatically as you type in the field.

2. Click the desired element to select it.

   The element will also be selected on the Timeline and on the Stage. If a scene or keyframe is selected, Flash takes you to that scene or keyframe.

3. From the options pull-down menu of the Movie Explorer panel, choose Edit in Place or Edit in New Window to go to symbol-editing mode for a selected symbol.

   or

   From the options pull-down menu choose Rename.

   The name of the element becomes selectable so that you can edit it.

   or

   Double-click the desired element to modify it. Flash makes the element editable or opens an appropriate window, depending on what type of element it is:

   Double-clicking a symbol (except for sound, video, and bitmaps) opens symbol-editing mode.

   Double-clicking ActionScript opens the Actions panel.

   Double-clicking a scene or layer lets you rename it. Double-clicking a frame opens the panels associated with frames (Actions, Frame, and Sound).

   Double-clicking a text selection lets you edit its contents.

USING THE MOVIE EXPLORER

373

To replace all occurrences of a particular font:

1. In the Find field of the Movie Explorer panel, enter the name of the font you wish to replace.

   All occurrences of that font appear in the display (**Figure 12.27**).

2. Select all the text elements, using shift-click to make multiple selections.

3. In the Character panel, choose a different font and style for all text elements.

   All the selected text elements change according to your choices in the Character panel (**Figure 12.28**).

To find all instances of a movie-clip symbol:

◆ In the Find field of the Movie Explorer panel, enter the name of the movie-clip symbol whose instances you want to find.

   All instances of that movie-clip symbol appear in the display (**Figure 12.29**).

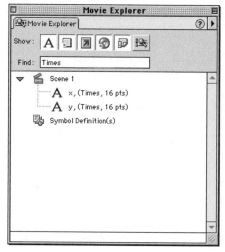

Figure 12.27 All the occurrences of the Times font appear in the Display window.

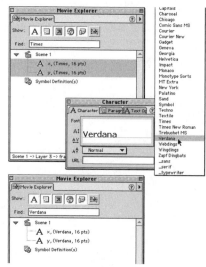

Figure 12.29 Entering the symbol name **ball** in the Find field displays all the instances of the ball symbol.

Figure 12.28 With the Times text elements selected, choose a different font, such as Verdana (top) from the Character panel. Flash changes those text elements from Times to Verdana (bottom).

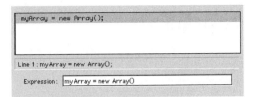

Figure 12.30 The object myArray is created from the new Array constructor function.

Listing Variables and Objects in the Output Window

While the Movie Explorer represents many of a movie's graphic elements and ActionScript, it doesn't display variables or object target paths. For this you use the Output window. Often, while your movie is playing, you will want to know the values of your variables and the target paths of movie clips to determine whether Flash is manipulating the information correctly. This is especially important when your movie is very complicated, perhaps involving many parameters passing between functions or having dynamically allocated variables. For example, say you want to initialize and populate an array object in the first frame of the Timeline. After assigning the ActionScript to the frame that does the job, you can test your movie, but you won't really know if Flash has correctly populated the array because there's nothing visual on the Stage. In order to see if the array is indeed filled up with the correct values, you can list the variables in the Output window in testing mode. The List Variables command displays all the variables in a movie with their scopes and values.

In the following task, you first create a simple array object, and then assign values to it using a looping statement. In testing mode, you list the movie's variables in the Output window to see the array's final values.

To list variables in the Output window:

1. Select the first frame of the main Timeline, and open the Actions panel.

2. Instantiate a new array object called myArray, as described in Chapter 11 (**Figure 12.30**).

(continued on next page)

LISTING VARIABLES IN THE OUTPUT WINDOW

3. Choose Actions > for. In the Init field, enter i=0. In the Condition field, enter i<5. In the Next field, enter i++ (**Figure 12.31**).

4. Choose Actions > set variable. In the Variable field, enter myArray[i]. In the Value field, enter i*5. Check the Expression box next to the Value field.

Each time the for statement loops, the value of i increases by 1. Flash assigns each entry in the myArray array the value of its index multiplied by 5. This loop populates the myArray array (**Figure 12.32**).

5. Test your movie. In testing mode, from the top menu, choose Debug > List Variables (Option-Command-V for Mac, Control-Alt-V for Windows).

The Output window opens, displaying all the variables in the movie. The first variable listed is $version, which contains information about the version of the Flash player and the system platform. The second variable is the myArray object. Flash lists its location (_level0.myArray), its data type (object), and all of its values in each index (0, 5, 10, 15, 20). The third variable is the counter variable, called i, that was used in the for looping statement (**Figure 12.33**).

✔ Tip

■ The List Variables command displays all the variables in a movie at the instant you choose the command from the menu. If the variables change as the movie plays, you need to choose List Variables again in order to see the latest values. For real-time display of variables, use the Debugger panel, described later in this chapter.

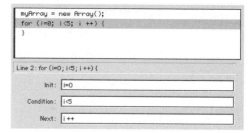

Figure 12.31 Create a loop that begins with i=0 and increases by 1 until it reaches 4.

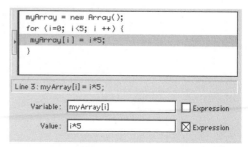

Figure 12.32 The object myArray is automatically filled with the values determined by the looping statement.

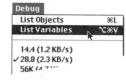

Figure 12.33 Choose Debug > List Variables in testing mode to see all the current variables. The myArray object and its values are listed, verifying the results of the looping statement.

LISTING VARIABLES IN THE OUTPUT WINDOW

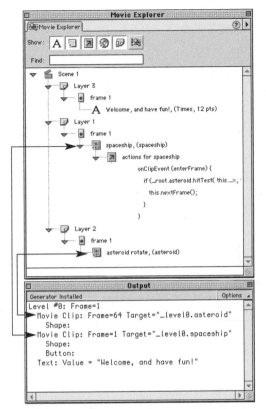

Figure 12.34 The same movie is displayed in the Movie Explorer (top) and the Output window (bottom). The Movie Explorer shows the spaceship movie clip, its button, and the actions assigned to that button. The Output window shows the target path of the spaceship movie clip, and tells you that there is a shape and a button inside it. The Output window shows that the asteroid movie clip is on Frame 64 at the time the List Objects command was selected.

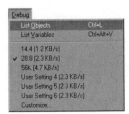

Figure 12.35 Choose Debug > List Objects in testing mode.

You can also use the Output window to display a list of the objects in the movie. While the Output window's display is not as graphically appealing as the display in the Movie Explorer, it gives you information about objects that you can't get from the Movie Explorer. The object information listed in the Output window includes the object's level, frame number, type of symbol (movie clip, button), and type of graphic (text, shape), and the absolute target path of movie clips. The target path of movie clips is the most important bit of information the Output window can tell you directly, although the Movie Explorer can tell you indirectly. A comparison of the typical information display for the same movie in the Movie Explorer and in the Output window is in **Figure 12.34**.

To list objects in the Output window:

◆ In testing mode, choose from the top menu bar Debug > List Objects (Command-L for Mac, Control-L for Windows) (**Figure 12.35**).

All the objects in the current state of the movie are displayed in the Output window.

✔ Tip

■ As in the command List Variables, the command List Objects only displays the movie's current status. If a movie clip disappears from the Timeline as the movie plays, you need to select List Objects again to update the display of objects in the Output window.

Tracing Variables in the Output Window

Sometimes you'll want to know the status of a variable or expression at a particular point during the playback of your movie. For example, imagine that you've created a game of Pong in which a movie clip of a ball bounces between two other movie clips of paddles. You want to find out, for testing purposes, the position of the paddle at the instant of a collision with the ball. Using the command List Variables would be very little help because of the rapidly changing variables for the paddle positions. The solution is to use the action trace. You can place the action trace at any point in the movie to have Flash send a custom message to the Output window during testing mode. The custom message is an expression you create that gives you tailored information at just the right moment. In the example of the game of Pong, you could write a trace statement that would look something like:

```
trace ("paddle X-position is " +
myPaddle._x);
```

```
trace ("paddle Y-position is " +
myPaddle._y);
```

Place these two trace statements in the if statement that detects the collision. When the condition holds true, Flash will send a message at the moment of collision to the Output window, and it would look something like:

```
paddle X-position is 25
```

```
paddle Y-position is 89
```

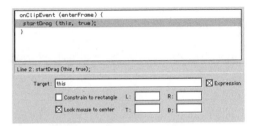

Figure 12.36 The startDrag action will make this movie clip follow the pointer.

```
onClipEvent (enterFrame) {
  startDrag (this, true);
  trace (this.hitTest(_root.rock));
}
```
Line 3: trace (this.hitTest(_root.rock));

Message: this.hitTest(_root.rock)   ☒ Expression

Figure 12.37 The trace action evaluates the expression in the Message field and displays the value in the Output window.

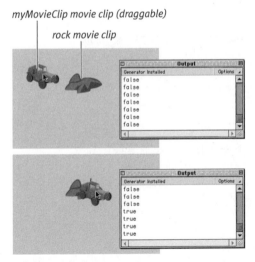

myMovieClip movie clip (draggable)

rock movie clip

Figure 12.38 The Output window displays false when myMovieClip is clear of the rock movie clip (top). The Output window displays true when there is a collision (bottom).

You can also use trace to monitor the condition of an expression so you can understand the circumstances that change its value. For example, in the following task, you'll create a simple draggable movie clip and another movie clip that remains stationary. You'll assign a trace action to display the value of the draggable movie clip's hitTest method, letting you see when and where the value becomes true or false.

To display an expression in the Output window:

1. Create a movie-clip symbol, place an instance of it on the Stage, and name the instance myMovieClip.

2. Create another movie-clip symbol, place an instance of it on the Stage, and name the instance rock.

3. Select the myMovieClip instance, and open the Actions panel.

4. Choose Actions > on. Select the enterFrame event in the Parameters pane.

5. Choose Actions > startDrag. Enter this in the Target field, and check the Expression box. Check the Lock mouse to center box (**Figure 12.36**).

6. Choose Actions > trace (Esc + tr).

7. In the Message field, enter the expression

   this.hitTest(_root.rock)

   Check the Expression box (**Figure 12.37**).

   Flash evaluates the hitTest method to see if the draggable movie clip collides with the movie clip called rock. The returned value is displayed in the Output window in testing mode.

8. Test your movie.

   The Output window opens, displaying the result of the trace action (**Figure 12.38**).

The **typeof** operator can be used in conjunction with the **trace** action in order to display the data type of a certain variable. This information is very useful when you begin to encounter problems with unexpected values in your variables. If you suspect that the problem stems from using a variable in ways that are incompatible with its data type, placing a **trace** action to display the data type will confirm or disprove your suspicions.

To determine the data type of a variable:

1. Continue with the file you created in the previous section, "Listing Variables and Objects in the Output Window." This is the file in which you created an array and populated the array with a looping statement. Select the first frame, and open the Actions panel.

2. Select the ending curly brace of the last statement in the Actions List.

3. Choose Actions > trace.

4. In the Message field, choose Operators > typeof.

    The **typeof** operator appears in the Message field with the argument expression highlighted.

5. Replace the highlighted word with myArray (**Figure 12.39**).

    Flash evaluates myArray and displays its data type in the Output window in testing mode.

6. Add two more **trace** actions with the **typeof** operator (**Figure 12.40**).

7. Test your movie. Flash displays the results of the three trace statements in the Output window in testing mode. The first displays the data type of myArray as an object. The second displays myArray[3] as a number, and the third displays myArray.toString() as a string (**Figure 12.41**).

```
myArray = new Array();
for (i=0; i<5; i++) {
  myArray[i] = i*5;
}
trace (typeof (myArray));
```

Line 5: trace (typeof (myArray));

Message: typeof (myArray)   ⊠ Expression

Figure 12.39 The data type of myArray will be evaluated.

```
myArray = new Array();
for (i=0; i<5; i++) {
  myArray[i] = i*5;
}
trace (typeof (myArray));
trace (typeof (myArray[3]));
trace (typeof (myArray.toString()));
```

Figure 12.40 Add trace actions to evaluate and display the data type of index 3 of myArray and the method toString of myArray.

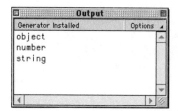

Figure 12.41 The results of the trace action in the Output window.

TRACING VARIABLES IN THE OUTPUT WINDOW

Using the Debugger

The Debugger panel lets you monitor and modify the values of all the variables and properties in your movie as it plays. You can also examine the values of objects that hold data, such as instances of the Date or Sound objects. Use the Debugger to verify that Flash is manipulating the information in variables the way you want it to, and to test certain conditions or the effects of certain variables quickly. For example, imagine that you created an animation with the variable myVelocity controlling the speed of a spaceship. In the Debugger panel, you can modify the variable myVelocity as the movie plays to see how it affects the motion of your spaceship. Increase or decrease the value of myVelocity until you are satisfied with the results.

The Debugger panel opens and is active in a special version of the Flash Player accessible from the Flash authoring environment. Once open and active, the Debugger displays information in two separate parts: a Display list at the top and Properties, Variables, and Watch lists at the bottom. The Display list shows the root Timeline and the hierarchy of movie clips in that Timeline. You can select the root Timeline or the other movie clips to see the properties belonging to that particular Timeline or to see all the variables within that particular scope (**Figure 12.42**).

Use the Control menu to rewind, play, and step forward or backward through your movie, frame by frame, as necessary to scrutinize the movie's properties and variables (**Figure 12.43**).

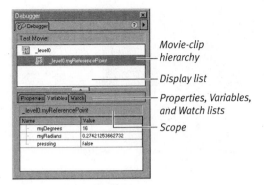

Movie-clip hierarchy

Display list

Properties, Variables, and Watch lists

Scope

Figure 12.42 The Debugger panel displays a hierarchy of movie clips and their properties and variables. The variables myDegrees, myRadians, and pressing are scoped to _Level0.myReferencePoint.

Figure 12.43 Use the Control menu to control the playback of your movie in testing mode.

To access the debugger:

1. From the Flash authoring environment, choose Control > Debug Movie (Shift-Command-Enter for Mac, Control-Shift-Enter for Windows) (**Figure 12.44**).

   Flash exports a SWF and enters testing mode. The Debugger panel opens and is activated.

   or

1. In testing mode of the authoring environment, in the Flash Player, or in a Web browser, Control-click (Mac) or right-click (Windows) the SWF movie.

   The Flash display menu appears on top of your movie (**Figure 12.45**).

2. Select Debugger from the display menu.

   The Debugger panel appears and is activated.

To modify a property or a variable in the Debugger panel:

1. In the Display list of the Debugger panel, select the movie clip whose properties or variables you wish to modify.

2. Select the Properties or the Variables tab.

3. Double-click the field in the Value column next to the property or variable you wish to modify (**Figure 12.46**).

4. Enter a new value.

   The new value must be a constant (a string, number, or Boolean value) rather than an expression that refers to another variable or property. For example, it must be 35 instead of 35 + myAlpha. The movie reflects the new value immediately.

✔ Tip

■ Certain properties are read-only and cannot be modified. For example, the property _totalframes is a fixed value determined by the number of frames in your movie.

Figure 12.44 Choose Control > Debug Movie.

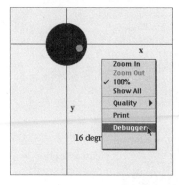

Figure 12.45 You can access the Debugger from the contextual display menu.

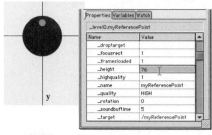

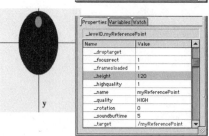

Figure 12.46 The values of properties can be selected (top) and modified (bottom), and your movie will reflect the change even while it plays.

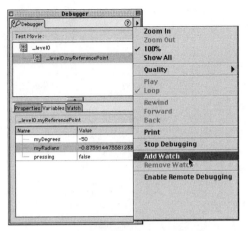

Figure 12.47 The selected variable (myRadians) is added to the Watch list using the pull-down menu.

Figure 12.48 The selected variable (myRadians) is added to the Watch list using the display menu.

Figure 12.49 Choose Add from the display menu on the Watch list to enter a variable by hand.

The Variables tab in the Debugger panel lets you watch only the variables within the same scope. If you want to watch variables belonging to different scopes, you can use the Watch tab to choose the variables you would like to observe. This lets you create a set of critical variables that are culled in one place for you to watch and modify. The variables in your Watch list are displayed with their absolute target paths in slash syntax.

To add variables to the Watch list:

1. In the Debugger panel, select the root Timeline or a movie clip from the Display list.

2. Select the variable from the Variables tab. From the options pull-down menu at the right-hand corner of the Debugger panel, choose Add Watch (**Figure 12.47**).

   A blue dot appears next to the variable, marking it to be displayed on the Watch list.

   or

2. Select the variable from the Variables tab. Control-click (Mac) or right-click (Windows) the variable. Choose Watch from the display menu that appears (**Figure 12.48**).

   A blue dot appears next to the variable, marking it to be displayed on the Watch list.

   or

2. From the Watch tab, Control-click (Mac) or right-click (Windows) in the empty list. Choose Add from the display menu that appears (**Figure 12.49**). Enter the absolute target path of the variable in slash syntax.

USING THE DEBUGGER

To remove variables from the Watch list:

◆ In the Watch list, Control-click (Mac) or right-click (Windows) the variable, and choose Remove from the display menu that appears.

◆ In the Variables list, Control-click (Mac) or right-click (Windows) the variable, and choose the check-marked Watch.

◆ In the Variables or Watch list, select the variable and then choose Remove Watch from the options pull-down menu at the top-right corner of the Debugger panel.

Optimizing Your Movie

Understanding the tools you use to create graphics, animation, sound, and ActionScript is important, but it's equally important to know how best to use them to create stream-lined Flash movies. To streamline a Flash movie, you use optimizations that keep the file size small, the animations smooth, and revisions simple. Many different factors affect the file size and performance of the final exported SWF. Bitmaps, sounds, complicated shapes, color gradients, alpha transparencies, and embedded fonts all increase the Flash file size and slow down the movie's performance. Only you can weigh the trade-offs between the quality and quantity of Flash content, and the size and performance of the movie. Keep in mind the audience to whom you're delivering your Flash movies—does your audience have Internet connections with T1 lines, or does your audience rely on 28.8 modems? Knowing the answer to this question helps you make more informed choices about what to include in your movie and how to build it.

The following strategies can help you work more efficiently and help you create smaller, more manageable, better performing Flash movies.

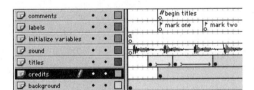

Figure 12.50 Well-organized layers like these are easy to understand and change.

To optimize your authoring environment:

◆ Use layers to separate and organize your content. For example, place all your actions on one layer, all your frame labels on another layer, and your sounds in still another layer. By doing so, you'll be able to understand and change different elements of your movie quickly (**Figure 12.50**). Having many layers does not increase the size of the final exported SWF file.

◆ Use a consistent naming practice for variables, movie clips, objects, and other elements that need to be identified. Avoid special punctuation within names. Consistent and simple names make the job that the variable performs more apparent.

◆ Use comments within your ActionScript to explain the code to yourself and to other developers who may look at your Flash file for future revisions. Use comments in keyframes as well to explain the different parts of the Timeline.

◆ Use dynamic text boxes as an addition to the Output window and Debugger panel to observe variables in your movie. Dynamic text boxes let you display expressions and variables in the context of your movie.

◆ Avoid using scenes in your movie. Although scenes are a good organizational feature for simple movies, Timelines that contain scenes are more difficult to navigate from movie clips. Also, movie-clip instances are not continuous between scenes. Use labels to mark different areas of the Timeline instead.

To optimize bitmaps and sounds for playback performance:

◆ Avoid animating large bitmaps. Keep bitmaps as static background elements if they are large, or make them small for tweening.

◆ Place streaming sounds on the root Timeline instead of within a movie clip. A movie clip needs to be downloaded in its entirety before playing. A streaming sound on the root Timeline, however, will begin playing as the frames download.

◆ Use the maximum amount of compression tolerable for bitmaps and sounds. You can adjust the JPEG quality level for your exported SWF file in Publish Settings. You can also adjust the compression settings for the stream sync and event sync sounds separately, so you can keep a higher-quality streaming sound for music and narration, and a lower-quality event sound for button clicks (**Figure 12.51**).

◆ Avoid using the Trace Bitmap command to create an overly complex vector image of an imported bitmap. The complexity of a traced bitmap can make the file size larger and the performance significantly slower than if you use the bitmap itself.

◆ Import bitmaps and sounds at the exact size or length that you want to use them in Flash. Although editing within Flash is possible, you want to import just the information you need to keep the file size small. For example, do not import a bitmap and then reduce it 50 percent to use in your movie. Instead, reduce the bitmap 50 percent first and then import it into Flash.

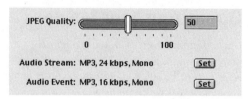

Figure 12.51 The JPEG quality and audio-compression options in the Publish Settings dialog box.

Figure 12.52 A symbol defined as separate groups (top left) contains more information (top middle) and can produce undesirable transparency effects (top right). A symbol defined as a shape (bottom left) contains less information (bottom middle) and will become transparent as one unit (bottom right).

- Optimize curves by avoiding special line styles (such as dotted lines) and using the pencil tool rather than the brush tool, and by reducing the complexity of curves with Modify > Optimize (Option-Shift-Command-C for Mac, Control-Alt-Shift-C for Windows).

- Use fewer font styles, and embed only the essential font outlines.

To optimize graphics, text, and tweening for playback performance:

- Use tweening wherever you can instead of frame-by-frame animation. In an animation, Flash only has to remember the keyframes, making tweening a far less memory-intensive task.

- Tween symbols instead of groups. Each group in the keyframes of a tween must be downloaded, whereas only the single symbol in a tween must be downloaded. Moreover, groups don't allow you to apply instance effects like Tint, Brightness, or Alpha. Using groups in tweens makes editing difficult because you have to apply the same edit on every single group in the keyframes of the tween.

- Avoid creating animations that have multiple objects moving at the same time or that have large areas of change. Both of these kinds of animations will slow the movie's performance.

- Break apart groups within symbols to simplify them. Once you're satisfied with an illustration in a symbol, break apart the groups into shapes to "flatten" the illustration out. Flash will have fewer curves to remember and thus have an easier time tweening the symbol instance. Alpha effects on the instance will also affect the symbol as a whole instead of the individual groups within the symbol (**Figure 12.52**).

- Use color gradients and alpha transparencies sparingly.

- Use the Effect panel to change the color, tint, and brightness of instances instead of creating separate symbols of different colors.

Avoiding Common Mistakes

When trouble-shooting your Flash movie, there are a few obvious places where you should look first to locate the problem. These mistakes usually involve some simple but critical element, such as overlooking quotation marks or a relative path term, or forgetting to name an instance. Pay close attention to the following warning list to ensure that all your Flash movies are free of bugs.

To avoid common mistakes:

◆ Double-check the data type of your values. Review the Actions List to make sure that quotation marks are only around string data types. The keyword `this` should not be within quotation marks. Movie-clip target paths can be within quotation marks, but it's good practice to keep them as expressions.

◆ Double-check the target paths for your movie clips, variables, and objects.

◆ Remember to name your movie-clip instance.

◆ Check to see if ActionScript statements are within the correct parentheses or curly braces in the Actions List. For example, statements belonging to an if statement or to an `onClipEvent` statement are contained within their curly braces.

◆ Check to see if the correct event has been selected for your button or movie-clip instance (mouse event or clip event).

◆ Place a `stop` action in the first keyframe of a movie clip to prevent it from playing automatically and looping.

◆ Make sure your button symbol contains a defined area in the Hit keyframe.

Figure 12.53 Access the Macromedia Dashboard panel from the Help menu for the latest news, tips, and tutorials.

◆ To test simple actions and simple buttons, remember to choose Enable Simple Frame Actions and Enable Simple Buttons from the Control menu.

◆ Remember that the default setting for your Flash movie in the testing mode is to loop.

✔ Tip

■ For additional help and advice on debugging your movie, check out the vast Flash resources on the Web. Begin your search from the Macromedia Dashboard, a window that links to Macromedia's Web site, where there is a searchable archive of tech notes and online versions of the user's manual and ActionScript dictionary (**Figure 12.53**). You'll also find links to Web sites with Flash tutorials, articles, FLA source files, bulletin boards, and mailing lists. Check out the CD that accompanies this book for more Flash links and resources.

APPENDIX

Summary of Object Methods and Properties

The following tables summarize the predefined Flash objects discussed in this book, along with their complete methods and properties. Parameter names are italicized.

Array Object

METHOD	DESCRIPTION	ARGUMENTS
new Array(*length*)	Creates a new array object.	*length*, optional argument for array length
concat(*array1,…,arrayN*)	Concatenates the specified values and returns a new array.	*array1,…,arrayN*, the elements to be concatenated in a new array
join(*separator*)	Concatenates the elements of the array, inserts the *separator* between the elements, and returns a string.	*separator*, a character or string
pop()	Removes the last element in the array and returns the value of that element.	
push(*value*)	Adds elements to the end of the array and returns the new length.	*value*, the elements to be added to the array
reverse()	Reverses the order of elements in the array.	
shift()	Removes the first element in the array and returns the value of that element.	
slice(*indexA*, *indexB*)	Returns a substring beginning with and including *indexA* and all the elements up to but not including *indexB*.	*indexA*, the starting element (included) *indexB*, the ending element (not included)
sort()	Sorts an array using the less than (<) operator. Numbers are sorted in ascending order, and strings are sorted alphabetically.	
splice(*index*, *count*, *elem1,…,elemN*)	Inserts or deletes elements from the array.	*index*, the beginning of the insertion or deletion *count*, the number of elements to be deleted *elem1,…,elemN*, the elements to be inserted
toString()	Returns a string with every element concatenated and separated by a comma.	
unshift(*value*)	Adds elements to the beginning of an array and returns the new length.	*value*, the elements to be added to the array
PROPERTY	DESCRIPTION	
length	Number of entries in the array.	

Color Object

METHOD	DESCRIPTION	ARGUMENTS
new Color(*target*)	Creates a new color object.	*target*, the target path of a movie clip
getRGB()	Returns the numeric value of the color of a movie clip assigned by getRGB.	
getTransform()	Returns the color-transform information of a movie clip assigned by setTransform.	
setRGB(*0xRRGGBB*)	Sets the color of the color object. color	*0xRRGGBB*, the red, green, and blue values for the
setTransform(*cxform*)	Transforms the color and alpha of the color object.	*cxform*, an object holding the color-transformation parameters ra, rb, ga, gb, ba, bb, aa, and ab

Date Object

Note: Universal Coordinated Time (UTC) is the same as Greenwich Mean Time.

METHOD	DESCRIPTION	ARGUMENTS
new Date(*year*, *month*, *date*, *hour*, *min*, *sec*, *ms*)	Creates a new date object.	*year*, *month*, *date*, *hour*, *min*, *sec*, *ms*, optional arguments for a specific date
getDate()	Returns the date of the month (1-31).	
getDay()	Returns the day of the week (0-6).	
getFullYear()	Returns the four-digit year.	
getHours()	Returns the hour of the day (0-23).	
getMilliseconds()	Returns the millisecond (0-999).	
getMinutes()	Returns the minute (0-59).	
getMonth()	Returns the month (0-11).	
getSeconds()	Returns the second (0-59).	
getTime()	Returns the number of milliseconds elapsed since midnight, January 1, 1970 UTC.	
getTimezoneOffset()	Returns the difference between the local time and UTC, in minutes.	
getUTCdate()	Returns the date of the month (1-31), UTC.	
getUTCday()	Returns the day of the week (0-6), UTC.	
getUTCFullYear()	Returns the four-digit year, UTC.	
getUTCHours()	Returns the hour of the day (0-23), UTC.	
getUTCMilliseconds()	Returns the millisecond (0-999), UTC.	
getUTCMinutes()	Returns the minute (0-59), UTC.	
getUTCMonth()	Returns the month (0-11), UTC.	
getUTCSeconds()	Returns the second (0-59), UTC.	
getYear()	Returns the year calculated from the current year minus 1900.	
setDate(*date*)	Sets the day of the month.	*date*, an integer from 1 to 31
setFullYear (*year*, *month*, *date*)	Sets the year, month, and date.	*year*, a four-digit integer *month*, an optional integer from 0 to 11 *date*, an optional integer from 1 to 31
setHours(*hours*, *minutes*, *seconds*, *ms*)	Sets the hour, minute, second, and millisecond.	*hours*, an integer from 0 to 59 *minutes*, an optional integer from 0 to 59 *seconds*, an optional integer from 0 to 59 *ms*, an optional integer from 0 to 999

Date Object

Note: Universal Coordinated Time (UTC) is the same as Greenwich Mean Time.

METHOD	DESCRIPTION	ARGUMENTS
setMilliseconds(ms)	Sets the millisecond.	ms, an integer from 0 to 999
setMinutes(minutes, seconds, ms)	Sets the minute, second, and millisecond.	minutes, an integer from 0 to 59 seconds, an optional integer from 0 to 59 ms, an optional integer from 0 to 999
setMonth(month, date)	Sets the month and date.	month, an integer from 0 to 11 date, an optional integer from 1 to 31
setSeconds(seconds, ms)	Sets the seconds and millisecond.	seconds, an integer from 0 to 59 ms, an optional integer from 0 to 999
setTime(value)	Sets the number of milliseconds elapsed since midnight January 1, 1970.	value, an integer representing the elapsed time
setUTCDate(date)	Sets the day of the month, UTC.	date, an integer from 1 to 31
setUTCFullYear (year, month, date)	Sets the year, month, and date, UTC.	year, a four-digit integer month, an optional integer from 0 to 11 date, an optional integer from 1 to 31
setUTCHours(hours, minutes, seconds, ms)	Sets the hour, minute, second, and millisecond, UTC.	hours, an integer from 0 to 59 minutes, an optional integer from 0 to 59 seconds, an optional integer from 0 to 59 ms, an optional integer from 0 to 999
setUTCMilliseconds(ms)	Sets the millisecond, UTC.	ms, an integer from 0 to 999
setUTCMinutes (minutes, seconds, ms)	Sets the minute, second, and millisecond, UTC.	minutes, an integer from 0 to 59 seconds, an optional integer from 0 to 59 ms, an optional integer from 0 to 999
setUTCMonth (month, date)	Sets the month and date, UTC.	month, an integer from 0 to 11 date, an optional integer from 1 to 31
setUTCSeconds (seconds, ms)	Sets the seconds and millisecond, UTC.	seconds, an integer from 0 to 59 ms, an optional integer from 0 to 999
setYear (year, month, date)	Sets the four-digit year.	year, a four-digit integer month, an optional integer from 0 to 11 date, an optional integer from 1 to 31
toString()	Returns a string of the values of a date object.	

Key Object

METHOD	DESCRIPTION	ARGUMENTS
getAscii()	Returns the ASCII value of the last key pressed.	
getCode()	Returns the key code of the last key pressed.	
isDown(keycode)	Returns true if the specified key is depressed.	keycode, the numerical code assigned to each key
isToggled(keycode)	Returns true if either the Caps Lock or Num Lock key is depressed.	keycode, the numerical code for Caps Lock (20) or Num Lock (144)
PROPERTY	**DESCRIPTION**	
BACKSPACE	Key code of the Backspace key	
CAPSLOCK	Key code of the Caps Lock key	
CONTROL	Key code of the Control key	
DELETEKEY	Key code of the Delete key	

Key Object

PROPERTY	DESCRIPTION
DOWN	Key code of the down arrow key
END	Key code of the End key
ENTER	Key code of the Enter key
ESCAPE	Key code of the Escape key
HOME	Key code of the Home key
INSERT	Key code of the Insert key
LEFT	Key code of the left arrow key
PGDN	Key code of the Page Down key
PGUP	Key code of the Page Up key
RIGHT	Key code of the right arrow key
SHIFT	Key code of the Shift key
SPACE	Key code of the spacebar
TAB	Key code of the Tab key
UP	Key code of the up arrow key

Math Object

METHOD	DESCRIPTION	ARGUMENTS
abs(*number*)	Calculates the absolute value.	*number*, any number or expression
acos(*number*)	Calculates the arc cosine.	*number*, a number from −1 to 1
asin(*number*)	Calculates the arc sine.	*number*, a number from −1 to 1
atan(*number*)	Calculates the arc tangent.	*number*, a number
atan2(*y*, *x*)	Calculates the arc tangent.	*y*, the *y* coordinate of a point *x*, the *x* coordinate of a point
ceil(*number*)	Returns the closest integer that is greater than or equal to the *number*.	*number*, a number of expression
cos(*number*)	Calculates the cosine.	*number*, an angle in radians
exp(*number*)	Calculates the constant e to the power of the specified *number*.	*number*, the exponent
floor(*number*)	Returns the closest integer that is less than or equal to the *number*.	*number*, a number or expression
log(*number*)	Calculates the natural logarithm.	*number*, a number or expression
max(*x*, *y*)	Returns the larger value of the two specified arguments.	*x*, a number or expression *y*, a number or expression
min(*x*, *y*)	Returns the smaller value of the two specified arguments.	*x*, a number or expression *y*, a number or expression
pow(*base*, *exponent*)	Calculates the value of *base* raised to the power of *exponent*.	*base*, a number or expression *exponent*, a number or expression
random()	Returns a random number between 0 and 1.	
round(*number*)	Rounds a number to the nearest integer.	*number*, a number or expression
sin(*number*)	Calculates the sine.	*number*, an angle in radians
sqrt(*number*)	Calculates the square root.	*number*, a number or expression
tan(*number*)	Calculates the tangent.	*number*, an angle in radians

Math Object

PROPERTY	DESCRIPTION
E	Euler's constant; the base of natural logarithms
LN2	Natural logarithm of 2
LOG2E	Base 2 of logarithm of e
LN10	Natural logarithm of 10
LOG10E	Base 10 of logarithm of e
PI	Ratio of the circle circumference to its diameter
SQRT1_2	Reciprocal of the square root of 1/2
SQRT2	Square root of 2

Mouse Object

METHOD	DESCRIPTION
hide()	Hides the pointer.
show()	Shows the pointer.
PROPERTY	DESCRIPTION
_xmouse	x position of the pointer
_ymouse	y position of the pointer

Movie Clip Object

METHOD	DESCRIPTION	ARGUMENTS
attachMovie(idName, newName, depth)	Attaches a movie clip from the Library to a movie-clip instance on the Stage.	idName, the identifier of the movie- clip symbol in the Library newName, the instance name of the attached movie-clip depth, the depth level
duplicateMovieClip(newName, depth)	Creates another instance of a movie-clip instance on the Stage.	newName, the instance name of the duplicate depth, the depth level
getBounds(targetCoordinateSpace)	Returns the minimum and maximum x and y positions of the movie clip in the coordinate space of the specified target. The returned object contains the properties xMin, xMax, yMin, and yMax.	targetCoordinateSpace, the Timeline whose coordinate space is the reference
getBytesLoaded()	Returns the amount of a movie clip downloaded, in bytes.	
getBytesTotal()	Returns the total size of a movie clip, in bytes.	
globaltoLocal(point)	Converts the global coordinates of the point object to coordinates relative to the movie clip.	point, an object that contains x and y coordinates.
gotoAndPlay(frame)	Sends the playhead to the specified frame or label and begins playing.	frame, the number of the frame or name of the label
gotoAndStop(frame)	Sends the playhead to the specified frame or label and stops.	frame, the number of the frame or name of the label

Movie Clip Object

Method	Description	Arguments
hitTest(x, y, shapeFlag) hitTest(target)	Returns true if the x and y coordinates intersect the movie clip. Returns true if the specified target movie clip intersects the movie clip.	x, the x coordinate y, the y coordinate shapeFlag, true or false parameter that determines if the coordinates intersect the shape of the movie clip (true) or its bounding box (false) target, the intersecting movie- clip instance
loadMovie(URL, method)	Loads an external SWF into the movie clip.	URL, the path to the external SWF file method, optional argument specifying the CGI GET or POST method
loadVariables (URL, method)	Loads external variables kept in a text file into the movie clip.	URL, the path to the external text file method, optional argument specifying the CGI GET or POST method
localtoGlobal (point)	Converts the coordinates of the point object from a movie clip to coordinates relative to the Stage.	point, an object that contains x and y coordinates.
nextFrame()	Sends the playhead to the next frame and stops.	
play()	Begins playing the movie movie-clip Timeline at the current position of the playhead.	
prevFrame()	Sends the playhead to the previous frame and stops.	
removeMovieClip()	Removes a movie-clip instance created with duplicateMovieClip or attachMovie.	
startDrag(lockCenter, left, top, right, bottom)	Makes the movie clip follow the pointer.	lockCenter, true or false parameter that determines if the center point of the movie clip is locked to the pointer left, top, right, bottom, values to constrain the movie clip's position
stop()	Stops the playhead.	
stopDrag()	Stops the movie clip from following the pointer.	
swapDepths(depth) swapDepths(target)	Switches the stacking order of movie clips.	depth, the depth level that contains a movie clip to swap target, the movie clip that swaps
unloadMovie()	Removes the loaded SWF file in a movie movie-clip instance or a movie clip that was attached to another movie movie-clip instance with attachMovie.	

Property	Description
_alpha	Alpha transparency from o (transparent) to 100 (opaque)
_currentframe	Current frame position of the playhead (read-only)
_droptarget	Target path of a movie clip that the draggable movie clip is dropped on (in slash notation, read-only)
_framesloaded	Number of frames that have been downloaded to the viewer's computer (read -only)
_height	Vertical dimension in pixels
_name	Name of the movie- clip instance
_rotation	Rotation in degrees, clockwise
_target	Target path of the movie- clip instance (read -only)
_totalframes	Total number of frames in the movie- clip symbol (read -only)
_url	The URL of the SWF file loaded into the movie clip (read -only)

Movie Clip Object

PROPERTY	DESCRIPTION
_visible	Visibility, either true or false
_width	Horizontal dimension in pixels
_x	x position
_xscale	Percentage of the horizontal dimension of the movie- clip symbol
_y	y position
_yscale	Percentage of the vertical dimension of the movie- clip symbol

Selection Object

METHOD	DESCRIPTION	ARGUMENTS
getBeginIndex()	Returns the index of the start of the selection.	
getCaretIndex()	Returns the index of the cursor position.	
getEndIndex()	Returns the index of the end of the selection.	
getFocus()	Returns the name of the currently focused text box.	
setFocus(variableName)	Sets the focus of a text box.	variableName, the name of the text box
setSelection (beginIndex, endIndex)	Sets the selection in an editable text box.	beginIndex, the start index of the selection endIndex, the end index of the selection

Sound Object

METHOD	DESCRIPTION	ARGUMENTS
new Sound (target)	Creates a new sound object.	target, the target path for a movie clip
attachSound(idName)	Attaches a sound file from the Library to a sound object.	idName, the identifier of your sound in the Library
getPan()	Returns the pan level assigned by setPan.	
getTransform()	Returns the sound- transformation information assigned by setTransform.	
getVolume()	Returns the volume level assigned by setVolume.	
setPan(pan)	Sets the left-right balance of the sound.	pan, a number from –100 (left) to 100 (right)
setTransform(sxform)	Sets how the left and right sounds are distributed through the left and right speakers.	sxform, an object holding the sound-transformation parameters ll, lr, rr, and rl
setVolume(volume)	Sets the percentage of the volume level.	volume, a number from 0 (silent) to 100 (loud)
start(secondsOffset, loops)	Plays the attached sound.	secondsOffset, the starting point of the sound (in seconds) loops, the number of times the sound loops
stop()	Stops the attached sound.	

String Object

METHOD	DESCRIPTION	ARGUMENTS
new String (*value*)	Creates a new string object.	*value*, the value of the string object
charAt (*index*)	Returns the character at a specific index.	*index*, the position of the character
charCodeAt (*index*)	Returns the character code at a specific index.	*index*, the position of the character
concat (*string1,…,stringN*)	Combines the contents of the specified strings.	*string1, …, stringN*, the strings to be concatenated
fromCharCode (*num1,…,numN*)	Returns a string made up of the specified elements.	*num1,…,numN*, the characters to be made into a string
indexOf (*searchString, fromIndex*)	Returns the index of the first occurrence of a specified character or substring.	*searchString*, the character or characters *fromIndex*, the starting index
lastIndexOf (*searchstring, fromIndex*)	Returns the index of the last occurrence of a specified character or substring.	*searchstring*, the character or characters *fromIndex*, the starting index
slice (*indexA, indexB*)	Returns a substring between the specified indices including *indexA* but not including *indexB*.	*indexA*, the start of the substring *indexB*, the end of the substring
split (*separator, limit*)	Returns an array of two or more substrings based on the *separator*.	*separator*, the character that separates the substrings *limit*, the maximum number of substrings to be put in the array
substr (*start, length*)	Returns a substring of a certain length starting at the specified index.	*start*, the starting index *length*, the length of the substring
substring (*indexA, indexB*)	Returns a substring between the specified indices.	*indexA*, the start of the substring *indexB*, the end of the substring
toLowerCase()	Converts the characters in a string to all lower case.	
toUpperCase()	Converts the characters in a string to all upper case.	

PROPERTY	DESCRIPTION
length	The number of characters in a string (read-only)

APPENDIX

Keyboard Keys and Matching Key Codes

Letters	
LETTER KEY	KEY CODE
A	65
B	66
C	67
D	68
E	69
F	70
G	71
H	72
I	73
J	74
K	75
L	76
M	77
N	78
O	79
P	80
Q	81
R	82
S	83
T	84
U	85
V	86
W	87
X	88
Y	89
Z	90

Numbers and Symbols

Key	Key Code	Key Object Property
0	48	
1	49	
2	50	
3	51	
4	52	
5	53	
6	54	
7	55	
8	56	
9	57	
Numbpad 0	96	
Numbpad 1	97	
Numbpad 2	98	
Numbpad 3	99	
Numbpad 4	100	
Numbpad 5	101	
Numbpad 6	102	
Numbpad 7	103	
Numbpad 8	104	
Numbpad 9	105	
Numbpad *	106	
Numbpad +	107	
Numbpad Enter	108	
Numbpad -	109	
Numbpad .	110	
Numbpad /	111	
Backspace	8	BACKSPACE
Tab	9	TAB
Clear	12	
Enter	13	ENTER
Shift	16	SHIFT
Control	17	CONTROL
Alt	18	
Caps Lock	20	CAPSLOCK
Esc	27	ESCAPE
Spacebar	32	SPACE
Page Up	33	PGUP
Page Down	34	PGDN
End	35	END
Home	36	HOME
Left arrow	37	LEFT
Up arrow	38	UP

Numbers and Symbols

Key	Key Code	Key Object Property
Right arrow	39	RIGHT
Down arrow	40	DOWN
Insert	45	INSERT
Delete	46	DELETEKEY
Help	47	
Num Lock	144	
;:	186	
=+	187	
-_	189	
/?	191	
`~	192	
[{	219	
|	220	
]}	221	
'"	222	

Function Keys

Function Key	Key Code
F1	112
F2	113
F3	114
F4	115
F5	116
F6	117
F7	118
F8	119
F9	120
F10	121
F11	122
F12	123

APPENDIX

Summary of the Actions Category

Descriptions of Actions

ACTION	SYNTAX	KEY SEQUENCE	DESCRIPTION
break	break;	Esc + br	Breaks out of a looping statement (for, for in, do while, or while).
call	call (frame);	Esc + ca	Performs the script attached to a specified frame label. This action is deprecated, so the action function should be used.
comment	// comment	Esc + //	Allows text to be included within the Actions List for commentary only.
continue	continue;	Esc + co	Makes Flash skip the rest of the actions within a looping statement and jump to where the condition is tested.
delete	delete variable;	Esc + da	Removes a variable.
do while	do { statement; } while (condition);	Esc + do	Creates a loop that performs statements as long as the specified condition is true.
duplicateMovieClip	duplicateMovieClip (target, newname, depth);	Esc + dm	Creates a copy of a movie-clip instance.

else	else {
	    statement;
	}
		Esc + el	Specifies the statements to be performed when the condition in an if statement is false.

else if	else if (condition) {
	    statement;
	}
		Esc + ei	Specifies the statements to be performed for an alternative condition.

evaluate	expression;	Esc + ev	Adds a new statement line in the Actions List to evaluate an expression.

for	for (init; condition; next) {
	    statement;
	}
		Esc + fr	Creates a loop that performs statements as long as the specified condition is true. The condition is usually a counter that increases or decreases with each loop.

Descriptions of Actions

ACTION	SYNTAX	KEY SEQUENCE	DESCRIPTION

for..in	for (*iterator* in *object*) {
	    statement;
	}
		Esc + fi	Creates a loop that performs statements on the properties of an object or elements in an array.

fsCommand	fscommand (*command*, *arguments*);	Esc + fs	Sends commands to JavaScript in the browser environment, or to the Flash Player or Projector to control playback.

function	function *name* (*parameters*) {
	    statement;
	}
		Esc + fn	Defines statements that perform a certain task given a set of parameters. Use function to create custom classes and methods.

getURL	getURL (*URL*, *window*, *variables*);	Esc + gu	Loads the file at a specified URL (absolute Internet address or relative path) in a browser window. Provides optional arguments specifying the CGI GET or POST method.

goto	gotoAndPlay (*scene*, *frame*);
	gotoAndStop (*scene*, *frame*);
	nextFrame();
	previousFrame();
	nextScene();
	previousScene();
		Esc + go	Sends the playhead to the specified scene, frame number or frame label, and plays or stops there.

if	if (*condition*) {
	    statement;
	}
		Esc + if	Specifies the statements to be performed when a certain condition is true.

ifFrameLoaded	ifFrameLoaded (*scene*, *frame*) {
	    statement;
	}
		Esc + il	Specifies the statements to be performed when a certain frame of a scene has been downloaded. This action is deprecated, so the property _framesloaded should be used.

include	#include (*path*)	Esc + in	Incorporates ActionScript from an external text document.
loadMovie	loadMovieNum or loadMovie (*URL*, *levelortarget*, *variables*);	Esc + lm	Loads an external SWF file into a level or into a movie clip. Provides optional arguments specifying the CGI GET or POST method.
loadVariables	loadVariablesNum or loadVariables (*URL*, *levelortarget*, *variables*);	Esc + lv	Loads variables from an external text document into a level or a movie clip. Provides optional arguments specifying the CGI GET or POST method.

on	on (*mouseEvent*) {
	    statement;
	}
		Esc + on	Specifies the statements to be performed when a certain mouse event or key event occurs. The on handler is always assigned to a button instance.

onClipEvent	onClipEvent (*clipEvent*) {
	    statement;
	}
		Esc + on	Specifies the statements to be performed when a certain clip event occurs. The onClipEvent handler is always assigned to a movie-clip instance.

play	play();	Esc + pl	Begins playing the movie from the current position of the playhead.
print	print (*location*, *boundingbox*);	Esc + pr	Prints the contents of frames.

Descriptions of Actions

removeMovieClip	removeMovieClip (*target*);	Esc + rm	Removes a duplicate movie-clip instance.
return	return *value*;	Esc + rt	Returns a value calculated from a function.
set variable	*variable* = *value*;	Esc + sv	Assigns a value to a variable.
setProperty	setProperty (*target*, *property*, *value*);	Esc + sp	Assigns a value to a property of a movie-clip instance or to a property of the entire movie.
startDrag	startDrag (*target*, *centered*, *L*, *T*, *R*, *B*);	Esc + dr	Makes the specified movie clip follow the pointer.
stop	stop();	Esc + st	Stops the playhead.
stopAllSounds	stopAllSounds ();	Esc + ss	Stops all sounds from playing.
stopDrag	stopDrag();	Esc + sd	Stops the movie clip from following the pointer caused by the startDrag action.
tellTarget	tellTarget (*target*) { statement; }	Esc + tt	Specifies the statements to be performed on a movie clip of a certain target path. This action is deprecated, so the with action or dot syntax should be used.
toggleHighQuality	toggleHighQuality ();	Esc + tq	Turns antialiasing on or off, affecting the entire movie. This action is deprecated, so the property _quality should be used.
trace	trace (*message*);	Esc + tr	Displays an expression in the Output window in testing mode.
unloadMovie	unloadMovieNum or unloadMovie (*levelortarget*);	Esc + um	Removes a loaded movie from a level or a movie clip.
var	var *variable* = *value*	Esc + vr	Defines local variables that are contained within a function.
while	while (*condition*) { statement; }	Esc + wh	Creates a loop that performs statements as long as the specified condition is true.
with	with (*object*) { statement; }	Esc + wt	Specifies the statements to be performed on an object or movie clip of a certain target path.

INDEX

New from Peachpit Press

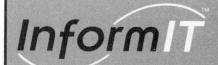